THIRD HANDBOOK OF PSYCHOLOGICAL AND SOCIAL INSTRUMENTS

About the Author

Professor D.M. Pestonjee is presently the L&T Chair Professor of Organizational Behaviour at the Indian Institute of Management, Ahmedabad, India. He is a psychologist by training having obtained his M.A. in Psychology with a First Class First and Ph.D. in Industrial Psychology from the Aligarh Muslim University.

He has over three decades of teaching experience and has successfully supervised sixteen Ph.D candidates. He is author/co-author of nine books and over 100 research articles. Among his better known works are : *Second Handbook of Psychological and Social Instruments* (1988), and the celebrated *Stress and Coping — The Indian Experience* (1992).

Professor Pestonjee has been active as a trainer and consultant in non-business sectors like, education and health. He has been Temporary Advisor to WHO, USAID, OXFAM. He was also an Individual Category Elected member of the International Social Service Council of the UNESCO to represent Management Sciences for three terms, 1980-83; 1983-86; 1986-88. He was also a Member of the Executive Committee of the International Sociology Association 1986-90. He served as a Regional Representative of the International Association of Applied Psychology.

He has served on several national bodies like the Indian Council of Social Science Research, the All India Council for Technical Education, and the Indian Council of Medical Research.

His current areas of interest are executive stress, coping and issues related to executive health, job satisfaction and morale.

Concepts in Communication
Informatics & Librarianship-75

General Editor : **S.P. AGRAWAL**

THIRD HANDBOOK OF PSYCHOLOGICAL AND SOCIAL INSTRUMENTS

Volume One

Edited and Compiled by

Prof. D.M. PESTONJEE

L&T Chair Professor of Organizational Behaviour & Chairman, OB Area
Indian Institute of Management, Ahmedabad

CONCEPT PUBLISHING COMPANY, NEW DELHI - 110059

ISBN 81-7022-652-X (Vol. 1)
ISBN 81-7022-653-8 (Vol. 2)
ISBN 81-7022-654-6 (Set)

First Published 1997
Reprinted 2003

Published and Printed by
Ashok Kumar Mittal
Concept Publishing Company
A/15-16, Commercial Block, Mohan Garden,
NEW DELHI-110059

Phones : 25351460, 25351794
Fax : 091-11-25357103
Email : publishing@conceptpub.com

General Editor's Introduction

Experimental psychologists have made valiant efforts to upgrade psychology to the level of exact sciences like physics, chemistry and biology. They have not been able till now to attain the desired goal. But they have achieved some success in this direction in the form of psychological testing which, by systematic use of tests, strives to quantify the psychological behaviour, abilities, and problems and to make predictions about psychological performance. Through the professionally developed tests we are now able to evaluate human abilities, aptitudes, educational achievements, skills, interests, attitudes, and the personality characteristics. As a matter of fact, the psychological testing accorded a respectability to psychology and revolutionized it by making it 'as a science objectively and quantitatively oriented, in contrast to the earlier orientation of more subjective and philosophical nature.' These psychological tests, which have been recognized as standardised instruments, have proved very much efficacious and have played important role in tackling the problems 'of the mentally retarded, of educating the slow-learning children, of classifying and training military personnel, of selecting and promoting personnel in industry and the government, and of helping maladjusted individuals adjust to the demands of life.'

The present publication, which is the third Handbook in the series of Handbooks on the instruments for measurement of behaviour and standardised in India, attempts to provide reliable and authentic information on the subject. It will prove a great boon to the researchers, teachers of psychology, education and sociology, pyschiatrist, guidance counsellors, personnel administrators and the serious students of psychology. The compilers of this Handbook (as also other two Handbooks brought out earlier) have made tremendous efforts to collect these instruments from various sources and obtain technical details about them from their authors. It is really a creditable job that most of the major instruments have been retrieved and made available to the users at one place.

The present Handbook comprises four parts, namely. Personality, Education, Organisational Behaviour, and Social Phenomena. Each part is divided into sections which include four categories of instruments: Instruments reproduced with information, instruments with technical information only, citations, and adaptations. Instruments dealing with personality dimensions are reported under five sections which are: (i) General, (ii) Adjustment and Problems, (iii) Anxiety, (iv) Self-Concept, and (v) Motivation. In all 95 instruments have been included in this part. Of these, 16 instruments have been reproduced here (14 of them are in the general category) and 15 are adaptations. Only technical information about the remaining 64 instruments has been provided in this part. The instruments pertaining to the second part of the different educational dimensions have also been categorised under five sections: (i) General Instruments, (ii) Student Problems and Adjustment, (iii) Interests and Preferences, (iv) Attitudes, and (v) Institutional Characteristics like climate, etc. In all, there are 64 instruments reported in this area of which 15 have been reproduced here. Technical information about other 47 instruments has been given in this part. The remaining two are adaptations. The instruments dealing with various dimensions of organizational behaviour have been reported under two sections: (i) Industrial Organizations, and (ii) Health Organizations. For instance, these instruments deal with job satisfaction, job motivation, organizational effectiveness, occupational and role stress, participation, role conflicts, and attitudes etc. There are in all 32 instruments listed under this part. Of these, 25 have been reproduced here. Only information has been provided for 6 instruments. The areas covered by the instruments reproduced here include managerial styles, interpersonal needs, motivational aspects in organizations, organizational effectiveness, job satisfaction, managerial behaviour, job anxiety, occupational and role stress, participation, performance rating, general personality of workers, and role conflict etc. The fourth and the last part reports instruments dealing with several social dimensions. These instruments have been categorised under six sections: (i) Values, (ii) Stratification, (iii) Social Distance and Group Attitudes, (iv) Modernization and Social Change, (v) Religion and Morality, and (vi) Other Social Attitudes. In all, 79 instruments have been reported in this part. 52 instruments have been originally reproduced here. Information has been provided for other 22 instruments. 3 are citations and 2 are adaptations.

S.P. AGRAWAL

PREFACE

There is a continual and felt need to have access to instruments for measurement of behaviour and social phenomena. It is precisely two decades now, since the First Handbook by Professors Udai Pareek and T. Venkateshwara Rao was published. This was followed in 1988 by the Second Handbook under the authorship of the present author. We are now presenting the Third Handbook of Psychological and Social Instruments.

In the present volumes, we have 270 entries. Of these, (A) 108 are complete instruments, (B) 140 are instruments with technical information only, (C) 03 citations, and (D) 19 are adaptations. Table is shown below :

Table: Break-Up of All the Instruments Included in the Handbook

Classification	Originals Reproduced	Only Information	Citations	Adaptations	Total
	A	B	C	D	
Personality	16	64	—	15	95
Education	15	47	—	02	64
Organisational Behaviour	25	07	—	—	32
Social Phenomena	52	22	03	02	79
Total	108	140	03	19	270

In preparing a Handbook of this nature, it is necessary to collect materials from various sources. Materials were sifted from back issues of various journals. A comprehensive questionnaire was sent to all Indian Universities (specially Heads/Deans of Faculty of Psychology and Education), Professors and teachers of Psychology, Education, and Sociology, and researchers in the field. In a majority of cases, three to four reminders were required. This delayed our efforts to put together the Handbook. However, we are thankful to all the scholars who provided their valuable materials.

On Using the Handbook

The classification system of the instruments is not based on theoretical distinctions, but it is a pragmatic one reflecting the number of instruments reported. The classification system of the instruments is the same as has been followed in the First Handbook (1974) and also in the Second Handbook of Psychological and Social Instruments (1988). The uniformity of the classification of instruments was maintained as the author wanted to make it easy for those people referring to the new edition, the easy accessibility of new instruments in their respective coding system, and also for those who are referring for the first time, this Handbook would be of extreme help to find out the latest instruments developed.

The coding is based on the following 3 tier classification :

Part indicates the field. The Handbook is divided into four parts:

1. Personality,
2. Education,
3. Organisational Behaviour, and
4. Social Phenomena.

Each Part is further divided into sections. The first numeral of the code number of the instrument indicates the *part* and the second numeral indicates the *section* under that part.

Under each Section, four categories of instruments are included:

A — Instruments reproduced with information,
B — Instruments with technical information only,
C — Citations, and
D — Adaptations.

The category is indicated by the letter codes mentioned above. In each category, the instruments are serially numbered. Thus, in numbering an instrument, the *Part* number occurs first, followed by the *Section* number, and Category (A, B, C, or D explained above) which is followed by serial number of the instrument. For example, 12A10 would indicate that the instrument is in Part 1, i.e., Personality, dealing with Adjustment (Section 2), is reproduced here with information (Category A) and has a serial number 10 in that category. Similarly, 31D2 indicates that the instrument is from Organisational Behaviour (Part 3), dealing with Industrial Organisation (Section 1), is an Indian adaptation (Category D) and has a serial number of 2 under that category.

Two indices are provided at the end of the *Handbook,* namely, instrument index and author index. These may be used by the reader for locating a desired instrument in the *Handbook*.

Preparing the Handbook is a patently time consuming activity which depends on cooperation of several academic collaborators. Thanks should be given to authors and publishers of several tests and instruments whose works are included here.

The project for preparing the Handbook was financed by a research grant from the Indian Council of Social Science Research (ICSSR). The ICSSR deserves the thanks of the whole Social Science community for encouraging and financing not only the present Handbook but also the earlier Handbooks.

The American Psychological Association (APA) has very graciously allowed me to incorporate the "Standards for Educational and Psychological Tests (1974)" in the present Handbook.

Lastly, I would like to thank Ms. Nina Muncherji for her help; I will also like to thank Ms.Havovi J Ginwala for her help in the project and also for having typed the whole Handbook having had to read literally several hundred types of handwritings.

Ahmedabad **D.M. PESTONJEE**

STANDARDS FOR EDUCATIONAL AND PSYCHOLOGICAL TESTS PROVIDED BY THE AMERICAN PSYCHOLOGICAL ASSOCIATION (APA)

Highlights

1. When a test is published or otherwise made available for operational use, it should be accompanied by a manual (or other published or readily available information) that makes every reasonable effort to follow the recommendations of these standards and, in particular the information required to substantiate any claims that have been made for its use.
2. A test manual should describe fully the development of the test: the rationale, specifications followed in writing items or selecting observations, and procedures and results of item analysis or other research.
3. The test and its manual should be revised at appropriate intervals. The time for revision has arrived whenever changing conditions of use or new research data make any statements in the manual incorrect or misleading.
4. The test, the manual, the record forms, and other accompanying material should help users make correct interpretations of the test results and should warn against common misusers.
5. The test manual should state explicitly the purposes and applications for which the test is recommended.
6. The test manual should describe clearly the psychological, educational, or other reasoning underlying the test and nature of the characteristic it is intended to measure.
7. The test manual should identify any special qualifications required to administer the test and to interpret it properly.
8. Evidence of validity and reliability, along with other relevant research data, should be presented in support of any claims being made.
9. Test developers or others offering computer services for test interpretation should provide a manual reporting the rationale and evidence in support of computer-based interpretation of scores.
10. The directions for administration should be presented in the test manual with sufficient clarity and emphasis so that the test user can duplicate the administrative conditions under which the norms and the data on reliability and validity were obtained.

11. Instructions should prepare the examinee for the examination : Sample material, practice use of answer sheets or punch cards, sample questions, etc., should be provided.
12. The procedures for scoring the test should be presented in the test manual with a maximum of detail and clarity to reduce the likelihood of scoring error.
13. Norms should be published in the test manual at the time of release of the test for operational use.
14. Norms presented in the test manual should refer to defined and clearly described populations. These populations should be the groups with whom users of the test will ordinarily wish to compare the persons tested.
15. In reporting norms, test manuals should use percentiles for one or more appropriate reference groups or standard scores for which the basis is clearly set forth; any exceptional type of score or unit should be explained and justified. Measures of central tendency and variability always should be reported.
16. Local norms are more important for many users of tests than are published norms. A test manual should suggest using local norms in such situations.
17. Derived scales used for reporting scores should be carefully described in the test manual to increase the likelihood of accurate interpretation of scores by both the test interpreter and the examinee.
18. If scales are revised, new forms added, or other changes made, the revised test manual should provide tables of equivalence between the new and the old forms. This provision is particularly important in cases where data are recorded on cumulative records.
19. Where it is expected that a test will be used to assess groups rather than individuals (i.e., for schools or programs), normative data based on group summary statistics should be provided.
20. A manual or research report should present the evidence of validity for each type of inference for which use of the test is recommended. If validity for some suggested interpretation has not been investigated, that fact should be made clear.
21. A test user is responsible for marshalling the evidence in support of his claims of validity and reliability. The use of test scores in decision rules should be supported by evidence.
22. All measures of criteria should be described completely and accurately. The manual or research report should comment on the adequacy of a criterion. Whenever feasible, it should draw attention to significant aspects of performance that the criterion measure does not reflect and to irrelevant factors likely to affect it.

23. A criterion measure should itself be studied for evidence of validity and that evidence should be presented in the manual or report.
24. The manual or research report should provide information on the appropriateness of or limits to the generalizability of validity information.
25. The sample employed in a validity study and the conditions under which testing is done should be consistent with recommended test use and should be described sufficiently for the reader to judge its pertinence to his situation.
26. The collection of data for a validity study should follow procedures consistent with the purposes of the study.
27. Any statistical analysis of criterion-related validity should be reported in the manual in a form that enables the reader to determine how much confidence is to be placed in judgments or predictions regarding the individual.
28. A test user should investigate the possibility of bias in tests or in test items. Whenever possible, there should be an investigation of possible differences in criterion-related validity for ethnic, sex, or other subsamples that can be identified when the test is given. The manual or research report should give the results for each subsample separately or report that no differences were found.
29. When a scoring key, the selection of items, or the weighting of tests is based on one sample, the manual should report validity coefficients based on data obtained from one or more independent cross-validation samples. Validity statements should not be based on the original sample.
30. To the extent feasible, a test user who intends to continue employing a test over a long period of time should develop procedures for gathering data for continued research.
31. If test performances is to be interpreted as a representative sample of performance in a universe of situations, the test manual should give a clear definition of the universe represented and describe the procedures followed in the sampling from it.
32. If the author proposes to interpret scores on a test as measuring a theoretical variable (ability, trait, or attitude), his proposed interpretation should be distinguished from interpretations arising on the basis of other theories.
33. The test manual or research report should present evidence of reliability, including estimates of the standard error of measurement, that permits the reader to judge whether scores are sufficiently dependable for the intended uses of the test. If any of the necessary evidence has not been collected, the absence of such information should be noted.
34. The procedures and samples used to determines reliability coefficients

or standard errors of measurement should be described sufficiently to permit a user to judge the applicability of the data reported to the individuals or groups with which he is concerned.

35. Reports of reliability studies should ordinarily be expressed in the test manual in terms of variances of error components, standard errors of measurement, or product moment reliability coefficients. Unfamiliar expressions of data should be clearly described, with references to their development.
36. If two or more forms of a test are published for use with the same examinees, information on means, variances, and characteristics of items in the forms should be reported in the test manual along with the coefficients of correlation among their scores. If necessary evidence is not provided, the test manual should warn the reader against assuming equivalence of scores.
37. Evidence of internal consistency should be reported for any unspeeded test.
38. The test manual should indicate to what extent test scores are stable, that is, how nearly constant the scores are likely to be if a parallel form of a test is administered after time has elapsed. The time interval to be considered depends on the nature of the test and on what interpretation of the test scores is recommended.

Standards for the Use of Tests

1. A test user should have a general knowledge of measurement principles and of the limitations of test interpretations.
2. A test user should know and understand the literature relevant to the tests he uses and the testing problems with which he deals.
3. One who has the responsibility for decisions about individuals or policies that are based on test results should have an understanding of psychological or educational measurement and of validation and other test research.
4. Test users should seek to avoid bias in test selection, administration, and interpretation; they should try to avoid even the appearance of discriminatory practice.
5. Institutional test users should establish procedures for periodic internal review of test use.
6. The choice or development of tests, test batteries, or other assessment procedures should be based on clearly formulated goals and hypotheses.
7. A test user should consider more than one variable for assessment and the assessment of any given variable by more than one method.
8. In choosing an existing test, a test user should relate its history of

research and development to his intended use of the instrument.

9. In general a test user should try to choose or to develop an assessment technique in which "tester-effect" is minimized, or in which reliability of assessment across testers can be assured.
10. Test scores used for selection or other administrative decisions about an individual may not be useful for individual or programme evaluation and vice versa.
11. A test user is expected to follow carefully the standardized procedures described in the manual for administering a test.
12. The test administration is responsible for establishing conditions, consistent with the principle of standardization, that enable each examinee to do his best.
13. A test user is responsible for accuracy in scoring, checking, coding, or recording test results.
14. If specific cutting scores are to be used as a basis for decisions, a test justification, or explanation of the cutting scores adopted.
15. The test user shares with the test developer or distributor a responsibility for maintaining test security.
16. A test score should be interpreted as an estimate of performance under a given set of circumstances. It should not be interpreted as some absolute characteristic of the examinee or as something permanent and generalizable to all circumstances.
17. Test scores should ordinarily be reported only to people who are qualified to interpret them. If scores are reported, they should be accompanied by explanations sufficient for the recipient to interpret them correctly.
18. The test user should recognize that estimates of reliability do not indicate criterion-related validity.
19. A test user should examine carefully the rationale and validity of computer-based interpretations of test scores.
20. In norm-referenced interpretations, a test user should interpret an obtained score with reference to sets of norms appropriate for the individual tested and for the intended use.
21. Any content-referenced interpretation should clearly indicate the domain to which one can generalize.
22. The test user should consider alternative interpretations of a given score.
23. The test user should be able to interpret test performance relative to other measures.
24. A test user should develop procedures for systematically eliminating from data files test-score information that has because of lapse of time, become obsolete.

CONTENTS

VOLUME ONE

PART 1 : PERSONALITY

PART 2 : EDUCATION

VOLUME TWO

PART 3 : ORGANISATIONAL BEHAVIOUR

PART 4 : SOCIAL PHENOMENA

PART ONE

PERSONALITY

INTRODUCTION

Instruments dealing with personality dimensions have been included in this part of the Handbook. The instruments are reported under five sections :-

1. General Instruments,
2. Adjustment and Problems,
3. Anxiety,
4. Self-concept, and
5. Motivation.

The classification system of the instruments is not based on theoretical distinctions, but it is a pragmatic one reflecting the number of instruments reported. The instruments measuring a particular dimension of personality, available in sufficient number, are treated separately. Thus, adjustment, anxiety, self-concept, and motivation emerge as separate dimensions. Anxiety and self-concept include instruments dealing exclusively with these variables whereas the sections on adjustment and motivation report instruments dealing with several types of adjustment and motivation respectively. The section on adjustment reports instruments mainly related to personality adjustment and problems. The instruments dealing with the other personality dimensions have been grouped under the title of general instruments of personality. The instruments dealing with extraversion, introversion, authoritarianism, locus of control, frustration etc. have been included in this group.

In all 95 instruments have been reported in this part of the Handbook. 16 instruments are reproduced here, 14 of them are in the general category; 15 instruments are adaptations. Only technical information about other 65 instruments is provided here. There have been no instruments which have been cited and where the information is not available. The detailed break-up of the instruments is given in the Table.

Table Number 1
Break-Up of Personality Instruments

Classification	Originals Reproduced	Only Information	Citation	Adaptation	Total
	A	B	C	D	
General	16	38	-	11	65
Adjustment	02	04	-	-	06
Anxiety	-	04	-	03	07
Self-Concept	-	10	-	01	11
Motivation	-	09	-	-	09
Total	18	63	0	15	98

General Instruments

In all 62 instruments are listed under this title. The instruments cover different personality dimensions. A few of these are multi-trait personality tests and cover more than a single personality dimension. Some of the instruments are exclusively meant to cover a single or a select few dimensions, like extraversion, introversion, neuroticism etc. The different dimensions covered by these general personality instruments include : security-insecurity, mental health, altruism, non-violence, authoritarianism, frustration, manifest hostility, punctuality, stress and strain, social conformity, locus of control, racialism, conservation, ego-identity, certainty of judgment, risk-taking, parental behaviour, menopausal symptoms, persistence and dominance etc. A few instruments for clinical diagnosis measuring psychiatric disability, psychosis, neurosis, paranoid tendencies etc. are also reported here. Out of 62 instruments, 11 are adaptations. Only technical information about the other 37 instruments is provided here. 14 instruments are originally reproduced here. No citations are available.

Instruments are available mainly for school and college students. Different techniques such as scales, checklists, questionnaires, inventories and tests, have been used in measuring the different dimensions of personality.

Regarding the standardisation measures, the reliabilities and validities of these instruments have been established. Split-half and test-retest are the most common forms of reliabilities.

The size of the sample on which the reliability coefficients are based, is mentioned only in a few instruments, hence, no significant conclusions can be drawn on these. However, the coefficients in most of the cases are very high and thus, these instruments can be considered as well standardised instruments.

As regards the validity, many of the instruments are not validated. A quarter of the instruments available do not report any validity. A few of them simply report that validity is established without giving any details. Validity by correlating the instruments with other standardised instruments seems to be the popular type. Concurrent and validity by ratings are also commonly used. The validity coefficients wherever reported are fairly high and encouraging. More attention needs to be paid on application of systematic techniques of validation.

There are 14 original instruments which will be reproduced here. Multi Dimensional Parenting Scale by N.S. Chauhan and C.P. Khokhar is meant for adults, and assesses deviant and non-deviant parenting. The Menopausal Experience Scale by Neelakshi Arvind Lavakare is a summated rating scale which is used for the diagnosis of Menopausal suffering and screening before treatment among women. It is useful to the middle aged women between 40-55 years. There is a Personality Inventory which measures the different dimensions of personality of educated subjects (10 years of Schooling).

There are some instruments which measure neuroticism and introversion.

There is a test called Childhood Psychopathology Measurement Schedule which measures psychiatric symptoms in children. The test is in both the languages English and Hindi. It can be used for screening children. There is another test called Temperament Measurement Schedule which is used for measuring the temperament of children seeking psychiatric help as well as normal children. Other tests reproduced here measure reactions to frustration, security insecurity, mental health, altruism, ascendence and submission among school and college students. Scales on assessing sex roles of college youth are also included in this section. The Coimbatore Androgyny Inventory (CAI) assesses the different sex-role identity as well as the response set variable "social desirability."

A few of the instruments reproduced here have reported norms. Most of the instruments do not report any norms and a few of them do not report any reliability and validity. These instruments have been reproduced for benefit of further researches.

There are 11 adaptations of some of the standard instruments in this area. Most of these instruments are meant for school or college students, or young adults. Samajik Pratikriya Soochi is an adaptation of the Original J.B. Rotter's test which measures the Internality-Externality (Locus of Control). This test is available both in Hindi and English. Then, among the other adaptations is the Adaptation of Cattell's Sixteen Personality Factors. This test is available in Gujarati. Another is Cattell's Early School Personality Questionnaire for Gujarati Children of Ages 6-8. Another one is High School Personality Questionnaire for ages 12-18. There is another adaptation of Cattell's Children Personality Questionnaire for Gujarati Children of ages 8-12 years. All these tests are available in the Gujarati language. Reliability and Validity have been reported for most of the instruments. Indian norms are also provided for these instruments.

Adjustment and Problems

There are 6 instruments which measure personality adjustment and problems. Two instruments will be available in their original forms and will be reproduced here. One instrument can be used mainly to measure the family adjustment of working women and another instrument can be used for measuring the marital satisfaction or the quality of marital life.

Information about the other 4 instruments is reported here which also measure adjustment.

The adjustment inventories are meant for measuring the adjustment in several areas like home, health, social, emotional and school adjustment of adolescents and college going students. Some other instruments are also available which measure neurotic tendencies and aggression etc. Reliabilities have been reported by 5 out of 6 instruments. Most of the instruments have reported both split-half and test-retest reliabilities. A few of them have reported only one type of reliability. The coefficients of reliabilities are quite high and are mostly above 0.70. Only for two instruments reliability data is not available.

As regards the validity, the instruments have reported validity by using Pearson Product Moment Correlation Formula, Spearman-Brown Formula (Split-half method), Internal validity, ratings, and the correlation of the scores of the instruments with other standardised instruments. Some instruments have reported concurrent and construct validity. One instrument has no validity data available.

On the whole, the coefficients of validity reported by these instruments seem to be at an acceptable level.

Two instruments have been reproduced here. Marital Satisfaction Scale by Brunda Amrithraj and Indira Jai Prakash assesses marital satisfaction or quality of marital life, and it reports highly significant reliability and validity data. Family Adjustment Inventory For Working Women is available in English and measures the family adjustment of married working women. On the whole, the adjustment inventories reported here seem to be fairly well standardised.

Anxiety

There are 7 instruments reported here which measure anxiety. No original scale is available which could be reproduced here. The scales are meant for high school and college students.

One instrument is available in Hindi and measures the symptoms of anxiety relating to social avoidance and distress. It also assesses the level of social anxiety. This test is meant for college going students. The other instrument is the Test-Anxiety Scale (TAS). The scale is available both in Hindi and English. The scale consists of 25 test situations, each provided with 5 alternatives to select from.

This test is mainly used to measure the level of test anxiety, indicating children who would at a later date experience the pre-dominantly disabling effects of anxiety. Another scale is Sinha's Comprehensive Anxiety Test (SCAT) by A.K.P. Sinha and L.N.K. Sinha. It measures the level of anxiety in the college students. There is an instrument called Academic Anxiety Scale for Children by A.K. Singh and A. Sen Gupta which measures the academic anxiety for children which relates to the impending danger from the environments of the academic institutions. Levels for whom it is meant are school students of class VIII to X, with age range of 13-16 years. There are 3 adaptations in this section. Two adaptations are the Sarasan's Test Anxiety Scale; and the Sarason's General Anxiety Scale for Children. All the three scales are in the Hindi version. All the anxiety instruments have reported high reliability and validity coefficients. All the tests have either reported split-half reliability coefficients or test-retest reliabilities.

Six instruments have been validated by correlating with other instruments and yield highly significant coefficients of correlation. Predictive validity has been found in one scale. Only one scale has no validity established. Norms in terms of 'T' Scores and 'Percentile' are prepared for all the instruments.

Self-Concept

There are 11 instruments available on this theme out of which there is not a single instrument which can be reproduced. There are 10 instruments which have only information and there is one adaptation. Information about 10 instruments are reported here which measure self-esteem, self-concept of illiterate adults, self-concept of normals, neurotics and schizophrenics (adults), personal worth, self-esteem, self-perception and self-identity.

There is a Self-Esteem Inventory by Nalini Rao which is an adaptation measuring appraisal of self-evaluation. The scale is useful in assessing self-attitude of subjects in parent, peer, personal interest and school contexts.

Reliabilities have been reported for all the instruments. Both the split-half and test-retest methods have been found to be very high. Only one instrument does not report either reliability or validity. Validity coefficients are reported in the rest of the instruments. Content validity, factorial validity, and clinical validation is reported in some instruments. Other instruments have been validated by correlation methods.

Motivation

There are 9 instruments listed on this theme. All the 9 instruments contain only information. The instruments in this area measure prolonged deprivation, personality need, encouragement given by parents, level of aspiration, power motive, achievement motivation and fear of failure motivation. There are 3 instruments on achievement motivation measuring the achievement motive of an individual, who may be adults, adolescents, or students. One instrument is a Projective test of Achievement Motivation. One is the Self-Expression Inventory, measuring sense of deprivation. The title has been faked so that the respondent cannot decipher the real purpose of the test, meant for high school students. One instrument is the Sports Motivation Inventory which measures the motivation of Indian sportsmen and sportswomen. It may prove to be a perfect test for selection, training, coaching, and skill improvement in pursuit of excellence in sports performance.

Reliabilities have been reported for all the instruments. Both the split-half and the test-retest methods have been used and the values have been found to be very high.

All the instruments report validity. Validity coefficients are found out by expert's ratings, content, criterion, and concurrent methods. Standardization data on these scales can be had from the authors.

General Instruments

A

11A(1)

Title of the Instrument : **Temperament Measurement Schedule.**

Purpose : Measures temperament of children.

Authors : Savita Malhotra and Anil Malhotra.

Languages : English and Hindi.

Availability : National Psychological Corporation, Kacheri Ghat, Agra-4.

Uses : Temperament assessment of children seeking psychiatric help as well as normal children. It may be used for research as well as for clinical assessment of children.

Level : Children who are normals as well as abnormals.

Main features : 15 items each on a 5 point scale with mid point (average) at 3.

Reliability : Test-retest reliability (8 weeks interval) = 0.83 to 0.94 ; Inter rater reliability=0.88 to 0.96.

Validity : Factorial validity and construct validity studied and was found satisfactory.

Time Limit : 30-40 minutes.

Norms : They are available in the manual which may be obtained from the publisher.

References :

1. Malhotra, S., Randhawa, A. (1982) : A Schedule for measuring temperament in Children. Preliminary data on Development and standardization. *Indian J. Clini Psychol* 9, 203-210.
2. Malhotra, S. Malhotra, A., Randhawa, A (1983). Children's Temperament : Factorial validity. *Indian J. Clini Psychol*, 10, 399-406.
3. Malhotra, S. Malhotra, A., Randhawa, A. (1983) Temperament as a discriminating variable between emotionally disturbed and normal children. *Indian J. Clini Psychol*, 10, 79-84.
4. Malhotra, S. (1984) Study of Temperament and its relationship with phenomenology of Childhood Psychiatric Disorders. Ph.D. thesis. Post-graduate Institute of Medical Education and Research.

Chandigarh, India.

5. Malhotra, S. Varma V.K., Varma S.K. (1986) Temperament as determinant of phenomenology of childhood psychiatric disorders. *Indian J. Psychiatry* 28 (4), 263-276.
6. Malhotra,S. (1989) Varying Risk Factors and Outcomes : An Indian Perspective in *Clinical and Educational Application of Temperament Research.* Eds. Carey W.B., Mc Devitt S.C. Pub. Swets & Zeit Linger B.V. Netherlands. (in press).

TEMPERAMENT MEASUREMENT SCHEDULE

No. Date

Name Age : Sex :

Education :

Residence : (Address)

Informant :

Instructions

Information is to be obtained regarding the child's temperament before the onset of symptoms if he has an illness or about when the child has been his most usual self if he has no illness. Informant should be one of the parents, preferably the mother. Each item explores into some area of routine activities of the child which may be repetitious at places but measures different aspects of the temperament. Items are generally the probes and minor elaborations are permitted wherever necessary. Score all items on a five point scale, where 1 and 5 denote the two extremes of frequency and intensity on the negative and positive direction with the average at point 3.

1=Hardly Ever; 2=Once in a while; 3=Sometimes; 4=Often; 5=Almost always

Activity Level

1. How active is your child? Do you find him so active that he runs rather than walks or is he so inactive that he hardly moves? 1 2 3 4 5
आपका बच्चा कितना चुस्त है ? क्या आपको ऐसा लगता है कि यह इतना चुस्त है कि चलने की बजाए भागता है या इतना सुस्त है कि हिलता ही नही ?
2. Can he keep still or does he have difficulty in doing so and keeps moving and fidgeting?
क्या यह टिक कर बैठ सकता है या हर समय हिलता-जुलता ही रहता है ?
3. Can he sit still while listening to story, joke or some interesting happening? 1 2 3 4 5
जब यह कोई कहानी, चुटकुला या मजेदार बात सुन रहा हो तो क्या यह टिक कर सुनता है या घूमता फिरता ही सुनता है ?
4. While playing does he run and jump about being actively involved or does he quietly move about? 1 2 3 4 5
खेलते समय यह काफी उछल-कूद, भाग-दौड़ करता है या चुपचाप एक तरफ रहता है ?
5. While eating does he eat staying still or does he keep moving about? 1 2 3 4 5
खाना खाते समय यह कितना हिलता-जुलता है ? आराम से बैठकर खाता है या पूरा समय हिलता-जुलता, छेड़खानी करता रहता है ?

Rhythmicity

1. Does your child feel hungry at approximately the same time every day?
Are you able to tell roughly at what time he is bound to feel hungry? 1 2 3 4 5
इसके भूख लगने का कोई नियमित (खास) समय होता है या किसी भी समय भूख लग जाती है ? क्या आपको पता होता है कि इसे किस समय भूख लगेगी ?

2. Does your child eat roughly the same amount of food every day or does it vary from one day to the next? Do you have an idea of how big or small an appetite he generally has? 1 2 3 4 5
आमतौर पर यह खाना रोज जितना ही खाता है या किसी दिन बहुत ज्यादा और किसी दिन बहुत कम खाता है? क्या आपको इसको भूख का अन्दाजा रहता है कि यह कितना खाना खायेगा?
3. Does your child go to sleep at approximately the same time every night? What time does he generally go to sleep?
क्या इसके सोने को कोई नियमित (खास) समय होता है? हर रोज कितने बजे सोता है? रोज इसी समय सोता है या इसके सोने का समय बदल जाता है?
4. At what time does your child wake up every morning? On weekends or holidays does your child wake up at the same time as on other (school) days or does the time change? 1 2 3 4 5
आपका बच्चा सुबह कितने बजे उठता है? इतवार को या छुट्टियों में यह किस समय उठ जाता है? हर रोज की तरह या समय बदल जाता है?
5. Does your child have the bowel movement at about the same time every day? 1 2 3 4 5
हर रोज टट्टी किस समय जाता है? इसका समय रोज वही रहता है या बदल जाता है

Approach-Withdrawal

1. What is your child's first reaction when he meets a stranger (relative, neighbour, doctor, shopkeeper, bus-conductor etc)? Does he approach the stranger, talk to him or does he feel shy, frightened? 1 2 3 4 5
जब इसको नये लोग मिलें जो पहले नहीं मिले (relative, neighbour, doctor, shopkeeper, bus-conductor etc.) तो यह एक दम क्या करता है? कैसे behave करता है? उनके पास जाता है, उनसे बातचीत करता है या डरता, शर्माता है?

2. What is your child's first reaction when he meets children of his age for the first time? Does he approach them, get friendly or does he feel hesitant, shy, frightened. 1 2 3 4 5

   अगर पहली बार अपनी उमर के बच्चों से मिले तो शुरू शुरू में क्या करता है? उनके पास जाता, घुल-मिल जाता है या शर्माता, डरता है?

3. If he is given a new food (or placed in a new situation) what is his first reaction, will he try it of does he refuse to do so? 1 2 3 4 5

   जब इसे कोई नई तरह का खाना दिया जाये (या कोई नई स्थिति में हो) तो क्या करता है? एक दम खा लेता है या पहले मना करता है?

4. When your child is introduced to a new game or activity does he join in at once or initially prefers to sit on the side and watch? 1 2 3 4 5

   जब इसे कोई नई खेल/(activity) बताई जाये तो क्या यह फटाफट से उसमें भाग लेने के लिए तैयार होता या पहले दूसरों को खेलते देखना पसन्द करता है?

5. What is your child's first reaction when he is offered a new toy, game or clothes? Does he accept it with enthusiasm or does he hesitate, watch from far, preferring his familiar toys, games and clothes. 1 2 3 4 5

   अगर इसे कोई नई चीज (खिलौना, कपड़ा) दिया जाये जो इसने पहले देखा न हो तो यह क्या करता है? एक दम शौक से पकड़ कर देखता है या दूर से देखता है? क्या यह अपनी पुरानी चीजें ही पसन्द करता है और नई की ओर ध्यान नहीं देता है?

Adaptability

1. Food that he refused earlier or disliked earlier does he still refuse it or has he now accepted it? After how long did he accept it? 1 2 3 4 5

   जो खाना इसे पहले पसन्द नहीं था क्या यह अब वो खाना खा लेता है? कितनी देर बाद आराम (खुशी) से खाने लग जाता है?

2. If your child has been shy with some stranger earlier, how long does it take him to get friendly? Just a few minutes or a long time. 1 2 3 4 5

अगर यह किसी से शुरू-शुरू में शर्माता हो तो कितनी देर के बाद उनसे दोस्ती कर लेता है या घुलमिल जाता है ? जल्दी से या काफी देर के बाद ?

3. If your child has been shy with some children earlier how long does it take him to mix up and get friendly just a couple of minutes or a long time? 1 2 3 4 5
   यह शुरू-शुरू में जिन बच्चों से शर्माता था क्या अब यह उनसे बातचीत करता है, घुलमिल गया है? कितनी देर के बाद उनसे दोस्ती कर लेता है?
4. If he initially hesitates to join a game how long does it take him to start participating in it? Immediately, after sometimes or never? 1 2 3 4 5
   अगर यह कोई नये खेल में भाग लेने से आनाकानी करता है तो कितनी देर के बाद यह खेल में अपने आप भाग लेना शुरू कर देता है? बहुत जल्दी ही या कुछ देर के बाद या बिल्कुल ही भाग नहीं लेता है?
5. Does he settle back into school routine quickly after a long holiday or does it take him a long time to do so? 1 2 3 4 5
   लम्बी छुट्यिों के बाद क्या यह स्कूल के कार्यक्रम में जल्दी ही घुलमिल जाता है या कुछ समय लेता है?

Mood

1. Is your child generally happy, satisfied or generally unhappy discontented? 1 2 3 4 5
   आमतौर पर यह बच्चा खुश-हंसता, मुस्कुराता रहता है या चिड़चिड़ा असन्तुष्ट रहता है?
2. When with other children does he seem to be happy and having a good time? Is he generally dissatisfied, angry, irritable? 1 2 3 4 5
   जब यह दूसरे बच्चों के साथ होता है तो क्या यह खुश होता है लगता है कि मजे में है या आमतौर पर चिड़चिड़ा और गुस्से में लगता है?
3. When playing with other children does he argue/ fight with them or does he not? 1 2 3 4 5

जब यह दूसरे बच्चों के साथ खेलता हो तो उनसे बहस झगड़ा करता है या बड़े प्यार व आराम से खेलता है?

4. If your child cannot have or do something that he wants, them for how long does he remain annoyed—only momentarily or for a long time? 1 2 3 4 5
जब इसे कोई चीज जो यह चाहता हो न दी जाय या कोई चीज जो यह करना चाहता हो और उससे मना किया जाये यह कितनी देर तक गुस्से में या नाराज रहता है? कुछ ही पल या काफी देर तक?

5. When he is given something that he is fond of and wants, what is his reaction? Is he happy, smiles only momentarily or for a long time? 1 2 3 4 5
यदि इसे कोई चीज दी जाये जो यह चाहता हो और पसन्द हो तो यह क्या करता है? धीरे से मुस्कुराता है या जोर से हंसता, बहुत खुश होता है? कितनी देर के लिए ऐसा रहता है कुछ ही पल या बहुत देर तक?

Intensity

1. What is his reaction if he is given some food which he likes very much. Is he very happy and eats it with relish or does it not make much of a difference to him? 1 2 3 4 5
What is his reaction if he is given some food which he dislikes? Does he turn up his nose at it, protests mildy, gets angry, throws his plate, on the floor? 1 2 3 4 5
अगर इसे कोई खाना बहुत अच्छा लगे तो यह क्या करता है? बहुत खुशी से मजे से खाता है या कोई खास फर्क नहीं?
और अगर इसे कोई खाना नापसन्द हो तो क्या करता है? सिर्फ मुंह बनाता है, बहुत गुस्सा करता या फैंक देता है?

2. If your child is taken away or stopped from an activity that he enjoys very much, how does he react? Does he protest mildy, gets annoyed, angry or starts crying? 1 2 3 4 5
यदि आप इसे कोई खेल या किसी कार्य से जो इसे बहुत पसन्द हो हटा दें तो यह क्या करता है- सिर्फ मना करता है, नाराज होता है या बहुत गुस्सा होता है या फिर रोने लग जाता है?

3. When he is not given something that he wants then how does he behave? Does not matter very much, gets a little annoyed, gets angry, cries and yells. 1 2 3 4 5
अगर इसे कोई चीज जो यह चाहता हो न दी जाए तो यह क्या करता है - ? सिर्फ मुंह बनाता है, बहुत गुस्सा करता, रोता चिल्लाता है या इसे कोई फर्क ही नहीं पड़ता ?
4. What is his reaction if he or his team loses a game? Does not mind very much, takes it lightly or gets upset, cries? 1 2 3 4 5
अगर यह बच्चा या इसकी टीम कभी किसी खेल में हार जाए तो यह कैसा महसूस करता है - एक दम झगड़ा करने या रोने लग जाता या बहुत महसूस नहीं करता?
5. What is his reaction if another child takes away his toy or book or any other possession? Does not matter much, gets upset, cries, fights with the other child. 1 2 3 4 5
अगर कोई दूसरा बच्चा इसकी कोई चीज या खिलौना किताब ले ले तो यह क्या करता है - नाराज होता, रोता है, मारपीट करता है, या इसे कोई फर्क नहीं पड़ता?

Threshold

1. Does he seem to bother about the minor noises or sounds around or does he ignore these? 1 2 3 4 5
अगर आस - पास छोटी - मोटी आवाजें या शोर हो तो क्या उनकी परवाह करता है या इसे कोई फर्क नहीं पड़ता जैसे की ध्यान नहीं देता ?
2. Does he ignore the temperature of food hot or cold? 1 2 3 4 5
अगर खाना बहुत गर्म हो या ठंडा हो तो क्या यह उराके बारे में कहता है या बिना कुछ कहे चुपचाप खा लेता है?
3. Does the child have to be seriously injured before he comments, cries about cuts, bruises? 1 2 3 4 5
जब इसे कोई छोटी - मोटी चोट लग जाये तो क्या यह आकर बताता है या तभी जिक्र करता जब कि चोट / जख्म ज्यादा हो?
4. Does the child not react if accidently touched pushed or lightly brushed by another child? 1 2 3 4 5
खेलते समय अगर इसको कोई धक्का दे दे या छू दे तो क्या यह उसकी शिकायत करता है, रोता है या परवाह नहीं करता?

5. If there is something new or different about things or people at home, does he notice it immediately or not? 1 2 3 4 5
यदि घर में कोई नई चीजें या घर के पास कोई नई तरह का सामान हो तो क्या इसका ध्यान एक दम उस तरफ जाता है या नहीं?

Distractibility

1. If he is annoyed or in a bad mood can he be easily joked out of it or is it very difficult to do so? 1 2 3 4 5
अगर यह कभी नाराज हो जाये या कुछ चिड़चिड़े (mood) में हो तो क्या यह मजाक इत्यादि करने से मान/बहल जाता है या बहुत मुश्किल होती है?
2. What does he generally do, if he is playing or is absorbed in some work, and there is a noise outside his window or on the road, will he keep on with his activity or will he be easily drawn away from it? 1 2 3 4 5
अगर यह खेल रहा हो या और कोई काम में लगा हो और खिड़की के बाहर या सड़क पर कोई शोर या ऊची आवाजें सुनाई दें तो यह क्या करता है - अपने काम में ध्यान लगा कर बैठा रहता है, ध्यान ही नहीं देता या एकदम उठकर देखने जाता है?
3. Is it easy or difficult to console him with a toy or story when he is crying? 1 2 3 4 5
जब कभी यह रोने लग जाये तब इसको खिलौने देकर (कहानी सुनाकर) आसानी से बहलाया जा सकता है या बहुत मुश्किल होती है?
4. Do you find that he is engrossed in an interesting task, you have to call out several times before he hears or responds? 1 2 3 4 5
अगर यह किसी दिलचस्प काम में लगा हो तो क्या ऐसा भी होता है कि जब तक आप इसे दो चार आवाजें न लगायें इसे सुनाई ही नहीं देता?
5. While the child is eating or reading if someone knocks at the door or comes does he immediately stop eating or reading or does he continue to do it? 1 2 3 4 5

मान लो यह पढ़ रहा हो या खाना खा रहा हो और घर में कोई मेहमान आ जाये तो क्या यह खाना या पढ़ाई छोड़ देता है या उनसे पल दो पल बात करने के बाद अपनी पढ़ाई या खाने पर वापिस आ जाता है?

Persistence

1. When your child starts on some project like painting etc. does he work at it completing it no matter how long it takes or does he give it up without completing it? 1 2 3 4 5
जब कभी यह कोई मनपसन्द काम शुरू करता है जैसे कि कोई तस्वीर बनाना इत्यादि तो क्या यह उसको पूरा करता है चाहे कि कितना भी समय लग जाये या उसको जल्दी की बिना पूरा किया छोड़ देता है?
2. If your child finds a game or a piece of work difficult, what does he do? Does he quickly turn to another activity or does he keep on trying until he learns that particular game or activity? 1 2 3 4 5
अगर बच्चे को कोई काम या खेल मुश्किल लगे तो यह क्या करता है–छोड़ कर कुछ और करने लग जाता या उसको किसी तरह सीखने की कोशिश करता रहता है?
3. For how long can he continue on the same activity? For about an hour or less than that? 1 2 3 4 5
अगर यह किसी काम में लगा हो तो कितनी देर तक उसे ध्यान लगाकर करता रहेगा? आम तौर पर अन्दाजन एक घंटा या उससे कम?
4. If he gets angry or annoyed how long does it take him to come out of it? Just a few moments or long time? 1 2 3 4 5
अगर बच्चा कभी नाराज हो या गुस्सा हो जाये तो कितनी देर में (mood) ठीक हो जाता है? जल्दी ही कुछ पल में या बहुत देर में ठीक होता है?
5. If you interrupt your child's activity does he try to go back to it or does he forget it? 1 2 3 4 5
अगर बच्चा कोई काम कर रहा हो या खेल में लगा हो और उस को कुछ समय के लिए हटा लिया जाये तो क्या करता है–उस काम या खेल पर दोबारा लग जाता या उसे भूल जाता है?

SCORING GUIDE

Activity	Score 1.	Completely still or very little movement
	5.	Always on the move, jumps rather than walks always fidgeting.
Rhythmicity	Score 1.	Very and always irregular
	5.	Very fussy about time even when away from home.
Approach withdrawal	Score 1.	Feels frightened, cries, withdraws physically
	5.	Goes and talks spontaneously, rushes into new places. spontaneously hold or touches new things.
Adaptability	Score 1.	No adaptability—doesn't accept change at all
	5.	Initial reaction of withdrawal is only momentary.
Mood	Score 1.	Always crying, angry, annoyed, irritable, discontented
	5.	Always laughing, giggling, contented, happy.
Intensity	Score 1.	Hardly any reaction
	5.	Roaring with laughter screaming with anger, crying loudly.
Threshold	Score 1.	Low threshold—easily bothered by noise, comments on temperature of food etc.
	5.	High threshold—not bothered by noise, ignores temperature of food etc.
Distractibility	Score 1.	Low distractibility—even on frustration and active effort can't be distracted.
	5.	Highly distractible on his own.
Persistence	Score 1.	No persistence—no effort at all
	5.	Continues till he achieves what he set out to.

11A (2)

Title of the Instrument : **Multi Dimensional Parenting (MDP-Scale).**
Purpose : Measures fathering and mothering.
Authors : Chauhan, N.S. ; C.P. Khokhar.
Languages : Hindi and (English version attached.).
Availability : MAPA (Meerut), D-69, Shastrinagar, Meerut.
Uses : Research in deviant and non-deviant parenting.
Levels : Adults.
Main Features : 5 point scale, 56 items.
Reliability : The internal consistency of the scale has been determined in two ways. Detailed reliability coefficients are given in the manual. The reliability of the whole scale was found to be 0.589 by the test-retest method and 0.62 for split half method. (Positive dimension. (B.) For the negative dimension Test-retest method was 0.878 and 0.921 for split-half method.
Validity : As no other test is available in the field the criterion-measure was used. The coefficient of validity was found to be for the Positive Dimension. The test as a Whole = 0.67, Negative Dimension As a whole = 0.72.
Time Limit : Unlimited.
Norms : Available in the manual.
References :

1. Baldwin, *et al.* : The appraisal of parental behaviour. *J. Psychol. Mono* 1949, 63 No.4.
2. Bandura, A. and Walters, R.H. : *Social learning and personality development*, New York, Holt, Rinehart and Wintson, 1963.
3. Baumrind, D. : Current patterns of parental authority. *Develop. Psychol. Monograph*, 1971, 4 (1, part 2). 1-103. u
4. Becker *et al.* ; Factors in parental behaviour and personality as related to problem behaviour in children. *J. Consult Psycho*, 1959 (23) 107-118.
5. Ghurye, G.S. : *Caste and Class in India*, Popular Book Depot Bombay, 1957 (31) 240.

(English Version)

SCALE FOR MULTI-DIMENSIONAL PARENTING (M.D.P. SCALE)

* Dr. N.S. Chauhan, Professor of Psychology, Meerut University.
* Dr. C.P. Khokhar & Dr. Vikram Singh.

Name	:	Education:
Age	:	Rural/Urban:
Sex	:	Eco. Status:
Occupation	:	Address:
Date:		

Instructions

1. The scale contains some statements about children.
2. Read each statement carefully; for answer tick the underlined from the agreement level whichever suits you.
3. The description of answers is as follows:

Agree Very much	Agree much	Agree Ordinarily	Agree Less	Agree Much less	Do Not Agree
( )	( )	( )	( )	( )	( )

4. You are to tick only one of the answers for each question.
5. Answer all questions.
6. All answers are to be taken as correct and will be kept confidential.

	Agree Very much	Agree much	Agree Ordi-narily	Agree Less	Agree Very Less	Do Not Ag.
	1	2	3	4	5	6
1. Thought about good food and arrangement of dress for my children, ponders over my mind.	—	—	—	—	—	—
2. I fulfil the need whenever it is felt by children.	—	—	—	—	—	—
3. I provide only limited pleasure and convenience to children.	—	—	—	—	—	—
4. The achievements of my children are inactive in promotion of my encouragement.	—	—	—	—	—	—
5. I reward children for each of their achievement.	—	—	—	—	—	—

(Contd.)

	1	2	3	4	5	6
6. I always exhibit sympathy for problems of children.	—	—	—	—	—	—
7. Due to my involvement in worldly affairs, I remain helpless in fulfilment of needs of children.	—	—	—	—	—	—
8. I pay scanty attention to loving of children.	—	—	—	—	—	—
9. I use to say something in praise whenever the child is seen doing something.	—	—	—	—	—	—
10. I keep in mind the interest, encouragement and recreation of children.	—	—	—	—	—	—
11. My order for children remains over and above their feelings etc.	—	—	—	—	—	—
12. I always like to see the work as complete, allotted to children and become angry if not done so.	—	—	—	—	—	—
13. I give a sympathetic answer to curiosity of children.	—	—	—	—	—	—
14. Children in the family enjoy full independence in expressing each of their ideas.	—	—	—	—	—	—
15. I put more the failures of children before them.	—	—	—	—	—	—
16. My pleasure remains without expression even on the success of my children.	—	—	—	—	—	—
17. My children enjoy full independence in selecting subject and school in education.	—	—	—	—	—	—
18. I surely take advice of children in matters related to them.	—	—	—	—	—	—
19. I tolerate my criticism made by my children.	—	—	—	—	—	—
20. The social relations of children are beyond my control.	—	—	—	—	—	—
21. My children have full independence in taking any decision about their game/ recreation.	—	—	—	—	—	—
22. I pay special attention to education, food and dress procurement of my children.	—	—	—	—	—	—
23. Modernity of the day is senseless. I tell my children to adopt those very old customs and traditions.	—	—	—	—	—	—

(Contd.)

	1	2	3	4	5	6
24. There remains a prohibition from my side against going of children to cinema or theatre.	—	—	—	—	—	—
25. I have seen the world, you are still a child. Do as I say.	—	—	—	—	—	—
26. School-dress of children is arranged as per my wish.	—	—	—	—	—	—
27. I take assistance of children for promotion of family income.	—	—	—	—	—	—
28. Due to reasons, I am helpless in providing most of things of children.	—	—	—	—	—	—
29. I always call my children by their surnames (e.g. Pappu, Guddu etc.).	—	—	—	—	—	—
30. Mostly on my way back to home, I embress and kiss children.	—	—	—	—	—	—
31. Curiosity of children are so many that it is impossible for me to provide answers to all.	—	—	—	—	—	—
32. Being perturbed from family affairs, I use bad words for children.	—	—	—	—	—	—
33. Motivating children involved in work, has become my habit.	—	—	—	—	—	—
34. I fulfil wishes of children after telling them feelings and wishes of my childhood.	—	—	—	—	—	—
35. Misbehaviour of children compels me to use bad words for them.	—	—	—	—	—	—
36. Going to cinema with children is done less frequently by me.	—	—	—	—	—	—
37. Whenever I go for a walk, I take children with me.	—	—	—	—	—	—
38. I enjoy unique pleasure in satisfying the maximum of wishes of my children.	—	—	—	—	—	—
39. Provision of punishment is right for rectification of mistakes. I use this in case of children.	—	—	—	—	—	—
40. I want to see the work allotted to children in time. Its negligence is intolerable for me.	—	—	—	—	—	—
41. I keep the pocket money of children in mind.	—	—	—	—	—	—
42. My children enjoy full independence for going to clubs and keeping friendship with age mates (boys/girls).	—	—	—	—	—	—
43. Asking something repeatedly by children does not appear palatable to me. I chide them for this.	—	—	—	—	—	—

(Contd.)

	1	2	3	4	5	6
44. Failures of children despite providing good conveniences, compel me to beat them.	—	—	—	—	—	—
45. In talking to children, I mind their feelings and wishes.	—	—	—	—	—	—
46. A correct criticism of mine by children is acceptable to me.	—	—	—	—	—	—
47. It is beyond my power to adopt a critical method before them while making assessment of children.	—	—	—	—	—	—
48. I remain indifferent towards complaints against children.	—	—	—	—	—	—
49. I allot responsibility to children according to their age alone.	—	—	—	—	—	—
50. I do full efforts to provide for children music education and journals.	—	—	—	—	—	—
51. I keep children in limited independence.	—	—	—	—	—	—
52. I usually say - keep satisfied within available conveniences and do not wish for more.	—	—	—	—	—	—
53. Children must seek permission from me for going to other houses and making friends.	—	—	—	—	—	—
54. Untimely taking of food and recreation of children compels me to become angry.	—	—	—	—	—	—
55. Putting repeatedly by children the needs that I can not satisfy, makes me angry.	—	—	—	—	—	—
56. I could not effect control over my children due to my inability.	—	—	—	—	—	—

11A (3)

Title of the Instrument : **Psychological Sex Role Orientation Inventory.**

Purpose : To assess the psychological sex role orientation of the individual.

Author(s) : Sudha Bhogle, Geeta Rao Gupta and Vinoda N. Murthy.

Language : English.

Availability : Dr. Sudha Bhogle, Department of Psychology, Bangalore University, Bangalore 560 056.

Uses : Helps to determine the psychological sex role orientation of the individual and categorise individuals as masculine, feminine, androgynous, or undifferentiated.

Levels : Adolescents and above.

Main Features : It is a self administered inventory, based on Bem's conception of masculinity and femininity as two different dimensions which can co-exist in an individual. It consists of 30 adjectives describing personality, of which 15 are 'masculine' adjectives and 15 are 'feminine' adjectives as determined for an Indian population. The Subject is asked to evaluate, on a 7 point Likert Scale, the presence or the absence of the trait in himself. Items are arranged such that odd numbered items (i.e., 1,3,5..) measure masculinity and even numbered items (i.e., 2,4,6..) measure femininity. Scores are totalled separately for the two dimensions are averaged to get the masculinity and femininity score, for the subject. Using the median split technique, the subject can then be categorised as masculine, feminine, androgynous, or undifferentiated in his sex role orientation.

Reliability : Test-retest : Masculinity Scale .80 $p < .01$

Femininity Scale .80 $p < .01$

Split Half Masculinity Scale .45 $p < .01$

(S-B Correction) Masculinity Scale .55 $p < .01$

Validity : Construct validity : between the two scales was .15 (n.s.) indicating that the two scales are independent.

With average :	Masculinity scale	.36 $p < .01$
rating to peers	Femininity scale	.37 $p < .01$
	Self rating : Masculinity scale	.16 n.s.
	Femininity scale	.34 $p < .05$

Time Limit : 10 minutes.

Norms : Available with the author.

References :

1. *B.S.R.I. (A) — An Indian Adaptation of the Bem Sex Role Inventory.*
2. *Personality Study and Group Behaviour*, 1982, 2(1), 1-10.

PSYCHOLOGICAL SEX ROLE ORIENTATION INVENTORY

Instructions: Given below are a list of adjectives describing personality. Read each adjective and mark on the 7 point scale next to it how well each adjective describes *you*. 1 represents one extreme — never or almost never true and 7 represents the other extreme — always or almost always true of you. In each case put a cross on the appropriate number. Please answer all items.

Items

1. Act as a leader
2. Adaptable
3. Aggressive
4. Emotional
5. Ambitious
6. Faithful
7. Arrogant
8. Generous
9. Assertive
10. Gentle
11. Competitive
12. Homely
13. Conceited
14. Innocent
15. Defend own beliefs
16. Love children
17. Dominant
18. Religious
19. Forceful
20. Sensitive
21. Independent
22. Shy
23. Individualistic
24. Submissive
25. Self-centered
26. Tender
27. Self-reliant
28. Tolerant
29. Self-sufficient
30. Willing to sacrifice.

11A (4)

Title of the Instrument : **A Questionnaire without Questions.**

Purpose : To measure response biases. To study dissatisfaction level.

Authors : S.K. Verma, B.L. Dubey, D.K. Menon, Anil Malhotra (PGI Chandigarh.).

Language : English.

Availability : Available with the author.

Uses : Mainly to measure response biases, also to study dissatisfaction level.

Levels : All educational levels (Orally to illiterates, Knowing English.)

Main Features : A simple 12 item questionnaire with varied response categories.

Reliability : Percentage agreement 50 to 100 per cent for different items. (Stability over time.).

Validity : Agreement with other studies (Burg and Rapoport Study and Heergen and Hoogstran Study.). Construct validity Percentage of responses changing in the predicted direction, Evidence of biases.

Time Limit : 10 minutes.

Norms : Available in terms of responses.

References : (a) Verma, S.K.; Menon, D.K. and Malhotra, A. (1980) Response tendencies in a questionnaire without questions. *Indian J. of Clinical Psychology*. 7,151-

155.

(b) Verma, S.K. and Dubey, B.L. (1983) : Stability of the responses Choices on a questionnaire without questions. *Psycho-Lingua*. 12(1). 61-64.

(c) Dubey, B.L. and Verma, S.K. (1985) : A Study of dissatisfaction index on a questionnaire without questions. *Indian J. of Clinical Psychology* 11, 19-21.

(d) Dubey, B.L. Verma, S.K. and Dwivedi, P. (1982) : Induced Frustration set, neuroticism and response biases on a questionnaire without questions. *Researches in Psychology*. 1(1) 23-30.

(e) Dubey, B.L.; Verma, S.K.; Uppal K.K. and Dwivedi, P. (1983) : Response tendency in business management trainees. *Panjab University Management Review*, 6, 37-43.

(f) Verma, S.K.; Menon, D.K.; Malhotra,A. and Dubey, B.L. (1982) : A Study of responses biases through a questionnaire without questions. *Journal of Education and Psychology* 49(1) 74-84.

A QUESTIONNAIRE WITHOUT QUESTIONS

Age :____________

Sex :____________

Education :____________

Instructions : In this investigation we want to determine *how well you can guess the answers to questions that are not known to you*. Below, you will find a group of possible answers. Sometimes these alternatives are words : in other cases they are figures or, characters. The question, however, is missing. You are to circle one of the alternatives, the one that you think is correct. You can be sure that in principle each of the option is a fitting response. Please work through the items in the order given. Try *not to skip items and circle one alternative per item only.*

Items	*Alternatives*			
I	Yes	No	Uncertain	
II	1	2	3	4
III	Very-Satisfied	Satisfied	Dissatisfied	Very-Dissatisfied

IV	First	Second	Third	
V	True	False		
VI	A	B	C	D
VII	Always	Sometimes	Never	
VIII	Agree	Indifferent	Disagree	
IX	0-1.5 cm	1.5-3.5 cm	3.5-6.5 cm	6.5-8.5 cm 8.5-10 cm
X	Very Certain	Indifferent	Very-Uncertain	
XI	No	Yes	Uncertain	
XII	False	True		

11A (5)

Title of the Instrument : **Menopausal Experience Scale.**
Purpose : Diagnosis of Menopausal suffering and screening before treatment.
Author : Neelakshi Arvind Lavakare.
Languages : English.
Availability : Jariwala Building, Ist Floor, 29, Bhulabhai Desai Road, Mahalaxmi Temple Lane, Bombay 400026.
Uses : A diagnostic tool before medical or psychological treatment.
Levels : 40-55 years.
Main Features : Summated rating. Total number of items are 30.
Reliability : .70 by Split Half method.
Validity : Judgement of 5 judges very high.
Time Limit : About 10-15 minutes.
Norms : In the process.
References : With the author.

MENOPAUSAL EXPERIENCE SCALE (FORM II)

Given here is a list of feelings which women often experience. The responses are categorized as 1. *No reaction* 2. *Mild* 3. *Strong*. Encircle the descriptive category of response which best describes your experience e.g. Cramps — 1, 2, 3, indicates that your feeling of cramps is mild. Even if none of the response categories fits you exactly, choose the one that closely describes your experience. Since there are no right and wrong answers, kindly give candid replies. Ensure that you answer all the items. Work as fast as possible. The items are to be treated in relation to your condition since January 1984.

	Feelings	Responses		
		No Reaction	Mild	Strong
1.	Anaemia	1	2	3
2.	Fatigue	1	2	3
3.	Blood Pressure - High/Low	1	2	3
4.	Illness Proneness	1	2	3
5.	Constipation/Diarrhoea	1	2	3
6.	Dizzy Spells	1	2	3
7.	Headache	1	2	3
8.	Weight Gain	1	2	3
9.	Palpitation	1	2	3
10.	Bodyache - Legs/Back	1	2	3
11.	Hot Flushes	1	2	3
12.	Feeling of Stagnation	1	2	3
13.	Irritability	1	2	3
14.	Crying Spells	1	2	3
15.	Loneliness	1	2	3
16.	Mood Swings	1	2	3
17.	Tension	1	2	3
18.	Inability to Take Decisions	1	2	3
19.	Anxiety	1	2	3
20.	Urge to Run Away	1	2	3
21.	Useless Thoughts	1	2	3
22.	Aversion to Self Criticism	1	2	3
23.	Disagreements	1	2	3
24.	Aversion to Social Activities	1	2	3
25.	Depression	1	2	3
26.	Insomnia	1	2	3
27.	Worry About Future	1	2	3
28.	Nervousness	1	2	3
29.	Restlessness	1	2	3
30.	Any Other (Physical)	1	2	3

Thank you very much for your cooperation

11A (6)

Title of the Instrument : **The Coimbatore Androgyny Inventory (CAI).**

Purpose : To assess the different Sex-Role identity as well as the Response set variable "Social Desirability."

Author : R. Balakrishnan.

Languages : English and Tamil.

Availability : R. Balakrishnan, Department of Psychology, PSG College of Arts and Science, Coimbatore - 641 014., Tamil Nadu, India.

Uses : For assessing masculine (M), feminine (F), and Androgynous

(A) Sex-role identity as well as the social desirability (SD) response set. Also used for Guidance and counselling.

Levels : College students and adults.

Main Features : The inventory consists of 48 items of which 20 items of each relate to masculinity (M) and femininity (F) and the remaining eight items bear on social desirability (SD). The items of the inventory were constructed on the basis of "Catch-phrase" methodology (Alpert and Sargent, 1941).

Reliability : The Split-Half reliabilities for the subscales of the CAI namely, MF and SD are .84, .78, and .83 respectively using the adult population. (Balakrishnan, 1985). In a post-graduate student population, the split-half reliabilities reported for M,F, and SD scales were .72, .64, and .81 (Padmalochini, 1988).

Validity : Content validity of the subscales of the CAI using eight college professors and seven clinical psychologists were examined. The validity of the concepts of Masculinity (M), femininity (F) and androgyny (A) and social desirability (SD) were worked out. The correlations between the scores on M and F was .09 and that between M and SD was .10; also the correlation between F and SD was .08. Besides, the positive and significant correlations between M and A (.19) and that between F and A (.14) showed that M and A (.19) and that between F and A (.14) showed that M and A, and F and A are related to each other (N = 204; Balakrishnan, 1985). Construct validity for the concepts of androgyny, masculinity and femininity have also been reported. The correlation of the masculinity score with the Realistic/ mechanical occupational interest score on the Vocational Preference Inventory among male post-graduate students was .40 (N = 50) and among female students .46 (N =40).

THE COIMBATORE ANDROGYNY INVENTORY

Instructions

A list of words and phrases related to human characteristics is given below. Please read them one by one. If you feel that a word or a phrase, generally describes yourself as you are, encircle the number "1" under the heading "Yes"; if not, encircle the number "2" under the heading "No". Please give your first reaction and avoid pondering for a long time over any single word or phrase. There is no right or wrong answer. Do not omit any word, phrase or sentence while answering the inventory. This is not a test of your intelligence or ability but simply a measure of the way you behave.

		Yes	No
1.	Capable	1	2
2.	Dependent	1	2
3.	Masculine	1	2
4.	Stable	1	2
5.	Never get angry	1	2
6.	Strong	1	2
7.	Not popular	1	2
8.	Unconventional	1	2
9.	Reserved	1	2
10.	Unassuming	1	2
11.	Yielding	1	2
12.	Flatterable	1	2
13.	Independent	1	2
14.	Always Courteous	1	2
15.	Not jealous	1	2
16.	Assertive	1	2
17.	Sensitive to the needs of others	1	2
18.	Always admit my mistakes	1	2
19.	Analytical	1	2
20.	Eager to soothe hurt feelings	1	2
21.	Forceful	1	2
22.	Soft spoken	1	2
23.	Risk taking	1	2

11A(7).

Title of the Instrument : **The Vocational Preference Inventory (VPI).**

Purpose : To measure the Holland's six occupational personality dimensions as well as the response set variable "Acquiescence."

Author : R. Balakrishnan.

Languages : English and Tamil.

Availability : R. Balakrishnan, Department of Psychology, PSG College of Arts and Science, Coimbatore — 641 014. Tamil Nadu, India.

Uses : 1. For measuring the six types of occupational personalities namely, Realistic (R), Investigative (I),

Conventional (C) as well as the Acquiescence (Ac) response set.
2. For giving vocational guidance and counselling.
3. For making employee selection.

Levels : High School, Colleges, Professional Colleges, University students as well as adults of both sexes.

Main Features : This is a semi-projective inventory written in English and Tamil. This can be self-administered. It may be administered individually or in group by an examiner. The inventory covers the six occupational personality dimensions namely R,I,A,S,E, and C as expounded by Holland (1973) as well as the acquiescence response set. Following Holland (1973, pp. 7-8) it was assumed that the interest inventory is a personality inventory. The inventory has 120 occupational titles of which 20 items of each relate to R,I,A,S,E and C dimensions as well as 10 imaginary occupational titles as formulated by the present writer conforming to the criteria set forth by Wiggins (1973) to assess the acquiescence disposition (Balakrishnan, 1979a,b). Each item which is checked 'yes' is awarded score of 'one'. The score on R,I,A,S,E,C and acquiescence dimensions can be separately scored by hand as well as by the use of relevant stencils.

Reliability : The split-half reliabilities for the subscales of the inventory are as follows : R =.76, I = .81; A = .85; S = .75; E= .84; C = .85; Ac = .85. And the related re-test reliabilities are : R = .82; I=.78; A = .78; S =.82; E = .84; C =.76; Ac = .80 (Balakrishnan, 1979b).

Validity : Content validity of the R,I,A,S,E and C subscales of the VPI were found out. Concurrent validities with the Self-Directed Search-Occupations Section (Holland,1973) were as follows : R =.38; I =.42; A =.42; S = .62; E = .41; and C = .51. Other Validities given in the manual.

Time Limit : No time limit is stipulated for taking this inventory. Ordinarily, an individual takes about 15 minutes to complete it.

Norms : Separate stanine grade norms for the sub-scales of the VPI for boys and girls of tenth standard are available with the author. However, it is recommended that the raw scores obtained by the individual may be used for the purpose of guidance and counselling.

References:
1. Balakrishnan, R. (1979a) : Vocational Choice in Relation to intelligence, Creativity and Sex.

Unpublished M.Phil Thesis, University of Madras, Madras.

2. Balakrishnan, R. (1979b): The Manual for Vocational Preference Inventory. Unpublished. Department of Psychology : PSG College of Arts and Sciences, Coimbatore.
3. Bernard, L.C. (1981): *The Manual for Multi-dimensional Sex-role Inventory*. University of Southern California : Los Angeles.
4. Holland, J.L. (1973): *Making Vocational Choices : A Theory of Carrers*. Englewood Cliffs. N.J., : Prentice Hall Inc.
5. Longanathan, M. (1981): A Study of Organizational Climate in Relation to Holland's Personality Types among Nurses. Unpublished MA Thesis, University of Madras, Madras.

THE VOCATIONAL PREFERENCE INVENTORY (VPI)

Name:	Occupation:
Age:	Income per Month:
Sex:Male/Female	Address:

Directions

This is an inventory of your feelings and attitudes about many kinds of occupations. Please read each occupational title and indicate your interest in it following the instructions given below:

1. If the occupation interests or appeals to you make a tick (◂) mark against 'Yes'.
2. If you dislike or feel uninterested in the occupation make a tick (◂) mark against 'No'.
3. Make no marks when you are undecided about an occupation.

1.	Actor/Actress	Yes	No
2.	Advertising Executive	Yes	No
3.	Agricultural Scientist	Yes	No
4.	Air Hostess/Steward	Yes	No
5.	Animal Trouble Worker	Yes	No
6.	Artist	Yes	No
7.	Auctioneer	Yes	No
8.	Auditor	Yes	No

9.	Auto Sales Dealer	Yes	No
10.	Banker	Yes	No
11.	Botanist	Yes	No
12.	Broker	Yes	No
13.	Building Gladiator	Yes	No
14.	Business Education Expert	Yes	No
15.	Carpenter	Yes	No
16.	Cashier	Yes	No
17.	Chemist	Yes	No
18.	Cinema Director	Yes	No
19.	Cinema Theater Manager	Yes	No
20.	Contractor	Yes	No
21.	Dance Teacher	Yes	No
22.	Dentist	Yes	No
23.	Detective	Yes	No
24.	Diplomat	Yes	No
25.	District Collector	Yes	No
26.	Drama Specialist	Yes	No
27.	Draughtsman/Women	Yes	No
28.	Drawing Farmer	Yes	No
29.	Dry Cleaner	Yes	No
30.	Dry Land Active Agent	Yes	No
31.	Educational Officer	Yes	No
32.	Electrician	Yes	No
33.	Elementary School Teacher	Yes	No
34.	English Specialist	Yes	No
35.	Exporter-Importer	Yes	No
36.	Eye Farmer	Yes	No
37.	Farmer	Yes	No
38.	Fashion Model	Yes	No
39.	Footwear Sales Manager	Yes	No
40.	Foreman/Woman	Yes	No
41.	Furniture Designer	Yes	No
42.	Furniture Dealer	Yes	No
43.	General Manager	Yes	No
44.	Geographer	Yes	No
45.	Glass Blower	Yes	No
46.	Governor of a State	Yes	No
47.	Headmaster/Headmistress/Principal	Yes	No
48.	High School Teacher	Yes	No

49.	Higher Secondary School Teacher	Yes	No
50.	Historian	Yes	No
51.	Hotel Manager	Yes	No
52.	Jeweller	Yes	No
53.	Judge	Yes	No
54.	Key Punch Machine Operator	Yes	No
55.	Labour Welfare Officer	Yes	No
56.	Lawyer	Yes	No
57.	Librarian	Yes	No
58.	Library Assistant	Yes	No
59.	Life Insurance Agent	Yes	No
60.	Life Insurance Clerk	Yes	No
61.	Mathematician	Yes	No
62.	Maths Teacher	Yes	No
63.	Mechanical Engineer	Yes	No
64.	Military Officer	Yes	No
65.	Mill Top Sawyer	Yes	No
66.	Mill Worker	Yes	No
67.	Minister	Yes	No
68.	Music Director	Yes	No
69.	Musician	Yes	No
70.	Newspaper Editor	Yes	No
71.	Novelist	Yes	No
72.	Nurse (Male/Female)	Yes	No
73.	Occupational Worker	Yes	No
74.	Office Manager	Yes	No
75.	Payroll Clerk	Yes	No
76.	Personal Secretary	Yes	No
77.	Petrol Bunk Manager	Yes	No
78.	Pharmacist	Yes	No
79.	Philosopher	Yes	No
80.	Photographer	Yes	No
81.	Physician	Yes	No
82.	Physicist	Yes	No
83.	Physiologist	Yes	No
84.	Poet	Yes	No
85.	Police Officer	Yes	No
86.	Politician	Yes	No
87.	Postal Clerk	Yes	No
88.	Post Master	Yes	No
89.	President of a country	Yes	No

90.	Printer	Yes	No
91.	Professor	Yes	No
92.	Proof Reader	Yes	No
93.	Psychiatrist	Yes	No
94.	Psychologist	Yes	No
95.	Radio/T.V. Commentator	Yes	No
96.	Radio/T.V. Repairer	Yes	No
97.	Rancher	Yes	No
98.	Receptionist	Yes	No
99.	Reservation Clerk	Yes	No
100.	Retail Merchant	Yes	No
101.	River Guider	Yes	No
102.	Sales Person	Yes	No
103.	Sales Manager	Yes	No
104.	Science Teacher	Yes	No
105.	Scientist	Yes	No
106.	Sculptor	Yes	No
107.	Ship Captain	Yes	No
108.	Singer	Yes	No
109.	Social Service Past Master	Yes	No
110.	Statistician	Yes	No
111.	Stenographer	Yes	No
112.	Surgeon	Yes	No
113.	Tailor	Yes	No
114.	Tamil Specialist	Yes	No
115.	Taxi Driver	Yes	No
116.	Telegraph Operator	Yes	No
117.	Telephone Mechanic	Yes	No
118.	Telephone Operator	Yes	No
119.	Telex Operator	Yes	No
120.	Temple Clerk	Yes	No
121.	Time Keeper	Yes	No
122.	Tourist Bureau's Clerk	Yes	No
123.	Tourist Guide	Yes	No
124.	Typist	Yes	No
125.	Veterinary Doctor	Yes	No
126.	Watch Repairer	Yes	No
127.	Wheel Rotation Expert	Yes	No
128.	Wholesale Dealer	Yes	No
129.	X-ray Technologist	Yes	No
130	Zoologist	Yes	No

Please check to see that you have answered all the items

For the Researcher Use only:
Ac — R — I— A — S — E — C —

11A (8)

Title of the Instrument : **The Learned Helplessness Scale.**
Purpose : To measure learned helplessness.
Author : Upinder Dhar, Sarvdeep Kohli and Santosh Dhar.
Language : English and Hindi.
Availability : Haryana Council of Psychological Research, Link Road, Vijay Nagar, Bhiwani-125021 (Haryana).
Uses : Gives a quick measure of learned helplessness for experimental (research), clinical and counselling programmes.
Levels : Age range of 15-18 years; both sexes. (For all age levels except childhood.).
Main Features : 15 items were developed.
Reliability : Test-retest reliability coefficient = 0.77, Split half method = 0.46.
Validity : Content validity = High.
Time Limit : No time Limit but it generally takes around 10 minutes for administration.
Norms : Given in the manual.
References : Given in the manual.

Scale of 11 A(8) LH-Scale is given on page 609

11A (9).

Title of the Instrument : **Illness Behaviour Questionnaire.**
Purpose : Measurement of illness behaviour in psychiatric patients.
Authors : V.K. Verma, Anil Malhotra, S.K. Chaturvedi.
Language : Hindi and English.
Availability : From the authors, Department of Psychiatry, PGI MER, Chandigarh.
Uses : To study illness behaviour patterns in the patient population.
Levels : For all educational levels. It can be given orally in cases of illiterates/low literates.
Main Features : 62 items with yes/No response pattern.
Reliability : Test-retest =.86 to .91 for the 4 factors for Hindi version, Test-restest =.896 to .936 for the 4 factors for English version.

Correlation of the two version = .71 to .92 for the 4 factors.

Validity : Factor analysis done. Revealed 4 meaningful factors which corresponded with the four out of seven factors reported by Pilowsky. (1971) Factor I General Hypochondriasis, Factor II Denial or problems, Factor III Effective Inhibition, Factor IV Affective Disturbance/Dysphobia.

Time Limit : 30-40 minutes.

Norms : Available with the manual, on 200 consecutive patients suffering from chronic intractable pain.

References :

1. Chaturvedi, S.K.; Verma, V.K. and Malhotra, A. (1984) : Non-Organic Chronic intractable pain : A Comparative Study. *Pain* 19, 87-94.
2. Varma, V.K.; Chaturvedi, S.K.; Malhotra, A. and Chari, P. (1983) : Psychiatric aspects of chronic intractable pain. *Indian Journal of Psychiatry*, 25, 173-179.
3. Varma, V.K.; Malhotra, A.K. and Chaturvedi, S.K. (1986) : Illness behaviour Questionnaire (IBQ) : Translation and Adaptation in India. *Indian Journal of Psychiatry*, 28 (1) 41-46.

ILLNESS BEHAVIOUR QUESTIONNAIRE

Here are some questions about you and your illness. For the purpose of this survey it is important that you complete Every question even though some of these questions may not be directly applicable to you.

Circle either Yes or No to indicate your answer to each question.

1. Do you worry a lot about health? Yes No
2. Do you think there is something seriously wrong with your body? Yes No
3. Does your illness interfere with your life a great deal? Yes No
4. Are you easy to get on with, when you are ill? Yes No
5. Does your family have a history of illness? Yes No
6. Do you think you are more liable to illness than other people? Yes No
7. If the doctor told you that he could find nothing wrong with you, would you believe him? Yes No
8. Is it easy for you to forget about yourself and think about all sorts of other things? Yes No

9.	If you feel ill and someone tells you that you are looking better, do you become annoyed?	Yes	No
10.	Do you find that you are often aware of various things happening in your body?	Yes	No
11.	Do you ever think of your illness as a punishment for something you have done wrong in the past?	Yes	No
12.	Do you have trouble with your nerves?	Yes	No
13.	If you feel ill or worried, can you be easily cheered up by the doctor?	Yes	No
14.	Do you think that other people realise what it is like to be sick?	Yes	No
15.	Does it upset you to talk to the doctor about your illness?	Yes	No
16.	Are you bothered by many pains and aches?	Yes	No
17.	Does your illness affect the way you get on with your family or friends a great deal?	Yes	No
18.	Do you find that you get anxious easily?	Yes	No
19.	Do you know anybody who has had the same illness as you?	Yes	No
20.	Are you more sensitive to pain than other people?	Yes	No
21.	Are you afraid of illness?	Yes	No
22.	Can you express your personal feelings easily to other people?	Yes	No
23.	Do people feel sorry for you when you are ill?	Yes	No
24.	Do you think that you worry about your health more than most people?	Yes	No
25.	Do you find that your illness affects your sexual relations?	Yes	No
26.	Do you experience a lot of pain with your illness?	Yes	No
27.	Except for your illness, do you have any problems in your life?	Yes	No
28.	Do you care whether or not people realise you are sick?	Yes	No
29.	Do you find that you get jealous of other people's good health?	Yes	No
30.	Do you ever have silly thoughts about your health which you can't get out of your mind, no matter how hard you try?	Yes	No

31.	Do you have any financial problems?	Yes	No
32.	Are you upset by the way people take your illness?	Yes	No
33.	Is it hard for you to believe the doctor when he tells you there is nothing for you to worry about?	Yes	No
34.	Do you often worry about the possibility that you have got a serious illness?	Yes	No
35.	Are you sleeping well?	Yes	No
36.	When you are angry, do you tend to bottle up your feelings?	Yes	No
37.	Do you often think that you might suddenly fall ill?	Yes	No
38.	If a disease is brought to your attention (through the radio, television, newspapers or someone you know) do you worry about getting it yourself?	Yes	No
39.	Do you get the feeling that people are not taking your illness seriously enough?	Yes	No
40.	Are you upset by the appearance of your face of body?	Yes	No
41.	Do you find that you are bothered by many different symptom?	Yes	No
42.	Do you frequently try to explain to others how you are feeling?	Yes	No
43.	Do you have any family problems?	Yes	No
44.	Do you think there is something the matter with your mind?	Yes	No
45.	Are you eating well?	Yes	No
46.	Is your bad health the biggest difficulty of your life?	Yes	No
47.	Do you find that you get sad easily?	Yes	No
48.	Do you worry or fuss over small details that seem unimportant to others?	Yes	No
49.	Are you always a co-operative patient?	Yes	No
50.	Do you often have the symptoms of a very serious disease?	Yes	No
51.	Do you find that you get angry easily?	Yes	No
52.	Do you have any work problems?	Yes	No
53.	Do you prefer to keep your feelings to yourself?	Yes	No
54.	Do you often find that you get depressed?	Yes	No

55. Would all your worries be over if you were physically healthy? Yes No
56. Are you more irritable towards other people? Yes No
57. Do you think that your symptoms may be caused by worry? Yes No
58. Is it easy for you to let people know when you are cross with them? Yes No
59. Is it hard for you to relax? Yes No
60. Do you have personal worries which are not caused by physical illness? Yes No
61. Do you often find that you lose patience with other people? Yes No
62. Is it hard for you to show people your personal feelings? Yes No

11A (10)

Title of the Instrument : **Childhood Psychopathology Measurement Schedule.**

Purpose : Measures psychiatric symptoms in children.

Author : Savita Malhotra.

Languages : English and Hindi.

Availability : From the author, address : Additional Professor of Psychiatry, Department of Psychiatry, PGI, Chandigarh.

Uses : Used for screening children. Psychiatric disturb and measure nature of psychopathology.

Levels : Children.

Main Features : 75 items with 'yes' or 'no' responses. Measures 8 factorially derived syndromes.

Reliability : Test-retest reliability = 0.78 to 0.91. Inter rater reliability coefficient = 0.88 to 0.96.

Validity : Factorial and Construct validity are high. Criterion validity is also found.

Time Limit : 20 minutes.

Norms : Yes, given in the manual.

References : Appended (Appendix Manual.

1. Malhotra, S.; Varma, V.K.; Verma, S.K., Malhotra, A. (1988) : Childhood Psychopathology Measurement Schedule : Development and Standardization. *Ind. J. Psychiat.* Oct issue, in press.

2. Malhotra, S. (1984) : Study of Temperament and its relationship with phenomenology of Childhood Psychiatric Disorders. Ph.D. Thesis. Postgraduate Institute of Medical Education and Research, Chandigarh — India.

CHILDHOOD PSYCHOPATHOLOGY MEASUREMENT SCHEDULE

No. Date

Name Age: Sex:

Education :

Residence : (Address)

Informant :

What are the main problems with the child which necessitates psychiatric consultation?

Complaints : (in chronological order) Duration

1.
2.
3.
4.

I will ask you certain questions regarding the child's illness and behaviour during the last 12 months. All the questions may not be applicable to your child but these are to be asked for the sake of completion. Please answer whether it is often true or very much true (score 2) sometimes true (score 1) or often not true (score 0)

Items given below are in the form of question. Please use additional probes wherever necessary. Score 8 if you are not sure.

1. Acts too young for his age. 0 1 2 8
   इसकी हरकतें अपनी उमर के बच्चों जैसी हैं या अपने से छोटों जैसी?
2. Does he go to school—Yes—No
   Poor School Work 0 1 2 8

पढ़ाई में कैसा है? ठीक है या कमजोर है?

3. Has your child ever repeated a grade? 0 1 2 8
क्या आपका बच्चा कभी फेल हुआ है?

4. Poorly coordinated or clumsy 0 1 2 8
क्या यह सलीके से काम करता है या बेसलीके से करता है जैसे कि चीजों को ठीक ढंग से नहीं पकड़ सकना या चीजें हाथ से अकसर छूट जाती है, बिखर जाती है या यह काम करते समय अकसर इधर उधर टकरा जाता है?

5. Prefers playing with younger children 0 1 2 8
क्या यह अपनी उमर से छोटे बच्चों के साथ खेलना पसन्द करता है?

6. Argues a lot 0 1 2 8
क्या इसको ज्यादा बहस करने की आदत है?

7. Clings to adults or too dependent? 0 1 2 8
क्या यह आमतौर पर माँ बाप व बड़ों से चिपका रहता है और उनका सहारा ढूंढता है?

8. Demands a lot of attention 0 1 2 8
क्या यह चाहता है कि इसकी बहुत देख भाल की जाए या हर समय घर के लोग इसी का ध्यान रखें?

9. Destroys his or her own things 0 1 2 8
क्या यह कभी अपनी चीजों की तोड़-फोड़ भी करता है?

10. Destroys things belonging to other family members or children 0 1 2 8
क्या यह दूसरे बच्चों या घर वालों की चीजें तोड़-फोड़ करता है?

11. Disobedience at school 0 1 2 8
क्या यह स्कूल में कहना मानता है या नहीं?

12. Disobedience at home 0 1 2 8
क्या यह घर वालों का कहना मानता है या नहीं?

13. Cruel to animals 0 1 2 8
क्या इसको जानवरों/कीड़ें मकोड़ों को मारने व परेशान करने की आदत है?

14. Cruelty, bullying, meanness to others 0 1 2 8
क्या इसको और बच्चों को तंग करने व चिढ़ाने की आदत है?

15. Physically attacks people 0 1 2 8
क्या यह मारपीट करता है?

16. Steals at home 0 1 2 8
क्या यह घर में चोरी करता है?

17. Steals outside home 0 1 2 8
क्या यह कभी घर के बाहर चोरी करता है?

18. Stubborn, obstinate, irritable 0 1 2 8
क्या यह जिद्दी व चिड़चिड़ें स्वाभाव का है ?

19. Threatens people 0 1 2 8
क्या यह कभी औरों को कोई धमकियां देता है ?

20. Gets in many fights 0 1 2 8
क्या यह आमतौर पर लड़ाई झगड़े कर बैठता है?

21. Impulsive or acts without thinking 0 1 2 8
क्या यह बिना सोचे-समझे अचानक कुछ कर बैठता है?

22. Runs away from home 0 1 2 8
क्या यह कभी घर से भाग जाता है?

23. Nervous, highstrung, tense 0 1 2 8
क्या यह जल्दी घबरा जाता है व परेशान रहता है?

24. Abnormal movements 0 1 2 8
क्या कभी कोई गलत हरकतें करता है?

25. Withdrawn, does not get involved with others 0 1 2 8
क्या यह आमतौर पर बिना किसी से मिले-जुले अकेला रहता है?

26. Gets hurt a lot, accident prone 0 1 2 8
कुछ बच्चे रोज के खेल व छोटे छोटे कामों में बहुत चोटें खाता है क्या यह भी ज्यादा चोटें खाता है?

27. Likes to be alone 0 1 2 8
क्या यह आमतौर पर अकेला रहना पसन्द करता है?

28. Cries a lot 0 1 2 8
क्या यह बहुत रोता है?

29. Deliberately harms self or attempts suicide 0 1 2 8
क्या इसने कभी अपने आप को जान बूझ कर नुकसान पहुंचाने की या खुदकुशी करने की कोशिश की?

30. Repeats certain acts over and over (compulsions) 0 1 2 8
क्या यह कुछ काम अपनी मर्जी के खिलाफ, बार-बार करता है जिससे कि इसको परेशानी होती है?

31. Screams a lot 0 1 2 8
क्या यह बहुत चिल्लाता है?

32. Fears certain animals, situations, places other than school 0 1 2 8
क्या यह कई जानवरों या जगहों से बहुत डरता है, इतना कि उनके पास जाने से बहुत घबराता वह कतराता है ?

33. Fears going to school 0 1 2 8
क्या यह स्कूल जाने से डरता है?
34. Too fearful or anxious 0 1 2 8
क्या यह बहुत डरा या घबराया रहता है?
35. Shy or timid 0 1 2 8
क्या यह बहुत शर्माता है?
36. Temper tantrum or hot-temper 0 1 2 8
क्या यह बहुत गुस्सा करता है?
37. Unhappy, sad or depressed 0 1 2 8
क्या यह अकसर उदास रहता है?
38. Worrying 0 1 2 8
क्या यह ज्यादा फिक्र करता है?
39. Can't concentrate or pay attention for long 0 1 2 8
क्या इसको ध्यान लगाकर काम करने में मुश्किल होती है?
40. Can't get his mind off certain thoughts (obsession) 0 1 2 8
क्या इसके मन में विचार बार-बार आते हैं जिन्हें कि यह मन से निकाल नहीं सकता?
41. Complaining of loneliness 0 1 2 8
क्या यह अकेलापन महसूस करता है?
42. Confused or seems to be in a fog 0 1 2 8
क्या कभी ऐसा लगता है कि यह कुछ खोया-खोया सा है, कुछ समझ नही पा रहा है ?
43. Day dreams or gets lost in his/her thoughts 0 1 2 8
क्या यह आमतौर पर अपने विचारों में खोया व मग्न रहता है?
44. Feels and complains no one loves him 0 1 2 8
क्या यह महसूस करता करता है कि कोई इसे प्यार नहीं करता?
45. Feels others are out to get him 0 1 2 8
क्या यह महसूस करता है कि लोग इसके पीछे पड़े हैं?
46. Feels worthless and inferior 0 1 2 8
क्या यह महसूस करता है कि वह बेकार (हीन) है?
47. Stares blankly 0 1 2 8
क्या यह कभी टक-टकी लगाकर खाली काफ़ी देर तक देखता रहता है?
48. Secretive, keeps things to self 0 1 2 8
क्या यह अपने मन की बात बता देता है या उसे मन में ही रखता है?

49. Strange behaviour, specify 0 1 2 8
क्या कभी इसने कोई अजीब हरकतें की, यदि हाँ तो किस तरह की हरकतें करता है?
50. Strange ideas, specify 0 1 2 8
क्या कभी इसने कोई अजीब विचार जाहिर किये; किस तरह के विचार?
51. Irrelevant talking 0 1 2 8
क्या कभी कोई बेमतलब (न समझ आने वाली) बातें करता है?
52. Talks about killing self 0 1 2 8
क्या कभी यह खुदकुशी करने की बात करता है?
53. Talks too much 0 1 2 8
क्या यह ज्यादा बोलता है?
54. Teases a lot 0 1 2 8
क्या यह औरों को बहुत चिढ़ाता है?
55. Poor memory 0 1 2 8
इसकी याददाश्त कैसी है, ठीक है या कम है?
56. Too concerned with neatness or cleanliness 0 1 2 8
क्या यह सफाई का बहुत अधिक ध्यान रखता है?
57. Does not eat well 0 1 2 8
क्या यह खाना ठीक से खाता है या नहीं?
58. Eats or drinks things that aren't food 0 1 2 8
यह यह कोई ऐसी चीज खाता है जो कि खाने की नहीं जैसे कि मिट्टी, कागज, लकड़ी
59. Over eating 0 1 2 8
इसकी भूख कैसी है, क्या यह ठीक खाना खाता है या ज्यादा खाता है?
60. Gets teased a lot 0 1 2 8
क्या यह खुद जल्दी चिढ़ जाता है?
61. Hangs around with children who get in trouble 0 1 2 8
क्या यह बुरे बच्चों, जो कि लड़ाई-झगड़े में पड़ जाते हैं, की संगति में रहता है?
62. Bites finger nails 0 1 2 8
क्या इसको नाखून चबाने की आदत है?
63. Nightmares 0 1 2 8
क्या यह रात में डर कर चिल्लाता है?
64. Sets fire 0 1 2 8
क्या कभी आग लगाता है?

65. Trouble sleeping 0 1 2 8
क्या इसको सोने में कोई मुश्किल होती है?
66. Sleeps less than most children 0 1 2 8
और बच्चों से कम सोता है?
67. Sleeps more than most children 0 1 2 8
क्या यह और बच्चों से ज्यादा सोता है?
68. Swearing or obscene language 0 1 2 8
क्या यह गंदी गालियां निकालता है?
69. Talks or walks in sleep 0 1 2 8
क्या कभी नींद में बोलता या चलता है?
70. Thumb sucking 0 1 2 8
क्या इसे अंगूठा चूसने की आदत है?
71. Wets the bed 0 1 2 8
क्या रात को बिस्तर पर पेशाब करता है?
72. Wets self during the day 0 1 2 8
क्या कभी दिन में कपड़ों में पेशाब कर लेता है?
73. Uses alcohol, tobacco or drugs 0 1 2 8
क्या शराब व सिगरेट पीने या और नशीली चीजें इस्तेमाल करने की आदत है?
74. Physical problem without known medical cause
क्या इसको (बिना किसी शारीरिक बीमारी के) कुछ शारीरिक तकलीफें रहती है जैसे कि-

Aches and pains—दर्द 0 1 2 8
Headaches—सरदर्द 0 1 2 8
Fits—दौरा 0 1 2 8
Nausea—मतली, मचली 0 1 2 8
Stomach aches—पेट दर्द 0 1 2 8
Vomiting—उल्टी 0 1 2 8
Overtired—ज्यादा थकावट 0 1 2 8
Constipated—कब्जी 0 1 2 8
Feels dizzy—चक्कर 0 1 2 8
Over-weight—मोटापा 0 1 2 8
Nervous movements & twitchings 0 1 2 8
Tics 0 1 2 8
Others 0 1 2 8

75. Any other physical complaints (specify) e.g. allergy, asthma, diarrhoea, epileptic fits 0 1 2 8
क्या इसको और शारीरिक बीमारी है? क्या है?

11A (11)

Title of the Instrument : **Simple Self-Reporting Questionnaire.**

Author : Rupashree Khubalkar, Department of Psychology, P.G.T.D. Nagpur University, Nagpur University, Nagpur—440010. M.S. (India).

Language : Marathi, English, and Hindi.

Availability : From the author. Address as above.

Uses : To find out the level of neuroticism in rural unsofisticated illiterate people. It screens neurotics from normals. It also helps in knowing psychological health problems in normals and neurotics. It helps in clinical diagnosis. It enhances the authority of diagnosis. It can be used as a measure neuroticism for research purpose.

Levels : Rural unsofisticated people.

Main Features : Complete test consists of 103 items. Responses are to be sought in 'yes' or 'no' form. Total score is based on 100 items. The last three items give definite idea about insight toward illness of the individual which facilitates further therapeutic probe.

Reliability : The test-retest reliability following a gap of 1 day through 8 days to 15 days ranges from 0.86 to 0.92. Split half reliability by using odd-even method with Spearman-Brown formula and Flannagan formula was found to be 0.96.

Validity : The phi-coefficient as a measure of validity was found to be 0.86 at cut-off point 30.

Time Limit : 15 minutes is the time limit but it takes usually between 10 to 20 minutes.

References :

1. Cattell, R.B. and Scheier, I.H. (1961) : *The meaning and measurement of neuroticism and anxiety*. The Ronald Press Co., New York, 1961.
2. Eysenck, H.J. (1955) : *Dimensions of Personality*, Lund Humphries, London, Bradford, Great Britain.
3. Edwards, A.L. (1970) : *The Measurement of Personality Traits — by Scales and Inventories*, Holt Rineheart and Winston, Inc., U.S.A.
4. Khubalkar, R.V.; Khubalkar, M.V. and Nafde, A. (1988) : Psychological seghalae in mastectomized

Patients suffering from carcinoma of breast (Unpublished).

5. Wig, N.N. and Verma, S.K. PGI Health Questionnaire N-1, a simple neuroticism scale in India. *Indian Journal of Psychiat*, 15.

SIMPLE SELF REPORTING QUESTIONNAIRE (SSRQ)

Name and Address :

Age : Sex : M F

Education : Marital Status :

Occupation : Date :

Referral : Total Score :

Diagnosis : Impression :

Instructions

This is a simple questionnaire containing 103 questions pertaining to your health. There is no right or wrong answer. The statement which is applicable to your present state of condition — to be marked 'yes' by putting a right mark [◂] as shown, in a square against it, under the column 'Yes'. If the statement is not applicable to you, put the mark under the column 'No'. Read all the statements carefully and report your true answer.

In these days :		Yes	No
1.	I often worry about something or other.	( )	( )
2.	I have often been worried about my health.	( )	( )
3.	I have at times been very worried about things which did not really matter.	( )	( )
4.	I often feel that I am suffering from chinta-rog (worry).	( )	( )
5.	I often feel my heart-beating fast.	( )	( )
6.	I often feel uneasiness (e.g. in bus, train, mob etc.).	( )	( )

		Yes	No
7.	I often get shooting type of pain in chest.	( )	( )
8.	I often get perspiration, sweating of palms and feet even in cool days.	( )	( )
9.	I often feel numbness and heaviness of extremeties — hands or legs etc.	( )	( )
10.	I often tremble (tremors of hands or fingers).	( )	( )
11.	I often get fulness of chest (breathlessness).	( )	( )
12.	I often feel tired.	( )	( )
13.	I often get burning sensation in some part of the body (such as eyes, chest, abdomen, throat etc.).	( )	( )
14.	I often get pain in abdomen (or stomach).	( )	( )
15.	I often feel thirsty (dryness of mouth).	( )	( )
16.	I frequently suffer from dry-cough.	( )	( )
17.	I often feel giddy (dizzy).	( )	( )
18.	I often get headaches.	( )	( )
19.	I often feel heaviness in head.	( )	( )
20.	I often feel pins in head.	( )	( )
21.	I often feel emptiness in head.	( )	( )
22.	I often feel that upper part of head is floating.	( )	( )
23.	I often get low back-ache/(back-ache).	( )	( )
24.	I often get tightening of neck.	( )	( )
25.	I frequently suffer from diarrhoea.	( )	( )
26.	I frequently suffer from constipation.	( )	( )
27.	I often get watering of eyes.	( )	( )
28.	I often find myself unable to do work.	( )	( )
29.	I often feel uneasy when I have to meet a stranger.	( )	( )
30.	I often become restless.	( )	( )
31.	I frequently suffer from gas trouble (gases in abdomen or stomach).	( )	( )
32.	I often face difficulty (fear) to 'start' the work.	( )	( )
33.	I often become too much emotional, feel like crying.	( )	( )
34.	It becomes impossible for me to bear loud voice (noise).	( )	( )
35.	I cry quite easily.	( )	( )
36.	I often feel speechless in tense situation.	( )	( )
37.	I often find life to be strenuous.	( )	( )

		Yes	No
38.	I often get confused, don't understand what to do.	( )	( )
39.	I often forget things.	( )	( )
40.	I often find difficulty in getting sleep.	( )	( )
41.	I often dream of death of some near and dear one, sometimes nightmares.	( )	( )
42.	I often get interrupted sleep.	( )	( )
43.	I fear the fate of my family after my death.	( )	( )
44.	I often wake-up too early in the morning (before usual timing).	( )	( )
45.	I often feel sleepy throughout the day.	( )	( )
46.	I often get poor appetite (loss of appetite), don't feel like eating.	( )	( )
47.	I have lost some body weight.	( )	( )
48.	I often get dysmenorrhoea./I often worry over khar (dhat) discharge.	( )	( )
49.	I often feel sad (depressed)	( )	( )
50.	I am unable to enjoy things, (or life)	( )	( )
51.	I often feel life is meaningless.	( )	( )
52.	I often get irritated easily.	( )	( )
53.	I often experience lack of energy (bodily weakness).	( )	( )
54.	I often like to be alone.	( )	( )
55.	I often find difficulty in taking decisions.	( )	( )
56.	I often get feeling of loneliness-even among many people.	( )	( )
57.	I often find difficulty to initiate and continue work.	( )	( )
58.	I often face difficulty in concentration.	( )	( )
59.	I often feel decrease in sex-desire.	( )	( )
60.	I at times feel to end my life.	( )	( )
61.	I often experience a sense of guilt over unknown sin, without any apparent reason.	( )	( )
62.	I often find difficult to restore my courage (lack of confidence).	( )	( )
63.	I feel that I will never be completely cured.	( )	( )
64.	I often get the feeling that I am suffering from some deadly disease.	( )	( )
65.	I frequently become restless to sit silently at one place.	( )	( )

		Yes	No
66.	I often get involved in hotch-potch thoughts to think fruitfully.	( )	( )
67.	I feel worse in the evening.	( )	( )
68.	I often brood over trivial-routine things.	( )	( )
69.	I do not feel fresh after getting up in the morning.	( )	( )
70.	I feel that present life is miserable.	( )	( )
71.	I often feel that other persons talk about me.	( )	( )
72.	I always feel that other persons do not think good of me.	( )	( )
73.	I often get involved in my own thoughts (day-dreaming).	( )	( )
74.	I find difficulty in mixing with other people.	( )	( )
75.	I often feel inferior to others.	( )	( )
76.	I frequently get temperature (hotness feeling of body).	( )	( )
77.	I suddenly get pains all over the body.	( )	( )
78.	I often get burning pain of sexual organ.	( )	( )
79.	I often suffer from involuntary movements like trembling or pendulum like movements of hand.	( )	( )
80.	I often get bad dreams, bad thoughts.	( )	( )
81.	I often feel insecure (feeling of being left alone).	( )	( )
82.	I feel numbness of some part of body.	( )	( )
83.	I sometimes feel ants crawling over skin (or over some part of body).	( )	( )
84.	I frequently feel pricking of needles in some part of body.	( )	( )
85.	I often suffer from loss of hearing (feel hard of hearing).	( )	( )
86.	I am unable to speak at times, can produce only whisper.	( )	( )
87.	I often get hiccoughs.	( )	( )
88.	I often get belching.	( )	( )
89.	I often get nauseating sensations, sometimes vomiting.	( )	( )
90.	I often suffer from distension of abdomen.	( )	( )
91.	I often get stiffness of limbs (hand or leg).	( )	( )
92.	I often get difficulty in swallowing.	( )	( )

		Yes	No
93.	I frequently get altered consciousness, attacks of fit.	( )	( )
94.	I often feel possessed of devils or God.	( )	( )
95.	I often find difficulty in seeing things (visual blurring, sometimes total blindness).	( )	( )
96.	I often feel lump in throat.	( )	( )
97.	I often feel lump moving inside the stomach.	( )	( )
98.	I often get सूं सूं चींचीं (nsoon-nsoon-nchiennchien) noise (peculiar voice) in the ear or head.	( )	( )
99.	I fear even over the 'name' of poisonous insects or thing eg. scorpion, snake etc.	( )	( )
100.	My illness does not improve even after various treatments.	( )	( )
101.	My trouble is physical.	( )	( )
102.	My trouble is mental (Psychological)	( )	( )
103.	My trouble is both physical as well as psychological.	( )	( )

11A (12)

Title of the Instrument : **Mental Health Inventory.**

Purpose : Assess individual's good mental health or psychological well being.

Author : Jagdish and A.K. Srivastava.

Languages : English and Hindi.

Availability : Dr. A.K. Srivastava, Department of Psychology, B.H.U.; Varanasi.

Uses : General.

Levels : Adults.

Main Features : The scale has six dimensions : 1. Positive self evaluation, 2. Realistic perception, 3. Integration of personality, 4. Autonomy, 5. Group oriented attitudes, 6. Environmental mastery.

Reliability :

Sub-scales	Reliability index	No. of items
1. Positive self-evaluation	.75	10
2. Realistic perception	.71	08
3. Integration of personality	.72	12

4. Autonomy	.72	06
5. Group oriented attitudes	.74	10
6. Environmental mastery	.79	56
7. The whole Scale	.73	

MENTAL HEALTH INVENTORY

Instructions

This inventory is meant for a psychological investigation. It consists of a number of statements relating to your feelings about yourself in every day life. You have got four alternatives to respond each of the statements. Choose either of the four alternatives responses, i.e. Always Most of time, Some times, Never, which most suitably indicate the frequency of your feelings, and views

Do not leave any statement unanswered.

Thanks.

		Always	Most of times	Some times	Never
1.	I feel lack of confidence.	( )	( )	( )	( )
2.	I get excited very easily.	( )	( )	( )	( )
3.	I am not able to take quick decision on any subject.	( )	( )	( )	( )
4.	I feel that situations are continuous in going against me.	( )	( )	( )	( )
5.	I have affection and attachment with my neighbours.	( )	( )	( )	( )
6.	I mould myself according to circumstances.	( )	( )	( )	( )
7.	I feel that I am losing self-respect.	( )	( )	( )	( )
8.	I use to worry even about trivial matter for a long time.	( )	( )	( )	( )
9.	I am not able to take decision about my next step.	( )	( )	( )	( )
10.	I hesitate in meeting with others.	( )	( )	( )	( )
11.	I do my duty well even in adverse circumstances.	( )	( )	( )	( )

(Contd.)

	Always	Most of times	Some times	Never
12. I feel that I am not able to fully utilize my abilities in performing my different duties.	( )	( )	( )	( )
13. In adverse circumstances, I act without keeping in view of the real facts,	( )	( )	( )	( )
14. I feel irritation.	( )	( )	( )	( )
15. I feel to be insecure.	( )	( )	( )	( )
16. I am much worried about my responsibilities.	( )	( )	( )	( )
17. I feel depressed/dejected.	( )	( )	( )	( )
18. I play important role in social ceremonies.	( )	( )	( )	( )
19. I utilize my reasoning even in difficult times.	( )	( )	( )	( )
20. I feel that my relations with others are not satisfactory.	( )	( )	( )	( )
21. My responsibilities are like burden to me.	( )	( )	( )	( )
22. I suffer from inferiority complex.	( )	( )	( )	( )
23. I am used to be lost in world of imagination.	( )	( )	( )	( )
24. I am and anxious about my future.	( )	( )	( )	( )
25. My friends/relatives remain ready to help me in the difficult times.	( )	( )	( )	( )
26. I make definite plans about my future.	( )	( )	( )	( )
27. I am enraged even by the slightest unfavourable talks.	( )	( )	( )	( )
28. I take decision easily even in difficult circumstances.	( )	( )	( )	( )
29. I am not able to behave in such a way as my friends expect from me.	( )	( )	( )	( )

(Contd.)

		Always	Most of times	Some times	Never
30.	I am satisfied with most of the aspects of my life.	( )	( )	( )	( )
31.	My friends and colleagues hale respect for me.	( )	( )	( )	( )
32.	My confidence varies highly in quantity.	( )	( )	( )	( )
33.	I am always ready to fight the problems.	( )	( )	( )	( )
34.	I make impressions about people or issue even in absence of facts and grounds.	( )	( )	( )	( )
35.	I am not able to concentrate fully in my works.	( )	( )	( )	( )
36.	I feel inclined towards opposite sex.	( )	( )	( )	( )
37.	I solve my problems myself.	( )	( )	( )	( )
38.	I fully cooperate in the important functions of my community.	( )	( )	( )	( )
39.	I am perplexed with my contradictory thoughts.	( )	( )	( )	( )
40.	I take decisions on the basis of facts even though they are contrary to my wish.	( )	( )	( )	( )
41.	I am not able to continue any task for long.	( )	( )	( )	( )
42.	I feel my self secured amidst my friends/group.	( )	( )	( )	( )
43.	I do not become hopeless even when I fail.	( )	( )	( )	( )
44.	I consider myself useful for society.	( )	( )	( )	( )
45.	I aspire for something without having in view of my short comings.	( )	( )	( )	( )
46.	I do not get influenced even by reasonable arguments.	( )	( )	( )	( )

(Contd.)

		Always	Most of times	Some times	Never
47.	I am not able to take such decision as I want to take.	( )	( )	( )	( )
48.	I am afraid of imaginary calamities.	( )	( )	( )	( )
49.	I feel that this world is a place good enough for passing life.	( )	( )	( )	( )
50.	I feel full of enthusiasm to think that I will certainly achieve my objectives.	( )	( )	( )	( )
51.	I do not get disappointed with the common worries of daily life.	( )	( )	( )	( )
52.	My mood changes momentarily.	( )	( )	( )	( )
53.	I myself decide what and how I should do.	( )	( )	( )	( )
54.	I feel that my intimacy with my group community is increasing gradually.	( )	( )	( )	( )
55.	I feel pleasure in taking responsibilities.	( )	( )	( )	( )

11A (13)

Title of the Instrument : **Personality Inventory.**

Purpose : To measure extraversion, psychoticism, emotional instability, depression, social desirability, and dimensions of personality.

Authors : B.L. Dubey, P. Dwivedi, S.K. Verma (Department of Psychiatry, PGI, 'Chandigarh and Department of Business Management, Punjab University, Chandigarh).

Language : English.

Availability : From the author. Also published in *Indian J. Clini. Psy.* (1988).

Uses : To measure certain well known dimensions of personality, viz. extraversion, psychoticism, emotional instability, depression, social desirability.

Levels : Educated subjects (10 years of schooling).

Main Features : A 50 item simple questionnaire.

Reliability : Test-retest = 0.46 to 0.82 for different dimensions, Internal consistency (E 1/3 value) of items satisfactory.

Validity : Correlation with other tests.

Time Limit : 20-25 minutes.

Norms : Available on 323 subjects (Public sector employees) and 175 graduate engineers.

Reference : Dudey, B.L.; Dwivedi, P. and Verma, S.K. (1988) : Some observations about business executives on a personality inventory. *Indian J. Clini. Psychology*, 15, 24-27.

Dubey, B.L. and S.K. Verma (1980) : A Personality Study of Business Executives, *Management Review*, 3 : 37-43.

Dubey, B.L., Verma, S.K. and Dwivedi, P. (1982) : Personality Profiles of Successful Business Executives, *Lok Udyog*, 16 : 21-24.

Eysenck, H.J. (1968) : *Genetic and Environmental Influences on Behaviour*. Oliver and Boyd. London.

Verma, S.K. (1978) : *Construction and Standardization of P.G.I. Health Questionnaire N-2*. Agra Psychological Research Cell, Agra.

Yates, J.E. (1976) : *Managing Stress*, American Management Association.

PERSONALITY INVENTORY

Please tick (✓) 'Yes' or 'No' whichever may be most suitable to you

1.	I generally get impatient if someone makes me wait.	Yes	No
2.	I do not have much enthusiasm in my work.	Yes	No
3.	Do you enjoy hurting the feelings of persons you love?	Yes	No
4.	Do you have a ready answer if someone asks you?	Yes	No
5.	Do you always keep your promise, no matter how inconvenient it might be for you?	Yes	No
6.	Sometimes I get so much angry that I cannot speak anything.	Yes	No
7.	I am easily upset by a small event of disappointment.	Yes	No
8.	Do people become offensive easily?	Yes	No
9.	I make friends easily.	Yes	No

10.	All my habits are good and desirable ones.	Yes	No
11.	I feel highly discouraged when my views differ from others.	Yes	No
12.	At times I feel that life is not worth living.	Yes	No
13.	Have you had an awful events of bad luck?	Yes	No
14.	I enjoy going out a lot than sitting inside.	Yes	No
15.	I am totally free from all sorts of prejudices.	Yes	No
16.	My mood usually changes without apparent cause.	Yes	No
17.	I worry too much when someone in the family gets sick.	Yes	No
18.	I feel lonely on most of the occasions even when I am with others.	Yes	No
19.	I think I am a talkative person.	Yes	No
20.	I do not get irritated whatever may happen.	Yes	No
21.	I often take very long time to recover from a strong emotion.	Yes	No
22.	When I see anyone sad I also feel sad.	Yes	No
23.	I don't care what happens to me.	Yes	No
24.	I like lots of hustle and bustle.	Yes	No
25.	I have never talked behind a person.	Yes	No
26.	I am quick temp red person.	Yes	No
27.	I generally think that I may not be successful in life.	Yes	No
28.	Do you remain worried about catching diseases?	Yes	No
29.	I do not hesitate to contact important persons.	Yes	No
30.	I have never been late for an appointment.	Yes	No
31.	I cannot tolerate people who are unreasonable to me.	Yes	No
32.	I do not feel confident in my ability.	Yes	No
33.	Do you loose your friends easily without your fault.	Yes	No
34.	I usually tell my problems to others.	Yes	No
35.	Do you always reply a personal letter soon after you have read it.	Yes	No
36.	My feelings are easily hurt by the comments and actions of others.	Yes	No
37.	For my past mistakes I feel very much unhappy.	Yes	No
38.	Do people say and do things to annoy you?	Yes	No
39.	I enjoy telling jokes to my friends.	Yes	No

40.	I never keep things pending for tomorrow what I need to do today.	Yes	No
41.	I very often worry over possible bad luck.	Yes	No
42.	I do my work slowly and leisurely.	Yes	No
43.	Do things sometimes look as if they were not real?	Yes	No
44.	I enjoy mixing with people.	Yes	No
45.	I never told a lie in my life.	Yes	No
46.	I often thought of running away from present circumstances.	Yes	No
47.	I am easily moved to tears.	Yes	No
48.	Are you generally not keeping good health?	Yes	No
49.	I like people around me.	Yes	No
50.	I never indulge in gossip.	Yes	No

11A (14)

Title of the Instrument : **PGI Well Being Scale.**
Purpose : To measure subjective well being. (Positive mental health).
Author :S.K. Verma, A.C. Moudgil, Kuldip Kaur, Madan Pal, B.L. Dubey, D.Gupta, Department of Psychiatry, PGI, Chandigarh.
Language : Hindi and English.
Availability : Published in *Indian J. Clini. Psychol.* (1986).
Uses : To measure positive mental health. (Subjective well being.)
Levels : All educational levels. (Orally to illiterates.)
Main Features : A simple 20 item scale.
Reliability : Inter-rater reliability = 0.86
Inter-score reliability = 0.10
Test-retest reliability = 0.86
Internal consistency (E 1/3 Value) of items is satisfactory.
Validity : Correlation with other tests, correlation with the original scale is significant.
Time Limit : 5-8 minutes.
Norms : Available.
References :

1. Moudgil, A.C.; Verma, S.K.; Kaur, Kuldip and Pal, Madan, (1986) : PGI Well Being Scale (Hindi Version). *Indian J. Clinical Psychology*, 13, 195-198.
2. Verma, S.K.; Dubey, B.L. and Gupta, D. (1983) : PGI General Well Being Scale : Some Correlates. *Indian J. Clini. Psycholo*. 10, 299-304.

P.G.I. GENERAL WELL BEING SCALE

Instructions: How do you feel these days (past one month)?
Kindly tick (✓) the items applicable to you.

1. In good spirits. ( )
2. In firm control of behaviour and feelings. ( )
3. Fairly happy in personal life. ( )
4. Sleeping fairly well. ( )
5. Interested in life a good bit of the time. ( )
6. Feeling emotionally stable & good bit of time. ( )
7. Feeling relaxed most of the time. ( )
8. Feeling energetic most of the time. ( )
9. Feeling cheerful most of the time. ( )
10. Not bothered by nervousness. ( )
11. Not bothered by anxiety or worry. ( )
12. Not easily tired. ( )
13. Not bothered by illness or pain. ( )
14. Not feeling depressed or dejected. ( )
15. Feeling satisfied with life in general. ( )
16. Not easily irritated most of the time. ( )
17. Feeling useful, wanted. ( )
18. Feeling productive, creative. ( )
19. Having a sense of belongingness. ( )
20. Being in good health. ( )

B

11B (1)

Title of the Instrument: **Behaviour Observation Check List.**
Purpose : To measure aggression and dependency in children 3-6 years.
Author : Shalini Bhogle.
Language: English (Can be translated).
Availability : Not printed here reach the demands, but I have enclosed a copy for your reference.
Uses: Can be used by any body by observation method.
Levels: 3 to 6 year old school going normal child.
Main Features : Four types of aggressive and four types of dependency behaviour are enclosed. A child to be observed on 8 occasions four in school four in the home 2 when adults are around and 2 when child is with siblings, peers. The observer ticks every behaviour seen in the span of 10 minutes.
Reliability : No need.
Validity : No need.
Time Limit : 10 minutes each observation total time 80 minutes.
Norms : Given in the manual.
References : Nil.

11B (2)

Title of the Instrument : **The Cognitive Failure Scale (CFS) in Hindi**
Purpose : To measure cognitive Failure in subjects.
Author(s) : S.K. Verma, B.L. Dubey, H. A. Khan.
Language : Hindi.
Availability : *Journal of Clinical Psychiatry*, India (1982) (scale is published in it).
Uses : To measure common mistakes that we make mainly in the areas of perception, memory, and motar functions.
Levels : All educational levels. (orally to illiterates.)
Reliability : Test-retest reliability =0.783. E1/3 Value. Internal consistency of items.
Validity : Correlation with other test (with depression = 0.43, Neuriticism = 0.75). Organic group scored significantly higher.) Independent of locus of control, achievement value index, paranoid

tendency, etc.

Time Limit : 5-7 minutes.

Norms : On normals and organic group.

References : Verma, S.K., Dubey, B.L. and Hasan, H.A. (1982). The cognitive failure scale (CFS) in Hindi—Some initial experiences. *Journal of Clinical Psychiatry*, India. 6.205-210.

11B (3)

Title of the Instrument : **P.G.I. Quality of Life Scale (Revised Form).**

Purpose: To quantity Positive mental Health (measure quality of life.)

Authors : Moudgil. A.C. Verma, S.K. and Kuldip Kaur., Dept. of Psychiatry, P.G.I. Chandigarh.

Language: Hindi.

Availability : Published in *Indian J. Clinical Psychology* (1986).

Uses : To measure positive mental health (measure quality of life).

Levels :All education levels (orally to illiterates).

Main Features : 26 items on 5-point scale.

Reliability : Test-retest = 0.79, Split-half = 0.72, Inter-scorer = 0.99, Inter-rater, = 0.89, Internal consistency (E1/3 value of items satisfactory.

Validity : Self-Rating validity = 0.81, Correlation with Achievement Value Index and Well Being Scales but not with other tests.

Time Limit : 10 minutes.

Norms : Available.

References :

1. Moudgil, A.C., Verma, S.K., and Kaur, Kuldip (1986) PGI quality of Life Scale (Revised form) *Indian Journal of Clinical Psychology*, 13,175-184.
2. Verma, S.K. (1986) : Identify indicators of quality of family life. International Conference on Health Policy: Ethics and Human Values, New Delhi.

11B (4)

Title of the Instrument : **Suicidal Intent Questionnaire.**

Purpose : To detect suicidal preoccupation or intent especially in the psychiatrically disturbed individuals.

Author(s) : S.C. Gupta, R. Anand, J.K. Trivedi, Dept. of Psychiatry, K.G. Medical College, Lucknow.

Availability : Directly from the first author (Dr. S.C. Gupta).

Uses : As specified above.

Levels : To be used for adults.

Main Features: The questionnaire comprised of items in English. Responses were recorded as often, 'sometimes', and 'never' and were scored as 2, 1, and 0 respectively.

Reliability : Not specified.

Validity : The validity of the Questionnaire by comparing the SIQ scores of definite communicators and non-communicators.

Norms: Available.

Time Limit : 15-20 minutes.

References : Used in a large number of research projects/M.D. or Ph.D. Thesis under the supervision of the test authors.

11B (5)

Title of the Instrument : **Shor Sanvedi Mapak.**

Purpose : It measures noise sensitivity level of subject.

Author(s) : Prabha Bhatia: Sunita Malhotra and I.S. Muhar.

Language(s) : Hindi and English.

Availability : National Psychological Corporation, 4/230, Kacheri Ghat, Agra – 4 (India.).

Uses : Noise in the environment in which we live and work affect behaviour, interpersonal interaction, studies of students etc. Apparently it is associated with learning difficulties, unnecessary fatigue, reduced work and productivity. The effect, however, differs from person to person indicating marked individual differences in sensitivity to noise. A recent study conducted by the authors (1988) of this test supported this viewpoint. This test ought to be useful in industrial personnel selection and inter departmental transfers so that high noise sensitivity workers could be put on low noise producing jobs and low noise sensitivity workers could be put on high noise producing jobs. Such procedure is likely to reduce the turnover rate, irritability, frustration, unnecessary fatigue and increase in the morale and identification of workers with the job.

By the same logic hostel accommodation allotment to shared rooms in consideration to the noise sensitivity levels of the partners could eliminate one of the common sources of rift amongst hostelers. In fact there is no end to the list of situations in which this test could be put to practical use.

Levels : It could be safely used in industries, schools, colleges.

Universities under any situation where the respondents can read Hindi (Only elementary knowledge is required). There is no other constraint with respect to its applicability.

Main Features : It consists of 21 items based on Likert Scaling technique. These items are presented on five point scale.

Reliability : Scale was standardized by working out the reliability and validity coefficients on a sample of 200 university/college students of M.D. University. Reliability was worked out by using test-retest method with a gap of four weeks. The reliability coefficient was 0.89- while the original version of Weinstein noise sensitivity scale had reliability coefficient of 0.79.

Validity : Validity of the scale was worked out by administering the original Weinstein scale in English to the same sample on between test-retest interval. Pearson's coefficient of correlation was calculated between the paired scores of the same subjects on the English and Hindi versions of the scale. A validity coefficient of 0.79 was found which was significant of 0.01 level.

Time Limit: There is no formal time limit. However, subject usually take 10-12 minutes for completing the test.

Norms: Norms of the test were prepared by administering the scale to 250 randomly selected male and female college/university students 16-25 years of age. They have been given in the manual. The following statistics were obtained: Mean 68.25, Median 68.71, SD 10.92, SK — 0.12, Ku 0.29, Q1 60.75, Q3 76.45.

Individuals scoring above 76 have high noise sensitivity while individuals scoring below 61 belong to low noise sensitivity levels. The middle range of scores indicate moderate degree of noise sensitivity.

11B (6)

Title of the Instrument : **Sex Role Preference Scale.**

Purpose : To measure Sex Role Preference of Children

Author : Sushila Srivastava.

Language : English. (Complete scale together with photographs attached.)

Availability : Dr. Sushila Srivastava, Professor and Head, Department of Child Development, JBAS Women's College, Madras - 600018.

Uses : To assess the Sex Role Preference of Indian boys and girls.

Levels : Children of 3-9 years.

Main Features :

1. Development of Toy Preference Scale:
2. A number of studies have been reported attempting to demonstrate that children's preference for toys, games, clothes, and activities may be employed variously as an index of SRP (Brown, 1956), as a measure of masculinity/femininity (Rosenberg and Sutton Smith, 1959) and as an index or psycho-sexual identification (Angerille, 1960). To determine the child's SRP, the use of toys is both feasible and valid. Evidence concerning the feasibility of using toys in delineating differential sex-role interest comes from a number of studies that have been conducted to discover children's preference among play materials (Benjamin, 1932), Van Alstyne, 1932; Vence and McCall, 1934; and Thompson, 1936.

   Majority of these studies employ one of the following two techniques. Subjects either directly designate their preference for items assumed to contain sex-appropriate content, or the designation is made indirectly by means of doll play. In the former situation, the subject is aware of his choice and in the latter the experimenter infers it from the subject's behaviour (Leftkowitz, 1962). In the preliminary testing carried out by the investigator, the child himself was asked to give his preference, revealed that confirmity to social expectation or pressure was more likely to be involved in child's own preference. Hence utilization of an indirect, Projective approach to the problem of measuring degree of SRF has been used and found to be effective. Hence this approach was chosen for this study.

Reliability : Two approaches were made for establishing the reliability of the SRP scale.

Split - Half Reliability Coefficients for the SRP Scale

Class	N	Age	Corre.Obt.	Correlated for Spearman-Brown	Level of Signi.
L.K.G.	20	3+	0.62	0.76	0.01
U.K.G	20	4+	0.67	0.80	0.01
I Grade	20	5+	0.82	0.90	0.01
II Grade	20	6+	0.76	0.85	0.01
III Grade	20	7+	0.88	0.93	0.01
IV Grade	20	8+	0.94	0.96	0.01
V Grade	20.	9+	8.94	0.96	0.01

On the whole, the reliability of SRP scale in high.

The table below shows the inter-correlations among whole and parts of the SRP scale.

Inter-correlations of Sub-tests of the SRP Scale and their Correlations with whole SRP Scale. (N = 140).

	whole Test	TPS	GPS	OPS	APS
Whole Test	—	0.71	0.64	0.68	0.70
TPS	—	—	0.57	0.54	0.44
GPS	—	—	—	0.66	0.55
OPS	—	—	—	—	0.62

It may be observed from the table above that all the intercorrelation coefficients are positive and significant at 0.01 level.

Validity : Validity is another important characteristic of an efficient psychological instrument. To assess the validity of the instrument, namely SRP scale, Thirty boys and 30 girls (from the pilot study sample) ranging in age from 3 to 9 years were administered the SRP scale which was constructed by the present investigator. After one week, in the second session, the same subjects were given Brown's (1956), 'IT' Scale for children to assess their SRP in the standard way which is an already established test in the Western Society. The co-efficient of correlation between these two tests was 0.61. Hence the scale constructed by the present investigated was taken as valid test and used in the final study of the present investigation.

Time Limit : 7 to 10 minutes.

Norms : Norms are not available.

References : NIL

11B (7)

Title of the Instrument : **Home Environment Measuring Scale.**

Purpose : To measure Adaptability to Home Environment among adolescents.

Author : Sushma Talesara, 172/12, Ashok Nagar, Udaipur - 313001. Telephone : 26698

Language : Hindi.

Availability : Dr. Sushma Talesara, 172/12, Ashok Nagar, Udaipur-313001.

Uses: The tool can be used by counsellors for diagnosing the adjustment problems of adolescent boys and girls in their relationship with parents. Adaptation may be initiated in response to the adverse as well as favourable parent child relations.

Levels : 12-18 years age group.

Main Features : It is a situational test covering five dimensions, viz. permissiveness vs. control, over protectiveness vs. freedom, reward vs. punishment, creative thinking vs. linear thinking and cognitive stimulation vs, suppression. Each dimension is to be judged through the reactions of the respondents. Scoring is done as over five point scale.

Reliability : The test-retest reliability of the tool is 0.72 and split-half reliability is 0.619.

Validity : The concurrent validity of the test is 0.64. Intrinsic validity ranged between 0.49 and 0.64.

Time limit : 25 minutes.

Norms : Under preparation.

References : Doctoral thesis, M.L. Sukhadia University, Udaipur, 1989.

11B (8)

Title of the Instrument : **Semi Projective Test, Test of Reactions to Frustration for the rural inhabitants.**

Purpose : To assess reactions to frustration of rural inhabitants.

Author : Surendra Nath Dubey, Ph.D.

Language : Hindi.

Availability : National Psychological Corporation, 4/230, Kacheri Ghat, Agra- 282004 (UP), India.

Uses : Social as well as for clinical purpose.

Levels : Adults.

Main features : Selection of protocols on the basis of interview and expert's suggestions. Number of items = 24.

Reliability :Test-retest reliability coefficients OD = 0.58, ED = 0.51, NP = 0.78, EA = 0.63, IA = 0.67, MA = 0.73.

Validity : Construct validity (three criteria) and Criterion-related validity has been reported.

Time limit : 25 Minutes.

Norms : Yes, on the basis of sample of 1000 adult subjects.

References : 20 references.

11B (9)

Title of the Instrument : **Literary Creativity Test, (LCT)**
Purpose : To Measure Literary Creativity among Adolescents.
Author : Sushma Talesara.
Language : Hindi.
Availability: Dr. Sushma Talesara, 172/12, Ashok Nagar, Udaipur-313001, Telephone; 26698.
Uses : 1. To guage the position of an adolescent in terms of his literary creativity. 2. The test can be used to measure creativity in general because the concurrent validity of the test with Mehdi's Verbal test of general creativity has been found to be 0.838.
Levels : 14-16 years of age group.
Main Features : The LCT consists of total nine activities. Five of these activities have two sub-tests under each activity. The dimensions of creativity covered are: Fluency, flexibility and originality. A detailed scoring key for originality dimension has been prepared. The test paper and response sheet are common.
Reliability : Split-Half reliability is 0.9575 K.R. formula 20=0.74.
Validity : Lawshe's C. VR. with 40 judges = 0. 62. Concurrent validity with Mehdi's Verbal Test of Creativity Thinking is 0.838.
Time Limit : 65 Minutes.
Norms : Under preparation.
References : Doctoral Thesis, M.L Sukhadia University, Udaipur, 1989.

11B (10)

Title of the Instrument : **Children's Approval Seeking Test (CAST).**
Author(s) : N.K.M. Tripathi and Ravi Ambast.
Availability : National Psychological Corporation, 4/230, Kacheri Ghat, Agra-4.
Language : English.
Level : School Children.
Uses : Very easy to administer, useful to finding out Children's approval.
Main Features : The test comprises of 50 items of which 25 items are in 'yes' form and remaining 25 are in 'no' form as an indicative of approval seeking. This form also comprised 25 items related with active approval seeking and rest with fear of disapproval.
Reliability : Split-Half reliability was found to be 0.78 on a large sample (N=600). Self correlation was estimated by correlating with

Spearman-Brown formula, and found the reliability coefficient of 0.88 with an index of reliability of 0.94.

Test-retest reliability N=250, CAST was readministered after one month interval. The correlation between the two sets of scores was 0.80 with an index of reliability =0.89.

Validity : Content, Intrinsic, concurrent, and Predictive as well as construct validity were established.

Norms: Percentile norms of younger and older children prepared (Boys & girls norms are separate.).

Time Limit : There is no time limit but it usually takes around 40-50 minutes to complete the test.

References :

1. Allaman, J.D.; Joyce, C.S., & Crandall, V.C. (1972): The antecedents of social desirabilities response tendencies of children and young adults. *Child Development*, 43, 1135-1160.
2. Ambast, R. & Tripathi, N.K.M. (1983) : Development of approval seeking tendency in relation to age, sex, types of family and religious group. Unpublished manuscripts, University of Gorakhpur.
3. Anastasi, A. (1968) : *Psychological Testing* (3rd Edition). London, Macmillan.
4. Boroson, W. (1970) : First born fortune's favorite? *The New York Times Magazine*, Dec. 13.
5. Calhoun, L.G.& Nikesell, R.H. (1972) : Biodata antecedents of the need for approval in male college freshman. *Developmental Psychology*, 7, 226.

11B (11)

Title of the Instrument : **PGI Visual Function Scale.**

Purpose : To scale the functional output (task performance level) of the subjects specialists help, reporting with visual problems.

Authors : H.O. Rastogi, MPA, Opt (Alig), Ph.D, and Prof. I.S. Jain, FRCS, DO (London), FAMS, Department of Ophthalmology, Post-graduate Institute of Medical Education & Research, Chandigarh-160 012, India.

Language : Hindi.

Availability : From the Authors.

Uses : Can be used for guidance, counselling and rehabilitation purposes for subjects with subnormal vision independent of other objective tools (Snellen's visual activity chart, Bjerrum Screen and the like) for scaling the adapted visual functions.

Can be used on subjects of complaining nature with normal physiological assets for the guidance of the clinicians for identifying right type of subjects for interdisciplinary referrals.

Levels : Adult male and female, literate (irrespective of number of years of formal education).

Main features : Total number of items 49 (visual function scale (T) comprising of 49 items) divided into three sub scales. :

1. Visual function (near) 15 items : 2. Visual function (distance) 12 items : 3 Visual function (orientation and mobility) 22 items. Range 0-33 for each function, score less than zero = zero, Total score 99.

Reliability : Split half reliability 0.89; Test-retest reliability=0.92 (6-8 weeks interval).

Validity : Good Face Validity, good concept validity. As anticipated subjects with clinically established severe pathological conditions obtained markedly low score as compared to the ones within normal limits subjects.

Time limit : 10-15 minutes.

Norms : Available with the authors.

References :

1. Assessment of residual vision and visual functions in literate visually handicapped. A Psychological study. Ph.D thesis in the department of Ophthalmology, Post-graduate institute of Medical Education and Research, Chandigarh-160012.
2. "Experiments in Optometric Psychometry" by Rastogi, Jain and Pershad, in the press, publisher Dr. N. Kumar, Editor *Optometry Today*, Post Box 2812, New Delhi, 110 005.

11B (12)

Title of the Instrument : **Boredom Proneness Inventory for College Students.**

Purpose : To measure the boredom proneness.

Author : Suman Nangia.

Language : Hindi.

Availability : From Author.

Uses : To measure boredom proneness in college students and for counseling.

Levels: College students.

Man Features : 36 items are to be marked true or false.

Reliability : Split-Half = 0.86, Test-retest = 0.83.

Validity : Validated against teachers and parent ratings = 0.79.

Time Limit : 25 minutes.

Norms : Available with the author.

References : Attached with the manual.

11B (13)

Title of the Instrument : **PGI Memory Scale**

Authors : Dwarka Pershad and N.N. Wig.

Availability : National Psychological Corporation, 4/230, Kacheri Ghat, Agra-4.

Language(s) : Hindi and English.

Level : Subjects who are above the age of 20 years.

Uses : Used in various fields of research. Used in the evaluation of memory functioning, in cannabis users, yoga exercises group relationships, with depression, differentiation of hemispheric lesion in epileptics, and neuro-psychological assessment of organic brain dysfunction. Used also in disertation thesis at master's level and doctoral level and the funded research projects.

Main Features : Short, simple, objective and valid test of memory. Standardised test in 1977. Equally valid for both sexes and applicable and acceptable to illiterates and unsophisticated subjects who constituted majority of subjects in Indian hospitals and clinics.

Reliability : Re-administration of the test was done on 40 subjects after an interval of one week. The test-retest reliability ranged between 0.70 and 0.84 for organic-psychotic groups. 0.48 and 0.84 for 'neurotic-normal' group (given in the manual table) Split-Half Reliability coefficient was found to be 0.91 and 0.83 respectively.

Validity : PGI Memory Scale was found to have a correlation of 0.71 with Boston Memory Scale and 0.85 with Wechsler Memory Scale. The test was compared with different famous scales like the Bhatia Scale and the WAIS (Given in the manual).

Norms : Norms provided here are based on the subjects who had no history of psychiatric/neurological illness, and are above the age of 20 years.

Time Limit : Administration takes nearly 15-20 minutes.

11B (14)

Title of the Instrument: **PGI Health Questionnaire N-1.**

Authors : S.K. Verma, N.N. Wig and D. Pershad.

Availability : National Psychological Corporation, 4/230, Kacheri Ghat, Agra-4.

Language : Hindi.

Level : Clinic population in India.

Uses : Useful as this test is short, simple test with low difficulty value for items, it can be used with illiterates, unsophicticated population also, it is medically oriented, hence more acceptable to the patient's population. Reflects a need for early psychiatric help and follow-up care.

Main Features : It has 38 items in Hindi which are very simple and easy to understand even by those who have not gone for higher education. Applicable to the patient's population.

Reliability : Test-retest (Full Scale) 1-2 weeks interval correlation was 0.88. Split half full test Correlated for length = 0.86.

Inter correlations	Correlations
- Physical and total	0.81
- Psychological and Total	0.86
- Physical and Psychological	0.56

Validity : Validity was established administering other well known tests of neuroticism concomitantly. Test was also cross-validated on fresh samples from Chandigarh, Ahmedabad and Rohtak.

Norms : Given.

Time Limit : Approximately within 5 minutes.

References : Given.

11B (15)

Title of the Instrument : **Risk Taking Questionnaire (R.T.Q.).**

Authors : Virendra Sinha and Premnath Arora (1983).

Availability : National Psychological Corporation, 4/230, Kacheri Ghat, Agra-4.

Language : Hindi.

Level : Male.

Uses : Measures the extent of 'risk' taken by a particular individual in his social life. This tool is capable of measuring or assessing the magnitude of 'risk' in different areas of life.

Main Features : Eight areas of risk are included in the tests, which are considered to be the most important number of sociologists, psychologists, and psychiatrists. Each area containing items pertaining to one particular area of risk in the sequence already stated.

Reliability : Rational Equivalence using the Kuder Richardson formula for different strata. Tables of reliability coefficients for Urban Male Adolescents for 14-20 years. Test-retest reliability coefficients for three age groups:

	N	rn	p	Range
Adolescents	37	0.79	0.01	—
Adults	55	0.83	0.01	0.66—0.83
Olds	17	0.66	0.01	—
Total N	109	0.785	0.01	

Validity : Face validity, construct, validity as well as Factorial validity, concurrent validity were found.

Norms : Age, caste, and economic status wise norms were computed on a sample of 1240 literate males of different places of Kumaun and Rohilkhand divisions of Uttar Pradesh.

Time Limit : No time limit is fixed.

References :

1. Arora, P.N. (1982) : A Psychological Study of Personality Pattern of Risk and Non Risk-Takers of Kumaun Region. Unpublished doctoral dissertation, Kumaun University, Nainital.
2. Bem, J. Darylt Wallach, M.A. & Kogan, N. (1965: Group decision-making under risk of adversive consequences, *J. Pers. Soc. Psychol.* 1(5), 543-460.
3. Chaubey, N.P. (1974) : *Motivational Dimensions of Rural Development : A Study of Risk-Taking Behaviour, risk avoidance and fear of failure in villagers*-Ahmedabad, Chaitanya Publishing House.
4. Hobrin (Ed) (1974) : *Advanced Learner's Dictionary.*

5. Knight, F.H. & Shackle, G.L.S. (1971) : *Risk Uncertainty and Profit,* Boston Houghton, Mifflin, N.Y. 197-232.
6. Kogan, N. & Wallach, M.A. (1967) : Risk-Taking as a function of situation, the person and the group *New Directions in Psychology* : New York, 211-273.
7. Wallach, M.A. & Kogan, N. (1964) : *Risk-Taking A Study on Cognition and Personality,* Holt, Rinehart & Winston, N.Y.
8. Yousuf, S.M.A., (1974) : A measure of risk taking. *Psychological Studies*, 19(1) 64-68.

11B(16)

Title of the Instrument : **Attitude Towards Androgynization of Roles Scale.**

Authors : Abha Rani Bisht.

Availability : National Psychological Corporation, 4/230, Kacheri Ghat, Agra-4.

Language : Hindi

Levels : Can be used on Teachers and adults.

Uses : Measures attitude towards androgynization of roles.

Main Features : There are 60 items. A three point scale of agree, uncertain, and disagree was incorporated in the scale. Four dimensions of androgynization of roles.

Reliability : Split half method was applied by S-B formula.

Norms : Given.

Time Limit :No time limit is fixed.

References :

1. Bem, S.L. (1974) : The measurement of psychological androgyny, *Journal of Consulting and Clinical Psychology*, 2. 155-62.
2. Lockheed, M.E. (1975) : *Research on women's acquisition of professional and leadership roles.* (ETSRB-75-39). Princeton, N.J.: Educational Testing Service.
3. Williams, J.E. and Best, D.L. (1982) : *Measuring sex stereotypes.* New Delhi : Sage Publications.

11B (17)

Title of the Instrument : **Dimension of Rigidity Scale.**
Purpose : Seven dimensions of Rigidity.
Author(s) : N.K. Chadha.
Language : English.
Availability : National Psychological Corporation, Agra-4.
Uses : Research and diagnosis.
Levels : 17-25 years.
Main features : Forced choice, 75 items.
Reliability : Test-retest and Split-half reliabilities of the present scale were found out. The scale was administered twice with a time interval of 15 days to an unselected sample of 120 subjects. The test-retest reliability coefficient for each dimension of the scale was found as follows:

S.No.	Dimensions	Retest reliabilities
1.	Intellectual Rigidity (A)	0.84
2.	Emotional Rigidity (B)	0.80
3.	Dispositional Rigidity (C)	0.69
4.	Social Rigidity (D)	0.71
5.	Behavioural Rigidity (E)	0.80
6.	Perceptual Rigidity (F)	0.78
7.	Creative Rigidity (G)	0.74
8.	Whole Test	0.94

The Split half reliability was found out by dividing the whole scale into two halves namely even-odd and first second halves for the whole scale. The split-half reliability found out in the case of even-odd items was 0.71 and for the 'first-second' halves was 0.69.

Validity : Validity of the present scale was found out with the help of two techniques : (1) Cross-validation, and (2), empirical/criterion validity. For cross validation, the scale was administered to two comparable groups of 100 subjects each in the age range of 18-21 years. The method of Pearson-Product Moment was applied. The results :

Sr. No.	Dimension	Correlation between two groups
1.	Intellectual Rigidity (A)	0.27
2.	Emotional Rigidity (B)	0.20

3.	Dispositional Rigidity (C)	0.33
4.	Social Rigidity (D)	0.38
5.	Behavioural Rigidity (E)	0.25
6.	Perceptual Rigidity (F)	0.22
7.	Creative Rigidity (G)	0.38

Time Limit : 30 minutes
Norms : N.P.C. Agra
References : Used in M.A. and M.Phil dissertation.

11B (18)

Title of the Instrument : **Emotional Stability Test for Children**
Authors : A. Sengupta and A.K. Singh.
Availability : National Psychological Corporation, 4/230, Kacheri Ghat, Agra-4.
Level : School going pupils of class VI and VII.
Language : Hindi.
Uses : To find out the emotional stability in School going pupils for their better development.
Main Features : 15 items testing emotional stability of children are included in this test.
Reliability : Test-retest method was computed sample was of 150 pupils with 14 days gap, correlation coefficient was found to be 0.70. Split half method reliabilities was also found. Sample was 150 pupils of both rural and urban population and again on 150 pupils (fresh sample) correlation was found to be 0.55.
Validity:

Test	Criterion	Corre. Coeff	N	P
Emotional	Neuroticism	0.53*	100	< 0.01
Stability	Singh & Sinha DPS	0.61*	100	< 0.01

* Significant

Norms : Percentile norms are available. N = 250.
Time Limit : Generally 12-15 minutes but no fixed time limit is there.
References: 1. Frandsen, A.N. *Educational Psychology. The principles of learning in teaching*, McGraw-hill

Book Company, Inc., 1961.

2. Guilford, J.P. *Fundamental Statistics in Psychology and Education*, New York : McGraw-Hill, 1954.
3. Jalota, S.S. & Kapoor, S.D. (1975), Manual of *Eysenck's Mandsley Personality Inventory* (MPI), New Delhi, Psycho Centre, 1975.

11B (19)

Title of the Instrument : **Social Maturity Scale.**
Authors : R.P. Srivastava
Availability : National Psychological Corporation, 4/230, Kacheri Ghat, Agra-4.
Level : Children and adolescents.
Language : Hindi.
Uses : For practical purposes and as a technique for research in the social sciences.
Main Features : Contains 17 parts and 130 items in all different ages are included in different parts.
Reliability : Test-retest method gives correlation coefficient of 0.782 & 0.62.
Validity : Still being developed or established.
Norms : Available in the manual.
Time Limit : No time limit fixed.
References :

1. Anderson, M.L., Administrative Uses of the Social Maturity Scale, *The Binet Review*, 6, 7-8 March, 1939.
2. Crow, L.D. & Crow, A., *Child Development : An Adjustment*. The Macmillan Company, New York, 1962.
3. Doll, E.A. A Genetic sale of social maturity, *American Journal of Orthopsychiatry*, 1935, 5, 180-188.
4. Embar, P. Effect of an educational and training programme on trainable mentally retarded child. In G.G. Prabhu (Ed.). Report of the third Asian Conference on mental retardation, New Delhi : *Federation for the Welfare of Mentally Retarded*, 1977, 165-173.

11B (20)

Title of the Instrument : **Sentence Completion Test.**
Authors : L.N. Dubey and Archana Dubey.
Availability : Ankur Psychological Agency, 22/481, Indira Nagar, Lucknow-16. (U.P.).
Level : 14-19 years age group boys and girls.
Language : Hindi.
Uses : Measures certain personality traits. Three personality characteristics are measured through the responses of the subjects.
Main Features : Main traits measured are: 1. Sociability, 2. Self-confidence, 3. Ambitious. Totally 50 items are there, sentences are to be completed by the subjects.
Reliability:

	Sociability	Self-confidence	Ambitious	Total
Split-Half	0.72	0.69	0.73	0.62
Test-retest	0.76	0.71	0.68	0.67

Validity : 1. Sociability- 0.66; 2. Self-confidence=0.73: 3. Ambitious=0.69.
The above are the coefficient of correlation.
Norms : Available in the manual.
Time Limit : No time limit.
References:
1. Anderson, H.H and Anderson G.S., *Techniques and other devices for understanding the Dynamics of Human Behaviour*, New York, Prentice Hall.
2. Bhargava, M., *Modern Psychological Testing and Measurement* (8th Edn.) Agra; Har Prasad Bhargava, 1985.
3. Lorge I and Thorndike, E.L. The values of responses in a completion test as indicators of personal traits. *J. Appl. Psychol.*, 1946, 30, 169-181.
4. Payne, A.F., *Sentence Completion,* New York, Guidance Clinic, 1928

11B (21)

Title of the Instrument : **Dimensions of Temperament Scale (DTS)**
Purpose : To measure fifteen dimensions of temperament.

Author(s) : N.K. Chadha and S. Chandana.

Language : English.

Availability : National Psychological Corporation, Agra.

Uses : Research and Diagnosis.

Levels : 16-25 years.

Main Features : Forced Choice, 152 items.

Reliability : Test-retest and Split half reliabilities of the present scale were found out. The scale was administered twice with a time interval of 25 days to an unselected sample of 100 samples. The test-retest reliability coefficient for each dimension of the scale was found out as follows:

Sr. No.	Dimensions		Retest reliability
1.	Sociability	A	0.86
2.	Ascendance	B	0.84
3.	Secretiveness	C	0.94
4.	Reflective	D	0.90
5.	Impulsivity	E	0.84
6.	Placid	F	0.82
7.	Accepting	G	0.85
8.	Responsible	H	0.88
9.	Vigorous	I	0.92
10.	Cooperative	J	0.84
11.	Persistence	K	0.86
12.	Warmth	L	0.83
13.	Aggressiveness	M	0.95
14.	Tolerance	N	0.88
15.	Tough-minded	O	0.94

Validity : Validity of the present scale was found out with the help of two techniques (1). Cross-validation and (2). Empirical validity. For cross validation the scale was administered to two comparable groups of 100 subjects each in the age range of 15-18 years. The data obtained on the first sample and second sample were correlated to test the validity of the scale. The method of Pearson Product Moment was applied. The results were as follows:

Sr. No	Dimensions		Correlation between Two groups
1.	Sociability	A	0.79

2.	Ascendence	B	0.84
3.	Secretiveness	C	0.80
4.	Reflective	D	0.92
5.	Impulsivity	E	0.91
6.	Placid	F	0.71
7.	Accepting	G	0.78
8.	Responsible	H	0.72
9.	Vigorous	I	0.75
10.	Cooperative	J	0.80
11.	Persistence	K	0.81
12.	Warmth	L	0.79
13.	Aggressiveness	M	0.74
14.	Tolerance	N	0.68
15.	Tough-minded	O	0.82

Overall cross-validation found out to be 0.81. The results indicate the these values are positive and highly significant. This confirms the validity of the present scale. The Empirical validity of the scale was found out by correlating the scale with some external criterion that is, Thorndike dimensions of temperament. Both the scale were administered to another sample of 50 subjects and correlation was found out between different dimensions. The dimensions which were common in both the scales indicated positive and significant correlations. Also the total score of the present scale is high and significantly correlated with Thorndike total score (r-0.73, $p < 0.01$). Hence forth, the present scale has got a validity coefficient of 0.73. The intercorrelations between the dimensions of Thorndike dimensions of temperament and present scale.

Norms : Percentile norm of each dimension and total temperament scale available.

Time Limit : 40 minutes.

References: Used in M. Phil thesis and few research papers.

11B (22)

Title of the Instrument. **Malhotra's Temperament Schedule (MTS).**

Authors : Savita Malhotra and Anil Malhotra.

Availability : National Psychological Corporation, 4/230, Kacheri Ghat, Agra-4.

Language(s) : Hindi and English.

Level : Children both normal as well as abnormal in the age group of 5-12 years were included. Both the sexes were included.

Uses : This test can be used on all child populations whether normal or abnormal within an age range of 4-14 years of both the sexes and any socio-economic class. Used to study the temperament profile of children to identify the children at greater risk of developing emotional problems later on. To evolve intervention strategies for parental counselling.

Main Features : In two languages that is in Hindi and in English. Five factors are included.

Reliability : Pearsons's Product Moment Correlation of Coefficient

	Test-retest 8 weeks interval N=10	Inter rater N=10
Activity	0.88	0.90
Rhythmicity	0.92	0.94
Approach withdrawal	0.94	0.96
Adaptability	0.84	0.92
Mood	0.90	0.96
Intensity	0.86	0.88
Threshold	0.86	0.88
Distractibility	0.83	0.82
Persistence	0.92	0.90

Validity : Face validity was found to be adequate. Factorial and Construct validities were also established.

Norms : Norms have been prepared on a group of 290 normal children in the age range of 4-14 years of both sexes and from all socio-economic classes.

Time Limit : No time limit fixed.

11B (23)

Title of the Instrument : **Personality Questionnaire.**

Authors : H.J. Eysenck : S.B.G. Eysenck : Jitendra Mohan & Paramjit Kaur Virdi.

Language : English.

Uses : To assess four dimensions of personality viz, Extra-version,

Neuroticism, Psychoticism, and Lie i.e., social-desirability.

Level : Graduates and Post-graduates.

Main Features : The scale consists of 89 items, divisible into four dimensions.

Reliability : Test-retest reliability (with one month intervening).

Extraversion : 0.93. Neuroticism : 0.96, Psychoticism : 0.85 Lie : 0.96.

Validity : Construct validity.

Norms : Available with the author

References :

1. Mohan J. & Virdi, P.K., (1985) : Standardization of P.Q. on Punjab University Students, *Indian Psychological Review*, Volume 28 (6) : 20-28.
2. Mohan, J., and Kaur, P. (1986), Standardization of P.Q. on Indian Students, *Journal of Personality and Clinical Students*, Volume 2(2), 121&123.
3. Mohan, J., Eysenck, H.J. and Eysenck, S.B.G. (1987) : The Eysenck Personality Questionnaire and Indian Experience. *Personality Study and Group behaviour*, Volume 1. (2).
4. Virdi, P.K., Standardization of Personality Questionnaire on Indian Students, Ph.D. thesis P.U. Chandigarh.

11B (24)

Title of the Instrument : **Nangia Person Perception Test**

Purpose : To test the extent to which physically attractive persons are treated as virtuous persons. To assess the correlation between beauty and personality as perceived by others.

Author (s) : Suman Nangia.

Language : English

Availability : Dr. S. Nangia, 1, Nashville Road, Dehra Dun 248001.

Uses : The test may be used in areas where interpersonal attraction is an important variable. It is useful to assess if individuals in fact have stereotyped notions of the personality traits possessed by individual of varying attractiveness and also to Judge the extent to which physically attractive stimulus persons are assumed to possess more socially desirable personality traits than unattractive persons.

Levels : All populations.

Main Features : Sketches of physically attractive and physically unattractive persons are to be judged against 6 point scale per

Cattell's 16 personality factors.

Reliability : Test-retest reliability established 0.93.

Validity: Validated against expert's rating= 0.89.

Time limit: 20 minutes.

Norms : Yes they are available with the author College students Parents of college students.

References:

1. Aronson, E. Some antecedents of interpersonal attraction in W.J. Armold & D. Levine (Eds.) *Nebraska Symposium on Motivation*, 1969, 17, 143-177.
2. Cross, J.F. & Cross, J. Age, sex, race and the perception of facial beauty. *Developmental psychology*, 1971, 5, 433-439.
3. Dion, K. & Berschied, E. "What is beautiful is good" *Journal of Personality and Social Psychology* (1972, 24, p. 285-290).
4. Hays, W.L. *Statistics for Psychologists*, New York: Holt, Rinehart & Winsgton, 1963.
5. Josselin de Jong, J.P.B. *Levi-Strauses theory on Kinship and Marriage*. Leiden, Holland : Brill, 1952.
6. Kirkpatrick, C., & Cotton. J. Physical attractive-ness, age, and marital adjustment. *American Sociological Review*, 1951, 16, 81-86.
7. Monahan, F. *Women in Crime*, New York : Ives Washburn, 1941.
8. Schiller, J.C.F. Essays, esthetical and philosophical, including the dissertation on the "Connexions between the animal and the spiritual in man." London: Bell- 1982.
9. Weight, B.A. *Physical disability—A Psychological Approach*, New York : Harper & Row, 1960.

11B (25)

Title of the Instrument : **Passi Tests of Creativity (Verbal) & (Non-Verbal).**

Author : B.K. Passi.

Availability : National Psychological Corporation, 4/230, Kacheri Ghat, Agra-4.

Level : School Children.

Languages : English and Hindi.

Uses : Test the creativity of school children. Research Studies in different parts of India have taken place. As the test is available in English and Hindi it is more applicable to a larger section of the population. Research studies are being conducted at the doctorate and master levels.

Main Features : Includes 6 test in the test battery, permits freedom of responses both qualitatively and quantitatively within specified time limits.

Reliability : Test-retest reliability coefficients and split half reliability coefficients of the PTC given in table format Test-retest reliability = 0.80.

Validity : Concurrent validity, factorial validity have been found.

Norms : Percentile Norms available for boys as well as girls for rural as well as urban population.

Time Limit: For each section, there are different time limits.

11B (26).

Title of the Instrument : **Language Creativity Test.**

Author(s) : S.P. Malhotra and Ms. Sucheta Kumari

Availability : National Psychological Corporation, 4/230, Kacheri Ghat, Agra-4.

Languages : English and Hindi.

Levels : Students of different grade levels right from VI Standard to B.A. Boys as well as girls are eligible.

Uses : Useful in measuring the language creativity of school as well as college (Undergraduate level). Useful test for researchers, teachers, creativity training institutes, and above all educationists. Measures the language creativity of students and have a purpose to develop their creative potential in English and Hindi. Can be used in all states of India.

Main Features : There are two languages creativity test, one in English and other in Hindi, "Creativity" Each language creativity has 5 sub-tests, namely 1. Plot building, 2. Dialogue Writing, 3. Poetic diction, 4. Descriptive Style, 5 Vocabulary test, 27 items are there in total in the test.

Reliability : Reliability coefficients ranging from 0.28 to 0.75 was found for Verbal Creativity test battery. Test-retest reliability coefficients of the test ranged from 0.71 to 0.93 over two weeks interval and from 0.35 to 0.73 over three years interval.

Validity : Construct validity of Language Creativity in English and Hindi are given.

Norms : Percentile mores available for boys as well as girls.

Time Limit : Generally takes two hours and twenty-seven minutes depending upon the grade leaves of the students.

11B (27)

Title of the Instrument : **Verbal Test of Scientific Creativity.**

Author(s) : V.P. Sharma and J.P. Shukla.

Availability : National Psychological Corporation, 4/230. Kacheri Ghat, Agra-4.

Language : Hindi.

Level : School Students.

Uses : To measure the scientific creativity among students.

Main Features : Consists of 12 items which have been classified into 4 sub-test namely 1. Consequences Test, 2. Unusual Uses Test, 3. New Relationship Test, 4. Just think why test. Under different sections, different items are classified.

Reliability : Reliability coefficients are as under : (N =230.)

1. Fluency (FI) = 0.729
2. Flexibility = 0.648
3. Originality = 0.774
4. Whole Test = 0.730.

Validity :

	Fluency	Flexibility	Originality	Whole Test
Fluency	*	0.9601	0.9461	0.9876
Flexibility		*	0.9587	0.9861
Originality			*	0.9880

Norms : Percentile norms for grades VII & VIII available for boys as well as girls separately.

Time Limit : For every tasks 15 minutes are given.

11B (28)

Title of the Instrument : **Fear Check List.**

Author : Ravinder Kaur.

Availability: National Psychological Corporation, 4/230, Kacheri Ghat, Agra-4.

Level : Adolescents in India.

Language(s) : English and Hindi.

Uses : Elicits information regarding the presence or absence of something used to collect data pertaining to human fears.

Main Features : 182 items are given. The subject has to respond to different situations pertaining to fear.

Reliability: Split-half reliability method and test-retest methods coefficients of correlations were found to be 0.84 and 0.78 respectively.

Validity : Validational Coefficients of the check list was found to be 0.78.

Norms : Available in the manual.

Time Limit : No time limit but it takes 10-12 minutes to complete the test.

References :
1. Buch, M.B. *Second Survey of Research in Education* 1972- 78. Society for Educational Research and Development, Baroda.
2. Geer, J.H. (1965) : '*The Development of a Scale to Measure Fear' Behaviour Res. Therapy*, 45-53.
3. Long, P.J. and Lazowick, A.D. (1954) : "Experimental desensitization of phobia" *Journal Abnormal and behavior problems of normal children between 21 months and 14 years*. Barkley and Los Angeles Univ. Cal. Press.
4. Wolpe, J.A. (1964) : Fear Survey Schedule for use in Behaviour Therapy, *Behav. Res. Thers.* 2, 27-30.

11B (29)

Title of the Instrument : **Frustration Tolerance (FRTO).**

Author : Dr. S.N. Rai.

Availability : Ankur Psychological Agency, 22/481 Indira Nagar, Lucknow-16.

Level : Children.

Language : English.

Uses : Both biologically as well as psychologically people differ greatly in their general vulnerability to stress as well as in general vulnerability to the type of stress to which they are most prone to.

This test is used to find out the frustration tolerance individually of different persons.

Main Features : Puzzle problems are given to the subject to solve in ten minutes fixed time. The Experimenter notes the exact time, the subject takes to solve the problem. The experimenter tries to see the frustration level of the subject.

Reliability and Validity : Not yet established.

Norms : Partially established.

Time Limit: 10 minutes.

References:

1. Andreanska, V. (1974) : Level of aspiration in weak sighted children under conditions of experimentally induced frustrating situations. *Psychologia*, 9, 345-359.
2. Cohen, S. and Spacapan, S. (1978). The after effects of stress : An attentional interpretation. *Environmental Psychology and Non-verbal Behaviour.* 3, 43-57. c
3. Dyek, D.G. Stove, V., and Lawrence, B.J. (1973) : Duration of failure, casual attribution for failure and subsequent reactions. *Journal of Experimental Social Psychology*. 25, 35-44
4. Rosenweig, S.(1960 a) : Consideration regarding reaction to frustration especially among adolescents. *Bolleltine de Psychologia Applicata*, 94, 3-12.
5. Thompson, J.W. (1978) : Frustration tolerance, parenting attitudes and perceptions of Parenting behaviour as factors in the incidence of child abuse. *Dissertation Abstract*. 38, 5598.
6. Wohlwill, J.F.; Nasar, J.L.; Dejoy, D.M. and Foruzani, H.H. (1976) : Behavioural effects of a noisy environment. Task involvement V/S Passive exposure. *Journal of Applied Psychology*.

11B (30)

Title of the Instrument : **Reactions to Frustration Scale.**

Author(s) : B.M. Dixit and D.N. Srivastava.

Availability : National Psychological Corporation, 4/230, Kacheri Ghat, Agra-4.

Language : Hindi.

Level : Individuals employed in the various fields of life and work.

Uses : To measure the reactions to frustration to the individuals employed in the various fields of life and work.

Main Features : Four reactions namely aggression, resignation, fixation, and regression, consists of 40 items out of which each reaction to frustration has 10 items equally divided into positive and negative items. Six alternative response options are graded on a six point scale.

Reliability : The reliability of RF's is determined by the method of the coefficient of stability by the test-retest method over one month and the *r* was found ranging between 0.64 to 0.82 in boys and 0.67 to 0.79 in girls.

Validity : Coefficient of correlation has been obtained 0.61 on the total frustration scale scores.

Norms : Percentile norms available.

Time Limit : 30 minutes.

11B (31)

Title of the Instrument : **Introversion = Extraversion Test.**

Purpose : To measure some aspects of personality.

Author : R.N. Singh.

Language : Hindi.

Availability : Manoviagnan Seva Kendra, Professor's Colony, Sakalenabad, Ghazipur -233001.

Uses : Provides measures of intraversion and extraversion dimension of personality alongwith its seven components.

Levels : Adults as well as adolescents.

Main Features : T.B. of 84 items, separate A>S> and scoring keys, profile sheet.

Reliability : Split-half reliability coefficients of 7 factors = 0.52 to 0.74; Repeat Split half reliability coefficients ranged from 0.60-0.76.

Validity : Data on internal validity provided.

Time limit : About 40 Minutes.

Norms : N-Sten norms available.

References :

1. Cattell, R.B. *et al* (1970) : *Handbook for The Sixteen Personality Factor Questionnaire*, Institute For Personality And Ability Testing, Champaign, Illinois.

2. Eysenck, H.J. (1970) : *The Structure of Human Personality*, Methuen & Co. Ltd. 11 New Fetter Lane, London.
3. Eysenck H.J. & Wilson, G., (1975) : *Know Your Personality*, Penguin Book Ltd, Harmondsworth, Mddlesex, England.
4. Hilgard, E.R. *et al.* (1975) : *Introduction to Psychology*, sixth edition, Oxford & IBH Publishing Co. New York.
5. Jung, C. (1976) : *Modern Man In Search of Soul*, Routledge and Kegan Paul, London, Reprint, 1976.
6. Singh, R.P. (1986) : *Under-Over Academic Achievement & Its Motivational Correlates*. Published by author himself, Faizabad, 1986.

11B (32)

Title of the Instrument : **Social Intelligence Scale.**
Purpose : Different dimensions of social intelligence.
Author(s) : N.K. Chadha and Usha Ganesan.
Language : English.
Availability : National Psychological Corporation, Agra-4.
Uses : Research and Diagnosis.
Levels : 20-35 years of age.
Main Features : 66 Items.
Reliability : In the present scale test, retest and split half techniques were employed to find the reliability coefficients. For finding the *split-half reliability* a sample of 150 (75 males and 75 females) was taken. The following coefficients were obtained.:
Split- half reliability coefficients.

1. Patience = 0.93
2. Cooperativeness = 0.91
3. Confidence = 0.89
4. Sensitivity = 0.90
5. Recognition of Social Environment = 0.95
6. Tactfulness = 0.91
7. Sense of Humour = 0.90
8. Memory = 0.96.

In order to determine the *test retest reliability* the previous sample used for split half was administered the scale after a period of 15 days. The following coefficients were obtained.

1. Patience = 0.94
2. Cooperativeness = 0.91
3. Confidence = 0.90
4. Sensitivity = 0.93
5. Recognition of Social Environment = 0.95
6. Tactfulness = 0.84
7. Sense of Humour = 0.92
8. Memory = 0.97.

Validity : The techniques used for finding out the validity of the scale = 1. Empirical Validity, and 2. Cross Validation.

Norms : Percentile norms are established for (150 males as well as 150 females.)

Time Limit : 30 minutes.

References : Used in M.A. and M.Phil dissertation.

11B (33).

Title of the Instrument : **Dysfunctional Analysis Qusestionnaire (DAQ).**

Purpose : To measure social, vocational, personal, family and cognitive, dysfunction through a questionnaire.

Author(s) : Parshad, D.; Verma, S.K., Malhotra, A; Malhotra S.; (Dept. of Psychiatry, P.G.I.; Chandigarh.)

Language : Hindi.

Availability : From Publisher National Psychological Corporation, Agra-4.

Uses : Evaluation of disabilities in the five areas.
Evaluation of progress of therapy.
Evaluation of rehabilitation measures after brain injury.
Guidance about rehabilitation.

Levels : All educational levels (orally to illiterates.)

Reliability : Test-retest reliability varies from 0.76 to 0.92 for dysfunction in five different areas viz. social, vocational, personal, family, and cognitive and split half reliabilities from 0.88 to 0.97.

Validity : Correlation with age, education occupation, and duration of illness have been reported separately for neurotic, psychotic and organic groups. (On 198, 132 and 90 subjects respectively.) High correlation between ratings by patients and by their relatives. Significant differences of dysfunction in the three groups of patients viz. neurotic, organics and psychotics. Correlation with psychiatric

Disability Scale. Factor Analysis. Correlation with work efficiency. Pre and post treatment comparisons.

Norms : On Neurotic (*n* = 198) < Psychotic (*n* =132), Organic (90 patients), amputes (*n* = 30), etc.

Time Limit : 10-15 minutes.

References :

1. Pershad, D.; Verma, S.K.; Malhotra, A.K. & Malhotra, S. (1985) : *Measurement of Dysfunction and Dysfunction Analysis Questionnaire* (DAQ) Agra, National Psychological Corporation.
2. Pershad, D.; Verma, S.K.; Malhotra, A.; Malhotra S; Das, K.; Khan H.A. & Khandelwal, S.K. (1982) Development of Dysfunction Analysis Questionnaire. *Indian Journal of Clinical Psychology*, 10, 445-450.

11B (34)

Title of the Instrument : **P.G.I. Locus of Control Scale.**

Purpose : To measure locus of control.

Author(s) : Menon, D.K.; Wig, N.N. & Verma, S.K. (Department of Psychiatry, PGI, Chandigarh.)

Language : Hindi.

Availability : Rupa Psychological Centre, B19/60 B, Deoriabir, Bhelupur, Varanasi 221010.

Uses : To Measure internal or external locus of control.

Levels : All educational levels (oral to illiterates)

Main Features : Items are on three point scale.

Reliability : Test-retest - 0.77, Inter scorer reliability =0.995.

Validity : With Psychiatric's rating = 0.792, Construct validity correlation with other tests.

Time Limit : 5-7 minutes.

Norms : On normals, post-graduate students, others of normal, mentally retarded and emotionally disturbed children, Acceptance and rejection of family planning. Breast cancer patients. Visually handicapped.

References : Menon, D.K.; Wig, N.N. & Verma, S.K. (1988) : *Manual for PGI Locus of Control Scale.* Rupa Psychological Centre, Varanasi.

11B (35)

Title of the Instrument : **Hindi PEN Inventory.**

Purpose : To measure personality dimensions.

Author(s) : D.K. Menon and S.K. Verma, Dept. of Psychiatry, PGI, Chandigarh.

Language : Hindi.

Availability : Rupa Psychological Centre, B 19/60 B Deoriabir, Bhelpur, Varanasi-221010.

Uses : To measure Psychoticism, Extraversion, Neuroticism and tendency to respond in a socially desirable way.

Levels : All educational levels (orally for illiterates.)

Main Features : 78 items in 2 response (yes/no) format, 20 items each for PEN and 18 items for Social Desirability Response Set.

Reliability : Test-retest = 0.6277 for P; 0.8875 for E, 0.6873 for N and 0.3370 for L scale.

Validity : Normal Vs. Psychiatric patients differentiated correlation with other tests.

Norms : Normals, Psychiatric patients.

Time Limit : NIL.

References : Menon, D.K. & Verma, S.K. (1988) : *Manual for Hindi PEN Inventory*. Rupa Psychological Center, Varanasi.

11B (36)

Title of the Instrument : **Self-Concept Inventory.**

Purpose : To construct and standardize self-concept inventory in Gujarati for pupils of grades IX and X.

Author : J.H. Shah.

Language : Gujarati.

Availability : Dr. J.H. Shah, Professor and Head, Department of Education, Gujarat University. Order to be placed at : Man-mapn. F/7 Swastik Apartments, Mr. N.N. Bus Terminus, Paldi, Ahmedabad-380007.

Uses : 1. To measure self-concept of pupil of grades VIII to X of Gujarat State 2. As a research tool 3. As a survey tool to locate pupils having very low self-concept and give them necessary counselling to up-lift his/her self-concept.

Level for whom it is meant : For pupils of grades IX and X in Gujarat state.

Main Features : On the basis of Personality Word List' of Pratibha Deo and self-concept inventory of Sagar Sharma, a new self-concept inventory was developed. Necessary try outs were carried out and expert's recommendation were taken into consideration while framing the inventory. Three criterion were taken into consideration for the inclusion of each word in the inventory. 1. It had to describe personality characteristic unambiguously either favourably or unfavourably. 2. It had to be intelligible to the average pupil. 3. It had to differentiate between pupils. The final inventory consists of 40 socially desirable adjectives and 40 socially undesirable adjectives. The weighted scores of positive words being 5,4,3,2,1, and those of negative ones being 1,2,3,4,5. Thus the range of scores was from 50 to 400.

Reliability : Test-retest method = (One month period) r =0.86 (n=75).

Validity : 1. Seven experts acted as judges in establishing its content validity. 2. Correlation between self-concept scores and 'ME' scores on '0.47 (n = 47) 3. Correlation with other variables : Self-concept and academic Ach. = 0.22 (N = 690.) Self concept and creativity = 0.25, Self-concept and locus of control = 0.35.

Time Limit : No time limit. However, it takes about 40-50 minutes for reading instructions and administering it.

Norms : No norm tables are provided. However, quartiles were taken into consideration. (The subjects of standards IX and X who would score 285 or below would be considered as having low self concept, between 285 to 330-moderate self-concept and above 330, as having high self-concept.

References :

1. Bhogayta, C. 'The Relationship among creativity, self-concept and loçus of control' (Unpublished Ph. D. Thesis) 'Saurastra University', 1988.
2. Shah, J.H. "Relationship of Self-concept to Academic Achievement of secondary school pupils" *Journal of Educational Research and Extension*, XVI, Ist July, 1979,70.
3. Shah, J.H. "Construction and Standardization of self-concept Inventories in Gujarat : For pupils of grades IX and X" *Experiments in Education*, XVII, 2, 1989, 31-36.

11B (37)

Title of the Instrument : **Self-Disclosure Inventory for Adolescent.**
Author : Virendra Sinha.
Availability : National Psychological Corporation, Agra-4.
Language(s) : Hindi and English.
Level : Adolescents 12-19 years of age both the sexes can be included.
Uses : It is a rating scale and the person judges himself/herself on the scale. It is used by the guidance workers, social workers, probation officers, clinicians, psychiatrists, teachers, and parents to know the nature and extent of self-disclosure of the adolescents and to guide them that optimum self-disclosure is an essential characteristic of the healthy mental personality.
Main features : Contains 80 items, (10 items in each area) and takes about 60 minutes to answer the whole inventory by an average testee. There is no right or wrong answer as it is a rating scale.
Reliability : Split-half reliability was calculated on a 200 mid adolescents sample including male, female, urban, and rural testees, and *r* was found to be 0.95 significant at 0.01 levels.
Validity : Construct validity was found.
Norms : Age norms were calculated.
Time limit : Average 70 minutes are required.
References :

1. Horney, K. (1936) : *The Neurotic Personality of Our Time* N.Y. Norton.
2. Jourard, S.M., (1959) : Self-disclosure and other Cathexis. *Journal of Abnormal & Social Psychology*. 59, 428-431.
3. Sinha, V. and Saun, G.S. (1979) : Role of Target-Figures in Self-disclosure of Hill region Urban Boys. *Journal of Perspectives in Psychological Researches*. 2 (1-2). 43-47.

[Note : Item 11C not reported]

D

11D (1)

Title of the Instrument : **Samajik Pratikriya Soochi.**
Purpose : To measure Internality-Externality (Locus of Control).
Author(s) : Original : J.B. Rotter
Adaptation : Y.P. Aggarwal.
Languages(s) : English and Hindi.
Availability : Dr. Y.P. Aggarwal, Prof., Chairman & Dean, Faculty of Education, Kurukshetra University, Kurukshetra - 132119.
Uses : To measure Locus of Control, Dimension of Personality.
Levels : High School/College Students and other young adults.
Main Features : 1. No. of items = 29 (including six fillers). 2. Each item has two alternative responses. 3. Scoring on externality dimension by adding on the scores on each item 4. Each item & scored as 1 to 0.
Reliability : Test, Retest reliability from point 0.86 to 0.95.
Validity : Validity coefficient on bilingual population and with original English version ranges from 0.80 to 0.83.
Time Limit : About 40 minutes.
Norms : Percentile norms on High School students/college students available in the manual.
References :

1. Aggarwal, Y.P. : A Study of Locus of Control & General Intelligence among scheduled castes and non-scheduled castes students, Report of a U.G.C. Financed Project, Kurukshetra University, 1975.
2. Aggarwal, Y.P. & Berry, P.: "Internal-External Control as a Determinant of Academic Achievement", *Kurukshetra University Research Journal* (Arts & Humanities), 1974, VII, 1 & 2, pp. 27-31.
3. Aggarwal, Y.P. & Kumari, M. : "A Study of Locus of control of Boys and Girls at various levels of socio-economic status", *Kurukshertra University Research Journal* (Arts and Humanities), 1975, IX, pp. 26-32.
4. Aggarwal, Y.P. & Mohinder Singh, "A Study of Locus of Control and Self-concept of Front-

benchers and Back-benchers." Mans, 1974, 21, 2, pp. 1-7.

5. Thukral, Manmohan Singh. A Comparative Study of Locus of Control, General Intelligence and Level of Vocational Aspirations of Scheduled Caste and Non-scheduled Caste High School Students. Doctoral thesis, Kurukshtra University, 1977.

11D (2)

Title of the Instrument : **C.M.I. Health Questionnaire (Hindi).**
Author(s) : N.N. Wig ; D. Pershad and S.K. Verma.
Availability : National Psychological Corporation, Agra-4.
Language : Hindi.
Uses : To study the physical and mental health of an individual.
Levels : All levels.
Main Features : There are two forms of the CMI, one for men and the other women. Questions are grouped into two basic sections: A to L section is called physical distress section, and M to R section is called emotional or psychological distress question. In every case a 'Yes' answer indicates that the patient claims to have the system. More than 25 items marked as 'yes' indicates a serious disorder.
Time limit : No time limit.

11D (3)

Title of the Instrument : **Intolerance of Ambiguity Scale (IA Scale).**
Author : P. Sarin.
Availability : Ankur Psychological Agency, 17-B, Narain Nagar, P.O. Building, Lucknow.
Language : Hindi.
Uses : To measure the subjects intolerance of ambiguity of the different kinds of situations.
Level : All levels.
Main Features : The scale consists of 16 items, each item represents a particular type of ambiguous situation. There are six response categories for each item. The responses are positive items are scored 7, 6, 5, 3, 2, 1, respectively and the scoring of negative items are done in the reverse direction. High score on this scale would be indicative of greater intolerance of ambiguity.

Reliability : Test-retest reliability established = 0.89.

Validity : Validity was determined by computing the coefficient of correlation between scores on Hindi version and English version. (original version = 0.72).

Time Limit : Approximately 15-20 minutes.

Norms : Norms are published in the manual.

References :

1. Budner, S. (1962) : "Intolerance of ambiguity as a personality variable" J. of Personality, 30, 82-83.
2. Garret, H.E. (1973) : "*Statistics in Psychology and Education*", Vakils, Feffer & Simon Pvt.
3. Millon, T. (1957) : "Authoritarianism intolerance of ambiguity and rigidity under ego and task involving condition. *Journal of Abnormal & Social Psychology*, 55.29-33.

11D (4)

Title of the Instrument : **Authoritarianism Scale.**

Author : P. Sarin.

Availability : Ankur Psychological Agency, 22/481, Indira Nagar, Lucknow.

Language : Hindi.

Uses : To Measure 'Authoritarianism' characteristic of an individual.

Level : All levels.

Main Features : There are 27 items in the scale. It is a 7 point scale, scoring skips from 3 to 5 points between between - 1 and + 1.

Reliability : The reliability was found to be 0.93.

Validity : The coefficient of correlation between Hindi version and English version was computed. It was found to be 0.63.

Time Limit : Approximately 15-20 minutes.

Norms : Norms are published in the manual.

References :

1. Adorno, T.W., Frenkel, Brurewick, Else; Levinson, B.J. and Sanford, R.N. (1950) : *The Authoritarian Personality*. New York : Harper & Row.
2. Garret, H.E. (1973) : *Statistics in Psychology and Education*. Vakils, Feffer, and Simons Pvt.

11D (5)

Title of the Instrument : **Aap Kis Prakar Ke Vyakti Hai? Parikshan.**

Authors : B. Nisha & K. Gupta.

Availability : National Psychological Corporation, 4/230, Kacheri Ghat, Agra.

Language : Hindi.

Uses : To study what kind of a person the individual is.

Main Features : There are 50 items contracted by pairing different characteristics of differing ranks and placed in forced choice format. In some cases the terms call the respondents to make a choice between two socially desirable characteristic on the other items. Similarly there are items in the test that differentiate between creative and non-creative individuals.

Reliability : Split-half reliability = 0.96; Rational Equivalence reliability = 0.94; Test-retest reliability = 0.68 to 0.90

Validity : Coefficient of correlation between the Hindi version of English version = 0.68.

Time Limit : 10-15 minutes.

Norms : Norms are published in the manual.

11D (6)

Title of the Instrument : **Social Preference and Social Behaviour Inventory (SPSBI).**

Author(s) : M.C. Joshi & J. Pandey.

Availability : National Psychological Corporation, 4/230, Kacheri Ghat, Agra-4.

Language : Hindi.

Uses : To measure two personality traits, Form P is called Inventory of Social Preferences and form B is called Inventory of Social Behaviour.

Main Features : There are two forms each with 3 items. The respondents have to make their choices on a 5 point scale. There are negative and positive items, the weightage is 5,4,3,2,8,1., it is reversed for negative items. High score indicates effective social preference and behaviour.

Reliability : Reliability for MISP :

Test-retest = 0.795 (75 days);

Test-retest = 0.845 (15 days);

Split-half = 0.685;

SEmmt = 5.87
Index of reliability =0.896.
Test-Retest = 0.520 (75 days).
Test-Retest = 0.740 (95 days).
Split-half = 0.915
SEmmt = 3.26
Index of Reliability = 0.95

Validity : External Validity of MISP & MISB are established by 1. Introversion-Extroversion Personality types as a criterion.

2. Discriminative Power as criterion.
3. Correlation with the Mooney Problem Check list Scores.

Time Limit : 30-40 minutes.

Norms : Norms are published in the manual.

References :

1. Edward, A.L. (1954) : *Statistical Methods for Behavioural Science*, New York, Rinehart.
2. Eysenck, H.J.(1961) : "Personality and Social Attitudes, *J. Soc.Psy.* Vol. 43.p 243.
3. Phillips, L. Fine, H.J.& Fulberson, S.C. (1955) : "Maladjustment and Social Attainment" *J. Ab. Soc. Psy.* Vol. 50.

11D (7)

Title of the Instrument : **Adaptation of Cattells Sixteen Personality Factor.**

Author : Sheela J.Emanuel. (available in Gujarati).

Age-Group and the Factors : The Sixteen Personality Factor Questionnaire was adapted for the age group 16 years to 21 years. It measures 16 primary personality factors.

Norms : Explore analysis developed by Skinner providing several multivariate results. Linear regression analysis, factor analysis solution, varimax, and oblique rotation etc. was implemented. Factor analysis was carried out for each form sex-wise, age-wise, as well as area-wise. The results of factor analysis clearly showed that Form A and Form B of the 16 PFQ were not parrellel and with respect to the variables of sex, age group and area, the factorial compositions varied from one group to another. So it was decided to report separate S-Sten norms for Form-A and Form-B, Sex-wise, age group wise as well as area wise.

Reliability : Reliability of the 16 PFQ was found out by following methods : A. Test-Retest after six days: The dependability coefficient ranged from 45 to 81.

2. Test-retest after three months : The stability coefficients of all the factors were less than dependability coefficients. The stability coefficient ranged from 44 to 76.

B. Equivalence Co-efficient = Co-efficienct of equivalence between Form A and Form B showed that out of 16 coefficients, the values of 13 were found below 0.50. Only three have higher values = 0.59, 0.64, 0.67. Factor N and Q2 were found having very low values, that is 0.26 and 0.33.

C. Method of Rational Equivalence = Reliability was also found out by using Kuder-Richardson formula. According to this formula the reliability co-efficients ranged from 0.34 to. 0.74.

D. The Index of Reliability : $r100 = r11$ where $r100$=index of reliability. The study showed that 0.90 was the highest correlation which this tests capable of yielding in its present form.

Validity : A Internal Consistency of items : Out of 187 coefficients in Form A, 161 were significant at 0.01 level and 26 at 0.05 level. While in Form B, 162 were significant at 0.01 level and the remaining 25 value at 0.05 level.

B. Concurrent Validity : The results showed that out of 12 validity coefficients, six were significant at 0.01 level while one was at 0.05 level. The remaining five factors A,B,C,E, and Q2 had very low values.

Availability : Dr. Sheela J.Christian. RH 1, Punyashree Apts. Mr. Kashiram, Agarwal Hall, Polytechnic Road, Ahmedabad-380015.

11D (8)

Title of the Instrument : **Excitability Rating Scale.**

Authors : K. Sinha & A.K.Sen.

Availability : National Psychological Corporation, 4/230, Kacheri Ghat, Agra-4.

Language : Hindi.

Uses : To study the behaviour characteristics of mentally retarded children.

Level : Mentally Retarded children.

Main Features : The scale consists of nine factors, graded on a five point scale. There are 38 items. The positive items are scored as 1,2,3,4, and 5 respectively and the negative items are reversely scored as 5,4,3,2, and 1. The nine factors are : 1. Emotional level, 2. Aggressive Behaviour, 3. Activity Level, 4, Variability of work Activity, 5. Verbal Activity, 6, Sociability, 7. Inter-personal responses, 8. Amenability, 9. Predictability.

Reliability : Reliability was established by administering the English and Hindi version of the test on the same group. The correlation between the two sets of scores was computed and the value was 0.63. Thus it was concluded that the reliability is high.

Time Limit : No time limit.

References :

1. Claridge, G.S. & O'Conner (1957) : "The Relationship between Incentive Personality Type and Improvement in Performance of Imbeciles." *J. of Mental Deficiency Research*, 33-35.
2. Garret, H.E. (1977) *Statistics in Psychology & Education*, New York.
3. Moser, C. & Kalton, G. (1979) : *Survey Methods in Social Investigation*, Heinmann Educational Books Ltd. London.

11D (9)

Title of the Instrument : **Adaptation of Cattell's Early School Personality Questionnaire for Gujarati children of ages 6 through 8.**

Authors : R.B. Cattell and R.W. Coan. Adapted by Bharat G. Dave.

Language : Gujarati.

Purpose : To measure thirteen dimensions of personality of Gujarati children of ages 6 through 8.

Availability : Dr. Bharat G. Dave, 2/3976 Opp: Kala Mehta's Sheri, Mahavir Hospital Road, Sanrampura, Surat - 39500.

Uses : The Present adapted ESPQ will be applicable to Gujarati speaking children.

1. The school can use it for the purpose of general survey, personality classification of pupils as well as personal and educational guidance.

2. It is useful in clinical practice.

Levels : As mentioned above it is used for early school children who are studying in grade 1, 2 and 3— of ages 6 through 8.

Main Features : In English version : It is available in form A. Gujarati version of Form A 1, & 2 are now available. There are thirteen factors in ESPO. For each factor 6 questions are asked. Factor B has 8 questions. All forms are provided with carefully designed answersheets to be used by the subjects which are scorable by hand with rapid stencil key.

(1) *Reliability* :

Method	Form	N	Range	Time interval.
Test-retest	A	100	0.29 to 0.67	One week.
	A	100	0.23 to 0.50	Two weeks
	A	100	0.18 to 0.45	Twelve weeks.
Method of Rational Equivalence	Al & A2	100	0.25 to 0.61	Same day
(2) *Validity* :				
ESPQ Form A with CPQ Form A		100	0.31 to 0.44	
ESPQ Form A with CPQ Form B		100	0.31 to 0.52	
Internal Consistency A of items		100	0.20 to 0.93	

By point biserial correlation Method. The level of significance 151 items at 0.01 level. 8 items at 0.05 level.

Time limit : It is a personality test. There is no time limitation in this test, but can generally be completed within 30 to 50 minutes per parts.

Norms : (are they variable) : Age-wise, Sex-wise, Form-wise and area-wise norms are available. "Adaptation of Cattell's Early School Personality Questionnaire for Gujarati children of ages 6 through 8.

References : 1. "Gujarati Adaptation of Cattell's Personality Questionnaires" was presented at the 75th Indian Science Conference held at Poona 7-12 Jan, 1989. This research paper has been accepted for publication in *Vidya* — A Humanities (Half-yearly Journal of Gujarat University, Ahmedabad).

11D (10)

Title of the Instrument : **An Adaptation of Cattell's High School Personality Questionnaire for Gujarati Children of Ages 12 through 18.**

Purpose : To measure fourteen dimension of Personality of Gujarati Children of Ages 12 through 18.

Authors : R.B. Cattell and Marry D.L. Cattell. Adapted by Dr. R.N. Thakur. (Gujarati version.)

Language : In Gujarati only.

Availability : Dr. R.N. Thakur, R.B. Sagar College of Education, Shativan, Paldi, Ahmedabad-7.

Uses : The present adapted HSPQ will be applicable to Gujarati speaking children.

1. The secondary and higher secondary schools can use it for the purpose of general survey, personality classification of pupils as well as personal and educational guidance.

2. This test can be of a good help in clinical practice.

3. In the light of this adaptation parent-teacher as well as parent-clinic co-operation will be eased and facilitated it would go a long way to focus the problems of a child.

4. An additional advantage is that with the same unit any personality concept and the almost similar population CPQ on one hand and the 16 PF on the other hand have already been adapted and standardized in Gujarati version.

Levels : As mentioned above, it is used for junior senior high school children of ages 12 through 18 years.

Main Features : 1. It is interesting to note that ESPQ, CPQ, HSPQ and very similar population of the whole Gujarat State. Only urban and semi urban areas are covered. The total sample on which HSPQ was standardized was 2342 (B =1254, G = 1088).

2. In English version, it is available in Four types of forms ABC and D. The Gujarati version of Forms A and Form B are now available.

There are fourteen factors in HSPQ and for each factor, the questions are asked the two questions nos. 1 and 142 are buffer questions. Total items in each form are 142. All Forms are provided with carefully designed answer sheets to be used by the subjects which are scorable either by hand with a rapid stencil key.

Reliability and Validity of adapted HSPQ.

Reliability :

Method	Form	N	Range	Time interval
Test-retest	A	70	.43 to .85	(One week.)
	B	70	.40 to .81	(One week.)
	A	70	.18 to .53	(Two weeks)

(Contd.)

Method	Form	N	Range	Time interval
	B	70	.19 to .40	(Two weeks)
	A	70	.10 to .35	(Twelve weeks)
	B	70	.10 to .49	
Parallel form method	A with B	100	.27 to .69	(the same day.)
Reliability by the method of Rational	A	100	.34 to .99	—
equivalence	B	100	.37 to .99	—

Validity :

Method	N	Form	Range
1. Correlation of HSPQ with CPQ	100	A with A	.29 to .58
	100	B with B	.28 to .43
2. Estimating correlation with 16 PFQ	80	A with A	.16 to .46
	80	B with B	.18 to. 40
3. Internal consistency of items		A .20 to. 96	
		B .20 to 99	
		A	Significant at. 01 level 115 items
			Significant at .05 level 25 items
		B	Significant at .01 level 120 items
			Significant at .05 level 20 items

Time Limit : It is a personality test. There is no time limit as such in this test, but it can generally be completed within 40 to 50 minutes per form.

Norms : Areawise-urban - semi urban ; Sex-wise—Boys— Girls; Form-wise A and B

Form wise A and B

An adaptation of High School Personality

Questionnaire for Gujarati Children

Age 12 through 18. PP 172 to 179.

References : "Gujarati Adoptations of Cattell's Personality Questionnaires" Presented at the 75th Indian Science Conference held at Pune 7-12 Jan'88. The same Paper has been accepted for publication in *Vidya* (A Humanities) Half Yearly Journal of Gujarat University, Ahmedabad.

11D (11)

Title of the Instrument : **Adaptation of Cattell's Children Personality Questionnaire for Gujarati Children of Ages 8 through 12.**

Purpose : To measure the personality of Gujarati Children of ages 8 to 12.

Author : R.S. Patel.

Language : Gujarati.

Availability : Er. R.S. Patel, M-177-2118, Surya Apartment, Sola Road, Naranpura, Ahmedabad-471823.

Uses : In School it can be used for the purpose of general survey, personality classification of pupils as well as guidance personal and educational. This test would be helpful in clinical practice. With the help of this test, parent-teacher and parenty-clinic co-operation is facilitated. To focus the problems of a child. This test-CPQ is a linkage between the ESPQ and HSPQ. One can have a meaningful continuous record of personality traits in the form of a profile of a tested from the age 6 to 20 years by using ESPQ, CPQ, HSPQ and 16 PFQ in turn. As all the four Questionnaires have been standardized on the almost similar population of the Gujarat Sate which we stratified into five regions-East, Central, North, and South.

Level : Ages 8 through 12.

Main Features : Questionnaire technique used. As stated earlier, CPQ has been standardized on the common sample drawn from the whole Gujarat State, for ESPQ, HSPQ, and 16 PFQ. The total sample on which it has been standardized is 2205 (B = 928 G = 1277).

Reliability :

1. Coefficient of stability by test-retest technique. Range : From A 0.53 to 0.90
   Range : From : 0.50 to 0.82
2. Coefficient of equivalence by the method of parrellel forms. Range : 0.27 to 0.48.
3. Method of rational equivalence by the method (Kuder Richardson Formula — 21.) Range Form : A : 0.21 to 0.73; Range Form : B : 0.29 to 0.57.

Validity : 1. Internal consistency a items in the rbis calculations out of 280 items 271 were significant at 0.01 level and remaining nine are significant etc 0.05 level. 2. Correlation with HSPQ. Form A :

Ranges from 0.29 to 0.58; Form B : it ranges from, 0.28 to 0.43..
4. factorial Validity analysis was carried out by using the programme "Explore" on Dec 10 in PRL.

Time Limit : It takes about one period nearly 30 minutes for each form of the part.

Norms : Sten Norms are prepared form-wise (A and B) (B and A) as well as area-wise.

References : The paper Cattell's personality questionnaires in Gujarati was presented at 75 the Indian Science Congress held at Poona 7-12 Jan. 1989 and has been accepted for publication in *Vidya*.

Adjustments and Problems

A

12A (1)

Title of the Instrument : **Marital Satisfaction Scale.**
Purpose : To assess marital satisfaction / Quality of marital life.
Author : Brunda Amrithraj and Indira Jai Prakash.
Language : English (attached.).
Availability : Dr. Indira Jai Prakash, Reader, Department of Psychology, Bangalore University, Bangalore-560 056.
Uses : Counselling and Research.
Levels : English knowing and Urban men and women.
Main Features : Maximum score possible in this scale was 60 and minimum score was 0. Content wise, the scale sampled social, emotional, interpersonal and sexual sources of satisfaction in marriage.
Reliability and Validity : The split-half reliability correlating odd even items applying Spearman-Brown formula was 0.94. Test-retest reliability was found to be 0.96. Validity of the test was found to be 0.77.
Time limit : 15 to 20 minutes.
Norms : They are available in the manual.
References : *Psychological studies*. 30 (2), 124-126, 1985.

MARITAL SATISFACTION SCALE

Given below are a number of questions related to different aspects of married life. Please read each statement and choose one of the responses given below the statement. There is *No* right or wrong answer. Be frank and choose an answer that best describes your feelings, experiences and thoughts. Your answers will be kept confidential.

1. Do you and your partner have friends in common?
   a. None b. a few c. Many
2. Do you feel that your partner understands you?
   a. Yes, many times b. At times c. No, rarely
3. Do you visit friends and relatives together ?
   a. Rarely b. Occasionally c. Always

4. Do you engage in outside hobbies and interests together?
   a. Always often b. occasionally c. Rarely
5. Are your needs being fulfilled in your married life?
   a. Very few b. Some of them c. Many of them,
6. Do you like your partner's friends ?
   a. Most of them b. Some of them c. None of them
7. Do you share with your partner the responsibility of looking after your child/children?
   a. Never share b. Occasionally c. Often, always
8. Compared to your life before marriage, is life at present ....
   a. Happier b. Same as before c. Unhappier
9. Are there things done by your partner which you dislike?
   a. a few b. Some c. Many
10. Does your partner actively try to make married life more harmonious?
    a. Never, not bothered b. At times c. Always
11. Do you derive satisfaction from sexual relations with your partner?
    a. Often, always b. At time c. Rarely
12. Do your parents-in-law have a holdover your partner?
    a. No b. At times c. Yes,
13. Do you get as much affection from your partner as you desire?
    a. Yes b. Cannot say c. No
14. If you could live your life all over again, would you like to marry the same person to whom you are married now?
    a. No, never b. Cannot say c.Yes
15. Are you frank regarding sexual matters with your partner?
    a. Often, always b. Occasionally c. Rarely, never
16. When you compare your family life with those of other do you feel disturbed?
    a. Never b. Sometimes c. Often
17. Have you ever wished you were not Married?
    a. Very often b. Occasionally c. No, never
18. Has your partner been unfaithful to you?
    a. Never b. Cannot say c. Often
19. Do you feel that your partner cares more for his/her relatives than for you?
    a. Very often b. At times c. Never
20. Have you ever wished you were married to some one else ?
    a. Never b. At times c. Often
21. Do you confide in your partner about your personal problems ?
    A. Rarely b. Occasionally c. Always

22. Do you have frictions with your partner over the use of money?
    a. Rarely b. Sometimes c. Often, always
23. Do you agree with your partner on essential matters related to your children (e.g., their schooling, career, friends, marriage etc.)
    a. Disagree often b. Agree sometimes
    c. Agree most of the times
24. Has your partner ever caused physical harm or injury to you ?
    a. Never b. Occasionally c. Often
25. Have you ever caused physical harm or injury to your partner ?
    a. Never b. Occasionally c. Often
26. Is your partner sensitive to your sexual needs and satisfaction ?
    a. Not sensitive b. At times c. Always sensitive
27. Do you feel that your partner depends on you rather than his/her relatives for advice on family matters ?
    a. Depends on me b. Cannot say c. Depends on relatives
28. Have you had disagreements with your partner about having children ?
    a. Often b. At times c.Never
29. Have you ever felt like leaving or divorcing your partner ?
    a. Often b. At times c. Never
30. Considering everything, would you say that your married life is ....
    a. Not satisfactory b. Neither satisfactory nor unsatisfactory c.Very satisfactory

Scoring Key

Item	A	B	C	Item	A	B	C
1	0	1	2	16	2	1	0
2	2	1	0	17	0	1	2
3	0	1	2	18	2	1	0
4	2	1	0	19	0	1	2
5	0	1	2	20	2	1	0
6	2	1	0	21	0	1	2
7	0	1	2	22	2	1	0
8	2	1	0	23	0	1	2
9	2	1	0	24	2	1	0
10	0	1	2	25	2	1	0

(Contd.)

Item	A	B	C	Item	A	B	C
11	2	1	0	26	0	1	2
12	2	1	0	27	2	1	0
13	2	1	0	28	0	1	2
14	0	1	2	29	0	1	2
15	2	1	0	30	0	1	2

References :
1. *Psychological Studies*, 1985, Vol. 30 (2), 124-126 for details regarding Construction, reliability and validity.
2. Anuradha, M.A. Sex role orientation and its relation to job and marital satisfaction in women. Unpublished M.A dissertation, Bangalore University, 1984.

Marital satisfaction scores of different S-R-O groups

	Masculine	Feminine	Androg-ynous	Undiffer-entiated
N	63	16	14	57
Mean	44.5	52.0	49.1	46.04
Median	44.95	42.80	51.60	45.95
S.D.	6.95	8.75	7.20	8.03

F. 1.7169 N.S.

Marital satisfaction of women in different occupations

	Clerks	Officers	Teachers	Lecturers	Doctors
N	30	30	30	30	30
Mean	44.66	49.00	43.16	43.83	47.16
Median	45.60	51.53	42.60	45.00	47.00
S.D.	7.94	8.32	7.38	6.52	7.14

F = 2.43*

t values between				
	1 & 2 = 2.08*	1 & 5 = 1.28	2 & 5 = 0.91	4 & 5 = 1.89
	1 & 3 = 0.76	2 & 3 = 2.87**	3 & 4 = 0.38	
	1 & 4 = 0.44	2 & 4 = 2.68*	3 & 5 = 2.04 *	

12A (2)

Title of the Instrument : **Family Adjustment Inventory for working women.**

Purpose : To know the family adjustment of married working women.

Author : Vishwa Vijaya Singh.

Language : English.
Availability : Dr. Mrs. V.V. Singh, Vidya Bhawen, Udaipur-313001. (Rajasthan).
Uses : To know adjustment in family of women in four professions i.e., Teaching, Medical, Clerical, and Administration.
Levels : Married Working Women
Main Features : There are 84 items. There are five areas i.e. self adjustment, Family adjustment, adjustment with children, adjustment with husband, and adjustment with Elders and Relations.
Reliability : a. Test-retest Method with interval of one month. Pearson Product Moment Correlation Formula was used. Reliability of the test by this method is =0.8.

b. Spearman Brown formula (Split-half Method) was used. Reliability by this method is 0.83.,
Validity : Family Adjustment Inventory scores and scores of Problem Check-List (developed by the author too) were used for validity by using Pearson Product Moment Correlation Formula. Validity is 0.57.
Time limit : No limit.
Norms : There are norms available with the author.

Family Adjustment Inventory for Working Women

1. I feel that life is full of difficulties and problems.
Agree/Disagree/Undecided
2. I often think of committing suicide.
Agree/Disagree/Undecided
3. I often feel very tired both mentally and physically
Agree/Disagree/Undecided
4. I feel that I am not getting enough liberty at home.
Agree/Disagree Undecided
5. I feel that I have an independent status of my won.
Agree/Disagere/Undecided
6. I feel I have too many worries. Agree/Disagere/Undecided
7. I feel I am making my contribution to society.
Agree/Disagere/Undecided
8. I feel I am contributing in raising the standard of my family.
Agree/Disagere/Undecided

9. I think that my employment has raised my status in my family. Agree/Disagere/Undecided
10. I am free to spend my salary as I wish. Agree/Disagree/Undecided
11. I feel that marriage is a hindrance in personal progress. Agree/Disagree/Undecided
12. I feel extremely bad when I am not able to do the domestic work properly. Agree disagree/Undecided
13. I face tension and strain being in Job. Agree/Disagree/Undecided
14. I face inner conflict due to dual responsibilities of my home and work Agree/Disagerее/Undecided
15. Left to myself I would never take up a job. Agree/Disagree/Undecided
16. Being in job, I am enjoying my life to the full. Agree/Disagree/Undecided
17. I am afraid I am losing my feminity and charm Agree/Disagree/Undecided
18. I feel happy when I am with the members of my family. Agree/Disagree/Undecided
19. It is impossible for me to live away from my family Agree/Disagree/Undecided
20. I cannot take decision on family matters. Agree/Disagree/Undecided
21. I have too many family responsibilities. Agree/Disagree/Undecided
22. The atmosphere of my family is very tense. Agree/Disagree/Undecided
23. There are many conflicts in my family. Agree/Disagree/Undecided
24 I feel that nobody in my family loves me. Agree/Disagree/Undecided
25. I feel sometimes like running away from my hame. Agree/Disagree/Undecided
26. I feel that members of my family do not appreciate my work. Agree/Disagree/Undecided
27. I feel there is too much interference from the members of my family in my personal affairs. Agree/Disagree/Undecided
28 I get affection and sympathy from my family. Agree/Disagree/Undecided

29. I am confident that my family will support me if I got into any trouble. Agree/Disagree/Undecided
30. My family members are proud of my job. Agree/Disagree/Undecided
31. I have a say in my family matters. Agree/Disagree/Undecided
32. Since I am supplementing the income of my family we enjoy the life better. Agree/Disagree/Undecided
33. I am continuing to work inspite of all discouragements from the members of my family. Agree/Disagree/Undecided
34. It is unjust on the part of the members of my family to expect so many domestic responsibilities from me when I am a working women. Agree/Disagree/Undecided
35. I wish our elders were more liberal in their outlook Agree/Disagree/Undecided
36. When I go to work I forget about the worries of any family life. Agree/Disagree/Undecided
37. I feel I am getting alienated (getting away) from my family. Agree/Disagree/Undecided
38. I think that I am not able to give the desired love and affection to my children Agree/Disagree/Undecided
39. I feel my children are being neglected because of my job. Agree/Disagree/Undecided

40 I feel that working women should not have children. Agree/Disagree/Undecided

41. I am very much worried about the future of my children. Agree/Disagree/Undecided
42. I am doing full justice to the duties towards children. Agree/Disagree/Undecided
43. I am able to guide and supervise the studies of my children. Agree/Disagree/Undecided
44. My children help me because I am earning for making their life better. Agree/Disagree/Undecided
45. My children are happy because they get good education. Agree/Disagree/Undecided
46. My children cooperate with me in all situations. Agree/Disagree/Undecided

46. My children adjust themselves in any unusual situation created due to my being in job. Agree/Disagree/Undecided

48. My children do not complain even if they are left alone in home. Agree/Disagree/Undecided

49. My children dislike my going out for job. Agree/Disagree/Undecided
50. My children are dissatisfied for not getting enough affection from me. Agree/Disagree/Undecided
51. My children complain for not being given proper attention and time. Agree/Disagree/Undecided
52. I feel my children have a grudge against me. Agree/Disagree/Undecided
53. I am not able to concentrate in my work because I am constantly re-minded of my children. Agree/Disagree/Undecided
54. My children are not developing along proper lines because I am not able to pay attention to them. Agree/Disagree/Undecided
55. I feel that my married life is happy. Agree/Disagree/Undecided
56. My husband is tolerant. Agree/Disagree/Undecided
57. My husband is very cooperative. Agree/Disagree/Undecided
58. My husbands attitude towards me is sympathetic. Agree/Disagree/Undecided
59. My husband always helps me in every difficulty. Agree/Disagree/Undecided
60. I discuss any personal problems with my husband. Agree/Disagree/Undecided
61. My husband helps me in house hold jobs. Agree/Disagree/Undecided
62. I feel that my being in job does not affect marital happiness. Agree/Disagree/Undecided
63. We respect each other as equals and have equal partnership in marital relationship. Agree/Disagree/Undecided
64. We share the burden and responsibilities of home and children. Agree/Disagree/Undecided
65. We both are conscious of our duties and responsibilities. Agree/Disagree/Undecided
66. We have considerations for each other's likes and dislike. Agree/Disagree/Undecided
67. My husband is an authoritarian person and therefore dominates me. Agree/Disagree/Undecided
68. My husband gets annoyed, when I am not able to give proper attention to his needs. Agree/Disagree/Undecided
69. I think I am not fulfilling my duties properly as a wife. Agree/Disagree/Undecided
70. My husband is very considerate towards me. Agree/Disagree/Undecided

71. My husband is keen to see me rise in my profession. Agree/Disagree/Undecided
72. Since both of us are busy throughout the day we eagerly look forward to the company of each other. Agree/Disagree/Undecided
73. Inwardly my husband does not want me to be in a job. Agree/Disagree/Undecided
74. I got along well with my relatives. Agree/Disagree/Undecided
75. I think my relatives are very orthodox. Agree/Disagree/Undecided
76. I think my relatives are suspicious about me. Agree/Disagree/Undecided
77. My relatives are in favour of my working Agree/Disagree/Undecided
78. I receive due attention and consideration from my in-laws. Agree/Disagree/Undecided
79. I am respected and admired by elders in the family. Agree/Disagree/Undecided
80. My in-laws are very considerate toward me because they understand the difficulties due to job. Agree/Disagree/Undecided
81. My in-laws always encourage me. Agree/Disagree/Undecided
82. I have to face sarcasm from relatives. Agree/Disagree/Undecided
83. Taking care of my in-law is hampering my responsibilities in the job. Agree/Disagree/Undecided
84. I feel the members of my family should share some of my responsibilities since I am a working woman. Agree/Disagree/Undecided

SCORE

AREAS	A	B	C	D	E	TOTAL SCORE

B

12B (1)

Title to the Instrument : **Vaivahik Jeevanache Manas-shastriys Drishtikonatoon Mulyamapan.**

Purpose : To study marital adjustment.

Author: Medha M. Kumthekar.

Language : Marathi.

Availability : Saleel Society, 21 Chintamani Nagar, Pune-411030.

Uses : Marital harmony of disharmony can be found out. Its antecedent factors can be known.

Levels : At any level of married life.

Main Features : 70 questions inclusive of 3 charts, each having 5 to 50 items. Total number of items—175. Few openended, few yes/no type, few quadruple alternative and few pentag alternative questions are included.

Reliability : No reliability coefficient. But cross-check items exist.

Validity : Nil.

Time Limit : Nil.

Norms : Yes, with the author.

References : It' s on the line of scales prepared by Burgees & Locke.

12B (2)

Title of the Instrument : **Mittal Adjustment Inventory. 1. School Form. 2. College Form.**

Purpose : To discriminate well adjusted and mal-adjusted individuals and groups.

Author : V.K. Mittal.

Language : Hindi.

Availability : Publishers, Manovigyan Kendra, 249, Noonia Street, Meerut Cantonment-250001.

Uses : Study of individuals and group differences., 2. Research and-Guidance.

Levels : Age of 11 years onwards. High School and College levels.

Main Features : Based on Bell pattern. It has 80 highly discriminative items. 20 each in each of the 4 areas. Scale has loading on two factors.

Reliability : 1. Split-half reliability = 0.94 2. Test-retest = 0.89 after one week. 3. Split half for 4 areas also reported.

Validity : Against Teacher's ratings = 0.68, 2. Against parents rating scale = 0.59, 3. Validity female school forum against Hindi check list. = .45 all college level against Rotter's ISB = .75.

Time Limit : 20 minutes on an average.

Norms : 1. Centile Norms, 2. Norms based on SD units.

References : Several research papers published in psychological researches.

12B (3)

Title of the Instrument : **Adjustment — Neuroticism Test.**

Author : R.N. Singh.

Language : Hindi.

Availability : Manovaigyanic Seva Kendra. Professor's Colony, Sakalenabad, Ghazipur-233001.

Uses : Provides measure of adjustment — neurotism dimension of personality along with its seven components.

Levels : Adults and adolescents.

Main Features : T.B. of 105 items, separate AS and scoring Key, profile sheet.

Reliability : Repeat reliability = 0.65 to 0.79.

Validity : Data on internal validity provided.

Time Limit : About 45 minutes.

Norms : N-sten norms.

References : Seven.

12B (4)

Title of the Instrument : **Marital Adjustment Inventory (Literate).**

Author : Har Mohan Singh.

Availability : National Psychological Corporation, 4/230, Kacheri Ghat, Agra-4.

Language : English.

Uses : To assess marital adjustment of married men and women.

Level : For literate adults.

Main Features : The inventory has two forms, Form-A, for husbands, and Form-B for wives. Each form contains ten questions, which may be answered in either 'yes' or 'no' only. Each 'yes' or 'no' is rated on a scale ranging from +10 (most favourable) to +1 (least favourable.) . Only selected answers are recorded and scored.

Reliability : The coefficient of reliability for six professions are calculated.

Validity : Internal validity was established by selecting items in terms of the degree to which they differentiate between the upper and lower fifteen per cent of the persons in a distribution of scores. The results of various professions were checked over a period of a year.

Time Limit : There is no time limit, approximately fifteen minutes are required.

Norms : Tentative norms are given for couples within range of 20 years to 30 years and above for both sexes.

References :
1. Arendt, H. (1958) : *The Human Condition*, Chicago, University Press.
2. Bach, G. & Deutch, R. (1970) : *Pairing*, New York, Avon Books.
3. Berne, E. (1964) : *Games People Play, the Psychology of Human Relationships*, New York, Grove Press.
4. Bellow, S. (1944) : *Laughing Man*, New York, Vanguard.
5. Bonner, H. (1965) : *On being Mindful of Man*, Boston, Houston Mifflin.
6. Broabdent, W.W. (1976) : How to be Loved, Englewood Cliff, New Jersy, Princeton Hall.

Anxiety

B

13B (1)

Title of the Instrument : **Hindi version of Social Avoidance and Distress Scale, and Fear of Negative Evaluation Scale.**

Author : Kamaluddin Sheikh and Sandhya Singh Kaushik.

Availability : Manovaigyanik Parikchhan Sansthan, UHB-28, Sanjay Nagar Colony, Chowka Ghat, Varanasi-2.

Language : Hindi and English.

Uses : To assess the level of Social Anxiety.

Level : College level and above.

Main Features : Hindi version of Watson and Friend's (1969) Scales as follows : 1. Social Avoidance and Distress Scale (SAD), and 2. Fear of Negative Evaluation Scale. In original format of SAD scale, there were 28 items and 30 items in FNE Scale. All these items of both scales are whored into 'true' and 'false' patterns. After the item analysis, there remain 28 items in each scale.

Reliability : Split-half (N = 357) = .77 for SAD and .88 for FNE Scale. Test retest (N=95) = .71 for SAD and 75 for FNE Scale.

Validity : To ascertain the validity of SAD and FNE Scales, the correlation coefficient has been obtained with some scales such as the coefficient of correlation between the SAD score and the scores of the Speilberger's State - Anxiety Inventory, Trait Anxiety Inventory, Singh's Social Self-Concept Inventory and the Sociability factors of Rastogi's Self-concept scale were found to be .49 (N=60), -.56 (N=94) and - .61 (N = 115) respectively. The coefficient of correlation between the scores of the FNE scale and the scores of above mentioned measures were found to be .41 (N = 60), -.63 (N = 60), -.45 (n = 94) and -.58 (N = 115) respectively.

Time limit : No time limit.

Norms : Available with the authors.

References :

1. Sheikh, K. (1989) : Behavioural Analysis and Treatment of Stage-fright in Orthopaedically handicapped youth. Unpublished Doctoral Dissertation, Banaras Hindu University.
2. Sheikh, K. and Kaushik, S.S. (1990) : Hindi

Adaptation of Social Avoidance and Distress Scale. *Journal of Personality and Clinical Studies*, 6 (2), 237-241.

3. Sheikh, K, and Kaushik, S.S (1991) : Hindi Adaptation of Fear of Negative Evaluation Scale. *Journal Psychological Research*. (in Press.)

13B (2)

Title of the Instrument : **Test-Anxiety Scale (TAS).**

Author : V.P. Sharma.

Availability : National Psychological Corporation, 4/230, Kacheri Ghat, Agra-4.

Language : Hindi and English.

Uses : To measure the level of test anxiety, indicating children who would at a later date experience the predominantly disabling effects of anxiety.

Level : College Students.

Main Features : The scale consists of 25 test situations, each provide with 5 alternatives to select from. The five alternative answers are assigned weights from 1 to 5. The sum of the weights on all the items would indicates the total anxiety score.

Reliability : 1. Coefficient of Stability by Test-Retest Method = .927. 2. Coefficient of Internal Consistency by Split Half Technique = . 876.

Validity : Predictive validity using : 1. Teacher's Rating = .768, 2. Internal Marks = .743.

Time Limit : 30 minutes.

Norms : Percentile Norms for both boys as well as girls have been established.

References :
1. Cattell, R.B. (1957) : *Personality and Motivation, Structure & Measurement*, New York.
2. Dollard & Miller N.E. (1956) : *Personality and Psychotherapy*, New York.
3. May, R. (1950) : *The Meaning of Anxiety*, Ronald Press, New York.
4. Mowrer, O.H. (1950) : *Learning Theory and Personality Dynamics*, Ronald Press, New York.
5. Saranon, S.B. & Mandler, G. (1950) : "Some correlates of test Anxiety", *J. of Abnormal & Social*

Psychology, 47.

6. Taylor, J.A. (1953) : 'A' Personality scale of manifest Anxiety," *Journal of Abnormal & Social Psychology*, 48.

13B (3)

Title of the Instrument : **Sinha's Comprehensive Anxiety Test (SCAT).**

Author(s) : A.K.P. Sinha & L.N.K. Sinha.

Availability : National Psychological Corporation, 4/230, Kacheri Ghat, Agra-4.

Language : Hindi.

Uses : To measure the level of anxiety.

Level : College Students. (Used as sample.)

Main Features : The test consists of 90 items. The subjects are required to respond to any item in terms of 'Yes' or 'No'. The 'yes' response to any item is indicative of anxiety.

Reliability : 1. Test-retest reliability = 0.85, 2. Internal consistency reliability was ascertained using odd-even procedure = 0.92.

Validity : The coefficient of validity was determined by computing the coefficient of correlation between scores on Comprehensive Anxiety test and on Taylor's manifest Anxiety Scale. It was .62.

Time limit : No time limit but usually takes 15-20 minutes.

Norms : Percentile norms are provided for boys and girls separately.

References :

1. Cattell, R.B. (1957) : The IPAT Anxiety Scale (self-Analysis Form), *Jour. Consult. Psychol*, 21,438.
2. Cattell, R.B. & Scheier, I.H. (1958) : "The Nature of Anxiety : A review of thirteen multivariate analysis comprising 814 variables." *Psychol. Rep.* 4, 351-388.
3. Martin, B. (1959) : 'The Measurement of Anxiety', *Jour. Gen. Psychol*, 61, 189-203.
4. Sarason, S.B. & Mandler, G. (1952) : "Some Correlates of Test Anxiety," *Journal Abnorm & Social Psychol*, 47, 810-817.
5. Taylor, J.A. (1953) : "A Personality Scale of Manifest Anxiety" *Jour. ABN & Social Psychol.* 48, 285-290.

13B (4)

Title of the Instrument : **Academic Anxiety Scale for Children (AASC).**

Authors : A.K. Singh & A. Sen Gupta.

Availability : National Psychological Corporation 4/230, Kacheri Ghat, Agra-4.

Language : Hindi

Uses : To measure the academic anxiety for children which relates to the impending danger from the environments of the academic institutions.

Levels : School Students of class VIII, IX, & X (age range : 13&16 years.).

Main Features : Scale consists of 20 items. There are positive items which are endorsed by subjects as 'yes' and all negative items No.4,9,16, and 18 which are endorsed by the subjects as 'No' are given a score of +1. A score of zero is awarded to all other answers.

Reliability : 1. Test-retest reliability = .60, 2. Split-Half reliability = .65.

Validity : The test has been validated against the Sinha anxiety test, Neuroticism scale of MPI & CAAT. Correlation coefficient against Neuroticism Scale = .31, Correlation coefficient against Sinha anxiety scale =. 41 Correlation coefficient against CAAT = .5/7.

Time Limit : No fixed time limit, but usually takes 10-15 minutes.

Norms : Percentile norms have been constructed for Rural as well as Urban students of class VIII, IX & X (Both sexes inclusive).

References :

1. Goodstein, L.D. & Lanyon, R.I. (1975) : *Adjustment Behaviour & Personality*. Addison Weekly Publishing Co. Inc.
2. Guilford, J.P. (1954) : *Fundamental Statistics in Psychology and Education*, New York : Mcgraw-hill.
3. Jayaswal, A. (1982) : 'Academic Anxiety among School students and its relation to occupational class, Co-education, and intelligence, Unpub. Ph. D Thesis, Patna University.
4. Kelly, T. L. (1939) : 'The Selection of upper and lower groups for the validation of test items *J. of Educational Psychol.* 30,17-24.
5. Sinha, D. (1976) : *Sinha-Anxiety scale.* Rupa Psychological Centre, Varanasi

D

13D (1)

Title of the Instrument : **Sarason's Test Anxiety Scale for Children (TASC)-Indian Adaptation.**

Author : A. Kumar.

Availability : National Psychological Corporation, 4/230, Kacheri Ghat, Agra-4.

Language : Hindi.

Uses : To help in locating the test anxiety level of children for guidance and counselling purposes.

Levels : For children upto the age of 17 years.

Main Features : The test consists of 30 items of Yes/No type. The questions are designed to elicit self-rating on items descriptive of anxiety reactions to the following areas. 1. Worries and tension 2. Fear and dreams, 3. Physical and physiological manifestations like feeling of pain heart beating, trembling etc. 4. Success or failure in tests. 5. Guilt and shame. etc. The total number on 'yes' answers, denotes the raw score of anxiety.

Reliability : 1. Split-half Reliability = 0.81, 2. KR Formula-20 = 0.83.

Validity : Validity was established by correlation between teacher's rating and anxiety scores on TASC for boys and girls = 0.31.

Time Limit : 20 minutes.

Norms : Norms are published in the manual.

13D (2)

Title of the Instrument : **Sarason's General Anxiety Scale for Children (GASC) – Indian Adaptation.**

Author : A. Kumar.

Availability : National Psychological Corporation, 4/230, Kacheri Ghat, Agra-4.

Language : Hindi.

Uses : To locate the anxiety level of children for the purpose of diagnosing and removing their problems.

Levels : For children upto the age of 18 years.

Main Features : The scale is in Hindi and has 45 items related to varied life situations. The items are of Yes/No type. The total number of 'Yes' answers denotes the raw score of anxiety. The GASC includes 11 items which are labelled as 'lie items', on the basis of which a child receiving a negative score of six or more is rejected because this reveals the lying tendency of the child.

Reliability : 1. Split-half Method = 0.79. 2. K-R Formula-20 Method = 0.81.

Validity : The scale was validated against the outside criterion of teacher's rating, the correlation was significant at .01 level. The scale. The scale was further validated against Sinha's Anxiety Scale. The validity coefficient was 0.739.

Time Limit : 15 minutes approximately.

Norms : Norms are published in the manual.

13D (3)

Title of the Instrument : **Hindi form of the Test Anxiety Inventory (TAI).**

Author : S. Sharma, A. Sud; C.D Speilberger.

Availability : Available with the first author.

Language : Hindi.

Uses : To assess individual differences in test anxiety as a situation-Specific Personality trait in students.

Level : High School and College students.

Main Features : It is a 20 item self-report psycho-metric scale. It also has 8-item subscales for measuring worry (W) and emotionality (E) components of test anxiety.

Reliability : The alpha reliability coefficients for the Hindi TAI are 0.83 and 0.89 for boys and girls respectively.

Time Limit : No time limit.

Norms : Percentile and T-scale norms for high school and college students are available.

References :

1. Sharma, S.; Sud, A; and Speilberger, C.D (1983): *The development of the Hindi form of the test anxiety inventory.*
2. Schwarzer, & Speilberger, C.D. (Eds.) : *Advances in Test Anxiety Research* : Vol. 2, Lisse : Swets & Zeitlinger, 183-190.
3. Speilberger, C.D. (1980) : *Test Anxiety Inventory: Preliminary Professional Manual*, Palo Atto, California : Consulting Psychologists Press.

Self-Concept

B

14B (1)

Title of the Instrument : **Self Concept Scale.**

Authors : Rajini M.R., S.V. Nagalakshmi & K. Sathyavathi.

Purpose : To Measure self esteem like personal, family and social self-esteem and self-confidence.

Language : English Kannada form work in progress.

Availability : Dr. S.V. Nagalakshmi, Department of Clinical Psychology, Nimhans, Bangalore-29.

Uses : For assessment of diagnosis and therapeutic purpose.

Levels : Adult sample 20-30 years. Education - minimum 12th standard and above.

Main Features : Five Point rating scale (Strongly Agree, Agree, Undecided, Disagree, and strongly Disagree). 80 items.

Reliability : Test-retest reliability on 45 subjects on normative sample. Personal self-esteem = 0.81, (reliability coefficient). Family self-esteem = 0.86, Social self-esteem = 0.79, self-confidence = 0.80.

Validity : Content Valididation : 220 items were given to five judges with more than 10 years of clinical and academic experience. Out of the 220 items were there was agreement among 3 or more judges. Only those items were retained.

Factorial Validity : Was done on 328 subjects with age group of 20-39 years with minimum 12 years of education on group of normals. Principal factor analysis followed by orthogonal varimax rotation was used in order to examine whether self-concept would emerge as unidimensional or multidimensional construct. 22 Factors emerged to which only the four factors were taken into consideration.

Factor I covered 17 per cent of total variance; Factor II covered 6.2 per cent of total variance; Factor III covered 5 per cent of total variance; Factor IV covered 3.7 per cent of total variance.

Factorial Revalidation : Was done on a sample of 430 subjects, 20-39 years with minimum 12 years of education. Again 22 factors emerged of which the first four factors accounted for major portion of variance.

Factor matching revealed that these factors are stable across the samples. The final varsion of the self-concept scale has 80 items.

Clinical Validation : Was done on 30 neurotics and 30 schizophrenics. Mean and SD was done on different aspects of self-esteem and self-Concept t test revealed significant difference between the normative group and schizophrenic group. In which both clinical samples score lower than the normals.

Time Limit : 30 minutes.

References : Dr. M.R. Rajini, The self-Concept Scale-unpublished Ph.D. thesis in Clinical Psychology, 1985, Bangalore University.

Norms : Available in the form of T-Score equivalence, Mean and SD for normative sample.

14B (2)

Title of the Instrument : **Personality Differential (PD).**

Author : K.G.Agrawal.

Availability : National Psychological Corporation, Agra-4.

Language(s) : Hindi, English, Bilingual.

Uses : To measure self-concept.

Levels : Normals, Neurotics and Schizophrenics (Adults).

Main Features : The Personality Differential is based on Semantic Differential Technique. There is a PD Short Scale where one concept is measured Four factors are used-Confirmity vs Tendermindedness; Normalcy; Tenseness. Four high loading scales are picked up from each of the four factors of PD.

The PD Full Scale measures 34 concepts. Both are bipolar scales with factor scores are worked out by summing scales scores for each individual factor. 7 step scale is between..

Time Limit: Administration of one concept PD form takes about 12 minutes. Administration of 34 concept forms takes about 40-50 minutes.

Norms : Not provided.

References :

1. Agrawal, K.G. (1970) : Personality Dimension as Revealed by Hindi Personality Differential. *Indian J. of Psychol*, 45, 23-37.
2. Cattell, R.B. (1965) : *The Scientific Analysis of Personality*, Middlesex : Penguin.
3. Kelly, G. (1961) :The Abstraction of human processes, Proceedings of the 14th International

Congress of Psychology. Copenhegan, 220-229.

4. Kuusinen, J. (1966) : Changes in the Structure of Personality ratings according to the relevance of objects. University of Jyvaskyla..
5. Osgood, C.E. (1962) : Studies on the Generality of Effective Meaning Systems. *American Psychologist*, 10-28.

14B (3)

Title of the Instrument : **Children's Self-Concept Scale (CSCS).**
Author : S.P. Ahluwalia.
Availability : National Psychological Corporation, Agra-4.
Language : Hindi and English.
Uses : To measure the self concept of children and adolescents.
Main Features : The test contains 80 items with 'Yes' or 'No' responses. It includes 14 lie items to detect whether the children and adolescents have filled it accurately.

There are six sub scales : 1. Behaviour, 2. Intellectual and School Status, 3. Physical Appearance and Attributes, 4. Anxiety, 5. Popularity, 6. Happiness and satisfaction.

The scale items are scored in a positive or negative direction to the reflect the evaluation dimension. A high score indicates a favourable self-concept.

Reliability : The test-retest reliability and split-half reliability have been established.
Validity : Face validity, concurrent validity and factorial validity have been established.
Time Limit : 15-20 minutes.
Norms : Norms are provided in the manual.
References :

1. Bhatnagar, R.P (1966) : Academic achievement as a function of one's self-concept & ego functions. *Educational & Psychological Review*. 6(4).
2. Combs, A.W. & Snyggs, D. (1959) : *Individual Behaviour: A Perceptual Approach to Behaviour* Revised Edition, New York; Harper & Row.
3. Cooley, C.H. (1964) : *Human Nature and Social Order*, New York : Schockers Books.

14B (4)

Title of the Instrument : **Swatva Bodh Parikshan (SBP).**
Author : G.P. Sherry; R.P Verma; P.K. Goswami.
Availability : National Psychological Corporation, 4/230, Kacheri Ghat, Agra-4.
Language : Hindi
Uses : To measure the self-concept of the school going adolescents of urban and rural areas.
Level : Adolescents.
Main Features : It is a 48 item test, yielding scores on eight different dimension of self-concept. The eight dimensions are : 1. Health & Physique, 2. Temperamental Qualities, 3. Academic Status, 4. Intellectual abilities, 5. Habits and Behavior, 6. Emotional Tendencies, 7. Mental Health, 8. Socio-Economic Status. The statements of the test are simple and declarative about self.
Reliability : Test-retest reliability established = .733, 2. Rational equivalence reliability established = .761.
Validity : Factorial Validity established.
Time Limit : 20 minutes.
Norms : Norms are provided in manual. Norms established for Rural and Urban boys as well as girls.

14B (5)

Title of the Instrument : **Kakkar Self-Acceptance Inventory (KSAI).**
Author : S.B. Kakkar.
Availability : National Psychological Corporation, 4/230, Kacheri Ghat, Agra-4.
Language : English.
Uses : Used to measure Self-acceptance through factors such as personal worth and satisfaction with self.
Level : For use with normal subjects in schools, colleges, business and industry, and in clinics and counselling agencies.
Main Features : its a 34-item inventory, covering a total set of 18 facets of personality including self-acceptance.
Reliability : Test-retest reliability = .94, Split-half reliability = .94, Kuder Richardson reliability = .77
Validity : The validity of the test was determined experimentally by finding correlation between the test and an independent criterion

(a rating scale) was .79 (males) and .86 (Females.).

Time limit : 10 minutes.

14B (6)

Title of the Instrument : **Self-Perception Adjective Checklist (SPA).**

Author : K.N. Sharma.

Availability : Ankur Psychological Agency, 22/481, Indira Nagar, Lucknow.

Language : Hindi.

Uses : To Measure Self-Perception of an individual by measuring his self-esteem and self-identity.

Level : Educated individuals.

Main Features : The Check list consists of 93 items in Hindi, indicating positive and negative qualities of human beings. The responses were to be given on a 3-point scale.

For positive items the scoring was 3,2,1, respectively and for negative items the scoring was inversed.

Reliability : The Test-Retest reliability was found to be 0.83.

Validity : Content Validity of the scale was established on the basis of ratings. Correlation with Kakkar's Self-Acceptance inventory was found to be .34.

Time Limit : Approximately 20 minutes.

Norms : Percentile norms were obtained from a sample of 200 subjects, Comprising of students, workers etc. with educational qualifications ranging from Primary to M.A. and with an age range of 17-30.

14B (7)

Title of the Instrument : **Self-Concept Scale for Adults.**

Authors : A. Kaur & T. Singh.

Availability : Centre for Adult and Continuing Education, Punjabi University, Patiala.

Language : Punjabi and English.

Uses : To measure the self-concept of illiterate adults.

Level : Illiterate rural adults.

Main Features : The scale consists of 50 items, consisting 25 positive and 25 negative statements about personality. Responses were elicited on a 3 point scale. The scoring for positive items was 1, 2, 3 to the 'Yes', 'sometimes', and 'No' categories respectively, and for negative items it was 3. 2. 1. respectively.

Reliability : Split-half reliability was calculated by using Spearman-Brown Prophecy formula, and was found to be .847.

Validity : Content validity was established by seeking experts' opinion. Intrinsic validity was established, represented by the index of reliability (0.847).

Time Limit : 15-20 minutes.

Norms : Percentile norms are published in the manual.

References :

1. Bhangoo, S. (1987) : 'Effectiveness of Selected Teaching Methods for Teaching Adult Rural Farm Women. Unpublished Ph. D. Dissertation, Punjabi University, Patiala.
2. Kaur, A. & Singh.T. (1982) : Development of Self-concept Scale. *Indian Journal of Adult Education*.
3. Multani, N.S. (1981) : "S.A. Profile of Male Adults Adult Education Centres in Punjab". Unpublished M.A. Dissertation, Punjabi University, Patiala.

14B (8)

Title of the Instrument : **Self-Concept Questionnaire (SCQ).**

Author : R.K. Saraswat.

Availability : National Psychological Corporation. 4/230, Kacheri Ghat, Agra-4.

Language : English.

Uses : To measure self-concept of adolescents.

Level : Adolescents.

Main Features : It is 48 item inventory to measure six separate dimensions of self-concept, viz. Physical, Social, Intellectual, Moral, Educational and Temperamental Self-concept. It also gives a total self-concept score. Each item is provided with five alternatives. These alternatives are arranged in such a way that the scoring system for all the items will remain the same i.e., 5, 4, 3, 2, 1, whether the items are positive or negative. High Score indicates a higher self-concept and a low score indicates a low self-concept.

Reliability : Test-retest reliability = .91. Reliability coefficients of its various dimensions varies from .67 to .88.

Validity : Expert opinion were obtained to establish the validity of the inventory. Items of highest agreement and not less than 80 per cent of agreement were selected.

Time Limit : 20 minutes.

Norms : S-C Questionnaire was standardized on 1000 students ranging from 14-18 years of both the sexes. Norms are published in the manual.

References :

1. Lowe, C.M. (1961) : The Self-Concept : Factor artifact? *Psychological Bulletin*, 58, 325-326.
2. Lynche, M.D. (1981) : *Self Contemplations-Self-concept : Advance in Theory and Research. Cambridge*, Mass Ballinger.
3. Pedersen, D.M. (1965) : Ego strength and discrepancy between conscious and unconscious self-concept. *Perceptual and Motor Skills*, 20,691-692.
4. Rogers, C.R. (1951) : *Client Centred Therapy—Its Current Practice, Implications and Theory*. Boston Houghton.
5. Saraswat, R.K. & Gaur, J.S. (1981) : Approaches for the Measurement of Self-concept : An Introduction. *Indian Educational Review*, 16 (3), 114-119.

14B (9)

Title of the Instrument : **Pandey Self-Confidence Inventory (PSCI).**

Author : D.D. Pandey.

Availability : Ankur Psychological Agency, 22/481, Indira Nagar, Lucknow.

Language : Hindi.

Uses : To measure self-confidence.

Level : Students in tenth grade with knowledge of Hindi.

Main Features : The test consists of 60 items, arranged in a systematic random order, The dimensions selected are subject's perceived ability about himself in the areas namely, 1. Social and Emotional Matureness, 2. Intellectual Adequateness, 3. Satisfaction, 4. Optimismness, 5. Independence, 6. Self-Assuredness, 7. Self-feelingness, 8. Evaluation about self, 9. Decisiveness. Only two responses are provided for each item either 'Yes' or 'No'. The items are Keyed in such a way that low score indicates a high self-confidence.

Reliability : Test-retest reliability = .882, Split-Half reliability = .892.

Validity : Face validity and construct validity established.

Time Limit : No fixed time limit.

Norms : Norms Published in the manual.

References :
1. Agnihotri, R. (1987) : *Manual for Agnihotri's Self-confidence Inventory*. National Psychological Corporation, Agra.
2. Allport, G.W. (1961) : *Pattern and Growth in Personality*, New York.
3. Basavunna, M. (1975) : *Manual for Self-confidence Inventory*. Rupa Psychological Centre, Varanasi.

14B (10)

Title of the Instrument : **Agnihotri's Self-Confidence Inventory (ASCI.)**

Author : R. Agnihotri.

Availability : National Psychological Corporation , 4/230, Kacheri Ghat, Agra-4.

Language : Hindi.

Uses : To assess the level of Self-Confidence among adolescents and adults.

Levels : Adolescents and Adults.

Main Features : Inventory consists of 56 items. Only two responses are provided for each item either 'Yes' or 'No'. Lower the score, Higher would be the self-confidence.

Reliability : Split-Half Reliability = .95, K-R Formula 20 = .94, Test Retest Reliability = .88

Validity : Item-analysis validity coefficients were determined for each item by biserial correlation method the inventory was also validated by correlating it with Basavanna's Self-confidence Inventory. The validity coefficient = .82.

Time Limit : Approximately 20 minutes.

Norms : Norms are published in the manual.

References :
1. Agnihotri, R. (1985) : Effects of sub-culture affliation and sex on self-confidence Paper presented at the International Seminar on Cross-Culture Perspectives on Problems of National Relevance, Aligarh Muslim University.
2. Agnihotri, R. (1986) : "Alienation in relation to self-Confidence, Scholastic attainment and level of aspiration," *Advances in Psychology.*
3. Agnihotri, R. & Gupta, R. (1985) : "Self-Confidence as a function of perceived maternal

child rearing behaviour". *Praachi Journal of Psycho-Cultural Dimension*, Vol. 1. No-2, pp. 30-33.

D

14D (1)

Title of the Instrument : **Self-Esteem Inventory (Adaptation of Coorsmith's SEI).**

Author : Nalini Rao.

Language : English.

Purpose : Appraisal of Self-evaluation.

Availability : Author.

Uses : It is useful in assessing self attitude of subjects in parent, peer, personal interest and school contexts.

Levels : Upper primary and secondary school students.

Main Features : The scale has four sub-scales namely, General Self-help, Social self-peer, Home-Parent, School academic; 2. It has a eight item built in lie scale. Warning technique to reduce 'faking good' is adopted. 3. The scale has 50 items which cycle in sequence the length of the Inventory.

Reliability : Test-retest reliability coefficient on a sample of one hundred after six week interval was .867 and after a ten week interval was .815. 2. Inter correlations between different sub-scales of the inventory ranged from .693 to .912.

Validity : The tool is validated against self confidence Inventory and the coefficient of correlation obtained was .725. 2. The inventory has shown considerable construct validity establishing theoretically consistent relationship with creativity, social maturity, parental treatment and sociological background variables.

Time Limit : There is no time limit.

Norms : No.

Development of the scale : A total sample of 1052 upper primary and secondary school students has been employed to adapt the tool.

References : Socio-psychological correlates of social development of high school children in grades VIII, IX & X in some schools of Bangalore City. Doctoral Dissertation in Education, Bangalore University, 1978. 2. "Socialization of children and youth" (In Press) Bhargava Book House, Agra.

Motivation

B

15B (1)

Title of the Instrument : **Achievement Motive Test (ACMT).**

Author : V.P. Bhargava.

Availability : National Psychological Corporation, 4/230, Kacheri Ghat, Agra-4.

Language : Hindi.

Uses : To measure the Achievement Motive of an individual.

Level : Adults and Adolescents.

Main Features : The test consists of 50 items of incomplete sentences which are to be completed by the subjects by putting a check-mark on any one of the three alternative responses give against each item Scoring.

Reliability : Test-retest reliability = .87, By comparing the responses on similar items =. 79.

Validity : Validity by correlating it with the test scores of SCT of B. Mukherji was. 80 and with Educational Achievement Test it was .75.

Time Limit : 30 minutes.

Norms : Percentile norms published in the manual.

References :

1. Aronson, (1956) : *The Need for Achievement as Measured* by Graphic Expression.
2. Atkinson (1954) : *An Introduction to Motivation*, Report on Nebraska Symposium on Motivation.
3. Bhargava, V.P. (1972) : "A Study of Level of Aspiration and Need for Achievement Motive." Ph.D. Dissertation, Agra University.
4. Brown (1953) : In *Current Theories and Research in Motivation*, Ed. M.R. Jones.

15B (2)

Title of the Instrument : **Deo-Mohan Achievement Motivation (n-Ach) Scale.**

Author : P. Deo and A. Mohan.

Availability : National Psychological Corporation, 4/230, Kacheri Ghat, Agra.

Language : English and Hindi.

Uses : To measure achievement motivation.

Level : Students.

Main Features : The Scale consist of 50 items, out of which, 13 are negative and 37 are positive items. Responses are to be made on a 5-point scale. A positive item carries the weights of 4,3,2,1 and 0 respectively for the 5 categories of Always, Frequently, Sometimes, Rarely, and Never. The negative item is to be scored 0,1,2,3, and 4 for the same categories.

Reliability : Test-Retest reliability = .69.

Validity: Item validity established by the high-low discrimination method. The coefficient of correlation between the scale and the projective test = .54. The coefficient of correlation between the scale and the Aberdeen Academic Motivation Inventory = .75.

Time Limit : No time limit.

Norms : Norms published in the manual.

References :

1. Bendig, A.W. (1964) "Factor Analytic Scales of Need Achievement." *J. Gen Psychol,* 70, 59-67.
2. Carrey, R.E. (1966) "The Effect of Situation Variables on the Measurement of Achievement Motivation. *Educ. Psychol. Meas*. 26,65-69.
3. Costello, C.G. (1967). "Two Scales to Measure Achievement Motivation." *J. Psychol*, 66, 231-235.

15 B (3) Details given on page 610

15B (4)

Title of the Instrument : **Sharma Academic Achievement Motivation Test (AAMT).**

Author : T. R. Sharma.

Availability : National Psychological Corporation, 4/230, Kacheri Ghat, Agra-4.

Language : Hindi.

Uses : To Measure academe achievement motivation.

Level : School children 11-15 years.

Main Features : The test consists of 38 items and provides a direct numerical score indicating how much a boy or girl is motivated in the field of academic achievement. The score range form 0-38.

Note : 15B(3) not included

Reliability : Split-Half reliability = .697, Test-retest reliability + Boys = .79; Girls =81.

Validity : Content Validity, Criterion Validity and Construct Validity established.

Time Limit : No fixed time limit.

Norms : Norms are published in the manual.

References :

1. Bisht, G.S. (1972) : A Study of the Levels of Educational Aspirations in Relation to Socio-Economic Conditions and Educational Attainment. Ph.D. Thesis, Agra University.
2. Ebel,R.L. (1959) : *Encyclopedia of Educational Research*. MacMillan Co. London.
3. *Gildford, J.R.*, (1965). : *Fundamental Statistics in Psychology and Education*. Mcgraw Hill Book Co.

15B (5)

Title of the Instrument : **Level of Aspiration Measures.**

Author : M.A. Shah and M.Bhargava.

Availability : National Psychological Corporation, 4/230, Kacheri Ghat, Agra-4.

Languages : Hindi and English.

Uses : To measure the level of aspiration.

Levels : Students.

Main Features : The Performance sheet has 50 circles which are arranged in five rows—ten in each row. Above and below of these rows, there are two boxes on the right side—the upper box is for writing the number of expected scored where as lower box is for putting the number of actual score of completed performance. Thus ten trials are needed for each subject besides practice trial. The respondent is asked to draw four lines in these circles, so that they appear like a eye, left eye, nose and mouth. And the respondent has to work from left to right across rows then proceed to the next line. Three types of scores are achieved. 1. Goal Discrepancy Score (GDS), 2. Attainment Discrepancy Score (ADS), 3. Number of Times the goal Reach Score. (NTRS).

Test-Retest Reliability : = .77 and split half reliability =.80 for Industrial Employees.

Validity : The factorial validity of the test has been calculated. The test has also been validated against two criterion groups.

Time Limit : 15 to 20 minutes.

Norms : Norms given in the manual for college students (boys and girls) and Industrial Employees.

15B (7)

Title of the Instrument : **Self-Expression Inventory.**

Author : R.P. Varma and U. Upadyaya.

Availability : National Psychological Corporation, 4/230, Kacheri Ghat, Agra.

Language : Hindi.

Uses : To measure sense of deprivation. The title has been faked so that the respondent cannot decipher the real purpose of the test.

Level : High School Students.

Main Features: The test contains 30 items and each item has two parts. The first part deals with the stem-question and the second part deals with four alternative responses, in which two of the alternatives are related to sense of deprivation, i.e. the 'yes' response to which shows that the respondents sense of deprivation and two of the alternatives are neutral statements, i.e. the 'yes' response to which does not show any sense of deprivation. Thus there are 60 responses related to sense of deprivation. 30 out of these 60 responses are related to sense of deprivation with respect to the home environment of the child and 30 responses are related to sense of deprivation with respect to school environment. The scale is based on forced choice technique. Scoring pattern mentioned in the manual.

Reliability : Split-Half reliability = .90, Test-retest reliability (after one month) = .89 (after six months = .87.

Validity : Cross-validity of the test was established as the value of critical ratio showed a non-significant difference between means.

Time Limit : No time limit.

Norms : Norms are published in the manual.

15B (8)

Title of the Instrument : **Self Actualization Inventory. (SEAI).**

Author : K.N. Sharma.

Availability : Ankur Psychological Agency, 22/481, Indira Nagar, Lucknow-16.

Language : Hindi.

Uses : To measure the self-actualization of an individual.

Levels : Adolescents and Adults.

Main Features : The inventory consists of 75 items. A three point rating scale is used. The weightage given to the three alternatives is 1,2,3.

Reliability : The test-retest reliability established = .85.

Validity : Content Validation has been established. A correlation of .27 was found against Kakkar's Self-Acceptance Inventory, and .29 with NCERT's Self-Perception Inventory.

Time Limit : Approximately 30 minutes.

Norms : Percentile norms are published in the manual.

References :

1. Cangemi, J.P. (1976) : "Characteristics of Self-Actualizing individuals." *Span Ravista Psychologia General Applicader*, 31, 138, 88-90.
2. Cangemi, J.P. and Englander, M.R. (1974) : "From self-awareness to Self-actualization," *College student J.* 82, 88-92.
3. Maslow, A.H. (1954) : *Motivation and Personality* N.J. Harper and Row.
4. Maslow A.H. (1962) : *Towards a Psychology of Being*. N.J.D. Van Nostrand.
5. Khurana, A. (1986) : *Self-Actualization among Teachers*. National Psychological Corporation, Agra.

15B (9)

Title of the Instrument : **Sports Motivation Inventory.**

Authors : S. Nangia and S. Jain.

Availability : Dr Suman Nangia, 1. Nashville Road, Dehra Dun-218001.

Language : Hindi.

Uses : To measure the motivation of Indian Sportsmen and sportswomen. The test is specially useful in coaching, skill improvement as well as in selection and training pursuit of excellence in sports performance.

Levels : All levels.

Main Features : It is a 48 item inventory which is rated on five-point Likert scale.

Reliability : Test-retest Reliability = .87; Split-Half Reliability = .89.

Validity : Criterion Validity = .87, Concurrent Validity = .91, Construct validity = .79 ; Judges Rating = .86.

Time Limit : 35 minutes.

Norms : Available with the first author.

References :

1. Kamlesh, M.L. and Sharma, T.R. (1986) : *Manual for Inventory of factors influencing sports career (IFISC)*. National Psychological Corporation, Agra.
2. Liewellya, J.H.; Lucker, B. and Judy, A. (1982) : *Psychological Coaching theory and Application*. Surjeet Publications, Delhi.
3. Nangia, S. (1981) : "The Personality Characteristics and Self-esteem of Indian Sportsmen and Sportswomen." Unpublished Ph. D. Thesis, Lucknow University.

PART TWO

EDUCATION

INTRODUCTION

This part of the handbook reports instruments dealing with different dimensions of education. The instruments are reported under five sections : General instruments, student problems and adjustment, interests and preferences, attitudes, and institutional characteristics like climate etc. This classification is also based on the number of instruments reported in each area. The different sections reported here represent only a broad classification of the instruments. Some instruments which could not be clearly classified have been included in the general category.

In all, there are 64 instruments reported in this area of which 15 have been reproduced here. Technical information about other 47 instruments is given here. The detailed break-up of the instruments is given in the Table.

Table : Break-Up of Instruments on Education

Classification	Originals Reproduced	Only Information	Citations	Adaptations	Total
	A	B	C	D	
General	05	13	—	01	19
Student Problems & Adjustment	03	13	—	01	17
Interests & Preferences	02	11	—	—	13
Attitudes	02	07	—	—	09
Institutional Characteristics	03	03	—	—	06
Total:	15	47	—	02	64

General Instruments

There are in all 19 instruments reported under this category of which 5 are reproduced here. About the other 13 instruments, only information is reported here. There is one adaptation also included in this section. These instruments cover several dimensions related to teacher's job satisfaction, classroom control and teacher leadership, teacher behaviour, school innovation, decision-making styles of principals, teacher efficiency and effectiveness, class teaching, purposes of higher education, teacher morale, job motivation, job anxiety, social characteristics and family climate of students, leadership styles of educational administrators and student activism. Of these instruments, 10 are meant for teachers, 1 for principals, and others are for students and schools. Majority of these instruments are meant for measuring the job satisfaction of teachers.

As regards the standardization, most of these instruments report high reliability and validity. Only 2 instruments do not report such data. Test-retest and split-half methods have been used in majority of the instruments. Face, content and concurrent validities have been reported for many of the instruments. A few have been validated against ratings and a few report inter-area coefficients of correlations.

Among the instruments reproduced here, one by Dr. (Mrs.) Jayalakshmi Indiresan is an instrument which provides a measure of the student learning orientation profile which can be used to understand both the factors affecting student learning. There is one Teacher Value Scale which measures the values of school teachers. There is also a Rating Scale For Student Evaluation of Teaching Effectiveness which assesses teaching effectiveness of college teachers by students.

There is a scale by Shavinder Kaur and Dr. Amarjit Singh called the Information Scale. Its main purpose is to measure the extent of use of information disseminated through the contents of the lessons of correspondence courses, which is available in Punjabi as well as English languages.

There are 13 instruments which are reported here with technical information only. Mostly these tests are meant for measuring teacher effectiveness in the school or college as also teacher values. The instruments reported here are mainly meant for teachers and measure job satisfaction and job anxiety of school teachers. A few instruments for student activism and social characteristics are also reported. There is one adaptation also reported. The adaptation by Dr. Badrun Nisha and Dr. Kiran Gupta is called the Classroom Boundary Questionnaire, which measures the classroom control and the aspect of teacher leadership in the classroom. The adaptation is from the original test called Morrison's C.B.Q. test.

Student Problems and Adjustment

Instruments on student's problems and adjustment are included under this section. There are 17 instruments reported in this section, of these

6 are originals reproduced, and 12 instruments in this section are reported along with technical information only. Only one adaptation is reported here. All instruments have reported standardization data. Test-retest and split-half reliabilities have been reported by most of the instruments. Some have reported more than two reliability coefficients. All the values reported are fairly high. More attention is also paid on validation of these instruments.

Among these instruments, there is an inventory called the Students Role Conception Inventory by Prof. M.B. Sharan in English and Hindi languages which measures the role concept on ideal level. Among its many uses, this test is useful in understanding role conception, role demands, and role performance of the college students. It is a five-point scale. Though the reliability in this test is fairly high, the validity is not established. Another good test is A Life Stress Scale for University Students by Manju Agrawal and R.K. Naidu. The scale has been developed for students of university level, however, after suitable necessary changes the scale can be used also with 10th and 12th grade students. The test finds out the amount and kind of life stresses encountered by university students. There are 9 different categories into which the test items are divided like Financial, Family, Social, Education, Ego Threat, Bereavement, Separation, personal set back, and health of others. It is a seven-point rating scale for the amount of distress.

There is a Youth Problem Inventory by Dr. (Mrs) Mithilesh Verma for youths between the ages of 16-20 years. This scale has lengthy reliability and validity coefficient of correlations have also been found. There is also a Teacher Adjustment Inventory (TAI) by Dr. S.K. Mangal which assesses the adjustment of teachers of both sexes. It segregates the poorly adjusted teachers from those who are better adjusted teachers.

Other instruments reported here are also meant for school and college students and report fairly high reliability and validity data. These are also well standardised instruments and could be used to measure students' adjustment and problems in their respective ways. In general, the instruments reported in this section seem to be well standardised instruments and are useful contributions to educational research.

Interests and Preferences

In this section, the instruments relating to curricular interests, reading interests, vocational interests, study habits and preferences are reported.

13 instruments have been reported of which 2 are reproduced here. These instruments are available for high school, higher secondary and college students. Majority of the instruments are on study habits and interests.

Reliability has been reported for all the instruments. All the instruments have been reported either split-half or test-retest reliabilities. The reliability coefficients wherever reported are fairly high. Validity has been established by different techniques. Face, content and construct validities seem to be commonly reported by the instruments. A few have used ratings and self-criterion for validational purposes.

Three instruments are reproduced here of which one is A Scale to Measure Job Preference and Job Satisfaction of the Faculty of Punjab Agricultural University for Teaching, Research and Extension, the second part of the test is A Scale to Measure Role Perceptions of the Faculty of Punjab Agricultural University for Teaching, Research and Extension. The purpose of this test is to measure job preference and job satisfaction as also the role perceptions of the faculty of Punjab Agricultural University.

The other instruments reported here are available in different languages and are meant for school and college students. These instruments measure students' liking, interests, and study habits. Reliability and validity reported for these instruments are also fairly high. These instruments are useful for guidance and counselling purposes.

Attitudes

The instruments dealing with attitudes of teachers and students towards various issues of education are reported in this section. These instruments measure attitudes of students towards mathematics, internal evaluation, N.C.C., strike and violence/non-violence. A few instruments are for teachers also and measure their attitudes towards their job.

In all 9 instruments have been reported out of which 2 have been reproduced here. Both the tests are studies on attitudes : (1) Scientific Attitude Study which is used to find out the scientific attitudes possessed by a student, and (2) Religious Attitude Scale for University Students by R. Krishnaraj and Dr. P.S. Balasubramanian which can be used with College/University students to study their attitudes towards religion. Both these instruments measure student attitudes. Both the tests give either split-half or test-restest reliabilities.

The first instrument gives good face validity, content validity, and also construct validity while the second instrument gives concurrent validity with Allport-Vernon which is above average validity coefficient.

All the scales have reported reliability and validity data. Except one instrument which does not report any validity coefficient. Split-half and test-retest reliabilities have been reported for almost all the instruments. For some scales, more than one reliability coefficient has been reported. All the coefficients are fairly high. Validity is also worked out for all the instruments. Tetrachoric, content, concurrent and such other types of validity coefficients have been used for validating the scales.

The other instruments are those where only information is provided. Here, 7 instruments are reported which consist of information only. These instruments are also well standardized instruments. There are five instruments here which measure some aspects of teachers' attitudes towards their profession, towards their students, or towards their training. One scale measures students' attitudes towards vocational maturity. Another scale is in cartoon form which measures attitudes of students towards teachers, learning process, mathematics and language arts. This scale has been devised by Dr. (Mrs) Kiran Gupta and Dr. (Mrs.) Badaron Nisha Khan.

Institutional Characteristics

There are 6 instruments available under this section. They mainly relate to the organizational climate of the institutions. 3 instruments are original and the other 3 are those where only information is provided.

The instrument by Dr. Virendra Singh is available in English and it is a rating scale for persons working in universities. The scale is devised to know the various administrative practices in the universities. No reliability or validity has been reported for this scale. Norms for this scale are available with the author. The items of the instruments are rated on a five-point scale. There is another scale by Ms. Shefali Pandya which measures students' perceptions of the psycho-social processes going on in the classroom. The scale describes the classroom climate in secondary schools as well as high schools. The scale reports high reliability correlation coefficients. Both split-half as well as test-retest methods have been used. The internal consistency reliability has also been established. Content validity has been reported.

There is another scale called the Structural Dimension Questionnaire which helps to identify the organizational structure of educational institutions. The scale has been devised by Dr. R. Krishnaraj and Dr. P.S. Balasubramanian. It can be administered to faculty members in college and university departments.

Three instruments are reported where only information is provided. They also report split-half or test-retest reliabilities and construct, content and face validities of tests have also been found out. School Environment Measuring Scale by Dr. (Mrs) Sushma Talesara is in Hindi and is found to be very useful by guidance workers and counsellors for diagnosing the adjustment problems of adolescent boys and girls in school situations. It is a situational test.

Reliability data in the form of test-retest and split-half reliability coefficients have been found to be sufficiently high. Concurrent as well as intrinsic validity have been reported.

Table : Break-Up of Personality Instruments

Classification	Originals Reproduced	Only Information	Citations	Adaptations	Total
	A	B	C	D	
General	14	37	-	11	62
Adjustment & Problems	02	04		-	06
Anxiety	-	04	-	03	07
Self-Concept	-	10	-	01	11
Motivation	-	09	-	-	09
Total	16	64	-	15	95

There are 7 instruments for which only information is provided.

Health Organizations

No instrument is available which can be included in this section.

General Instruments

A

21A (1)

Title of the Instrument : **Student Learning Orientation Profile (SLOP).**

Purpose : As part of an international study involving six countries namely, Japan, Malaysia, U.K., Nigeria, Sri Lanka, and India, an instrument was developed to measure the Student Learning Orientation Profile.

Author(s) : Jayalakshmi Indiresan.

Language : English

Availability : Senior Consultant, Asian Centre for Organisation Research and Development, C-126, Greater Kailash I, New Delhi-110 048, and from June 1,1989, Professor in Higher Education, National Institute of Educational Planning & Administration, 17-B, Sri Aurobindo Marg, New Delhi-110016.

Uses : This instrument which provides a measure of the student learning orientation profile can be used to understand both the factors affecting students learning and factors affected by students learning. Various antecedent factors of socio-economic background, type of school, and other personal variables, study habits etc. would affect the learning orientation. This instrument can also be used to study the relationship between student learning orientation and other attitudes. For example, preliminary studies have shown that the work orientation is related to learning orientation.

Levels for whom it is meant : High school and university students.

Main Features : (Scaling Techniques used, number of items, etc.) : Drawing from earlier studies in this area, preliminary interviews with students, teachers, parents and a pilot study, 122 items were developed and administered to 462 students in the 9th and 11th standard from various types of schools in a metropolitan city. A factor analysis of these 122 items yielded seven meaningful scales. Based on the item total correlations, a 56 item inventory with 8 items in each scale was arrived at.

8 (a). Administering and Scoring : For convenience the items are grouped under the various scales. While administering the test, the items may be presented in a random order.

The items are in a Likert format on a four point scale with the response categories strongly agree, agree, disagree and strongly disagree, scored from 4 to 1. The scoring of items with the negative sign is to be reversed and added to get the scale score for each dimension.

Instruction: Below you will find a number of statements made by students. You will find that you agree with some of the statements, but disagree with others. Please read the statements, and decide whether you strongly agree, agree, disagree or strongly disagree with the statements. Please answer as honestly, carefully and quickly as you can. There are no right or wrong answers. We simply want to know how you feel about these statements.

Reliability data : Split-half Reliability with Spearman Brown Correlation.

Scales	r
Personal Development Orientation (PEDOL)	.804
Assessment Domination in Learning (ADOL)	.622
Intrinsic orientation in Job getting & Learning (INJOL)	.632
Apathy in Learning (APAL)	.586
Involvement in Learning (INVOL)	.743
Extrinsic Orientation in Learning (EXOL)	.702
Significant other orientation in Learning (SIGOL)	.609

Validity data : The item total correlations were all high and significant indicating the internal homogeneity of the scales.

Time required for administering the test : About 30 minutes.

Norms : Not available.

References on the instruments, its development and use :

1. SLOG, 1985, Students Learning Orientation and Adult Work. The SLOG Project. International *Journal of Educational Development*. 5 (3) p. 217-222.
2. Why do Students Learn? *IDS Research Reports* Rr 17, April 1987, Brighton, England.

STUDENT LEARNING ORIENTATION PROFILE (SLOP)
PERSONAL DEVELOPMENT ORIENTATION—PEDOL

Item			Item total r.
1.	(+)	Class room lessons teach us to become self-disciplined individuals	.614
2.	(+)	I consider exams. to be a necessary part of learning.	.680
3.	(+)	I like doing exams. because I think it develops my character.	.731
4.	(+)	I like exams because they help me to organise my thoughts	.780
5.	(+)	Studying in class develops in us the ability to cooperate with one another	.621
6.	(+)	I like participating in classroom lessons because they help me to organise my thoughts	.689
7.	(+)	Exams. teach us to become self-disciplined individuals.	.699
8.	(+)	Preparing for exams. develops in me the ability to persevere.	.552

Assessment Domination in Learning—ADOL

Item			Item total r.
1.	(-)	What is most important is that I should enjoy my studies even if I do not do well in the exam.	.394
2.	(+)	I Study just to pass exams.	.583
3.	(+)	If there was a choice, I would select subjects in which it is easy to score marks even if I am not interested in them.	.621
4.	(-)	Studying for exams. interferes with the subjects I am really interested in.	.195*
5.	(+)	I study because my parents make me do so.	.494
6.	(+)	I study only those topic prescribed in the syllabus for the exams.	.472
7.	(+)	I study in order to do well in my exam. rather than for the interest in the subject.	.634
8.	(+)	The only reason for my studying is to pass exams.	.710

* Though a correlation of .195 is statistically significant the value is rather low.

Intrinsic Orientation in Job Getting and Learning - INJOL

Item			Item total r.
1.	(+)	I want to find a job where I can be creative and original	.506
2.	(+)	Doing well in class gives me a great deal of pleasure	.664
3.	(+)	I want to find a job where I can develop my interests	.582
4.	(+)	Passing well in exams gives me a great deal of pleasure	.619
5.	(+)	I want to find a job where I can demonstrate and develop my abilities and skills.	.611
6.	(+)	When I am not doing well in class I try harder	.690
7.	(+)	I chose the subjects I am studying because I enjoy studying them	.591
8.	(+)	Learning is an important personal experience.	.567

Apathy in Learning - APAL

Item			Item totle r.
1.	(+)	My mother does not worry about tests scores and reports	.488
2.	(+)	It will not worry me too much if I end up in a job that is not terribly interesting.	.424
3.	(+)	I do not like studying because the subjects are really boring.	.514
4.	(+)	I do not care very much about doing well in exams.	.669
5.	(+)	Taking exams. does not interest me	.502
6.	(+)	It will not worry me too much if I do not get a job when I finish my education.	.511
7.	(+)	I do not care very much about doing well in my studies.	.643
8.	(+)	Taking exams makes me feel helpless	.526

Involvement in Learning— INVOL

Item			Item total r.
1.	(+)	I do extra reading in the subjects I like	.524
2.	(+)	I enjoy taking exams.	.626
3.	(+)	I like exams. because they help me in my learning	.558
4.	(+)	I like studying because most of my school subjects are really interesting	.646
5.	(+)	I prefer quite difficult and challenging lessons rather than easier ones.	.587
6.	(+)	I will continue to study the subjects I like even after the exams. are finished.	.541
7.	(+)	I prefer quite difficult tests rather than easier ones.	.554
8.	(+)	I find most of my subjects really exciting and gripping.	.613

Extrinsic Orientation In Learning—EXOL

Item			Item total r.
1.	(+)	It is important that I find a job when I finish my studies	.534
2.	(+)	I hope to find a job that is highly regarded by others.	.622
3.	(+)	I am learning now to enter a prestigious University/Job	.573
4.	(+)	I hope to find a job that provides great opportunities for advancement	.629
5.	(+)	The exams. will determine how successful I am in later life.	.509
6.	(+)	I like to do well in exam. because it will help me to get better job qualification	.619
7.	(+)	Exam. success is what I have aimed for throughout my learning	.569
8.	(+)	I hope to find a job that brings great financial benefits.	.617

Significant Other Orientation—SIGOL

Item			Item total r.
1.	(+)	People look up to you if you do well in exams.	.479
2.	(+)	When I do not do well in exam. my mother gets quite upset	.445
3.	(+)	I work hard to please my parents	.585
4.	(+)	If I fail in my exams. my family will be disgraced.	.429
5.	(+)	I try to score high marks in exams. so that my friends will not think I am dull	.622
6.	(+)	I study hard in class to compete with my classmates.	.625
7.	(+)	I would like to do well in class so that my teachers will be pleased.	.634
8.	(+)	If I do not work hard in class, my classmates will get ahead of me.	.592

21A (2)

Title of the Instrument : **Teacher Value Scale.**

Purpose : Measurement of teacher values of school teachers.

Authors : S.M. Nayyer.

Languages : English and Hindi.

Availability : Dr. S.M. Nayyer, 56 Fatehpura Kharol, Udaipur-313001.

Levels : School teachers.

Main Features : No. of items 31, seven point scale. Scores 5,6,7 assigned to positive responses. Scores 1, 2, 3 assigned to negative responese score 4 to neutrals.

Reliability Data : Reliability calculated by split half method using Guttman formula reliability co-efficient ,82.

Validity Data : Content and Face Validity. Also logical keying approach used.

Time required for administration of test : No time limit Approximately 40 minutes.

Norms : Not developed.

References : Still not published.

TEACHER VALUE SCALE

Some statements are given below. The statements express ideas or beliefs. State on the basis of your own thinking and experience how is each idea. Is it valuable or useless? If it is not valuable, is it useless or are you certain about it and so can't say. If the ideas is valuable how much valuable it is ? Is it extremely valuable or very valuable or, just valuable ? How do you find the idea—express this by encircling any of seven alternate responeses given against each statement. For example if an idea is very valuable, then encircle very valuable. If it is extremely useless, encircle extremely useless. Only encircle one of the responses.

1.	Educating about Indian Culture by the teacher.	Extremely useless	Very useless.	Useless.	Un-certain	Valuable	Very Valuable	Extremely valuable
2.	Democratic behaviour by the teacher i.e. allowing students freedom to dissent or criticise.	Estremely useless.	very useless.	Useless.	Un-certain	Valuable	Very Valuable	Extremely valuable
3.	Teacher to know and use research find-ings according to need or to conduct research.	Extremely useless.	Very useless.	Useless	Un-certain	Valuable	Very Valuable	Extremely valuable
4.	Teacher to love discipline i.e. Meet students on committed time. Reach in the class or elsewhere in time.	Extremely useless	Very useless	Useless.	Un-certain	Valuable	Very Valuable	Extremely valuable
5.	Development of ideas, attitudes and values appropriate to the objective of social change in students by the teachers.	Extremely useless.	Vert useless	Usekess.	Un-certain	Valuable	Very Valuable	Extremely valuable
6.	Development of nationalistic ideas in students in or outside class by the teacher.	Extremely useless	Very useless	Useless.	Un-certain	Valuable	Very Valuable	Extremely valuable
7.	Developing in student the ability to think or act originally by the teacher	Extremely useless	Very useless	Useless.	Un-certain	Valuable	Very Valuable	Extremely valuable

(Contd. . .)

8.	Impartial and equal behaviour with every student by the teacher.	Extremely useless	Very useless	Useless	Un-certain	Valuable	Very Valuable	Extremely valuable
9.	Honest and moral behaviour by the teacher in every situation.	Extremely useless	Very useless	Useless	Un-certain	Valuable	Very valuable	Extremely valuable
10.	Development of scholarship in oneself by the teacher.	Extremely useless	Very useless	Useless	Un-certain	Valuable	Very valuable	Extremely valuable
11.	Regular study by the teacher of current journals.	Extremely useless	Very useless	Useless	Un-certain	Valuable	Very valuable	Extremely valuable
12.	Establishing the relations of mutual trust with community by the teacher.	Extremely useless	Very useless	Useless	Un-certain	Valuable	Very valuable	Extremely valuable
13.	Non-materialistic outlook towards life.	Extremely useless	Very useless	Useless	Un-certain	Valuable	Very valuable	Extremely valuable
14.	Dedicated effort by the teacher to master any topic/subject matter.	Extremely useless	Very useless	Useless	Un-certain	Valuable	Very valuable	Extremely valuable
15.	Polite behaviour by the teacher with the students in or outside class in school.	Extremely useless	Very useless	Useless	Un-certain	Valuable	Very valuable	Extremely valuable
16.	Maintaining patience by the teacher while working.	Extremely useless	Very useless	Useless	Un-certain	Valuable	Very valuable	Extremely valuable
17.	Using various modes for effective presentation of one's ideas.	Extremely useless	Very useless	Useless	Un-certain	Valuable	Very valuable	Extremely valuable
18.	Wearing simple cloths and simple living by the teacher.	Extremely useless	Very useless	Useless	Un-certain	Valuable	Very valuable	Extremely valuable
19.	Working with self-responsibility in the school.	Extremely useless	Very useless	Useless	Un-certain	Valuable	Very valuable	Extremely valuable
20.	Diligence of teacher in each of the activities of the school.	Extremely useless	Very useless	Useless	Un-certain	Valuable	Very valuable	Extremely valuable
21.	High thinking by the teacher.	Extremely useless	Very useless	Useless	Un-certain	Valuable	Very valuable	Extremely valuable
22.	Giving due consideration to individual differences.	Extremely useless	Very useless	Useless	Un-certain	Valuable	Very valuable	Extremely valuable

(Contd. . .)

23.	Generation of respect towards all religions in students by the teacher.	Extremely useless	Very useless	Useless	Un-certain	Valuable	Very valuable	Extremely valuable
24.	Emphasize learner's progress and personality development by the teacher.	Extremely useless	Very useless	Useless	Un-certain	Valuable	Very valuable	Extremely valuable
25.	Special attention by the teacher in developing healthy habits and behaviour in students.	Extremely useless	Very useless	Useless	Un-certain	Valuable	Very valuable	Extremely valuable
26.	Mutual cooperation in increasing profe-ssional efficiency of teacher.	Extremely useless	Very useless	Useless	Un-certain	Valuable	Very valuable	Extremely valuable
27.	Social recognition.	Extremely useless	Very useless	Useless	Un-certain	Valuable	Very valuable	Extremely valuable
28.	Salvation.	Extremely useless	Very useless	Useless	Un-certain	Valuable	Very valuable	Extremely valuable
29.	Self-respect.	Extremely useless	Very useless	Useless	Un-certain	Valuable	Very valuable	Extremely valuable
30.	Inner harmony.	Extremely useless	Very useless	Useless	Un-certain	Valuable	Very valuable	Extremely valuable

31. Mark 1 (one) against the Profession you consider best for you and 2 (two) against the profession you consider last but best. Similarly marks 3 to 7 in decreasing order of preference.

a. Doctor ________ b. Engineer ________ c. Administrative officer ________
d. Bank officer ________ e. teacher ________ f. any other ________ any other ______

Your Name ________

Teaching subject ________ Teaching Experience.

Qualification ________ Caste ________

(Last Examination passed)

21A (3)

Title of the Instrument : **Leadership Behaviour Pattern Questionnaire (LBPQ).**

Author(s) : R. Krishnaraj and P.S. Balasubramanian.

Language : English.

Purpose : To identify the leadership behaviour of college principals and heads of departments.

Availability : Dr. R. Krishnaraj, Lecturer in Education, Alagappa University, Alagappa Nagar, Karaikudi.

Uses : To be used with faculty members to find out the perception of leadership behaviour of heads of institutions.

Levels : Faculty members in colleges and university departments.

Main Features (Scaling technique used, number of items, etc.) : Questionnaire with 53 items measuring leadership behaviour in 15 dimensions. Responses are required on a five point scale for each statement : always, often, sometimes, rarely, never.

Reliability Data : Reliability measures; alpha = .958, theta = .958 and Omega = .901.

Validity Data : Content and Factorial validity are established.

Time required for administering the test : 45 to 60 minutes.

Norms (are they available ? If yes, from where — give sources.) : Nil. Not available.

References on the instruments, its development and use : NIL

LEADERSHIP BEHAVIOUR PATTERN QUESTIONNAIRE (LBPQ)

The following items describe the behaviour of the head of your institution.

(i) Please read each item carefully ; there is no right or wrong answer.

(ii) Please think about how frequently the Principal would engage in the behaviour described by the item

(iii) Decide whether he would *always*, *often*, *sometimes*, *rarely* or *never* act as described by the item.

(iv) Please tick off any one of the alternatives to show the answer you have selected.

	Always	Often	Some-times	Rarely	Never
Eg : The Principal would do personal favours to teachers					
1. The Principal encourages the staff members to keep abreast of new development and innovations in their field.					
2. He encourages teachers to keep up professional ethics and morale.					
3. Through his action, he proves to be an example for others in					
(a) Academic affairs					
(b) Administrative matters					
(c) In the introduction of innovations					
(d) In the adoption of new methods of teaching					
(e) His relationship with other staff					
(f) His relationship with communtiy					
4. The Principal renders ready help when teachers approach him for solutions to problems in					
(a) getting equipments for teaching					
(b) arranging for curricular programmes					
(c) arranging for co-corricular activities					
(d) classroom					

(Contd.)

	Always	Often	Some-times	Rarely	Never
5. He would bring to the notice of his subordinates					
(a) high level changes in policy and important decisions taken at the management level					
(b) innovations in teaching-learning process					
(c) the progress made by the institution in achieving its goals					
(d) the outcome of his meeting with higher authorities					
(e) important government decisions concerning teachers					
6. He clearly defines goals of the institution					
7. He helps teachers understand their role in achieving these goals					
8. He gives feedback to teachers about their performance in the class					
9. He identifies future needs of the institution					
10. He informs teachers about					
(a) job description					
(b) rules and regulations governing the institution					
(c) their role and responsibility in the total college programme					
(d) their powers in the classroom					
(e) their limitations					

(Contd.)

	Always	Often	Some-times	Rarely	Never
11. He represents the rights and feelings of teachers to appropriate authorities on the following issues: (a) promotions (b) job assignment (c) transfers (d) teacher grievances (e) teachers' rights and privileges					
12. He brings teachers together into a cohesive. cooperative group					
13. He discusses with teachers any problem situations that they have encountered.					
14. He creates appropriate climate for communication between disputants.					
15. He suggests procedures and ground rules to resolve conflicts					
16. He is a co-operative team worker with other higher administrators					
17. He has free access to his higher authorities					
18. The views put by him are patiently heard by higher authorities					
19. His help and guidance are required by higher authorities whenever needed					
20. His opinions and suggestions are respected by higher authorities					
21. He adheres to rules and regulations of the institution					

(Contd.)

	Always	Often	Some-times	Rarely	Never
22. Rule deviants are severely dealt with by him.					
23. He highly regards the formal restrictions that have been imposed on him by rules and regulations in operation.					
24. Environmental turbulance will not easily make him relax existing rules, procedures and policies.					
25. He never enforces rules to meet his own personal needs					
26. He gives instruction or assistance when needed					
27. He develops specific methods for checkng and evaluating in the total group performance					
28. He takes steps to direct teachers towards working in a well defined manner					
29. He gives instruction and supervision for (a) setting standards of performance (b) assisting teachers to achieve established goals					
30. He would provide tools and materials necessary to task performance					
31. He makes best efforts for planning the work to be done to achieve goals					
32. He motivates teachers to optimum performance					

(Contd.)

	Always	Often	Some-times	Rarely	Never
33. He establishes performance criteria					
34. He generally will					
(a) find time to listen to teachers					
(b) take necessary steps to promote faculty improvement					
(c) look out for the personal group members					
(d) take efforts to maintain the status of the teacher in the society					
(e) commend teachers' well suggested ideas in times of crises					
35. He will encourage open discussion for issues and problems confronting the institution					
36. He consults his subordinates for setting goals of the institution					
37. He will do what can be done to make teachers feel important and involved					
38. He will be available for discussion of any problem they face					
39. He will discuss with teachers in defining roles and spelling out tasks of teachers					
40. He will encourage the use of uniform procedures					
41. He will ensure that the activities of all teachers are co-ordinated with each other					
42. He will give guidance and assistance when needed by teachers					

(Contd.)

	Always	Often	Some-times	Rarely	Never
43. He lets teachers know what is expected of them					
44. He would see to it that each teacher is working up to his capacity					
45. He would maintain the organisation in good enough shape that it can continue to function without yielding to outside pressures					
46. He would take the initiative to move the teacher group toward goals of the institution overcoming all difficulties in his path.					
47. He would not yield to the pressure of teachers and students for their unreasonable cause					
48. He would be authentic while exhibiting a relatively consistent behaviour pattern					
49. He will give recognition to teachers whenever innovative suggestions and ideas are made					
50. He can administer sanctions and punishments to those who do not co-operate with him					
51. He will initiate appropriate action against teachers when they are incompetent					
52. He will discuss subordinate's behviour and performance in private rather than in front of fellow teachers and others while disciplining.					
53. To obtain co-operation of teachers, he will rely upon persuation and good personal relations.					

LBPQ : Dimensions and No. of Items

Dimension	S.No.in the LBPQ	Total No. of statements
1. Inspiration	1 to 3	8
2. Work Facilitation	4	4
3. Information Dissemination	5	5
4. Goal setting	6 to 10	9
5. Representation	11	5
6. Integration	12 to 15	4
7. Influence with superiors	16 to 20	5
8. Rule Orientation	21 to 25	5
9. Direction	26 to 29	5
10. Performance Emphasis	30 to 33	4
11. Consideration	34	5
12. Consultation	35 to 39	5
13. Structure Initiation	40 to 44	5
14. Role Retention	45 to 48	4
15. Inducement	49 to 53	5
	Total	78

Reliabiltiy of LBPO
Internal Consistency Measures of LBPQ

College	Co-efficients		
	Alpha	Theta	Omega
Autonomous	0.958	0.958	0.901
Affiliated	0.958	0.964	0.901

VALIDITY OF LBPQ

(i) Content Validity
(ii) Factorial Validity

21A (4)

Title of the Instrument : **Rating Scale For Student Evaluation of Teaching Effectiveness (RASSETE).**

Purpose : Assessing Teaching Effectiveness of College Teachers by Students.

Author(s) : Ethel S. Balachandran and E.G. Vedanayagam.

Languages in which available : English.

Availability : Dr. (Mrs.) Ethel Selina Balachandran, Lecturer, Department of Education, University of Madras. Madras-600005.

Uses : Assesses Teaching effectiveness.

Levels for whom it is meant : College students — undergraduate students of the academic courses.

Main Features (Scaling techniques used, Number of items.) : Likert type rating scale of 5 points consisting of 35 items. It includes 8 overlapping dimensions—Intellectual Kindling, Responsiveness, Motivating, Commitment to Teaching, Effective Communication, Concern for Student Progress, Impartiality and Informal academic help.

Reliability Data : Item reliability ranges between values .67 to .88 Test-retest reliability for the tool is .87.

Validity Data : Item validity (factor loading for the general component in factor analysis) ranges between .35 to .8. Concurrent validity (with self evaluation of teachers) for the tool is .78.

Time required for administering the test : About 30 minutes.

Norms : Nil

References on the instruments, its development and use : Teaching Effectiveness and Student Evaluation of Teaching—Ph.D. (Education) Thesis submitted to the University of Madras-1981.

RATING SCALE FOR STUDENT EVALUATION OF TEACHING EFFECTIVENSS (RASSETE)

The rating scale for student evaluation of teaching effectivenss consists of 35 teacher characteristics of teaching behaviours which are perceived by students as important in contributing to effective teaching. Please rate your teacher on each characteristic on a five point scale which forms a continuum with 5 denoting 'very good' at the highest and 1 denoting 'very poor' at the lowest end.

1. Very poor; 2. Poor; 3. Average; 4. Good; 5. Very Good.

Please indicate your rating for your teacher on each characteristic, by drawing a circle around the appropriate number among those given against it.

Eg. Punctuality 1 2 3 (4) 5

Circle around '4' as shown above' if you think the punctuality of the teacher is 'Good'.

1.	Giving clear explanations	1	2	3	4	5
2.	Moral integrity'	1	2	3	4	5
3.	Providing more matter than in the text book	1	2	3	4	5
4.	Capability to clear doubts of students	1	2	3	4	5
5.	Command of language	1	2	3	4	5
6.	Encouraging students consistently in their studies	1	2	3	4	5
7.	Being cheerful in the class	1	2	3	4	5
8.	Concern for each student's understanding of what is being taught	1	2	3	4	5
9.	Encouraging students to ask questions	1	2	3	4	5
10.	Coming well prepared for the class	1	2	3	4	5
11.	Duty consciousness					
12.	Being kind and courteous to students	1	2	3	4	5
13	Gearing teaching to the level of students	1	2	3	4	5
14.	Holding the attention of students throughout the class	1	2	3	4	5
15.	Knowledge of the subject	1	2	3	4	5
16.	Being interested in the progress of students	1	2	3	4	5
17.	Puntuality	1	2	3	4	5
18.	Making learning important and interesting to students	1	2	3	4	5
19.	Giving useful explanations while returning answer papers and assignments	1	2	3	4	5
20	Willingness to help students even out of class	1	2	3	4	5
21.	Encouraging discussion in the class	1	2	3	4	5
22.	Not misunderstanding students when they argue on matters relating to study	1	2	3	4	5
23.	Respect for student opinion	1	2	3	4	5
24.	Appreciating students as and when deserving	1	2	3	4	5
25.	Being patient in understanding the thoughts and difficulties of students	1	2	3	4	5

26.	Clear and audible voice	1	2	3	4	5
27.	Encouraging students to think for themselves	1	2	3	4	5
28.	Giving interesting illustrations	1	2	3	4	5
29.	Impartiality	1	2	3	4	5
30.	General knowledge	1	2	3	4	5
31.	Teaching with enthusiasm	1	2	3	4	5
32	Awareness of recent developments in the subject	1	2	3	4	5
33.	Reviewing the lesson of the previous class	1	2	3	4	5
34.	Having enthusiasm in the subject	1	2	3	4	5
35.	Emphasizing important points in the lesson	1	2	3	4	5

21A (5)

Title of the Instrument : **Information Scale.**

Purpose : To measure the extent of use of information disseminated through the contents of the lessons of correspondence courses.

Author(s) : Shavinder Kaur and Amarjit Singh.

Languages in which available : Punjabi and English.

Availability : Unpublished Ph.D Dissertation, Punjab Agricultural University, Ludhiana.

Uses : To study the extent of use of information disseminated through correspondence course by the trainees.

Levels for whom it is meant : Rural ladies who can read and write.

Main features : Three point continuum, 25 items.

Reliability Data : Reliability of the scale was found out by using Cronback formula, and the reliability coefficients came out to be .79.

Validity data : N.A.

Norms : Extent of use of Information Scores :

Always 3
Seldom 2
Never 1

References on the Instruments, its development and use : Erdos, R.F. (1967) : *Teaching by Correspondence*, London, Longmans , p. 10.

INFORMATION SCALE

Extent of use of Information

Some statements have been given below. Express your opinion in the extent of use of information which you have comprehended. Please insert the check mark (✓) in the appropriate column.

S. No.	Statement	Extent of use of information		
		Always	Seldom	Never
1	2	3	4	5
1.	Use of protein rich diet to prevent Kwashiorkor			
2.	To take germinated pulses to have vitamin C in the diet.			
3.	Use of fruits and vegetable in diet to get vitamins and minerals			
4.	Use of Malathion or clordane in the control of houseflies.			
5.	Use of eggs as an essential constituent of balanced diet.			
6.	Use of glycerine to remove coffee stain.			
7.	Vaccination of children against whooping cough, tetanus and dyptheria			
8.	Application of acetone to remove nail polish stain from the clothes			
9.	Use of ether to remove grass stain from the clothes.			
10.	Application of Sevin insecticide to kill the cockroaches			
11.	Use of green manure to make the soil fertile.			
12.	Preparation or buying of poultry feed on the basis of per bird consumption			
13.	To estimate the total expenditure of poultry farm keeping in view the per bird expenditure.			
14.	Preparation of recommended size of kitchen garden on the basis of the needs of the family.			
15.	Use of balanced ration for the cattle			

16. Preparation of Amla preserve from *Banarsi* variety.
17. Preparation of recommended sizes of compost pits.
18. Application of Aldarin insecticides to kill black ants.
19. To take whole pulses to have vitamin B in the diet.
20. Arranging pictures on the walls according to their sizes.
21. Construction of *Chullah* at the recommended height.
22. Scientific storage of grains.
23. Testing of soil to know the nutrients requirements of the crops.
24. Preparation of mango pickle. according to the recommended methods.
25. Providing first food to the neo-nate after 6-8 hours of birth.

Development of the Instrument : The scale has been standardized on a total sample of 2132 students from grades VI through XII, employing rigorous psychometric procedures.

References :

1. Sources : "A study of the Socio-psychological correlates of social development of high school children in unpublished Doctoral Dissertation in Education, Bangalore University, 1978.
2. "Socialization of children and Youth" (in press). Agra : Bhargava Book House.

21 B (1) Details given on page 611

B

21B (2)

Title of the Instrument : **Mangal Teacher Adjustment Inventory (MTAI)**
Author : Dr. S.K. Mangal.
Availability : National Psychological Corporation; 4/230, Kacheri Ghat, Agra-282004 (India)

Note : 21B(1) not included

Languages : Hindi and English.

Uses : It assesses the adjustment or maladjustment of the teachers of both sexes belonging to the Indian schools. It is in short form and therefore proves to be very useful. It is being widely used by the research investigators and teachers.

Level : Teachers of Indian Schools.

Main Features : 1. It has very few items, 70 only in comparision to the long form containing 253 items.

2. The mode of response provides only two alternatives in the form of yes or no (forced choice) instead of three as provided in the long form.

3. Scoring procedure has been simplified in the following ways:

(a) By assigning one mark to the response showing adjustment and zero for showing maladjustment.

(b) The Items of the inventory for which 'Yes' response shows adjustment (total 10 in number) have been made distinctive from the rest of the inventory items by putting ✓ mark in the beginning of the statement of the item. Where for these 10 items the 'yes' responses show adjustment and 'No' as maladjustment, for the remaining 60 items, 'No' responses show adjustment and 'Yes' as maladjustment.

(c) In the long form it was needed to compute 5 types of area of factor-wise scores for the calculation of total adjustment scores of an individual teacher. The present small form directly yields the total adjustment scores ranging from 0 to 70 without computing any factor or area-wise scores.

4. In the long form of the inventory, it was essential to arrange the items of the same nature in one place to facilitate area or factor-wise scores but here in the present form the items have been arranged in a random order and thus possibility of hallo and echo effects etc. have been minimised.

5. Interpretation of the subjects scores has been very much simplified by providing a five fold categorization (separately for male and female teachers) in the form of very good, good, average, poor, and very poor adjustment.

Reliability of the Inventory : It was estimated through test-retest and split-half methods. Number was 100 and the reliability Coefficient was 969 and 983.

21B (3)

Title of the Instrument : **Teacher Rating Scale (T R S).**
Author : Dr. R.C. Deva
Language(s) : English
Availability : National Psychological Corporation, 4/230, Kacheri Ghat, Agra-282 004.
Uses : It is used for the assessment of student teaching effectiveness
Level : School level teachers.
Main Feactures : The rating scale consists of 17 dimensions. They are grouped under 3 Major heads for help in locating them. 3000 "Critical Incidents were coded, scrutinised, classified and categorized to evolve these dimensions.
Reliability : Inter-rater reliability coefficient was found to be equal to .91
Validity : Coefficient of Correlation of .85 was obtained between the present scale and the Judgement given by the Experts.
Norms : Not available.
References :
1. Beery, J.R. : *Professional Preparation and Effectiveness of Beginning Teachers*. Florida; University of Miami, 1960.
2. Deva, R.C. : Prediction of Student Reaching Success, Unpublished Doctoral Dessertation, Aligarh : Aligarh Muslim University, 1967.
3. Flanagan, J.C : 'Critical Incidents Technique' 51 *Psychological Bulletin*, Vol. 51, 327-358, 1954.

21B (4)

Title of the Instrument : **General Teaching Competency Scale (GTCS).**
Author : B.K. Passi and M.S. Lalitha.
Availability : National Psychological Corporation, 4/230, Kacheri Ghat, Agra-4.
Language : English.
Uses : The Scale is generally used for measuring teaching competency of a teacher individually by a reliable observer or a group of reliable observers making direct observation of his classroom behaviour for the entire teaching period. It can also be used to train teachers both at preservice and inservice level. A teacher can use the tool for self-evaluation purposes also. It has not only been

used widely by researchers for doctoral studies but also in the national projects undertaken by the National Council of Educational Research and Training (Das, Passi. and Singh. 1976, 1977,1977). These projects are related to the study of effectiveness of microteaching in developing genaral teaching competence among teacher trainees belonging to teacher training institutions all over the country. The recent project is on studying the effectiveness of defferent stratagies of integrating teaching skills on general teaching competence. The scale has been used in all these projects to measure the criterion.

Levels for whom it is Meant : School teachers.

Main Features : There are 21 items related to 21 teaching skills which encompass the entire teaching-learning process in the classroom. They are related to five major aspect of classroom teaching, namely, Planning, Presentation, Closing, Evaluation and Managerial. The items are such that they are centred around teacher classroom behaviour in relation to pupil behaviour. It is a 7-point rating scale measuring the use of the skill by the teacher in the classroom corresponding to each item ranging from 1 for 'Not at all' to '7' for 'very much'.

Reliability : Since this is an observation tool, the more appropriate type of reliability is the inter-observer reliability. This scale has been used for doctoral research and the reported inter-observer reliability coefficients range for .85 to .91. Inter-observer reliability can be better established when the observers train themselves for using the GTC scale.

Validity : The scale has content validity, Factorial validity is also available. Scott's coefficient of inter-observer agreement ranging from 0.78 to 0.82.

Norms : Not available.

References :

1. Allen, D.W. and Ryan, K.A, *Micro Teaching.* Addison-Wesley Reading, Massachusetts, California, 1969.
2. Baral, D.P., Snow, R.D. and Allen, D.W., *A Taxonomy of Teaching Behaviour.* Stanford Center for Research and Development in Teaching, 1968 (Mimeo).
3. Biddle, B.J., "The Integration of Teacher Effectiveness Research". In B.J Biddle and W.J. Ellena (Eds.) *Contemporary Research on Teacher*

Effectiveness Holt, Reinehart and Winston, New York, 1964.

4. Bhattacharya, S.P. *Review of Research on Theory of Teaching,* Centre of Advanced Study in Education, M.S. University, Baroda, 1974.
5. Brown, G. Microteaching : *A Programme of Teaching Skills,* Methuen, London, 1975.

21B (5)

Title of the Intrument : **Indore Teaching Assessment Scale (ITAS).**

Author : B.K. Passi, Manohar Deshmukh and S.K. Sharma.

Availability : National Psychological Corporation, 4/230, Kacheri Ghat, Agra-28004 (U.P.).

Language : English.

Uses : Used for assessing the ability to integrate the teaching skills through well designed teaching based activities. Used to assess the ability of teachers to integrate the skills involved in teaching, directly, and to know how well competent he will be with teaching as a vocation. Also can be used for measuring the effectiveness of teacher education programme.

Main Features : The ITAS is a five-point rating scale to assess the ability to integrate teaching skills. The tool can be used by self or peer supervisors or college supervisors or researchers or educational administrators who have got the training in observation. The tool consists of four parts. Part A explains how to rate the observations and includes instructions. There are five possible responses from 'Not at all' to 'To a great extent'. The meaning of these categories are given for understanding and to have high inter-observer reliability. Part B is body of the tool. It contains 20 statements, each one of them represents observable behavioural events exhibited during the process of integration of skills. Part C of the tool gives Observational guidelines to observers. Part D is the glossary consisting of definiton and meaning for the terms given in the body of the tool. They have been arranged in chronology as in the rating scale.

Reliability : It has been observed that mature observers obtain an inter-observer reliability of .85 by carefully following the definition of the terms given in the glossary.

Validity : Content Validity has been established by carrying out discussions and interviewing teacher educators of different states of the country belonging to various levels of teacher education.

Norms : Key for scoring positive and negative items has been given.

Time required : No time limit.

References :

1. Jangira, N. K : *Towards a model for Integration of Skills*, Department of Teacher Education NCERT, 1979 (Mimeo).
2. NCERT : *National Project on Strategy for the Integration of Teaching Skills*, 1979.
3. Passi, B.K. : *Becoming Better Teacher*, Ahmedabad, Sahitya Mudranalaya, 1976.
4. Passi, B.K. & Sharma, K.K.: Integration of Skills, Paper presented at the Second Research Semiar on Microteaching, held at Indore University, Indore, 1979.
5. Singh, L.C. : *Micro-Micro-Teaching*, Agra National Psychological Corporation. 1979.

21B (7)

Title of the Instrument : **Mukhopadhyay's Change Proneness Inventory (MCPI).**

Author : M. Mukhopadhyay.

Availability : National Psychological Corporation , 4/230, Kacheri Ghat, Agra-282004.

Languages : English.

Uses : To measure Change Proneness in the Education System.

Level : School teachers and principals.

Main Features : Each item is provided with a five point scale where each question can be answered from 'Always' to 'Never' through 'frequently', 'Sometimes' and 'Seldom'. Total test items are 45 in number. Instructions are given as follows : "You are requested to answer the questions by putting a tick mark in appropriate cell which best represents your position."

Reliability : Split half reliability was found by using Spearman-Brown prophecy formula which was found to be equal to 0.82 which is significant at 0.01 level.

Validity : Content Validity of the inventory was established.

Norms : Not available.

Time Limit : No fixed time limit has been given.

References : 1. Agarwal M : 'A Study of Innovative Proneness of Secondary School Teachers in Relation to Certain Demographic and other Selected Characteristics,' Unpublished M.Ed. Dissertation, M. S. University, Baroda, 1974.

2. Havelock, R.G., *et al* : Planning for Innovation through Dissemination and Utilization of Knowledge, Ann Arbor, Michigan : Institute for Social Research, University of Michigan, 1973.

3. Mukhopadhyay, M: Change Proneness of Teachers, *Journal of Indian Education*, III (5), January, 1978

4. Rai, Kamal : 'Factors affecting Diffusion of Innovations in Secondary Schools,' Unpublished Ph.D. Thesis, M.S. University, Baroda, 1972.

5. Thorndike, R.L. and Hagen, E. : *Measurement and Evaluation in Psychology and Education*, New York : John Wiley and Sons, 1961.

21B (8)

Title of the Instrument : **Kakkar Interest in Teaching Scale (KITS).**

Author : S. B. Kakkar.

Availability : National Psychological Corporation, 4/230, Kacheri Ghat, Agre-282004 (U.P.) India.

Language : English.

Uses : Assesses interest in teaching of teacher trainees before admission to the teacher training progremme. Primarily it was constructed to be administered to the candidates—matriculates and high secondary passed—who aspired to be elementary school teachers.

Level : Teacher trainees before admision to the teacher training programme.

Main Features : This test is developed through the use of item analysis. High School, higher secondary, and college samples were used during its development. Consists of 27 multiple choice items. Such things as a person's reading interests, hobbies, school subjects, recreational interests likes for different types of people. loves, present personality, etc.

Reliability : Reliability by test-retest method was found to be 0.72 significant at 0.01 level. Test-retest = 0.69 and Kuder Richardson = 0.62.

Validity : The predictive validity was equal to r = 0.69 significant at

0.01 level. Validity of the criterion score was r = 0.64. Congruent validity coefficient = 0.71, Predictive validity = 0.69. In terms of reliability index = 0.71. item Validity- (given in Manual Table. 6.)

Norms : Grade Norms available.

Time: Takes an average of twenty minutes for testing.

References :

1. Anne, Anastasi . *Psychological Testing*. The Macmillan Company, New York, p. 517.
2. Barr, A.S. *Encyclopaedia of Educ. Research*. By W.S. Monroe, Revised New York, 1956, p. 889, 1447.
3. Boweres, Henry. *Manual descriptive of the Aptitude Test for Elementary School Teachers-in-taining*. J.M. Dent and Sons, Toronto, 1948, p.8.
4. Craig, D.R. (1924-25) : "The Preference Interest Questionnaire in Slecting retail Sales- women." *Journal of Personality Research,* 1942 pp. 31-39.
5. University of Minnesota *Minnesota Interest Inventory*. Department of Psychology. New York University, N.Y.

21B (9)

Title of the Instument : **Statistics Achievement Test (SAT).**

Author : R.C. Deva and A. Kumar.

Availability : National Psychological Corporation, 4/230 Kacheri Ghat, Agra-282004. (U.P.) India.

Language : Hindi.

Uses : Measures Knowledge, understanding, application objectives of cognitive domain. Measures achievement of high school and also B.Ed. students in the content area of 'Measures of Central Tendency' i.e. mean, median, and mode in both groups as well as ungrouped data.

Level : High School as well as B.Ed students.

Main Features : 40 items of multiple choice and completion type. These items measure knowledge, understanding, and application objectives of cognitive domain. Each objective is given weightage according to their importance attached in the context. One simple and another difficult, both the types of items on one subject matter area were included in the achievement test.

Reliability : The coefficient of reliability by the split half method was corrected by the Spearman — Brown Prophecy Formula which was = 0.84.

Validity : A validity coefficient of 0.82 was obtained.

Time Limit : One hour strictly.

Norms : Given in the Manual.

21B (10)

Title of the Instrument : **Teacher Values Inventory.**

Authors : Harbhajan L. Singh and S.P. Ahluwalia.

Availability : National Psychological Corporation 4/230, Kacheri Ghat, Agra -4.

Language : Hindi and English.

Uses : Exploring complex personality variables, Multiple uses.

Levele for whom it is meant : Primary to College levels.

Main Features : Semantic Differential Technique (S.D.), 7-point scale. 58, 58, and 30 items respectively for 'Teacher', 'Taught' and 'Teaching'.

Reliability: Not applicable.

Validity : Not applicable.

Time Limit : Teacher (30 Minutes.) Taught (30 Minutes).

21B (11)

Title of the Instrument : **Test of Personality Characteristics for Teachers.**

Purpose : To know personality characteristics of teachers relevent to success in teaching.

Author : N.S. Yadav.

Languages : English and Hindi.

Availability : 'Manasayan', 32, Netaji Subhash Marg, Daryaganj, New Delhi-110002.

Uses : This test is useful for both males as well as females of all age groups, Selection of higher secondary teachers discrimination of efficient and non-efficient selection of B. Ed trainees and teachers.

Levels for whom it is meant : Higher Secondary School teachers and B.Ed trainees — freshers and in service.

Main Features : Objective type verbal situational test forced choice with 50 items.

Reliability : Split half reliability with Spearman Brown Prophecy formula= 0.92 Test-retest reliability = 0.91.

Validity : With Ratings by Principals = 0.32 used through criteria with

Public Examination results = 0.52 with Teaching marks = 0.46.
Time Limit : 45 minutes.
Norms : Percentile and Stanine Norms are available.
References : Post-Doctoral work developed test for scoring, placement and selection of higher secondary school teachers.

21B (12)

Title of the Instrument : **Seven Point S.D. Scales**
1. Teacher, 2. Taught, 3. Teaching
Purpose : Ph. D. Work in Education
Author : Urmila Singhvi
Languages : English and Hindi.
Availability : Dr. (Miss.) Urmila Singhvi, 480, 4th A Road, Sardarpura, Jodhput (Raj) Pin-342001.
Uses : Exploring complex personality variables, multiple uses.
Level : Primary to college levels.
Main Features : Semantic Defferential Technique (S.D.) ; 7 Point Scale, 58,58 and 30 items respectively for 'Teacher', 'Taught', and 'Teaching'.
Reliability : Not applicable.
Validity : Not applicable.
Time Limit : Teacher = 30 minutes taught = 30 minutes. and Teaching = 15 minutes.
Norms : Ipsative scores, Norms not required.
References : Osgood, C.D.; Suci, G.J. and Tannenbaum, P.H. : *The Measurement of Meaning*, Urbana, University of Illinois, 1978, pp. 1-188, 217-317.

21B (13)

Title of the Instrument : **A.H—Mapni.**
Purpose : Identify students with deviant behaviour.
Author (s) : R.S. Wangu and J.B.S. Manral.
Language : Hindi.
Availability : Dr. R.S. Wangu, Head, Department of Education, North Eastern Hill University, Mizoram Campus, Aizawl 796007, India.
Uses: Identify students with a tendency to deviate in their behaviour under different situations of university life.
Levels : College and University students both boys and girls.
Main Features : Scale-Product Technique, No. of items = 90.

Reliability : Test-Retest reliability for the total test was 0.78.

Validity : Factorial validity and Internal consistency was established.

Time Limit : Approximately 30 minutes.

Norms : Locally developed.

References :

1. Wangu, R.S. Socio-Psychological correlates of Disciplined-Indisciplined behaviour among, University Students. *Dissertation Abstract International*. 43A (8), 1983 (Feb) pp 2612-2613.
2. Manral, J.B.S. A study of Indisciplined Behaviour in Kumaon and Garhwal University students as related to creativity, Intelligence and personality. Unpublished Ph.D Thesis, Kumaon University, Nainital, March (1985).

D

21D (1)

Title of the Instrument : **Class Room Boundary Questionnaire.**

Authors : Badrun Nisha and Kiran Gupta.

Availability : National Psychological Corporation, 4/230, Kacheri Ghat, Agra-282004.

Language : Hindi.

Uses : Measures the classroom control and the aspect of teacher leadership in the classroom.

Level : School Teachers.

Main Features : This test is an adapted version in Hindi and these test items are converted into Hindi from Morrison's test items. There are 25 multiple-choice item with three or four possible subsequent course of action three kinds of boundaries : Space boundary, time and behaviour boundary.

Reliability : Split half reliability was 0.88. Rational Equivalence method = 0.82; Test-retest reliability = 0.77.

Validity : Teacher (Variables) Instruction r = 0.62.
Teacher Permission : r = 0.59.
Child Initiation : r = 0.53.
Teacher Control (Total Score) r = 0.57.
Validity Coefficient of Kaksh Niyantran Prashnavalli against the Morrison's C.B.Q test which was found to be 0.70.

Time Limit : Generally 20-30 minutes (No rigid time frame.)

Norms : Percentile Norm's available.

Students Problems & Adjustments

A

22A (1)

Title of the Instrument : **Students Role Conception Inventory (S R C Inventory).**
Purpose : To measure role concept on ideal level.
Author(s) : M.B. Sharan.
Languages : English and Hindi.
Availability : Prof. M.B. Sharan. Dept. of Humanities and Social Sciences, I.I.T., Kharagpur-721 302.
Uses : To understand role conception, role demands, and role performance of the college students.
Levels for whom it is meant: College Students.
Main Features : Five-point scale (1 to 5), No. of items : 50.
Reliability : Test-retest reliability : 0.77 (N=105; Interval-6 weeks.)
Validity : Since it was a measurement on ideal level. Validity was not checked.
Time required for administering the test : About 10 minutes.
Norms : No.
References : A study of role conflict and its influence on role Performance (Firma KLM, Calcutta).

STUDENTS ROLE CONCEPTION INVENTORY

Now read each characteristic and give both the answers simultaneously.

	Answers (In what degree do you possess it?)					Answers (How do you feel about it?)				
	V.M.	M	C.S.	L	V.L.	V.G.	G.	C.S.	B.	V.B.
1. Simplicity	5	4	3	2	1	5	4	3	2	1
2. Self-confidence	5	4	3	2	1	5	4	3	2	1
3. Waywardness	1	2	3	4	5	5	4	3	2	1
4. Alertness	5	4	3	2	1	5	4	3	2	1

(Contd.)

	Answers (In what degree do you possess it?)					Answers (How do you feel about it?				
	V.M.	M	C.S.	L	V.L.	V.G.	G.	C.S.	B.	V.B.
5. Anger	1	2	3	4	5	5	4	3	2	1
6. Honesty	5	4	3	2	1	5	4	3	2	1
7. Discipline	5	4	3	2	1	5	4	3	2	1
8. Zeal	5	4	3	2	1	5	4	3	2	1
9. Boastfulness	1	2	3	4	5	5	4	3	2	1
10. Laziness	1	2	3	4	5	5	4	3	2	1
11. Obedience	5	4	3	2	1	5	4	3	2	1
12. Self-dependence	5	4	3	2	1	5	4	3	2	1
13. Nervousness	1	2	3	4	5	5	4	3	2	1
14. Virtuousness	5	4	3	2	1	5	4	3	2	1
15. Obstinacy	1	2	3	4	5	5	4	3	2	1
16. Concentration	5	4	3	2	1	5	4	3	2	1
17. Envy	1	2	3	4	5	5	4	3	2	1
18. Regularity	5	4	3	2	1	5	4	3	2	1
19. Aspiration	5	4	3	2	1	5	4	3	2	1
20. Co-operation	5	4	3	2	1	5	4	3	2	1
21. Flattery	1	2	3	4	5	5	4	3	2	1
22. Curiosity	5	4	3	2	1	5	4	3	2	1
23. Modesty	5	4	3	2	1	5	4	3	2	1
24. Selfishness	1	2	3	4	5	5	4	3	2	1
25. Dedication	5	4	3	2	1	5	4	3	2	1
26. Goodwill	5	4	3	2	1	5	4	3	2	1
27. Quarrelsomeness	1	2	3	4	5	5	4	3	2	1
28. Courage	5	4	3	2	1	5	4	3	2	1
29. Insight	5	4	3	2	1	5	4	3	2	1
30. Irritability	1	2	3	4	5	5	4	3	2	1
31. Competition	5	4	3	2	1	5	4	3	2	1
32. Shyness	1	2	3	4	5	5	4	3	2	1
33. Diligence	5	4	3	2	1	5	4	3	2	1
34. Tolerance	5	4	3	2	1	5	4	3	2	1
35. Inferiority Feeliing	1	2	3	4	5	5	4	3	2	1

V.M = Very much; M = Much; C.S. = Cannot say; L = Little; V.L. = Very little; V.G. = Very good; G = Good; B = Bad; V.B. = Very bad.

22A (2)

Title of the Instrument : **A Life-stress Scale for University Students.**

Authors : Manju Agrawal and R.K. Naidu.

Availability : Department of Psychology, University of Allahabad, Allahabad. To be published by Rupa Psychological Association, B 19/60 B Deoriabir, Bhelpura, Varanasi 221010.

Language : English, Hindi.

Levels : The scale has been developed for students of University level. However, after suitable necessary changes the scale can be used also with 10th and 12th grade students.

Main Features : The objective of the stress scale is to find out the amount and kind of life stresses encountered by university students. The scale consists of 58 items describing undesirable experiences and events likely to occur in the lives of university students. The items of the scale have been divided into 9 major categories : Financial, Family, Social, Education, Ego threat, Bereavement, Separation, Personal setback, and Health of others. The subject has to check those events of the scale which she/he had encountered in the previous one year. The subject has to also rate each checked item on a 7 point rating scale for the amount of distress. The scale ranges from 1, not at all distressing to 7, unbearably distressing.

Reliability : The test-retest reliability of the scale at an interval of 6 weeks was 0.88.

Validity : The scale has construct validity. Various measures of stress correlated significantly with the predictor variable strains. These correlations are much higher than those found in previous Western or Indian studies. Life stresses in previous Western studies have been reported to account for less than 10 per cent of Variance in strains (Rabkin & Struening, 1976, Andrews, Tennant, Hewson, & Vaillant, 1978) while stress measured by this scale accounted for 18 per cent to 24 per cent variance in strains. Construct validity was also indicated by very high correlations among various measures of stress (r = 0.93-0.94) ; these correlations were very much higher than the correlations of stress measures with the predictor variable strains (r=0.39-0.50).

Time Limit : Although there is no time limit but the scale usually takes 15-20 minutes to complete.

Norms : Percentile norms are available on 657 University students separately for both the sexes.

References : 1. Unpublished D. Phil dissertation, Department of Psychology, University of Allahabad, Allahabad.

2. Agrawal, M. & Naidu, R.K. Impact of desirable and undesirable events on health, *Journal of Personality and Clinical Studies*, 4,1,53-62.

LIFE STRESS SCALE FOR UNIVERSITY STUDENTS

	1	2	3	4	5	6	7
Scale:	Not at all distre-ssing	Very less distre-ssing	Less dis-tre-ssing	Average distre-ssing	Much dis-tre-ssing	very much distre-ssing	Unbe-arably distre-ssing

Sl. No.	Items
1.	Major decrease in outings and social activities (meeting people)
2.	Started living at friends' or relatives' place
3.	Started living in a hired room.
4.	Engagement was broken.
5.	Apprehended for a simple breach of law.
6.	Teacher scolded.
7.	Relations with an authority (hostel warden, teacher etc.) deteriorated.
8.	Parents favoured siblings.
9.	Serious differences arose with a friend or neighbour.
10.	I was not honoured for the commendable work I did.
11.	Parents scolded or beat.
12.	Family members interfered in personal matters.
13.	People behaved indifferently towards me.
14.	Family members frequently suffered from minor illnesses.
15.	Physical beauty diminished.
16.	Theft of wealth and property.
17.	Parents did not trust me on certain occasions.
18.	Theft or loss of a personally valuable possession.
19.	Relations with some family member got strained.
20.	People misunderstood me.
21.	I had inconvenience in finding means of conveyance to the University.
22.	Family income decreased heavily.

Sl. No. Items

23. A family member was jailed.
24. Lectures were incomprehensible.
25. Compared to others, I found myself inferior.
26. Indiscipline increased in the University.
27. A pet died.
28. I had to choose subjects I was not interested in.
29. I was blamed for no fault of mine.
30. A close friend or relative developed a serious desease.
31. Family environment got tense.
32. Indisciplinary action was taken against me.
33. Major financial trouble arose.
34. Major deterioration in health of a family member (though not hospitalized)
35. A close relative died.
36. Examinations were held late.
37. Appeared in examination despite ill health.
38. A family member was admitted in the hospital.
39. Adequate facilities not available in the laboratory.
40. Family environment interferes in studies.
41. Separated form some one near and dear.
42. Course was not completed in the class.
43. Failed in examination.
44. Could not secure admission in an important class or course.
45. My family was dishonoured.
46. Important books were not available in the library.
47. I do not get adequate time for studies.
48. Relations with a girl/boy friend got strained.
49. Neighbourhood environment interferes in studies.
50. Teacher acted partially.
51. A family member developed mental illness.
52. Aspirations of my life remained unfulfilled.
54. Could not appear in examination due to illness or some other reason.
55. Passed examination with poor marks.
56. A family member was missing.
57. A close family member died (mother/father/brother/sister-in-law)
58. Could not marry the person I loved.

Note (the items have been listed here on the basis of their mean severity ratings. The item with the lowest severity rating has been listed as 1 and the item with the highest severity rating is at S.No. 58).

22A (3)

Title of the Instrument : **Assessment of some aspects of Academic stress and symptoms in 10-16 year old students.**

Author : Suman Varma and Joyeeta Gupta.

Languages : English.

Availability : Dept. of Child Development, Government Home Science College, Chandigarh.

Uses : As a current problem in the educational issues of our country, this tool will help to explore the basic academic pressures burdening the school going child. It will help to identify flaws in the educational system.

The interview schedule can be used effectively by researchers, counsellors, teachers and parents to identify academic stress in children and assist them in coping with it. Further a better understanding of stress can assist students to manage stress. Increasing awareness and understanding among students regarding academic stress will not only help them in coping effectively with it but also may help in relieving other stressors. Awareness of the same among parents and teachers could help eliminate the problems related to conflicts and misunderstanding between the students and their parents or teachers.

Levels : 10-16 year old students.

Main features : Variable measured : Academic stressors and Type of measure : interview schedule-cum-check-list.

Applicability : Can be used with children between ages 10-16 years. The interview schedule-cum-checklist addressed to children is open ended and unstructured. It consists of questions under the following major components:

A. Categories as factors of Academic Stress are —Examination system ; Home work; Attitude of teachers and attitude of parents.

B. Symptoms of Academic Stress include a variety of indicators that can be classified into three categories — physiological, psychological and behavioural. Many of the symptoms are inter-related and may fit in more than one category.

Reliability : Test-retest reliability for the measure has been established (a 86 per cent agreement was obtained).

Validity : Comparision of responses on the open-ended interview and check-list has shown an 82 per cent agreement.

Time Limit: One to one and a half hours.

Norms : Nil.

References :

1. Agarwal, M: A Survey of Life stress for an Indian Sample. Project Report submitted to the Department of Psychology, University of Allahabad, 1976.
2. Elkind, D. : Stress and the middle grader. Special Issue : Counselling middle grade students. *The School Counselor*, 1986 (Jan) , Vol. 33 (3), 196-206.
3. Eysenck, H.J. and Rachman, S. : *The Causes and Cures of Neurosis*. San Diego : Knapp, 1965.
4. Farnsworth, B.J. and Garcia, I.M.: Do our elementary schools teach what society wants? Psychology : *A Quarterly Journal of Human Behaviour*, 1984, Vol. 21 (3-4), 59-64.
5. Gross, N. : *Exploration in Role Analysis : Studies of the School Superintendency Role*. New York: Wiley, 1972.
6. Gupta, K. and Khan, B.N. : Anxiety level as factor in concept formation. *Journal of Psychological Reports*, 1987, Vol. 31 (3), 187-192.
7. Kuczen, B. : *Childhood Stress*. New York : Delacorte Press, 1982.
8. Malhotra, P.L. : Cited by I. Badhwar and A. Pratap. The burdened child. *India Today,* 1987 (Nov.) 78-85.
9. Omizo, M.M. ; Omizo, S.A. and Suzuki, L.A. Children and Stress : An exploratory study of stressors and symptoms. *The School Counselor*, 1988, (Mar), vol. 35 (4), 267-274.
10. Price, J.H. A Model for explaining adolescent stress: *Health Education*, 1986, Vol. 16(3), 36-40.
11. Shah, M.L. Academic climate and its concept. : *The Progress of Education*, 1988 (Aug.) Vol. 62 (1), 13-15.
12. Singh, A.K. and Sengupta, A. : *Academic Anxiety Scale for Children*, Agra : National Psychological Corporation, 1986.
13. Smith, M.S. Evaluation and Management of Psychosomatic symptoms in adolescence. *Clinical Pediatrics*, 1986 (Mar), vol. 25 (3), 131-135.

22 A (3) Further matter of this scale is given on page 612

B

22B (1)

Title of the Instrument : **Youth Problem Inventory (YPI).**

Author : Mithilesh Verma.

Avaiability : National Psychological Corporation, 4/230, Kacheri Ghat, Agra-4.

Language : Hindi.

Level : 16-20 years of age. (Youths.)

Main Features : Contains 80 statements belonging to four areas and a number of sub-areas under each main area. The exhaustiveness of the inventory has been verified from the answers of an additional question "Do you think you have mentioned all of your problems in this Inventory" at the time of standardization of the final form of Y.P.I. The areas are as follows : A. Family Problems, B. School/ College Problems, C. Social problems, D. Personal Problems & Over Sensitivity.

Uses : It covers a sufficiently large range of all types of Problems of youths. It can be conveniently used in its full form as well as in its partial form that is only for a particular area. It has been also used for M.ED. thesis by a student of Kanpur.

Reliability : The reliability has been found only through test-retest method. Retest was given within a short period gap ranging from 15 to 20 days to avoid more changes in problems as the nature of problems is dynamic. The reliability coefficient of Y.P.I. is as follows:

Areas	Reliability coefficient
'A'	0.85
'B'	0.86
'C'	0.76
'D'	0.81
Entire Inventory	0.80
Range	0.76-0.86

Validity : Validity coefficients of Y.P.I. have been found with a number of standardized tests and also with certain other suitable techniques as mentioned below:

Sr. No.	Tests\Techniques	Sample size	Validity coefficients
1.	Problem check list Dr. N. Bhagia	764	0.75
2.	Adjustment Inventory Prof. H. Asthana	450	0.72
3.	Youth adjustment analyser Km. Mehru D. Bengali	400	0.68
4.	Mooney Problem check list	632	0.69
5.	Affirmative answers of the question concerning coverage of problems	720	87%
6.	Known cases	45	Range of scores 69-152

Time Limit : There is no time limit for this test.

Norms : Stanine norms available, also Percentile Rank and Percentile Band available for all the areas.

22B (2)

Title of the Instrument : **Teacher Adjustment Inventory (TAI)**

Author : S.K. Mangal

Availability : National Psychological Corporation, 4/230, Kacheri Ghat, Agra-4, India.

Languages : English and Hindi.

Uses : This test assesses the adjustment of teachers of both sexes. It segregates the poorly adjusted teachers from those who are better adjusted teachers. Teachers who are reasonably satisfied and adjusted thus may be entrusted with the task of bringing efficiency and improvement in Education. Helps teachers in modifying and adjusting their behaviour according to the demands of the situations.

Levels : School Teachers.

Main Features : 387 items were selected. Item analysis.

Factor analysis, Five factors or areas of teacher's adjustment :

(a) Adjustment with academic and general environment of the institution.

(b) Socio-psycho-physical adjustment.

(c) Professional relationship adjustment.

(d) Personal life adjustment.

(e) Financial adjustment and job satisfaciton.

Twenty-One dimentions of the sub-test are arranged as to yield factor wise and total adjustment scores with more ease and convenience.

Reliability : Reliability of the Inventory was estimated through test-retest and split-half methods.

Table : Reliability coefficients of the inventory

Methods used	I	II	III	IV	V	Total adjustment
Test-Retest (N=200)	.99	.99	.98	.99	.97.	.99
Split half (N=200)	.98	.98	.94	.98	.97	.99

Validity : Three types of Validity have been established for inventory: 1.Content validity ; 2. Construct or factorial validity; Criterion related validity.

Table : Validity coefficients of the Inventory against Headmaster's Ratings (N=270)

	Factors or areas of adjustment					Total
	I	II	III	IV	V	Adjustment
Value of 'r'	.945	.986	.967	.929	.957	.969

Norms : Percentile norms were computed separately for both male and female teachers with respect to their adjustment in each of the five areas of factors of teachers adjustment and also in terms of their total adjustment.

References : Nil.

22B (3)

Title of the Instrument : **Adjustment Inventory for College Students (AICS).**

Authors : A.K.P. Sinha and R.P. Singh.

Availability : National Psychological Corporation, 4/230, Kacheri Ghat, Agra- 282004.

Languages : English and Hindi.

Uses : The test segregates normal from poorly adjusted college students of all grades in respect of five areas of adjustemnt : Home, Health, Social, Emotional and Educational.

Screens the poorly adjusted students who may need further psychodiagnostic study and counselling.

Level : College students.

Main Features : Prepared in Hindi as well as English, it has 102 items : Home= 16, Health = 15, Social = 19, Emotional =31 and Educational =21. Simple Hindi words of everyday use is utilised so understandable to everybody.

Reliability : Coefficient of reliability was determined by (i) Split-Half method ; (ii) Hoyt's analysis of variance method (iii) K-R Formula-20. Test-retest reliability was also determined by administering the test after a period of 3 weeks on 228 students which is 10per cent of the total sample.

Table : Reliability coefficients of the inventory by using different Methods

Mathod used	Reliability Coefficients					
	Home	Health	Social	Emotional	Educa-tional	Total
	a	b	c	d	e	
Split half	.87	.83	.96	.95	.97	.94
Test-retest	.85	.82	.95	,94	.96	.93
Hoyt's Method	.86	.85	.95	.95	.94	.94
K-R Formula 20	.84	.82	.92	.94	.93	.92

Validity : In item analysis validity coefficients were determined for each item by biserial correlation method and only such items were retained which yielded biserial correlation with both the criterion (i) total score and (ii) area score, significant at .001 level. Intercorrelations among the five areas of the inventory were calculated. The correlation matrix is presented below in the table:

Table: Correlation Matrix of the five areas

	Areas	a	b	c	d	e
a.	Home	—	.22	.16	.26	.25
b.	Health	.22	—	.14	.25	.22
c.	Social	.16	.14	—	.21	.20
d.	Emotional	.26	.25	.21	—	.32
e.	Educational	.25	.22	.20	.32	—

Norms: Percentile norms were computed for both males and Educational separately as also for the inventory as a whole.

Time Limit : No time limit, but it takes around 18 minutes to complete the test.

22B (4)

Title of the Instrument : **Obedient -Disobedient Tendency Scale.**

Authors : C.S. Mehta and N. Hasnain.

Availability : National Psychological Corporation, 4/230, Kacheri Ghat, Agra-4 (U.P.).

Language : Hindi.

Uses : To find out obedient and disobedient behaviours in the context of increasing indiscipline in school and colleges in modern age so that teaching guidance and counselling is possible.

Level : High School and intermediate students of age range from 14 to 17 years.

Main Features : 36 items are there. Responses to be given in Yes/No. Those items which had a validity index between 0.25 and 0.75 were included.

Reliability : (1) The split-half reliability (N = 100) by Spearman-Brown formula was computed. The reliability coefficient of correlation was = 0.57.

(2) The Test-retest method (N=100) coefficient of correlation between the test score and the retest score was = 0.68.

Validity : The construct validity was calculated by extreme groups method. The Chi square value was found to be 10.91 which is found to be significant at 0.01 level. Construct validity was also found by comparing high and low groups with the help of 't' test. The 't' test value was found to be 6.81 with 46 degrees of freedom which was significant at 0.01 level.

Time Limit : No time limit but it takes usually around 15 to 20 minutes.

Norms : Norms prepared on a sample of 260 students of high school and intermediate. (Available in the manual.)

References :

a. Garret, H.E. : *Statistics in Psychology and Education*, Bombay : Vakils, Feffer & Simons Pvt. Ltd.

b. Mehta, C.S. A comparative study of adjustment of obedient and disobedient boys and girls *Perspectives in Psychological Researches*, 1981 a, 5, 49-52 scores

c. Mehta, C.S. A study of adjustment of obedient and disobedient student in relation to family size and economic status. Paper sent to Educational trend, Ajmer, 1981b.

d. Mehta, C.S. and Hasnain, N. Personality types and sex defferences in obedient/disobedient behaviours of students. Paper sent to *Asian Journal of Psychology and Education*, 1981.

e. Mehta, C.S. Caste and adjustment differences among the obedient and disobedient students. *Indian Psychological Review*, 1982, 22, 1-5.

f. Mehta, C.S. Personality types and family size among obedient-disobedient students *Perspectives in Psychological Researches*, 1982, 5, 35-36.

g. Mehta, C.S. Adjustment and Personality types among obedient/disobedient sutdents. Accepted for publication in the *Indian Psychological Review*, 1983, 24, (2).

22B (5)

Title of the Instrument : **The Test for Social Acceptability Among Peers (TSAAP). (A Socio-Metric Measure.)**

Author : S.L. Chopra.

Availability : National Psychologial Corporation, 4/230, Kacheri Ghat, Agra-4.

Language : Hindi.

Uses : It makes the student aware of their social position. The students should be acceptable to their class mates and the teachers pay adequate attention to the phenomenon of social acceptability so as to be able to help those who are socially less acceptable.

Level : Students from school levels.

Main Features : Students were asked to select only three of their class fellows for each of the four activities. No distinction is made between different levels of preferences and each choice was given a weightage of one.

Reliability : Newstertter Feldstein and New Comb (1938) had observed a stability coefficient of 0.95 for four successive weeks with five choices on criterion of test mates in a summer camp. Zeleney (1939) had observed stability coefficients of 0.90 to 0.95 on readministering a socio-metric test to college level discussion groups on sucessive days. The stability coefficient was = to 0.94.

Validity : The socio-metric test is unlike the usual mental tests in that it does not attempt to measure behaviour of certain types by eliciting related responses but employs a sample of actual behaviour studied. As such the sample is directly meaningful and need not be validated by relating it to an external criterion does not apply to socio-metric tests. It may, however, be considered whether a socio-metric test is valid in the sense that the behaviour which it is intended to elicit actually appears without falsification of responses on the part of the subject. The question here is how stable the behaviour is to be regarded as valid.

Time Limit : No time Limit.

Norms : Not available.

References :

a. Beckman, C.W. and Secord, P.F. Liking selective interaction and misperception in congruent interpersonal relations. *Sociometry*, 1962.25 321-335.

b. Bjerstedt, A. A field force model as a basis for prediction of social behaviour. *Human Relations*, 1958, 11, 331-340.

c. Bonfenbrenner, U. A constant frame of reference for sociomerric research Pt. II Experiment and Inference. *Scoio-metry*, 1944, 7, 40, 75.

d. Borgatta, E.S. The stability of Interpersonal judgements in independent situations. *J. Abnor. and Soc. Psychology*. 1960, 60, 188-194.

e. Cohn, T.S. Yee, W and Brown, V. Attitude change and interpersonal attraction. *J Soc. Psy*. 1961, 55, 207-211.

f. Davitz, J.R. Social perception and sociometric choice of children. *J. Abnor and Soc. Psychology*. 1955, 50, 173-76.

g. Fishbein, M. Prediction of interpersonal preferences and group member satisfaction : Estimated attitudes. *J, Per. and Soc. Psychology*, 1965, 663-667.

h. Gronlund, N. E. Generality of sociometric status over criteria in the measurement of social acceptability. *Elementary School Journal*, 1955.56, 173-186.

i. Gronlund, N.E. : The relative stability of calss room social status with unweighted and weighted sociometric status scores. *J. Edu. Psy*. 1955, 46, 345-54.

j. Haythorn, W. The influence of individual members on the characteristics of smaller groups. *J. Abnorm, Soc. Psy.* 1953,48, 276-84.

k. Hotowitz, Frances, D. The Relationship of anxiety, selfconcept and sociometric status among fourth, fifth and sixth grade children. *J. Abnorm. and Soc. Psy.* 1962,65,212-214.

l. Izard, C.E. Personality similarity and friendship. *J. Abnor. and Soc. Psy*. 1960, 61, 47-51.

m. Lott, B.F. and Lott, A.J. The formation of positive attitude toward group members. *J. Abnorm. and soc Psy*. 1960,61 292-300.

n. Mann, J.H. The influence of race prejudice on sociometric choices and perceptions. *Sociometry*. 1958, 21, 150-158.

o. Zeleney, L.D. Sociometry of Morale. *American Sociological Review*, 1939,4, 799-808.

22B (6)

Title of the Instrument : **Student Alienation Scale (SAS).**

Author : R.R. Sharma.

Availability : Ankur Psychological Agency, 22/481, Indira Nagar, Lucknow-16.

Language : Hindi.

Uses : Measures the alienated behaviour of college students.

Level : College Students.

Main Features : This scale has been developed on the basis of five dimensions of alienation (Powerlessness, Self-estrangement, Isolation, Meaninglessness, and Normlessness. It contains 54 items.

Reliability : Three indices of reliability were found out. Firstly, its reliability was determined by split-half method and was found to be= 0.61; secondly it was calculated by K.R. (Kuder Richardson) method and was found 0.84, and thirdly it was determined by test-retest method. Two test-retest reliabilities were determined : one after an interval of three months and the other of 6 months and the values were found 0.75 and 0.71 respectively. Thus, all this is a clear indication of adequate reliability of the scale.

Validity : Discriminant Validity was determined on the score of students obtained on Sharma Student Activism Scale developed by Sharma

(1988) and it was found to be .07, which shows that there is no agreement between the two measures. Secondly, its validity was determined by calculating correlation coefficient between the scores on total Student Alienation Scale and the scores on its five different demensions. Table is given below:

TABLE 2

Discriminant validity N = 30	Validity via correlation coeffivalidity cients. N = 30 Dimensions of Alienation				
	Powerlessness	Isolation	Self estr-angement.	Meaning-lessness	Norm-less-ness.
.07	.69	.60	.77	.62.	.72

Time Limit : Twenty minutes.

Norms : Percentile Norms for both males and females of all five dimensions of Student Alienation Scale and also for the Scale as a whole has been found.

References :

a. Aiken, M. and Hage, (1966). Organizational Alienation : A Comparative Analysis, *ASR*, 31, Aug.

b. Cline, S. (1960). *Organizational Psychology*, Rose Publication, Cinciniti.

c. Conger, J.J. (1977). *Adolescence and Youth*, Harper & Row Publishers, London.

d. Durkheim, E., (1966). *The Rules of Sociological Method*, Translated by Sarah A. Solovay & John H. Mueller, Edited by George, E.G. Catlin, New York, The Free Press.

e. Garrett, H.E., (1979). *Statistics in Psychology and Education*, Vakils Feffer and Simins Ltd. Bombay.

f. Josephson, Eric & Mary, *Man Alone*, (1962) Alienation in Modern Society (eds.), New York, Dell Publishing Co.

g. Kohen, L., (1970). *Organizational Behaviour,* Hplt Rine Hart Publication Washington.

h. Merton, R.K. (1938). Social Structure and Anomie, *American Sociological Review*, 3, Oct.

i. Oppenheimer, M., (1968). The Student Movement as a Response to Alienation, *Journal of Social Relations* 16 (First quarter).

j. Peter, K., (1973). *Studies in Organizational Roles,*

Interact Press, Pennsylvania.

k. Porter, L. (1976). Nature and Consequences of Organizational Complexities, *International Journal of Psychology*, 6(14).

l. Schacht, R. (1971). *Alienation*, Garden City, Doubleday.

m. Seeman, M. (1959). On the Meaning of Alienation, *American Sociological Review,* Vow. 24, Dec.

n. Sharma, R.R. (1988). *Sharma Student Activism Scale*, Lucknow, Ankur Psychological Agency.

o. Zillenger, R., (1977). Role Confusion as an Effect of Organizational Complexties, *Research Journal of Psychology* 9. (37).

22B (7)

Title of the Instrument : **Diagnostic Test in Decimal System and Percentage (DTDSP).**

Authors : V.P. Sharma and J.P. Shukla.

Availability : Ankur Psychological Agency. 22/481, Indira Nagar, Lucknow-16.

Language : Hindi.

Uses : It reveals a Person's strength and weakness in one or more areas of field being tested. Diagnostic testing can contribute much towards the qualitative improvement of education. Teachers can determine the strengths and weaknesses of indiviuals in specific areas of the course content and modify and improver their instructional materials with a view to suit the needs and demands of the classroom teaching.

Level : Middle School Children as well as any other grade.

Main Features : Two very important areas of Arithmetic that is, decimal system and percentage and have been primarily focussed on the fundamentals of mathematical knowledge and skill in these two areas. The scale consists of 25 items in Hindi.

Reliability : Reliability coefficient has been calculated in terms of coefficient of internal consistency by split half technique and it was estimated to be equal to 0.63

Validity : Predictive validity coefficients on coefficient of correlations between scores on the test and scores on Internal Examination in Mathematics as well as scores on Progressive Matrices (Raven's) was found to be +0.78 & 0.45 respectively.

Time : There is no time limit for this test.

Norms : Main Percentile Norms have been prepared for males and females respectively.

References : Not Available.

22B (8)

Title of the Instrument : **Guidance Needs Inventory (GNI).**

Author : J.S. Grewal.

Availability : National Psychologial Corporation, 4/230, Kacheri Ghat, Agra-282004 (India) 1982.

Language : English

Uses : This test can be used for personal guidance of students in group or individual settings. It can also be used in research where the scores on five guidance need areas can be treated either separately or collectively.

Level : Adolescents studying in secondary schools.

Main Features : Five different areas can be measured :

1. Physical, 2. Social, 3. Psychological, 4. Educational 5. Vocational. 65 items in English are included in this test. Each Need item of the GNI consists of asking the respondents to place a check mark (cross mark against one of the five multiple choice answers with a response and a scoring pattern.

Reliability : The Test-retest reliability was estimated to be 0.82 by administering it to a group of 50 students over an interval of 4 weeks.

Validity : Content Validity was ensured through method of selection and classification of items.

Time: No time limit has been fixed for this test.

Norms : Norms can be available from the manual.

References :

a. Martins, John J. Psychological needs, of engineering, prelaw, medical and undecided College freshmen, *Journal of College Student Personnel*, Vol. 12, No. 5 Sept., 1971.

b. Maslow, A.H. *Motivation and Personality*, Now York : Harper & Row, 1970.

c. Muley, R.S. *A Study of Needs and Problems of Adolescents*, Nagpur University Training College, 1971.

d. Murray, H.A. *Explorations in Personality*. New York: Oxford University Press, 1938.
e. Płasane, M.N., Some problems and Perceptions of College Students *Education and Psychology Review*, 1969, 9 (4), pp. 175-182.
f. Sharma, Meena. A Study of Guidance Needs of Secondary School Students, Unpublished M. Ed. Dissertation, Bhopal University, 1979.
g. Shipley, T.E. and Veroff, J.A. Projective Measure of need for affiliation, *Journal of Experimental Psychology*, 43, 1952 pp. 341-356.
h. Veroff. J., Development and Validation of Projective Measure of power Motivation, *Journal of Abnormal Social Psychology*, 54, 1957, pp.1-8.
i. Waters, L.K. and Roach, Darrell : A Factor Analysis of Need Fulfilment Items Designed to Measure Maslow need Categories. *Journal of Personnel Psychology*, 26, 1973, pp. 185-190.

22B (9)

Title of the Instrument : **Adjustment Inventory for School Students (AISS.)**

Authors : A.K.P. Sinha and R.P. Singh.

Availability : National Psychological Corporation, 4/230, Kacheri Ghat, Agra-282004. (U.P.).

Language : Hindi and English.

Uses : Segregates well adjusted students in three areas of adjustment: Emotional, Social and Educational.

Level : Hindi Knowing School students of India. (14-18 years age group.

Main Features : It is a 60 item inventory. Measures three areas of adjustment : Emotional, Social, and Educational. Questions indicating the significant problems of school students in the three areas were prepared. Questions were to be answered in Yes/No format. Simple easy to understand language was used in this test.

Reliability : Coefficient of reliability was determined by 1. Split Half Method, 2. Test-retest method and 3. K-R formula-20.

Table : Reliability Coefficients of the Inventory

	Method used	Emotional	Social	Educational	Total
1.	Split-half	0.94	0.93	0.96	0.95
2.	Test-Retetest	0.96	0.90	0.93	0.93
3.	K-R Formula-20	0.92	0.92	0.96	0.94

Validity : In item analysis validity coefficients were determined for each item by biserial correlation method and only such items were retained which yielded biserial correlation with both the criteria (i) total score, and (ii) area score, significant level being 0.001. Inter-correlations among the three areas of the inventory were calculated. The correlation matrix is being presented in the table below :

Table : Correlation Matrix of the three areas

	Areas	I	II	III
1.	Emotional	—	0.20	0.19
2.	Social	0.20	—	0.24
3.	Educational	0.19	0.24	—

The inventory was also validated by correlating inventory scores with ratings by the Hostel Superintendent. This was done on the data of 60 pupils living in the hostel of Patna Collegiate Multipurpose Higher Secondary School. The Hostel Superintendent rated the pupils on a five point scale, namely, Excellent, Good, Average, Poor, and very poor in respect of their adjustments. The product moment coefficient of correlation between inventory scores and superintendent's ratings was obtained to be 0.51.

Norms : Percentile Norms available for both males and females of all the three areas. (Emotional, Social, Educational.)

Time : No time limit (Around ten minutes.)

References : Not given.

22B (10)

Name of the Instrument : **Pupil's Problem Inventory (for stds. XI and XII.)**

Author : J.H. Shah.

Languages : Gujarati.

Purpose: To locate problems faced by pupils in six different areas and the information gathered can be used for guidance and counscelling.

Availability : Dr.j.H. Shah, Professor and Head, Department of Education, Gujarat University, Ahmedabad. Order to be Placed at : "Manomapan", C/o. Ms. Hema S. Shah, F/7, Swastik Apartments, Near N.N. Bus Terminus, Paldi, Ahmedabad - 380007.

Uses : i. To facilitate counscelling interviews. ii.As a survey tool, to locate students in need of help, iii. To know what are the most prevalent problems at higher secondary level. iv. To increase teacher understanding in regular classroom teaching. v. To know the prevalent rate of problem children at XI and XII levels. vi. As a research tool.

Levels for whom it is meant : Higher Secondary school pupils of Gujarat (stds. XI and XII).

Main Features: Open-end statement form was used to collect the various problems faced by pupils. Also pupil's problem inventory for secondary school pupils was also administered to two classes of each standard (Total : 213). Wherein they were asked to tickmark those problems they seemed to be facing at the end, they were asked to write their other problems not covered in the inventory. From these, 262 items, in all, were gathered. Out of these, 175 items, were selected on the basis of internal consistency (N=100). The six areas covered by the inventory are : 1. Health 2. Money matters 3. Personal (Emotional) problems 4. Social (family, friends, society, etc.) 5. Religious and moral problems and 6. Educational problems.

Reliability : Test-retest reliability =0.91 (N=120, interval 1 week). The frequency with which each of the items was marked at the first administration was correlated with the frequency with which each of the same items was marked on the second administration.

Validity : It was decided by i. Responsiveness of the pupils (pupils checked a wide range of problems) (ii) Coverage of problems i.e. content validity and (iii) usefullness (In 1988-89, one student has worked on it at the M.Ed. level finding will be available in July 1989.)

Time required : No time limit, however, it takes about 30-35 minutes for administration including the time for administrations.

Norms : There is no need to have norms on this inventory. However, quartiles have been reported sex-wise, area-wise and grade-wise.

References : Nil.

22B (11)

Title of the Instrument : **School Environment Inventory.**

Author : Karuna Shankar Misra.

Availability : Ankur Psychological Agency : 17, B Narain Nagar, Lucknow-6.

Language : Hindi.

Uses : Measures the Psycho-social climate of schools as perceived by the pupils. It provides a measure of the quality and quantity of the cognitive, emotional, and social support that has been available to the students during their school life in terms of teacher-pupil interactions.

Level : School Students.

Main Features : SEI has items belonging to six dimensions of the school environment. This test contains 10 items related to the six dimensions of school environment, i.e. concept intuitively judged relevent to the social psychology of the classroom. 20 items belong to the CRS Dimension while each of the remaining 5 dimensions has 10 items belonging to it. Responses are to be given 'Always', 'Often', 'some times', 'rarely' and 'never'.

Reliability: The 'School Environment Inventory' was administered to 113 students (54 boys and 59 girls) studying in Intermediate classes of five schools situated in city areas of Agra and Mainpuri. The split-half reliabilities (corrected for length for various dimensions of the school environment are as follows :

Table : Split-half Reliability Coefficients (For Six Scales of SEI)

Scale dimension		Reliability Coefficient
A.	Creative Stimulation	0.919
B.	Cognitive Encouragement	0.797
C.	Acceptance	0.823
D.	Permissiveness	0.673
E.	Rejection	0.781
F.	Control	0.762

Intercorrelations among Scales : Scale intercorrelations for SEI scores are shown in the table below:-

Table : School Environment Inventory Scale Intercorrelations

Scale	A	B	C	D	E	F
A. Creative Stimulation	—					
B. Cognitive Encouragement	.77	—				
C. Acceptance	.74	.89	—			
D. Permissiveness	.58.	.47	56	—		
E. Rejection	-01	-.03	-.22	.11	—	
F. Control	.51	52	45	37	20	—

Observation of the table shows that four of the scales are substantially interrelated. However, they may be treated independently in analyses, provided conservative statistical tests are employed. At present we are suggesting for an overall SEI score.

Validity : School Environment Inventory has been found to possesss content validity as measured with the help or views expressed by judges. Because of the lack of appropriate external criteria criterion related validity could not be estabished. During its short history, the inventory has been used in four research studies.

Norms : Stanine Scores norms are established for boys and girls.

Time : No time limit.

References :

a. Anderson, G.J. : Effects of Classroom Social climate on Individual Learning. Unpublished Doctoral Dissertation, Harvard University, 1968.

b. Misra, K.S. Effect of Children's Perception of Home and School Environments on their Scientific Creativity. Doctoral Dissertation, Rajasthan University, 1981.

c. Misra, K.S. Effect of Teacher's Control on Students' Scientific Creativity, *AYRE Journal of Eduction.*, 1 (2), 1982.

d. Misra, K.S. Anti-Creativity Climate, *Creativity Newsletter*., 1978-79, 7-8 (2,1), 41-43.

e. Shukla, M. Effect of Intelligence and School Environment on Achievement in Biology. M.Ed. Dissertation, Allahabad University, 1983.

f. Walberg, H.J. and Anderson, G.J. Classroom Climate and Individual Learning, *Journal of Educational Psychology*, 1968, 59, 414-419.

22B (12)

Title of the Instrument : **Pupils Problem Inventory. (Stds. VIII to X.)**

Purpose : To locate the problems faced by pupils in six different areas and the information gathered can be used for guidance and counscelling.

Author : J.H. Shah.

Languages : Gujarati.

Availability : Dr. J.H. Shah, Professor and Head, Dept. of Education. Order to be placed at : Mano-Mapan, F/7, Swastik Society, Near N.N. Bus Terminus, Paldi, Ahmedabad-380007.

Uses :
- a. As a Survey tool to screen problem children and provide counselling, if available.
- b. In researches : To know the prevalent rate of problem children : to correlate with other variables.
- c. To increase teacher understanding in regular classroom teaching.

Levels for whom it is meant : Secondary School Pupils of the Gujarat State. (Stds. VIII to X.)

Main Features : Open ended statement form was used to collect some concentious teachers were interviewed, but of 230 items, 140 items were selected on the basis of internal consistency.

The six areas in which the inventory is divided are : (a) Physical health (b.) Money Matters, (c) Individual (emotional) Problems (d) Social (family friends), etc. problems, (e) religious and morality and (f) educational problems (The manual is avaliable).

Reliability : Two administrations were undertaken at the interval of one week. The frequency with which each of the items was marked at the first time was correlated with the frequency with which each of the same items was marked at the second time. A correlation coefficient of 0.89 was found (n=153).

Validity : It was decided by (1) Responsiveness of pupils (2). Coverage of problems and (3) Usefulness at the M.Ed. level Researches.

Time required for administering the test : No time limit : However, it takes about 20-25 minutes.

Norms : It being an inventory there is no need to establish, howsoever, qualities have been reported sex-wise, area-wise, and standard-wise. Those who are having scores above 03 (in specific area or as a whole) need some help (Counselling) in a specific area or as a whole.

References : It has been used in researches at the M.Ed. level in the Department of Education of Gujarat University as well as south Gujarat University, Surat.

Note : Name of the publisher : "Mano-mapan" C/o Ms. Hema S. Shah, F/17 Swastik Apartments, Near N.N Bus Terminal, Paldi, Ahmedabad-380007.

(Price catalogue will be available on request).

22B (13)

Title of the Instrument : **Self-concept and Self-satisfaction (SC& SS) Inventory.**

Purpose : To measure self-concept and self-satisfaction.

Author(s) : M.B. Sharan, Dept. of Humanities & Social Sciences, I.I.T., Kharagpur-721302.

Languages : English and Hindi.

Availability : Prof. M.B. Sharan, Dept. of Humanities & Social Sciences, I.I.T., Kharagpur - 721302.

Uses : To understand perceived self-concept and self-satisfaction of the college students and others.

Levels : College students and others.

Main Features : Five-point Scale (1 to 5), No. of items : 35.

Reliability : Self-concept Inventory =0.84, Self-satisfaction Inv. = 0.82, (Test-retest reliability ; N = 90 ; Interval- 9 weeks.)

Validity : Self-concept Inv.=0.73; Self-satisfaction Inv. not checked.

Time required for administering the test: About 10 minutes for each Inventoy.

Norms : Not available.

References : A study of role conflict and its influence on role performance (Firma KLM, Calcutta.)

D

22D (1)

Title of the Instrument : **Problem Check List (Hindi Adaptation).**

Authors : M.C. Joshi, and Jagdish Pandey.

Availability : National Psychological Corporation, 4/230, Kacheri Ghat, Agra - 282004. (India.)

Language : Hindi.

Uses : Used for gathering information about the problems of adolescents, helps the students in expressing their personal problems.

Level : High School Students (Adolescents.)

Main Features : The scale covers 11 wide areas of adolescents problems. For each area, there are 30 items. There are in all 330 items. All the items are translated in Hindi. All statements are in a simple easy to understand language.

Reliability: The reliability of PCL has been demonstrated in the following four ways :

1. Co-efficient of Stability (Test-retest)
2. Co-efficient of homogeneity (Split-half, odd-even)
3. Standard error of measurement is a direct indicator of the probable extent of error in any score in the set to which it applies, and
4. Index of reliability which indicates correlations between obtained and true scores have been calculated.

Summary of Different Reliability Co-Efficients of PCL N=73.

Reli-bility types.	HPD	FLE	SRA	CSM	SPR	PPR	MR	HF	FVE	ASW	CTP	TOTAL
Test-Retest 10 wee-ks int-erval.	.641	.604	.812	.543	.682	.499.	494	.631	.832	.571	.589	.710
Split Half	.826	.809	.890	.880	.813	.851.	718	.742	.837	672	.835	.900
SE mmt.	2.09	2.54	1.64	1.46	2.52	2.33	3.15	2.79	2.30	3.93	2.55	8.97
Index of re-liability-	.91	.89	.94	.90	.92	.85	.86	.92	.86	.92	.86	.91 .95

Validity : Four major aspects of validity have been established for the PCL.

1. Extermal Validity
2. Criterion (1) Saxena's Vyaktitwa Parakh Prasnawali.

Table : Correlation co-efficients with Se,between Saxena Inventory and Problem Check list. (N=35)

Common Areas		Corr.Co-effis.	Corrected r coffs.
1.	Home	0.23+/-.15	-.032
2.	Health	-.840+/-.15	-.097
3.	Social	-.094+/-.15	-.103
4.	Emotional	-.407+/-.15	501
5.	School	-.226+/-.15	-.286
6.	Total	-.145+/-.15	-.204

Table : Correlation of scores on PCL with five factors of 16 P.F. Test. **N = 57**

Total PCL Scores	16 PF test Factors	Coor.Coeff.s withe SER
1. Criterion	A	-.008+/-.136
2. "	H	-.060+/-.136
3. "	L	+.109+/-.136
4. "	M	+.212+/-.136
5. "	Q	+.022+/-.136

Other Validity Tables also given in the Manual.

Norms : The PCL yield a count for each person for each of the areas and for the total list of items. However, it should be remembered that this count is not a real score, it is not a sum of points on a trait scale or a total of "Maladjusted" Choices on some trait key. No Norms available.

References :

1. Carrigon, M., (1960) : Extroversion and Introversion as a Dimension of Personality. *Psychol. Bull*, Vol. 5, No.5.
2. Joshi, M.C., (1964) : A Factorial Study of the Problems of Adjustment., *Ind. Psygl. Rev*. Vol.1, No.1.
3. Leach, K., (1949) : In Mooney, R.L., and Gordon, L.V.: Manual The Mooney Problem Check-List, Forms C.H. and *J.Rev.* (1950) New York : The Psygl. Corpn.
4. Mooney, R.L., and Gordon, L.V. (1950) : *Manual, The MPCL Forms C,H and J,* New York : The Psygl.Corpn.
5. Mooney, R.L., and Gordon, L.V. (1950) : *Ibid* (a).
6. Mooney, R.L., and Gordon, L.V. (1950) : *Ibid* (b).

Interests and Preferences

A

23A (1)

A. *Title of the Instruments* : **1. A Scale to Measure Job Preference and Job Satisfaction of the Faculty of Punjab Agricultural University for Teachnic, Research and Extension.**

B. A Scale to Measure Role Perceptions of the Faculty of Punjab Agricultural University for Teaching, research and Extension.

Purpose : For Master level thesis in the discipline of Extension Education.

Author : Kanchan Sharma.

Languages in which available : English only.

Availability : Head, Department of Extension Education, Punjab Agricultural University, Ludhiana - 141004.

Uses : For research on an extension organization.

Levels for whom it is Meant : Teachers of an Agricultural University.

Main Features : Constructed through paired comparision technique for determining relative preference of roles. Rank ordering was done on the basis of mean scores expressed in standardized form. Number of items in both the tests are 7 and 6 respectively.

Reliability :

	Scales	
	1	2
Reliability Coefficient (rtt)	.80	.84
Validity :		
Intrinsic validity	.89	.90

Time required : 12-15 Minutes.

Norms : Norms are available in the thesis of the author "A Study of Faculty Perceptions and Perceptions and Preferences for Extention as compared to Teaching and Research Roles at an Agricultural University", Department of Extension Education, Punjab Agricultural University, Ludhiana.

A SCALE TO MEASURE JOB PREFERENCE AND JOB SATISFACTION

1. Why did you join the present Job ? Please checkmark (✓)
   Others asked you to do this
   Your own liking
   The only job you could get
   Better Prospects
   Any other reason (please specify)
2. How did you acquire your present position: Check (✓) One.
   Through personal promotlon
   Through open advertisement
3. How do you feel about the work load you carry on your present position? Indicate your opinion by putting a checkmark (✓) on any point on the five point continuum which runs between *very inadequate* to *very excessive*.

Very Inadequate	Adequate	Optimal	Excessive	Very excessive
—	—	—	—	—

4. (a) Indicate your level or job satisfaction on the present position by putting a checkmark (✓) for the most suitable response on the five point scale indicated below:

Highly Satisfied	Satisfied	Just so	Dissatis-fied	Highly dissatisfied
—	—	—	—	—

   (b) Please Indicate the reason(s) for above response

   ____

   ____

   ____

   ____

5. (a) Would you prefer a change in your job/role on which you are serving at Present (i.e.teaching/research/extension) ?
   Yes — No —
   If yes, and given a choice, which role would you prefer the most to take up? Please tick (✓) only one item out of the following :
   Teaching ________________
   Research ________________
   Extension ________________
   (b) Please give at least three reasons for the above choice :
   (i) ________________________________
   (ii) ________________________________

(iii) ______________________________

6. Please rank order (the following roles as 1, 2 and 3 in your order of preference;

Roles	Rank
Teaching	__________________
Research	__________________
Extension	__________________

7. Please rank order your preference as 1 and 2 for each one of the role pairs/combinations listed below:

Role combination	Rank
(a) Teaching	—
V/s	—
Research	—
(b) Teaching	—
V/s	—
Extension	—
(c) Research	—
V/s	—
Extension	—

A Scale to Measure Role Perceptions of the Faculty of Punjab Agricultural University for Teaching Research and Extension

1	2	3	4	5	6	7	8	9	10	11	12	13	14	15	16
(ii) Outside the Organisation	—	—	—	—	—	—	—	—	—	—	—	—	—	—	—
(d) Opportunity to gain fame	—	—	—	—	—	—	—	—	—	—	—	—	—	—	—

2. Fllowing are certain statements constructed to know your perceptions regarding the opportunities embeded for professional enhancement in all the three roles (i.e. teaching research and extension. Please Indicate your level of agreement on the four point scale running between *very inadequate* to *Very adedquate*

Statements	Response category											
	Teachirg				Research				Extension			
	Very inade-quate	Inade-quate	Ade quate	Very ade-quate	Very inade-quate	Inade-quate	Ade-quate	Very ade-quate	Very inade-quate	Inade-quate	Ade-quate	Very ade-quate
1	2	3	4	5	6	7	8	9	10	11	12	13
(a) Opportunities for professional growth	—	—	—	—	—	—	—	—	—	—	—	—
(b) Scope for Independent Innovative work	—	—	—	—	—	—	—	—	—	—	—	—

Following statements are proposed to measure your perceptions for all the threse roles on five point scale which varies from very low to very high. Indicate your degree of agreement by putting a checkmark (✓) (one each for teaching researnch and extension) on any one point on the contnuum, against each statement and which your feel best reflects your response for each of the different statements of the situation.

Statements	Response category														
	Teaching					Research					Extension				
	Very low	Low	Ave-rage	High	Very high	Very low	Low	Ave-rage	High	Very high	Very low	Low	Ave-rage	High	Very high
1	2	3	4	5	6	7	8	9	10	11	12	13	14	15	16
(a) Status (it refers to the position of an individual in relation to other professional roles)	—	—	—	—	—	—	—	—	—	—	—	—	—	—	—
(b) Opportunity to develop contacts with people of high status	—	—	—	—	—	—	—	—	—	—	—	—	—	—	—
(c) Prestige (prestige here refers to the respect which people accord to a person by virtue of his/her position/role)	—	—	—	—	—	—	—	—	—	—	—	—	—	—	—
(i) Inside the organisation	—	—	—	—	—	—	—	—	—	—	—	—	—	—	—

23A (2)

Title of the Instrument : **Occupational Preference Scale.**

Purpose : Measurement of occupational interests of students.

Authors : Achala Umapathy and Mary Paul, Department of Psychology, Bangalore University.

Language : English.

Availability : Dr. Achala Umapathy, Reader in Psychology, Bangalore University, Bangalore-560 056.

Uses : Occupational Preferences and Career Orientation of students may be assessed for vocational Guidance.

Levels for whom it is meant : For all age levels above 10 years.

Main Features : The scale contains 176 titles of occupations classified into thirty groups based on International Standard classification of occupations, Titles and codes (1972) published by the International Labour Office, Geneva (pp.269-288). The preference for each occupation is indicated on a seven point rating scale with the description ranging from 'dislike very much' to 'like very much' with a neutral preference point at the centre.

Reliability : Test-retest reliability index was obtained for a group of high school (N=30) with a retest interval of one month. Product moment correlation coefficient between the two tests was 0.91 when mean rating of the group for each occupation was considered. Correlation coefficients from the above data were also obtained for each of the thirty randomly selected list of occupations on the basis of the scatter matrix for the ratings obtained for each occupation on the two occasions. The product moment correlation coefficients for different occupations vary from 0.31 to 0.98.

Validity Data : Significant group difference were noticed in the mean ratings given for occupations by younger (8th standard and older (10 standard) high school students, boys and girls, and students with defferent socio-economic status background.

Time required : 40 to 60 minutes.

Norms : Mean and standard deviation of preference rating for each occupation for a representative sample of 320 high school students in 8th and 10th standards and for boys and girls are available with the authors.

References on the instruments and its development and use : Mary Paul : A Study of Vocational Choice Patterns in adolescents : A function of age socio-economic status and sex. Unpublished M.A. (Psychology) Dissertation, Bangalore University, 1988.

OCCUPATIONAL PREFERENCE SCALE

School .... Age .... Sex............

Class .... Roll/Sl.No ....

Here are a series of occupations. You are to read each one carefully and indicate your preference for the occupation on the 7 point scale, by putting a "Tick" Mark. If you like the occupation very much, you can put a 'TICK' Mark over the number 7 in the 7 point scale. However, No. 1 on the scale would indicate "Dislike very much". Number 4 on the scale would indicate that you neither "Like nor Dislike" the occupation. Thus in between these numbers the degree of like or dislike decreases or increases accordingly.

	Dislike very much						Like very much
I. Accountants							
1. Accountants	1	2	3	4	5	6	7
2. Chartered Accountant	–	–	–	–	–	–	–
3. Auditor	–	–	–	–	–	–	–
II. Administrative and Managerial Workers							
4. Government official	–	–	–	–	–	–	–
5. General Manager	–	–	–	–	–	–	–
6. Production Manager	–	–	–	–	–	–	–
7. Research and Development Manager	–	–	–	–	–	–	–
8. Sales Manager	–	–	–	–	–	–	–
9. Budgeting and Accounting Manager	–	–	–	–	–	–	–
10. Personnel Manager	–	–	–	–	–	–	–
11. Hotel Manager	–	–	–	–	–	–	–
III. Agriculture, Animal Husbsndry, Forestry: Managers/Officers							
12. Farm Manager	–	–	–	–	–	–	–
13. Forest Officers	–	–	–	–	–	–	–
14. Fisheries Officers	–	–	–	–	–	–	–

(Contd.)

	Dislike very much					Like very much
IV. Agriculture Animal Husbandry, Forestry Workers						
15. Fishermen	–	–	–	–	–	–
16. Farm worker	–	–	–	–	–	–
17. Vineyard, Orchard workers	–	–	–	–	–	–
18. Dairy farm worker	–	–	–	–	–	–
19. Poultry farm worker	–	–	–	–	–	–
20. Gardeners	–	–	–	–	–	–
21. Forest ranger	–	–	–	–	–	–
V. Authors/Media	–	–	–	–	–	–
22. Authors	–	–	–	–	–	–
23. Editors	–	–	–	–	–	–
24. Journalists	–	–	–	–	–	–
25. News reader (TV & Radio)	–	–	–	–	–	–
26. Announcers	–	–	–	–	–	–
27. Short storywriters	–	–	–	–	–	–
28. Poet	–	–	–	–	–	–
29. Sound recording Operator	–	–	–	–	–	–
30. Radio/TV Transmitting Operator	–	–	–	–	–	–
31. Mike Operator	–	–	–	–	–	–
32. Advertising	–	–	–	–	–	–
33. Modelling	–	–	–	–	–	–
VI. Aircraft and Ship Officers						
34. Aircraft Pilot	–	–	–	–	–	–
35. Flight Engineer	–	–	–	–	–	–
36. Ship Pilot	–	–	–	–	–	–
37. Ship Engineer	–	–	–	–	–	–
VII. Clerical						
38. Stenographer	–	–	–	–	–	–
39. Typist	–	–	–	–	–	–
40. Bookkeeping Clerk	–	–	–	–	–	–
41. Cashier	–	–	–	–	–	–
42. Computer Operator	–	–	–	–	–	–

(Contd.)

	Dislike very much						Like very much
43. Receptionist and Travel Agency Clerk	–	–	–	–	–	–	–
44. Library and Filing clerks	–	–	–	–	–	–	–
VIII. Composers and Performing Artists							
45. Dancer	–	–	–	–	–	–	–
46. Actor	–	–	–	–	–	–	–
47. Movie Director	–	–	–	–	–	–	–
48. Producer	–	–	–	–	–	–	–
49. Circus Performer	–	–	–	–	–	–	–
50. Musician	–	–	–	–	–	–	–
51. Orchestra Conductor	–	–	–	–	–	–	–
52. Singer	–	–	–	–	–	–	–
IX. Creative Artists	–	–	–	–	–	–	–
53. Painter	–	–	–	–	–	–	–
54. Sculptors	–	–	–	–	–	–	–
55. Interior Decorators	–	–	–	–	–	–	–
56. Photographers	–	–	–	–	–	–	–
57. Movie/TV Cameramen	–	–	–	–	–	–	–
58. Choreographer	–	–	–	–	–	–	–
X. Food and Beverage Processors							
59. Grain Miller	–	–	–	–	–	–	–
60. Sugar Refiners	–	–	–	–	–	–	–
61. Meat preparer	–	–	–	–	–	–	–
62. Dairy product processor	–	–	–	–	–	–	–
63. Tea, Coffee or Cocoa preparer	–	–	–	–	–	–	–
64. Wine Makers	–	–	–	–	–	–	–
XI. Industrial and Related Workers							
65. Miners & Quarry men	–	–	–	–	–	–	–
66. Metal Plant workers	–	–	–	–	–	–	–
67. Refinery/factory worker	–	–	–	–	–	–	–
68. Construction worker	–	–	–	–	–	–	–
69. Contractor	–	–	–	–	–	–	–
70. Borewell Driller	–	–	–	–	–	–	–

(Contd.)

	Dislike very much						Like very much
XII. Engineers							
71. Architects	–	–	–	–	–	–	–
72. Civil Engineers	–	–	–	–	–	–	–
73. Electronics Engineers	–	–	–	–	–	–	–
74. Mechanical Engineers	–	–	–	–	–	–	–
75. Metallurgist	–	–	–	–	–	–	–
76. Computer Engineer	–	–	–	–	–	–	–
XIII. LAW							
77. Lawyer	–	–	–	–	–	–	–
78. Judge	–	–	–	–	–	–	–
XIV. Medical							
79. General Physician	–	–	–	–	–	–	–
80. Specialist	–	–	–	–	–	–	–
81. Surgeon	–	–	–	–	–	–	–
82. Dietician	–	–	–	–	–	–	–
83. Dentist	–	–	–	–	–	–	–
84. Optician	–	–	–	–	–	–	–
85. Veterinary Doctor	–	–	–	–	–	–	–
86. Pharmacist	–	–	–	–	–	–	–
XV. Other Professionals							
87. Librarians	–	–	–	–	–	–	–
88. Museum Curator	–	–	–	–	–	–	–
89. Social Worker	–	–	–	–	–	–	–
90. Counsellor	–	–	–	–	–	–	–
91. Astrologer	–	–	–	–	–	–	–
92. Shop Keeper	–	–	–	–	–	–	–
XVI. Physical Scientist							
93. Physicist	–	–	–	–	–	–	–
94. Chemist	–	–	–	–	–	–	–
95. Geologist	–	–	–	–	–	–	–
96. Biologist	–	–	–	–	–	–	–
97. Soil Scientist	–	–	–	–	–	–	–
98. Horticulturist	–	–	–	–	–	–	–
99. Marine Biologist	–	–	–	–	–	–	–
XVII. Protective Service							
100. Policemen	–	–	–	–	–	–	–
101. Prison guard	–	–	–	–	–	–	–

(Contd.)

	Dislike very much					Like very much
102. Watchmen	_	_	_	_	_	_
103. Security Personnel	_	_	_	_	_	_
104. Fire Fighter	_	_	_	_	_	_
105. Detective	_	_	_	_	_	_
XVIII. Religious						
106. Priest	_	_	_	_	_	_
107. Missionary	_	_	_	_	_	_
108. Faith Healer	_	_	_	_	_	_
XIX. Sales Workers						
109. Wholesale/Retail Managers	_	_	_	_	_	_
110. Sales Supervisors	_	_	_	_	_	_
111. Manufacturers Agent	_	_	_	_	_	_
112. Insurance/Real Estate/Securities/ Salesmen	_	_	_	_	_	_
113. Advertising Salesmen	_	_	_	_	_	_
114. Auctioneer	_	_	_	_	_	_
115. Pawn Broker	_	_	_	_	_	_
116. Salesmen/Shop Asst.	_	_	_	_	_	_
XX. Services						
117. House Maid	_	_	_	_	_	_
118. Caretaker	_	_	_	_	_	_
119. Waiter	_	_	_	_	_	_
120. Housekeeper	_	_	_	_	_	_
121. Cook	_	_	_	_	_	_
122. Dry Cleaner	_	_	_	_	_	_
123. Beautician	_	_	_	_	_	_
124. Baby sitter	_	_	_	_	_	_
125. Hair Dresser/Cutter	_	_	_	_	_	_
XXI. Services						
126. Electrician	_	_	_	_	_	_
127. Mechanic	_	_	_	_	_	_
128. Travel Agent	_	_	_	_	_	_
129. Travel Guide	_	_	_	_	_	_
130. Postman	_	_	_	_	_	_
131. Undertaker	_	_	_	_	_	_

(Contd.)

	Dislike very much						Like very much
132. Plumber	–	–	–	–	–	–	–
133. Welder	–	–	–	–	–	–	–
XXII. Skilled Workers							
134. Carpenter	–	–	–	–	–	–	–
135. Stone Cutter	–	–	–	–	–	–	–
136. Black Smith	–	–	–	–	–	–	–
137. Gold Smith	–	–	–	–	–	–	–
138. Gem Cutter	–	–	–	–	–	–	–
139. Glass Cutter	–	–	–	–	–	–	–
140. Potter	–	–	–	–	–	–	–
XXIII. Social Scientist							
141. Economist	–	–	–	–	–	–	–
142. Sociologist	–	–	–	–	–	–	–
143. Psychologist	–	–	–	–	–	–	–
144. Geographer	–	–	–	–	–	–	–
XXIV. Sportsman/Athelete							
146. Sportsmen	–	–	–	–	–	–	–
147. Sports Coach	–	–	–	–	–	–	–
148. Referee	–	–	–	–	–	–	–
XXV. Teaching							
149. Teacher at College level	–	–	–	–	–	–	–
150. Middle School Teacher	–	–	–	–	–	–	–
151. Nursery Teacher	–	–	–	–	–	–	–
152. Special Education (like Handicapped Schools)	–	–	–	–	–	–	–
153. Educational Officers	–	–	–	–	–	–	–
154. School Inspector	–	–	–	–	–	–	–
XXVI. Telephone Telegraph Operator							
155. Radio/Telephone Operator	–	–	–	–	–	–	–
156. Ship Radio Operator	–	–	–	–	–	–	–
157. Flight Radio Operator	–	–	–	–	–	–	–
XXVII. Textile and Leather Workers							
158. Spinners	–	–	–	–	–	–	–
159. Weaver	–	–	–	–	–	–	–
160. Dyer	–	–	–	–	–	–	–
161. Tanner	–	–	–	–	–	–	–
162. Tailor	–	–	–	–	–	–	–

(Contd.)

	Dislike very much						Like very much
163. Shoe maker	–	–	–	–	–	–	–
XXVIII. Technicians							
164. Surveyor	–	–	–	–	–	–	–
165. Draughtsman	–	–	–	–	–	–	–
166. Factory Foremen	–	–	–	–	–	–	–
167. Laboratory Technician	–	–	–	–	–	–	–
168. Medical Assistant	–	–	–	–	–	–	–
169. Nurse	–	–	–	–	–	–	–
170. Physiotherapist	–	–	–	–	–	–	–
XXIX. Transport Service Supervisors							
171. Railway Service Supervisor	–	–	–	–	–	–	–
172. Road Transprt Service Supervisor	–	–	–	–	–	–	–
173. Postal Service Supervisor	–	–	–	–	–	–	–
XXX. Transport Service Workers							
174. Passenger Train Guard	–	–	–	–	–	–	–
175. Engine Driver/Conductor	–	–	–	–	–	–	–
176. Porter	–	–	–	–	–	–	–

B

23B (1)

Title of the Instrument : **Educational Aspiration Scale (EAS) Form (P).**

Authors : V.P. Sharma and Anuradha Gupta.

Availability: National Psychological Corporation, 4/230, Kacheri Ghat, Agra-282004.

Language : Hindi.

Uses : Measures the Educational Aspiration of pupils of different grades of the educational cadder. It has a wide application in the measurement of level of aspiration, regardless of their grade of age.

Level : Secondary School Pupils and for universal use.

Main Features : It has wide application. It can widely be used over other samples by interpreting the raw scores obtained in terms of levels of educational aspirations. It has been developed on the rationale that : i. past experience, ii. Amount of efforts (Ae) made in the examination, iii. Ability and capacity.

By resolving these primary variables into different factors which could be effective in the past, present, and future, 45 items designed in a paired comparision form have been developed. These items have been refined several times from the point of view of the phraselogy, structure and presentation.

Reliability : Coefficient of stability by Test-retest method was rtt = 0.98.

Coefficient of Internal Consistency by Odd-Even technique using S-B Formula ....rtt = 0.803.

Validity : (a) Against Scholastic Achievement (Board Exam) r = 0.596.

Norms : Percentile norms available.

Time limit : No time limit but it takes around 20 minutes.

References :

a. Grewal, J.S. : *Manual for Occupational Aspiration Scale,* National Psychological Corporation, 1975.

b. Gardner, J.W. : The Use of term Level of Aspiration, *Psychological Review*, 47, 59-68, 1940.

c. Haller, A.O. and Miller, I.W. *Occupational Aspiration Scale : Theory, Structure and Correlates*, Deptt. of Rural Sociology, University of Wisconsin, Madison, 1967.

d. Haller, A.O. *Occupational Aspiration Scale*, East Lansing Michigan State University, 1957.

e. Hunt, J. Mc. V. (Ed.) *Personality and Behaviour Disorders*, New York, Vol.I., 1944, 333-378.

f. Shah, M.A. and Bhargava, M. : *Level of Aspiration Test*, Agra, National Psychological Corporation, Agra 1971.

23B (2)

Title of the Instrument : **Educational Aspiration Scale (EAS) Form (V).**

Authors :V.P. Sharma and Anuradha Gupta.

Availability : National Psychological Corporation, 4/230, Kacheri Ghat, Agra-282004. (India.)

Uses : Measures the educational aspiration of pupils in different grades of the educational cadre.

Level : College youth.

Main Features : This test has been designed on the concept and technique of Haller and Miller (1963). It has been designed on the strength of the list of degrees, diplomas, certificates, etc. The list figures 300 educational status of different levels. 275 different qualifications written separately, in the test material. Levels of expressions-realistic (R), And Idealistic (I). Goal periods are Long Range (L) and Short Range (S).

Reliability : (a) Coefficient of Stability test-retest method rtt= 0.798.

(b) Coefficient of Internal consistency by Split half technique using SB formula : (a) :. Between R and I items = rtt =0.671. (b) Between S and L Items = rtt = 0.817.

Validity : (1) The EAS has been validated against Scholastic Attainment : r = 0.758.

(2) It has also been validated against the judges opinion (n=15)

(3) Coefficient of Predictive Validity as judged on EAS, Form P, r = 0.542.

Norms : Percentile Norms for males as well as females are available in the manual.

Time Limit : No time limit is fixed, but it usually takes around 25 minutes for the test to complete.

References :

1. Grewal, J.S. : *Manual for Occupational Aspiration Scale*, National Psychological Corporation, 1975.
2. Cardner, J.W. The Use of term Level of Aspiration, *Psychological Review*, 47, 57, 68, 1940.
3. Haller, A.O. and Miller, I.W. : *Occupational Aspiration Scale : Theory. Structure and Correlates*, Deptt. of Rural Sociology, University of Wiscosin, Madison, 1967.
4. Haller, A.O.: *Occupation Aspiration Scale*, East Lansing, Michigan State University, 1957.
5. Hunt, J. Mc : V. (ed) *Personality and Behaviour Disorder*, New York, Vol.I, 1944, p. 333-378.
6. Shah, M.A and Bhargava, M. : *Level of Aspiration Measure*. National Psychological Corporation, Agra, 1971, 1987.

23B (3)

Title of the Instrument : **Sodhi and Bhatnagar Interest Inventory (SBII) for Girls.**

Authors : T.S. Sodhi and H. Bhatnagar.

Availability : National Psychological Corporation, 4/230, Kacheri Ghat, Agra-4.

Languages : Hindi and English.

Uses : To find out the interests that is the vocational interests of girls of India. Also used by many students of M.Ed and M. Phil.degrees for the conduct of their reseatch problems. Measures the fields of interests in the girls.

Level : Adolescent girls.

Main Features : The inventory consists of 136 items both in English and Hindi languages simultaneously. The inventory is divided into 11 interest areas and the items are divided amongst them.

Reliability : (A). Test-Retest Method : Coefficients of Correlation for the 11 interest areas ranged from 0.592 to 0.866 and were significant at 0.01 level of confidance.

(B) Split Half Method : Reliability Coefficients of correlation was renging from 0.792 to 0.894 and were significant at 0.01 levels.

Validity : Content and Criterion related validity as well as validity of Interest inventory by Teacher Ratings, Construct Validity. Biserial coefficients of correlation ranged from 0.448 to 0.656 and significant at 0.01 levels. Coefficient of Correlation between the scores on similar areas of present interest inventory and Chatterjee's Non language preference record range from 0.337 to 0.513. All are significant at 0.01 levels.

Norms : Regional Norms (Percentile Rank Norms available. Rural as well as urban students norms also available.

Time Limit : No time limit is fixed, but it takes around half an hour to take this test.

23B (4)

Title of the Instrument : **Science Interest Test (SIT).**

Authors : L.N. Dubey and Archana Dubey.

Availability : Ankur Psychological Agency, 222/481, Indira Nagar, Lucknow-16.

Language: Hindi.

Uses : Used in Educational and Voctional guidance. It enables the Teacher to know the level of interest in the subject of Science in the child. The higher interest in the subject is positively correlated with higher achievment. To know the interest in Science Subject in order to guide the student to offer science as one of the optional subjects for higher studies. This test will enable the guidance worker to know the cause of low achievement in Science subject. This test will be useful to the teachers in teaching science effectively.

Level : School Children.

Main Features : There are in all 64 statements in the test. 32 statements show a liking for the science subject, while 32 statements indicate disliking. The responses are given in 'Yes' and 'No' respectively.

Reliability : (1) Coefficient of Stability by Test-retest Method with an interval of 6 months : 0.68.

2. Coefficient of Internal Consistency by Split Half Method: 0.71.

Validity : 1. The test scores were validated against achievement scores in Science r=0.63.

2. It has been validated with teacher's rating r = 0.51.

Time limit : It takes 20 minutes to take this test.

Norms : Percentile norms available.

23B (5)

Title of the Instrument : **Political Interest Scale.**

Authors : Suresh Kumar Singh and B.B. Pandey.

Availability : National Psychological Corporation, 4/230, Kacheri Ghat, Agra-280004.

Language : Hindi

Uses : To know the political interest in the students so that they may be made aware of their interests.

Level : Under graduate Students.

Main Features : 38 items concerning political interests is given. Items showing significant t-ratio were retained in the final form of the test. The item analysis was done on the basis of responses of 25 per cent high scoring and low scoring 25 individuals of the sample.

Reliability : Test-retest reliability was found to be 0.84. Split Half reliability was = 0.78.

Validity : Validity was determined on the basis of opinion of experts.

Norms : The percentile norms are established for boys and girls students.

Time Limit : There is no fixed time limit for this test, but it takes around 20-30 minutes.

References : 1. Adelson, J. and Neil, R. : (1966) The Development of Political thoutht in adolescence. A sense of community. *Journal of Personality and Social Psychology,* 295-3080.

2. Appadorai (1971) : *Political Ideas in Modern India Impact of the West.*
3. Garret, H. E. (1971) : *Statistics in Psychology and Education*, New York, David Mekay Comp. 1966. Indian reprint.
4. Guilford, J.P. (1965) : *General Psychology.*
5. Pareek, U. (Ed.) : *Indian Psychological Abstracts* No. 1, Vol. 15, Bombay, Somiya Publication (1972 to 1978).
6. Saxena, A.K. (1980) : Construction and Standardization of a Hostility Scale, *Indian Psychological Review,* 19, (4) 8-16.
7. Singh, S.K. (1987) : *A Study of Political Interest of Students of Eastern U.P. in relation to their Socio-Economic status and Personality Traits.* Ph.D Thesis in Education Gorakhpur University.

23B (6)

Title of the Instrument : **Palsane & Sharma Study Habits Inventory (PSSHI).**

Authors : M.N. Palsane and Sadhana Sharma.

Availability : National Psychological Corporation, 4/230, Kacheri Ghat, Agra-280 004. (U.P.) (1989).

Language : Hindi

Uses : (i). When students want to know about their study habits they can use this inventory to find out whether they should make any improvements and if so in what direction. (ii). This inventory can be used by the teachers and counsellors for giving proper guidance to the students in the optimum use of their valuable time and energy. (iii). Parents can also use this inventory to guide their children.

Level : Students from school or college levels.

Main Features : The Study Habits of the individual are covered and the items are distributed among the 8 areas. The study habits of the individual cover mainly the reading habits, learning techniques, memory, time-schedule, physical conditions, examination, evaluation, etc. The eight areas are as follows:

1. Budgeting Time, 2. Physical Conditions for Study, 3. Reading Ability, 4. Note Taking, 5. Factors in Learning Motivation, 6. Memory, 7. Taking Examinations, (a) Preparation for examination, (b) Use of Examination Results, 8. Health.

Reliability : 1. Test-retest mothod = 0.88 with an interval of 4 weeks, sample of 200 male students of undergraduate classes. 2. The reliability coefficient was found to be 0.67 with an interval of three months on a sample of 60 girls.

3. Split Half technique, Sample Size = 150 boys of intermediate and undergraduate classes, the coefficients of correlation was found to be 0.56 between odd and even items.

Validity :

	Name of the other tests	N	Validity coefficients
1.	Study habit Inventory	80	0.69.
2.	Test of study Habits and attitudes	80	0.67.
3.	Study Habit Inventory	80	0.74.
4.	Study Involvement	80.	0.83.

Norms : Norms obtained on both the sexes.

Time Limit : No time limit. It takes around 20-25 minutes.

References :

1. Ahuja, G.C. and Ahuja, Pramila (1989) : *Manual for Reading Comprehension Test*. Agra, National Psychological Corporation.
2. Bhargava, V.P. (1984) : *Manual for Achievement Motive Test* (AMT). Agra, National Psychological Corporation.
3. Batnagar, Asha (1982) : *Manual for Study Involvement Inventory* (SII). Agra National Psychological Corporation.
4. Deo, Pratibha and Mohan, Asha (1986) : *Manual for Deo-Mohan Projective Test of Achivement Motivation*, Agra, National Psychological Corporation.
5. Mathur, C.P. (1974) : *Manual for Test of Study Habits and Attitudes*, Dehradun, ISPT.
6. Morgan, C.T. and James Deese (1957) : *How to Study*. New York, Mcgraw Hill.

7. Mukhopadhyay, M. and Sansanwal, D. N. (1983) : *Manual for Study Habit Inventory*, Agra, National Psychological Corporation.
8. Palsane, M.N. (1963) : *A Guide to Study Habits*, Baroda, Good Companions.
9. Palsane, M.N. (1977) : *Manual for Study Habits Inventory*. (Marathi Version.) Pune, Anand Agencies.
10. Petitt, Lincoln (1960) : *How to Study and Take Examination*, Rider Publications.
11. Preston, R.C. and Morton, Botel (1956) : *How to Study*, Chicago, Science Research Associates.
12. Shah, M.A.and Bhargava, M. (1987) : *Manual for Level of Aspiration Measure*. Agra, National Psychological Corporation.
13. Writesston, J.W. (1956) : *How to be Better Student*. Chicago, Science Research Associates.

23B (7)

Title of the Instrument : **Study Habit Inventory.**

Authors : M. Mukhopadhyay and D.N. Sansanwal.

Availability : National Psychological Corporation, 4/230, Kacheri Ghat, Agra-282004 (U.P.) (1983).

Language : English.

Uses : Used sucessfully in a few studies conducted on college students, polytechnic and Engineering college students.

Level : College Students.

Main Features : The Study habits have been considered to be constituted of nine different Kinds of Study behaviours. 52 statements or items are included with multiple choice answers.

Reliability : Split-Half method was used which gave coefficient of correlation = 0.91.

Norms : Given in the Manual.

Time Limit : No time limit.

References :

1. Abraham, M. *Some factors relating to under-achievement in English of Secondary School Pupils*, Ph. D. Thesis in Education, Karnataka University, 1974.
2. Beedawat, S.S., *A Study of academic under-*

achievement among students, Ph.D. thesis in Education, Rajasthan University, 1976.

3. Bhaduri, A., *A Comparative study of certain psychological Characteristics of the over and the under-achievers in higher secondary schools*, D. Phil thesis in Psychology, Calcutta University, 1971.
4. Chhabra, N., *A Study of certain social, psychological variables relating to teachers morale at secondary and college levels,* Ph.D. thesis in Psychology, Meerut University, 1975.
5. Jain S.K., *Study habits and academic attainments in Uttar Pradesh Colleges*, Ph.D. thesis in Psychology, Agra University, 1967.
6. Jamuar, K.K., *Investigation of some psychological factors underlying the study habits of college students*, Ph.D. thesis in Education Patna University, 1961.
7. Lalithamma, K.N. *Some factors affecting achievement of secondary school pupils in Mathematics*, Ph.D. Thesis in Education, Kerala University, 1975.
8. Mukherjee, N., *Talent Search*, Deptt. of Applied Psychology, Bombay University, 1967.
9. Patel, A.D. *Development and tryout of auto-instructional progames for class VIII*, Ph. D. thesis in Education, Sardar Patel University, 1977.
10. Prakash Chandra, *A study of the problems of high school students in the Varanasi Educational Region of U.P. and their relative effect on achievement*. Ph. D. thesis in Education Gorakhpur University, 1975.
11. Sinha, J.N., *Construction of a study habits and attitude Q sort test*. Ph.D. Thesis in Psychology, Patna University, 1972.

23B (8)

Title of the Instrument : **Indian Classificatory System of Vocational Expression.**

Authors : S.S. Chadha, H.K. Nijhawan, and Dwarka Pershad.

Availability : National Psychological Corporation, 4/230, Kacheri Ghat,

Agra-282004.

Language : English.

Uses : Classifies the vocational expressions may be aspirations, Preferences, choices, etc. of high school students. Classifies the specific expressions of the students who intend to enter certain vocations, they have in mind and it is not merely a categorisation of broad vocational fields.

Level : High School Students.

Main Features : Two dimensional classificatory system is there : 1. Non-hierarchical based on common interest areas.

2. Hierarchical related to appropriate occupations which can be generated within a single interest area. 232 Occupational titles were distributed into10 interest areas.

Reliability : Table

Agreement on repeated testing after a gap of one month

Vocational Fields	Initial Expression (n)	Repeat Expression (n)	Percent age Agreement
Engineering	100	80	80
Medical 7 Health	27	23	85
Artistic	7	7	100
Sales	12	9	75
Others	10	7	70
N	156	126	80.7%
Occupational Level			
I	47	45	97.7
II	77	70	90.9
III	32	25	78.1
Total	156	140	89.7

Validity : Two different approaches were followed to test the validity of the newly developed occupational classificatory system. Firstly, by finding out the relationship between the Interest areas (as measured by Strong's Vocational Interest Blank and Vocational Expression as elicited on Vocational Aspiration Blank and Secondly, by testing the hypothesis mentioned earlier.

References :

1. Caplow, T. (1954) : *The Sociology of work Minneapolis* University of Mannesotta Press.
2. Chadha, S.S. (1977) : Challenges to career guidance

workers under 10+2+3 System of Education, *Haryana Reviews*, XI, 18-21.

3. Chadha, S.S. (1979) : A study of some psychological and social factors as related to vocational aspirations of rural and urban high school children, Ph. D. thesis, Punjab University, Chandigarh.
4. Chadha, S.S (1980) : Concept of Aspiration vis-a-vis Vocational Aspiration, *News letter*, Central Institute for Research and Training in Employment Service New Delhi, 15,3,1-6.

23B (9)

Title of the Instrument : **Educational Interest Record (EIR).**

Author : S.P. Kulshrestha.

Availability : National Interest Test play a very significant role in educational guidance. To help a student develop and accept an integral and adequate picture of himself and a clear undertaking of his problems and of his role in the world of education. Therefore, Guidance is needed at all stages of education, (from Nursery to College).

Level : Students from graduates and post-graduate levels.

Main Features : Contains 98 educational subjects and activities belonging to 7 different educational interest areas.

Reliability : Test-retest reliability coefficient is obtained which was = 0.76., with a time interval of 15 days.

Validity : Test scores were correlated with teacher's opinion and follow up study and r = 0.90 and 0.70 was calculated respectively. The coefficient of validity is found 0.78 when this record was validated with Labh Singh's Educational Interest Inventory.

Norms : Revised Norms provided.

Time : No fixed time limit, but it takes around 7-10 minutes to complete the whole test.

References :

1. Bhargava, Mahesh : *Modern Psychological Testing and Measurement* (1982). Agra.
2. Mehdi, Baqer : *Vocational and Educational Guidance.* NIE Series for Teachers.
3. Katiyar, P.C : *Values and Vocational Preferences.* Baroda; Society for Educational Research and

Development, 1982.
4. Kulshrestha, S.P. : *Interest Patterns of Boys at Agra* (1967) Manika.
5. Kulshrestha, S.P. : Values and Vocational Interest of Intermediate Students. M. Ed. Dissertation, Agra University. (1968).
6. Pandey, R.S. : *Our Adolescents and their Interest.* (1965), Agra.
7. Puhan : *Issues in Psychological Measurement*, Agra, National Psychological Corporation, 1982.
8. Singh, Labh : Interest Patterns of Adolesents, Ph. D. Thesis, (1969). Agra University.
9. Thurstone, L.L. : Manual of Thurstone's Interest Schedule. Survey of Interest tools (1978) : Report Published by ISPT Dehradun.

23B (10)

Title of the Instrument : **Vocational Interest Record (VIR).**

Author : S.P. Kulshrestha.

Availability : National Psychological Corporation, 4/230, Kacheri Ghat, Agra-4. (U.P.).

Language : Hindi.

Uses : Helps students to adjust themselves to the careers/Jobs/Vocations, by making wise choices. Measures vocational interests, to enable the pupils to select such subjects in schools which are according to their preferred vocations. Used also by the research workers guidance counsellors and psychologists and found suitable for delta and higher secondary students.

Levels : Delta and Higher secondary students as well as for the students of colleges and also for young adults out of school and colleges.

Main Features : Contains 200 vocations belonging to 10 different vocational interest areas. They are as follows : 1. Literary (L), 2. Scientific (SC), 3. Executive (E), 4. Commercial (C) 5. Constructive (Co.) 6. Artistic (A), 7. Agriculture (AG), 8. Persuasive (P), 9. Social (S), 10. Household (H). Thus, this test includes 10 Vocational areas. Each of these areas has twenty jobs/ vocations/assignments on the record, 10 in horizontal and 10 on vertical side.

Reliability : The Test-retest reliability coefficient is obtained 0.69 with a time interval of 15 days.

Validity : 1. Initially only highly valid items were selected from Thurstone's Interest Schedule, Strong's Vocational Interest Blank, Kuder's Preference Record Form C etc.

2. The scores on the record were correlated with parent's teacher's and friend's opinion about the interests of the pupils and coefficient of validity was found 0.81, 0.83 and 0.85 respectively.

3. The coefficient of validity is found 0.74 when this record is validated with Labh Singh's Vocational Interest Inventory.

4. The comparision of results also done with the results of follow up study of the students and the coefficients of correlation was found about 0.80 which is significant at 0.01 levels.

Norms : Revised Norms Provided.

Time Limit : No fixed time limit but it takes around 7 to 10 minutes to complete the whole test.

References :

1. Bhargava, Mahesh : *Modern Psychological Testing and Measurement* (1978) Agra.
2. Mehdi, Baqer : *Vocational and Educational Guidance,* NIE Series for Teachers.
3. Kulshrestha, S.P. : *Interest Patterns of Boys at Agra* (1967) Manika.
4. Pandey, R.S. : *Our Adolescents and their Interests.* (1965), Agra.
5. Thurstone, L.L. : *Manual of Thurstone's Interest Schedule.*
6. Survey of interest tools (1978): A Report Published by ISPT Dehradun.

23B (11)

Title of the Instrument : **Study Habits Inventory.**

Purpose : To Know and Improve study habits of higher secondary students.

Author : N.S. Yadav.

Languages : English and Hindi.

Availability : Manasayan, 32, Netaji Subhash Marg, Daryaganj, New Delhi-110002.

Uses : (i) As a Screening instrument (ii). As a diagnostic instrument (iii). As a teaching aid and (iv). As a research tool.

Levels : For higher secondary students from Class IX to Class XII.

Main Features : Statements to be marked on a three point scale. In all 150 statements covering five areas of Planning. Reading Notes taking, Revision and Examination on Habits.

Reliability : Split Half Reliability = 0.93.

Test-retest reliability = 0.89.

Validity : With Examination Marks = 0.59.

With Teacher's ratings =0.53.

Time required : 30 minutes.

Norms : Norms are available from Manasayan, 32, Netaji Subhash Marg, Daryaganj, New Delhi - 110002.

References : Developed while counselling students as well as an aid for better performance for school achievement of students.

Attitudes

A

24A (1)

Title of the Instrument : **Scientific Attitude Study (S A S).**

Purpose : To find out the scientific attitude possessed by a student.

Author : D.N. Dani, M.Sc., M. Ed., Ph,. D.

Language : Hindi and English.

Availability : Dr. D.N. Dani, Co-ordinator, Vidya Bhawan G.S. Teachers College, Udaipur - 313001.

Uses : It can be used for measuring scientific attitude of adolescent students (Single or Group.)

Levels : Secondary and Higher Secondary Students, Early middle and late adolescents, Residing in Village, Middle classtown and big city Boys and Girls.

Main Features : 1. Prepared on Likert technique. 2. It has three parts related to three domains of attitude i.e., cognitive, action, and affective, which generally the other instruments lack. 3. It has only 60 items based on situations related to home, school and society. 4. Techniques of tryout and item analysis were used for refining the test. 5. Norms are obtained on 1265 cases.

Reliability Data : Split Half Reliability =0.768.
Test Retest Reliability = 0.805.

Validity : It has good face validity, content validity and construct validity as seen from factory analysis.

Time : Time limit is between 10-15 minutes.

Norms : Percentile Norms, Standard scores, Normalized T scores and stanine Norms are available.

References : Dr. Dani, D.N. *Scientific Attitude and Cognitive Styles*. New Delhi, Northern Book Centre, 1989.

SCIENTIFIC ATTITUDE STUDY

The main objective of this questionnaire is to study the scientific attitude. It has been divided into three parts. Instructions and examples have been given to illustrate how the questions in each part are to be answered. Please read all the question carefully and answer them on a *separate answer sheet*, provided for this purpose. Write your name and other particulars in the appropriate blanks on the answersheet.

Please do not write anything on this sheet.

FIRST—PART

You have to express your opinion about each statement by putting a tick mark (✓) in the most appropriate column against the statement concerned. *It May be remembered that every person has his own way of thinking.* If you agree fully with a statement put a tick mark (✓) against the relevent statement number under the column entitled "fully agree." If you generally agree with a statement put a tick mark against the relevant statement number in the column entitled "agree". Similarly put tick marks against relevant statement numbers in the columns entitled "undecided", "disagree" and 'fully disagree" according to your opinion.

Example: Statement — 'To err is human'

Suppose you fully agree with this statements, hence a tick mark (✓) has been put in the column "Agree" against the serial number `Ex' on the answer sheet. Answer the following statements in the same way.

1. One should decide quickly instead of wasting time in worrying about the results.
2. We should associate ourselves only with those whose ideas are similar to our own.
3. It is better to give money to the poors rather than pay taxes to the Government.
4. There are some problems which can't be solved.
5. Student-life is a period of merry making. One should not worry much about one's dress.
6. It is not necessary for a student to discover the reasons of natural events.
7. After the solution of a problem has been found it is a waste of

time to seek another solution.

8. If luck favours a student can pass an examination in the first division without any hard work.
9. The whole day is spoiled if one meets a one eyed person early in the morning.
10. It is not beneficial to visit a holy place which is related to the religion other than our own.
11. It is a waste of time to see a magic show.
12. It is not right to doubt the facts published in books.
13. A broken mirror in a house causes family quarrels.
14. Hiccups indicate that some one remembering us.
15. Most of the ideas published in books and journals are meaningless.
16. One must give one's correct opinion to the teacher even if it is against the views of the teacher.
17. The problem of student-unrest can be solved.
18. Good children believe that whatever their parents say is completely true.
19. It is wise to hide the truth if it save one from the forthcoming danger.
20. A good student-leader is one who calls for a strike whenever the principal punishes a student.

SECOND—PART

Instructions :- Some situations have been mentioned below. How will you work under these situations ? The possible answers are 'Yes', 'No' and ' I can't say'. Please put a tick-mark (✓) in the appropriate column, against each question-number according to yout opinion.

Example :- **Question**-"If you are allotted the room No. 13 in a hostel or hotel, would you request the authorities to change the room?"

Suppose you want to answer this question in 'Yes', hence a tick mark (✓) has been put in the column under 'Yes against the question number 'Ex'. Please answer the rest of the questions similarly.

1. Do you have a tendency to ask questions when the teacher's statements are not clear to you?
2. The last date for submitting application for a job of higher studies is very close. If you wait till tomorrow your application may not reach in time. Would you like to take risk by mailing the application tomorrow which is the auspicious day?
3. In order to maintain the reputation of your school, do you try to

win a match by fair means or foul?

4. Having failed to solve a mathematical problem twice or thrice, do you still want to make more efforts to solve it ?
5. Do you understand the working system of a ball pen?
6. Do you have a tendency to revise a letter after you have written it?
7. Do you have a tendency to solve mathematical problems by using different methods?
8. If you drop a book or an exercise book just before an examination, do you lift it and bow your head to it in reverence ?
9. In order to maintain your prestige, do you stick to your statement even after discovering your error?
10. It there is an accident on the road, do you have a tendency to get away from the scene, quickly in order to avoid police inquiry and harrassment ?
11. You are very hungry. Just when the food has been served and you are ready to start, you remember that your hands are not washed. Do you have a tendency to get up to wash your hands?
12. Whenever a great man's birth-day is celebrated in your school do you want to know more about his life?
13. If you lose all the matches to a player of your status. Do you believe that the day was not auspicious for you?
14. In an important deciding match, you are out. But the umpire gives a wrong decision in your favour through inadvertence. Would you like to tell the correct situation to the umpire?
15. You have prepared a plan for the cleanliness of your colony, but other colony members do not cooperate. Would you give up the idea of your plan?
16. While describing incidents do you have a tendency to exaggerate things?
17. When the reports of events in newspapers and magazines are not clear to you, do you discuss them with your friends of teachers for clarification?
18. While cutting a piece of paper in two, do you take care that the edges are parallel?
19. During an educational tour, you have the option either to go for a boating or visit a museum. Would you prefer boating to the visit to the museum?
20. Do you want all the older and younger members of your family to accept your views?

THIRD—PART

Instructions : Consider the following questions or statements. You have to respond to each statement or question by putting a tickmark (✓) in the appropriate column against the serial number of the question concerned in the answer sheet. You have to choose one of the three answers, 'Yes' 'No' and 'l can't say'.

Example : "I hate the persons who never keep the time".

Suppose you want to answer this question in 'No'. Hence a tick mark (✓) has been put in the column under 'No' against the serial No. (Ex) in the third part of the answer sheet. Answer the questions given below in the same manner:

1. I like the persons who accept my views without question or discussion.
2. I like the persons who don't take quick decisions.
3. I get angry when all my suggestions are rejected by my friends.
4. I am afraid of magicians.
5. I like people who continue their efforts even after failling to achieve their objectives three or four times.
6. I like to be treated by a doctor for small-pox instead of worshipping Goddess Shitla for a cure.
7. I boil with anger when the other people do not accept their mistakes.
8. If your friend steals an article from an old periodical and gives it as his own to the school magazine, would you like to report this theft to your teacher?
9. I generally prefer the cinema to an exhibiton.
10. While participating in religious ceremonies. I like to examine the scientific basis behind them.
11. Are you annoyed when the teacher does not a once punish the boy against whom you have complained?
12. Whenever I am defeated in a game by a player I admire his game.
13. Would you like to complain against a very close friend of yours who has taken some beautiful pictures from a library book?
14. Would you appreciate the action of your headmaster of parents if they postpone taking decision on your suggestions ?
15. I am afraid of going into the hostel room where a student committed suicide some years ago.
16. I like Mohan because he never gives up but completes his assignment inspite of several failures.

17. I like to have up-to-date information about the various political events.
18. If someone asks where I am going immediately after I leave home for important business, I am very much annoyed with them.
19. Do you like the people who point out your mistakes ?
20. I am perturbed at the news of accidents to my close and dear friends and relatives.

24A (2)

Title of the Instrument : **Religious Attitude Scale for University Students (RASUS).**

Purpose : To measure the attitude of College University students towards religion.

Author : R. Krishnaraj and P.S. Balasubramanian.

Language : English.

Availability : Dr. R. Krishnaraj, Lecturer in Education, Alagappa University, Alagappa Nagar, Karaikudi.

Uses : May be used with College/University students to study their attitude towards religion.

Level : College/University students.

Main Features : Likert Type: 5 point scale, 34 items with anchoring points, strongly agree, agree, undecided, disagree, and strongly disagree.

Reliability : Test-Retest = 0.743; Internal consistency (KR) =0.867.

Validity : Concurrent Validity with Allport Vernon = 0.65.

Time Required : 30-40 minutes.

Norms : (are they available? If yes, from where — give sources.) : NIL.

Referencess : Nil.

RELIGIOUS ATTITUDE SCALE FOR UNIVERSITY STUDENTS (RASUS)

	Strongly Agree	Agree	Un-decided	Dis-agree	Strongly Disagree
1. Civilization has become possible only through religion.	SA	A	U	D	SD
2. Religion curbs all creative powers	SA	A	U	D	SD

(Contd.)

	Strongly Agree	Agree	Un-decided	Dis-agree	Strongly Disagree
3. Pious people prosper in the long run	SA	A	U	D	SD
4. No rational person will believe in the existence of God	SA	A	U	D	SD
5. Service to humanity is more laudable than service to God	SA	A	U	D	SD
6. The existence of God is a myth, not a reality	SA	A	U	D	SD
7. God is our ultimate Saviour	SA	A	U	D	SD
8. Religious books talk about unscientific, fictious things only	SA	A	U	D	SD
9. Religion makes people moral	SA	A	U	D	SD
10. Religion promotes man's inner discipline	SA	A	U	D	SD
11. The great religious teachers have shown us the best ways of life	SA	A	U	D	SD
12. Religion leads to self-realization	SA	A	U	D	SD
13. True wisdom lies in religion	SA	A	U	D	SD
14. There is no heaven or hell	SA	A	U	D	SD
15. The pure in heart shall see God	SA	A	U	D	SD
16. Religion breeds enmity among peoples	SA	A	U	D	SD
17. Religion helps to develop the optimistic spirit	SA	A	U	D	SD
18. The greatest contribution to literature has been by mean of religion	SA	A	U	D	SD
19. Religion has been responsible for meaningless rituals	SA	A	U	D	SD

(Contd.)

	Strongly Agree	Agree	Un-decided	Dis-agree	Strongly Disagree
20. Religion teaches one to love all in the world	SA	A	U	D	SD
21. Religion fails to explain the facts of nature	SA	A	U	D	SD
22. If one practizes the principles of one's religion, one is bound to find life worthliving	SA	A	U	D	SD
23. Religion makes people non-rational	SA	A	U	D	SD
24. Faith in God makes one fearless	SA	A	U	D	SD
25. Man's highest thoughts are his religious thoughts	SA	A	U	D	SD
26. Religion leads humanity to chaos	SA	A	U	D	SD
27. Money spent on religious Institutions is a public waste	SA	A	U	D	SD
28. Religion makes man the noblest of God's creation	SA	A	U	D	SD
29. Religion impedes social and economic development	SA	A	U	D	SD
30. Religion makes life miserable	SA	A	U	D	SD
31 Religion makes people fanatic	SA	A	U	D	SD
32. Religion explains that science cannot	SA	A	U	D	SD
33. Religious books have been written for eternity and are valid for ever	SA	A	U	D	SD
34. A man can be good without religion	SA	A	U	D	SD

Scoring :- Item Nos 1, 2, 7, 9, 10, 11, 12, 13, 15, 17, 18, 20, 22, 24, 25, 28, 32, 33, = scores from 5 to 1.

Item Nos 2, 4, 5, 6, 8, 14, 16, 19, 21, 23, 26, 27, 29, 30, 31, 34 = scores from 1 to 5.

Reliability: (i) Test-retest co-efficient 0.743

(ii) Internal consistency co-efficient 0.867.

Validity : (1) Content Validity

(2) Concurrent validity : RASUS scores with the religious values scale of all port, vernon Lindzey (1960) correlation coefficient is 0.65.

SEMANTIC DIFFERENTIAL SCALE (SEDIS) "RELIGION"

	Very much	Gener-ally	Neu-tral	Gene-rally	Very much	
1. Good	—	—	—	—	—	Bad
2. Impractical	—	—	—	—	—	Practical
3. Aggressive	—	—	—	—	—	Withdrawing
4. True	—	—	—	—	—	False
5. Confused	—	—	—	—	—	Harmonious
6. Pleasant	—	—	—	—	—	Unpleasant
7. Gentle	—	—	—	—	—	Severe
8. Difficult	—	—	—	—	—	Easy
9. Strong	—	—	—	—	—	Weak
10. Positive	—	—	—	—	—	Negative
11. Useless	—	—	—	—	—	Useful
12. Thoughtful	—	—	—	—	—	Thoughtless
13. Disreputable	—	—	—	—	—	Reputable
14. Passive	—	—	—	—	—	Active
15. Straight	—	—	—	—	—	Crooked
16. Erratic	—	—	—	—	—	Errorless
17. Graceful	—	—	—	—	—	Disgraceful
18. Violent	—	—	—	—	—	Non-violent
19. Rigid	—	—	—	—	—	Flexible
20. Unacceptable	—	—	—	—	—	Acceptable
21. Dividing	—	—	—	—	—	Unifying
22. Dark	—	—	—	—	—	Light
23. Simple	—	—	—	—	—	Complex
24. Meaningless	—	—	—	—	—	Meaningful
25. Optimistic	—	—	—	—	—	Pessimistic

Scoring Item Nos 1,4,6,7,9,10,12,15,17,23,25, = Scoring is 5 to 1

Item Nos : 2,3,5,8,11,13,14,16,18,19,20,21,22,24, = Scoring is 1 to 5.

Reliability : (i) test-retest correlation co-efficient 0.675

(ii) Internal consistency co-efficient 0.865

Validity : (1) Concurrent validity : Correlation between SEDIS Scores and RASUS scores.

The correlation coefficient is 0.74.

25A (3) **This scale (page no 245-259) should be read after page 282**

Title of the Instrument : **Structural Dimension Questionnaire (SDQ).**

Purpose : To identify the organisational structure of educational institutions.

Author(s) : R. Krishnaraj & P.S. Balasubramanian.

Language : English.

Availability : Dr. R. Krishnaraj, Lecturer in Education, Alagappa University, Alagappa Nagar, Karaikudi.

Uses: To find out the organisational structure of educational institutions.

Levels : Faculty Members in Colleges and University Departments.

Main Features : Consists of 6 subscales, specialisation, formalisation centralisation consultation, integration, and autonomy.

Reliability data : Test-retest reliability ranges from 0.675 to 0.765 for the various subscales and internal consistency co-efficient from 0.782 to 0.842.

Validity : Content validity is established.

Time limit : One hour.

Norms : Nil.

References : Nil.

STRUCTURAL DIMENSION QUESTIONNAIRE (SDQ)

(a) Socialization Scale

Some curricular, co-curricular and administrative activities are listed below. Please state the extent of involvement of staff in these activities. You may indicate the prevailing practice by a tick mark in the appropriate column against each activity. Columns 4 to 10 present the possible reasons for entrusting the activity to a few or a particular person. If more than one reason could be attributed for the practice, all such reasons may please be indicated in the respective columns by tick marks.

Areas of Specialization	All are involved	Only a few are involved	Only one person is involved	Basis of entrusting the work to a few or a particular individual: Service (seniority)	Special training	Special ability	Special linking for the job	Favoured by the supervisor	No specific reason	Please state any other
	1	2	3	4	5	6	7	8	9	10
I 1. Selecting students for admission to the course										
2 Planning the work load of teachers.										
3. Being in-charge of attendance										
II. 1. Time-Table Planning for the class										
2. Planning curriculum										
3. Undertaking Project works										
4. Organising examinations										

(Contd.)

	1	2	3	4	5	6	7	8	9	10
5. Question paper setting										
6. Valuing answer scripts										
III. Being in-charge of										
(a) N.C.C.										
(b) N.S.S.										
(c) National service league										
(d) Community progress										
(e) Sports Clubs like Leo Club, Rotract Club etc.										
(g) Department associations										
(h) Moral and religious instructions										

(Contd.)

	1	2	3	4	5	6	7	8	9	10
(i) Programmes of continuing (adult) edn.										
(j) Cultural progress										
(k) Exhibitions and other national and international events.										
IV. 1. Giving guidance and counselling to students										
2. Being in-charge of										
(i) College elections										
(ii) College canteen										
(iii) College co-opperative stores										

(Contd.)

	1	2	3	4	5	6	7	8	9	10
(iv) Student concession facilities and scholarships										
V. 1. Supervising										
(a) the work of subordinates										
(b) student study projects										
(c) gardening										
(d) Research and development (Extension) programme										
2. Planning for the in-service training for teachers										
3. Being in-charge of										
(a) Hostel administration										
(b) Magazines and journals										
(c) Framing college calendar										

(Contd.)

	1	2	3	4	5	6	7	8	9	10
(d) Purchasing of books										
(e) Purchasing of materials and equipments										
(f) Maintaining buildings										
(g) Looking after the equipments and materials										
4. Being in-charge of examinations.										

(b) Formalization Scale

Rules and Regulations are specifically framed regarding the general structure of the organisation or the practice of various activities in the college. Please indicate whether such rules and regulation exist regarding the various items listed and if existing in what form (conventional or in written form). If there are breaches from these conventional or written codes, please indicate how often these breaches in general were made in the past two years in the college/Depatment/ classroom.

Whether specific procedures, rules and regulation are laid down regarding	Not Existing	If existing		Any breaches from laid down procedures rules and regulations if so, how frequent they are			
		conventional	in writing	Often	At times	rarely	never
I. 1. Organisational structure (hierarchy in the positions held by the staff)							
2. Aims and objectives of the institution							
3. Policies of the institution							
II. 1. Prescription of work load to teachers							
2. Approval for educational decisions made by the teacher in classroom teaching							
3. Notification of principal-staff meetings.							
4. Welfare measures for teachers							
5. Welfare measures for students							
6. Assignment of additional (extra curricular) responsibilities to teachers.							
7. Publication of journals and magazines							
8. Inspection of the institution.							
9. Professional assistance to teachers when needed.							
II. 1. Guidelines for teachers while planning curriculum							
2. Planning for new courses of study							
3. Planning for change in the existing course							

(Contd.)

Whether specific procedures, rules and regulation are laid down regarding	Not Existing	If existing		Any breaches from laid down procedures rules and regulations if so, how frequent they are			
		Conventional	in writing	Often	At times	rarely	never
IV. Student admission to							
1. College							
2. Hostel							
V. 1. The student elections							
2. Code of ethics for teachers							
3. Students Discipline							
4. Conduct of Students							
(a) Inside the class room							
(b) Outside the class room							
VI. 1. For the intimation of							
(i) Class tests							
(ii) Terminal examinations							
(iii) Final examinations							
2. For the methods of valuation							
3. Question Paper setting							
4. Revaluation							
5. Announcement of results							

(c&d) CENTRALIZATION AND CONSULTATION SCALES

In administration in classroom management, decisions are taken often. In the following cases please indicate *who is the most junior person* on whose decision action is normally taken and the most junior person who will be consulted in the decision-making process.

Please indicate your response by putting a tick mark (✓) in the relevant column against the person concerned.

S.No.	Activities	The junior person whose decision comes into force	The junior person who will be consulted
1.	Selection of students		
	(a) Above principal	(a)	a)
	(b) Principal	(b)	(b)
	(c) Head of the Dept.	(c)	(c)
	(d) Teacher	(d)	(d)
2.	Deciding syllabus for a subject		
	(a) Above Principal	(a)	(a)
	(b) Principal	(a)	(b)
	(c) Head of the Dept.	(c)	(c)
	(d) Teacher	(d)	(d)
	(e) Students	(e)	(e)
3.	Departmental activities for the year	(a)	(a)
	(a) Above Principal	(a)	(a)
	(b) Principal	(b)	(b)
	(c) Head of the Dept	(c)	(c)
	(d) Teacher	(d)	(d)
	(e) Students	(e)	(e)
4.	Appointment of a teacher		
	(a) Above Principal	(a)	(a)
	(b) Principal	(b)	(b)
	(c) Head of the Dept.	(c)	(c)
	(d) Other teachers	(d)	(d)
5.	Appointment of non-teaching staff		
	(a) Above Principal	(a)	(a)
	(b) Principal	(b)	(b)
	(c) Head of the Dept.	(c)	(c)
	(d) Teachers	(d)	(d)
	(e) Administrative Officer	(e)	(e)

(Contd.)

S.No.	Activities	The junior person whose decision comes into force	The junior person who will be consulted
6.	Promotion of Teacher		
	(a) Above Principal	(a)	(a)
	(b) Principal	(b)	(b)
	(c) Head of the Dept.	(c)	(c)
	(d) Other Teachers.	(d)	(d)
7.	Promotion of Non-teaching Staff.		
	(a) Above Principal	(a)	(a)
	(b) Principal	(b)	(b)
	(c) Head of the Dept.	(c)	(c)
	(d) Teachers	(d)	(d)
	(e) Administrative Officers (if there are)	(e)	(e)
8.	Spending of unbudgeted or unallocated money on capital items		
	(a) Above Principal	(a)	(a)
	(b) Principal	(b)	(b)
	(c) Head of the Dept.	(c)	(c)
	(d) Teacher	(d)	(d)
9.	To alter the responsibilities and areas of work of teachers		
	(a) Above Principal	(a)	(b)
	(b) Principal	(b)	(b)
	(c) Head of the Dept.	(c)	(c)
	(d) Teacher	(d)	(d)
10.	To decide dismissal of a teacher		
	(a) Above Principal	(a)	(a)
	(b) Prinipal	(b)	(b)
	(c) Head of the Dept.	(c)	(c)
	(d) Teacher	(d)	(d)
11.	To decide the dismissal of a non-teaching staff		
	(a) Above Principal	(a)	(a)
	(b) Principal	(b)	(b)
	(c) Head of the Dept.	(c)	(c)
	(d) Teacher	(d)	(d)
	(e) Administrative Officer	(e)	(e)

(Contd.)

S.No.	Activities	The junior person whose decision comes into force	The junior person who will be consulted
12.	To decide the dismissal of a student		
	(a) Above Principal	(a)	(a)
	(b) Principal	(b)	(b)
	(c) Head of the Dept.	(c)	(c)
	(d) Teachers	(d)	(d)
	(e) Other students	(e)	(e)
13.	Planning the curriculum		
	(a) Above Principal	(a)	(a)
	(b) Principal	(b)	(b)
	(c) Head of the Dept.	(c)	(c)
	(d) Teacher	(d)	(d)
	(e) Students	(e)	(e)
14.	To re-open the institution		
	(a) Above Principal	(a)	(a)
	(b) Principal	(b)	(b)
	(c) Head of the Dept.	(c)	(c)
	(d) Teacher	(d)	(d)
	(e) Students	(e)	(e)
15.	Purchasing teaching aids. books, materials and equipments		
	(a) Above Principal	(a)	(a)
	(b) Principal	(b)	(b)
	(c) Head of the Dept.	(c)	(c)
	(d) Teacher	(d)	(d)
	(e) Students	(e)	(e)
16.	Representing the institution in national and regional meets (cultural, sports etc.)		
	(a) Above Principal	(a)	(a)
	(b) Principal	(b)	(b)
	(c) Head of the Dept.	(c)	(c)
	(d) Teacher	(d)	(d)
	(e) Students	(e)	(e)
17.	Introducing new innovations		
	(a) Above Principal	(a)	(a)
	(b) Principal	(b)	(b)

(Contd.)

S.No.	Activities	The junior person whose decision comes into force	The junior person who will be consulted
	(c) Head of the Dept.	(c)	(c)
	(d) Teacher	(d)	(d)
	(e) Students	(e)	(e)
18.	Providing Welfare Measures for teachers and students		
	(a) Above Principal	(a)	(a)
	(b) Principal	(b)	(b)
	(c) Head of the Dept.	(c)	(c)
	(d) Teacher	(d)	(d)
19.	Deciding the selection of teachers for in-service training and faculty improvement programme		
	(a) Above Principal	(a)	(a)
	(b) Principal	(b)	(b)
	(c) Head of the Dept.	(c)	(c)
	(d) Teacher	(d)	(d)
20.	Deciding the closure of institution in times of emergency		
	(a) Above Principal	(a)	(a)
	(b) Principal	(b)	(b)
	(c) Head of the Dept.	(c)	(c)
	(d) Teacher	(d)	(d)
	(e) Students	(e)	(e)
21.	To institute a commission of enquiry on a teacher		
	(a) Above Principal	(a)	(a)
	(b) Princial	(b)	(b)
	(c) Head of the Dept	(c)	(c)
	(d) Other Teachers	(d)	(d)
22.	Deciding the institution of a new department		
	(a) Above Principal	(a)	(a)
	(b) Principal	(b)	(b)
	(c) Head of the Dept.	(c)	(c)
	(d) Teachers	(d)	(d)

(Contd.)

S.No.	Activities	The junior person whose decision comes into force	The junior person who will be consulted
23.	Deciding Celebration of National and International functions		
	(a) Above Principal	(a)	(a)
	(b) Principal	(b)	(b)
	(c) Head of the Dept.	(c)	(c)
	(d) Teacher	(d)	(d)
	(e) Students	(e)	(e)
24.	Deciding to hold elections to various bodies of college council		
	(a) Above Principal	(a)	(a)
	(b) Principal	(b)	(b)
	(c) Head of the Dept.	(c)	(c)
	(d) Teacher	(d)	(d)
	(e) Students	(e)	(e)

(e) INTEGRATION SCALE

Often we help others and get help from others also. Departments co-operate with each other in administrative, curricular and co-courricular activities.

Of the two alternatives given select any one which best describes the conditions existing in your department. Remember, there is no right or wrong answer.

1. Co-ordinating with other departments in relation to General administration Yes/No
2. Seeking help of other department for admission and selection purpose Yes/No
3. Consulting other departments while Planning the curiculum Yes/No
4. Consulting other department while Planning time-table for whole academic year Yes/No
5. Utilising teaching aids, materials and equipments of other departments Yes/No
6. Seeking help of other departments when evaluation of students is done Yes/No
7. Lending support to other departments when seminar, symposium and other departmental functions are organised Yes/No

8. Utilising classrooms of other departments Yes/No
9. Jointly working with other departments in times of crises Yes/No
10. Allowing department library for the use of staff and students of other departments Yes/No
11. Seeking the help of other departments while organising community and other social services Yes/No

(f) AUTONOMY SCALE

The following statements describe the relationships of your Department with others in the college and outside. State to what extent the statements describe the conditions existing in your Department. Remember there is no right or wrong answer.

	Definitely true	Mostly true	Neutral	Mostly false	Definitely false
1. The Department works independently of other departments					
2. The activities of the Dept. are not influenced by the college.					
3. People outside the Dept. decide on what work the Dept. is to do.					
4. The Dept. follows the examples set by similar Depts. in other Colleges/University.					
5. The Dept. cannot plan its activities without help from outside.					
6. The things the Dept. does are approved by the higher authorities in the college administration.					
7. The Dept. does not join with other Depts. in carrying out its activities.					

(Contd.)

	Definitely true	Mostly true	Neutral	Mostly false	Definitely false
8. The Dept. is a small part of the institution.					
9. The Department is under outside pressure.					
10. Members are not disciplined by outside groups.					
11. The Dept. is kept under constant vigil by higher authorities above the Dept.					

DIMENSIONS OF SPECIALIZATION SCALE

I. Classroom
II. Curriculum
III. Co-curriculum
IV. Student Welfare
V. Administration

DIMENSIONS OF FORMALIZATION SCALE

I. Administrative Structure
II. Activities
III. Curriculum
IV. Student Admission
V. Discipline
VI. Examinations

RELIABILITY OF SDO

S.No.	Scales	Test-retest co-efficient	Internal consistency co-efficient (Ferguson, 1976)
1.	Specialization	0.744	0.842
2.	Formalization	0.752	0.824
3.	Centralization	0.756	0.835
4.	Consultation	0.765	0.826
5.	Integration	0.694	0.796
6.	Autonomy	0.675	0.782

B

24B (1)

Title of the Instrument : **Teacher Attitude Inventory.**

Author : S.P. Ahluwalia.

Availability : National Psychological Corporation, 4/230, Kacheri Ghat, Agra-4. (U.P.).

Languages : Hindi and English.

Uses : To measure the teacher's attitude towards his/her profession and towards their respective class students.

Level : Prospective teachers, students of B.Ed. or school and college teachers.

Main Features : 90 item Likert instrument consisting of six sub-scales. These sub-scales were developed by the Likert summated ratings procedure. Each scale has 15 statements that pertain to a particular aspect of prospective and practicing teachers Professional attitudes.

Reliability : Split Half (odd-even) method was found to be 0.79 (Correlated to 0.88) for a sample of 239 prospective teachers. The test-retest method reliability coefficients after the interval of three months and nine months, are found to be 0.59, (N = 102), and 64 (N= 290.)

Validity : The inventory appears to have content validity. The validity was also determined through stimulus group technique.

For Determining the concurrent validity the scores on TAI were compared with the scores on the MTAI developed by Dr. M.C. Joshi. The obtained correlation coefficients for prospective teacher (n = 79) came out to be positive but low.

Norms : Norms have been computed State-wise and area-wise for the five Hindi speaking States. State-wise, and sex-wise percentile norms have been computed.

Time Limit : No time limit has been fixed for this test.

References :

1. Adaval, S.B. "Teacher Education" in *National Council of Educational Research Third Indian Year-book* (New Delhi : NCERT 1963).
2. Allport, C.W. "Attitudes" in Martin Fishbe in (ed.) *Readings in Attitude Theory and Measurement* (New York : Wiley, 1967).
3. Bernbaum, G. *Social Change and the Schools*

1916-1944 (London : Routledge and Kegan Paul. 1967)

4. Brim, B.J. "Attitude Changes in Teacher Education Students", *Journal of Educational Research*, 59 : 441-45 (1966).
5. Buch, M.B. "The Measurement of Attitudes of Secondary School Teachers Towards the Teaching Profession", *Journal of Educ. and Psychology*. 1959, 17 (3).
6. Butts, David P. and Raun, Chester B., *A Study in Teacher Attitude Change* (Austin University of Texas Research and Development Centre for Teacher Education, 1973).
7. Change in Teacher-pupil Attitudes related to training and experience *Educational and Psychological Measurement,* 1950, 10, 718-727.
8. Campbell, D.E., "Dimensional Attitude Changes of Student Teachers" *JER 1967*, 61,4, 160-162.

24B (2)

Title of the Instrument : **Teacher Attitude Scale (TAS).**

Author : J.C. Goyal.

Availability : National Psychological Corporation, 4/230, Kacheri Ghat, Agra-4 (U.P.)

Languages : English.

Uses : This test measures the attitude of teachers towards the profession of teaching, taking into consideration various components of the profession and also measures attitude of secondary, elementary and pre-primary level teachers, attitudes of student teachers, measures change in attitudes of students teachers during the training. Compares attitudes of different categories of teachers, types of teachers, and teachers working in different types of schools and student teachers under training in different types of teacher training institutions.

Level : School Teachers.

Main Features : Consists of 22 items. It has been developed by Thurstone technique of attitude scale construction. It measures attitude towards the profession of teaching. First of all the investigator collected statements of opinion, about the teaching

Profession from teachers on the basis of their teaching experience. Table showing Scale and Q-values of favourable and unfavorable statements were given.

Reliability : Reliability of the scale was determined by the Split-half method. It was found to be 0.90 by the Pearson Product-Moment Correlation Method. When corrected by Spearman-Brown Formula, its coefficient of correlation was 0.95.

Validity : Content Validity of the scale was ensured by the judges who carefully rated each item. The validity of the scale was also determined by self-rating by subjects on a graphic continuum of the scale. It was found to be 0.78.

Norms : On the basis of the data collected from 300 teachers the means and standard deviations of different groups of subjects were calculated and Norms established.

Time Limit : No time limit was fixed for this test.

References :

1. Ahluwalia, S.P. *Teacher Attitude Inventory*, TAI, Agra, National Psychological Corporation, 1978.
2. Allport, G.W. "Attitudes" in Martin Fishbein (Ed.) *Readings in Attitude Theory and Measurement*. New York : John Wiley and Sons Inc. 1967.
3. Bhogle, S. "Attitudes Towards Teaching Profession", in U. Pareek and T.V. Rao. *Handbook of Psychological and Social Instruments*, Ahmedabad: Samashti, 1974.
4. Buch, M.B. "The Measurement of Attitudes of Secondary School Teachers Towards the Teaching Profession." *Journal of Education and Psychology*, 1959 17 (3).
5. Buch, M.B. (Ed) *Second Survey of Research in Education*. Baroda : Society for Educational Research and Development, 1979.
6. Cook, W.W.; Leeds, C.H. and Callis, R. *Minnesota Teacher Attitude Inventory*, New York : Psychological Corporation. 1951.
7. Dawes R.M. *Fundamentals of Attitude Measurement,* New York : John Wiley and Sons, Inc. 1972.
8. Edwards, A.L. *Techniques of Attitude Scale Construction*. Bombay Vakils, Feffer and Simons. 1969.

9. Goyal, J.C. "A Study of the Relationship among Attitudes, Job Satisfaction, Adjustment and Professional Interests of Teacher Educators in India. Ph.D. Thesis , Delhi University, 1980.
10. Himmelfarb, S. and Eagly, A.H. *Reading in Attitude Change*, New York: John Wiley and Sons, Inc. 1974.
11. Naidu, V.R. : "Teachers Attitude Towards Teaching Profession". *Indian Journal of Applied Psychology*, 1975, 12 (1).
12. Thurstone, L.L. and Chave, E.J.: *The Measurement of Attitude*, Chicago University Press, 1929.
13. Travers, R.M.W.: *Second Handbook of Research in Teaching*, Chicago, Rand McNally Publishing Co. 1973.
14. Samantroy, G.K. : A Study of teacher attitude and its relationship with teaching efficiency. Ph.D. Thesis, 1970.

24B (3)

Title of the Instrument : **Attitude Scale Towards Education (ASTE.)**

Author : S.L. Chopra.

Availability : National Psychological Corporation, 4/230, Kacheri Ghat, Agra-4

Language : Hindi.

Uses : To measure relationship of attitude towards education and academic achievement.

Level : Teachers and teacher trainees.

Main Features : The inventory has 22 items which are to be responded in 'Yes' or 'No'. The statements have been arranged in a random order and suitable instructions have been provided for administration of the scale. The subjects are to indicate their agreement or disagreement with each of the statements.

Reliability : The reliability coefficient reported between the two forms of the scale gave 0.93. Split Half method gave the 'r' correlated by the Spearman Brown method was 0.89.

Norms : Given.

References :

1. Ahluwalia, S.P. : *Manual for Teacher Attitude Inventory*. Agra, National Psychological Corporation, 1978.

2. Baker, D.G. : Attitude towards Guidance. *Guidance and Personnel Journal*, 1966.
3. Bird, C. : *Social Psychology*. New York : Appleton Century Crofts, 1940.
4. Edwards, L. and Kenney, K.C. : A Comparison of the Thurstone and Likert Techniques of Attitude Scale Construction. *J. Appli . Psy.*, 1946, 30, 72-83.

24B (4)

Title of the Instrument : **Attitude Tests (Cartoon Form).**

Purpose : To measure Attitudes Toward Teachers, Learning Process, Mathematics and Language Arts.

Authors : Kiran Gupta and Badaron Nisha Khan.

Language : Hindi.

Availability : Indian Psychological Corporation, Shanti Sadan, Ras Behari Lal Road, Lucknow.

Uses : This test taking behaviour is considered to be a particular advantage in obtaining valid data on pupils with negative attitude.

Level : Secondary level (Class 9 to 12).

Main Features : There are four tests for measuring attitudes towards Teachers, Learning Process, Mathematics and Language Arts. In each test there are 15 items including 7 cartoon and 8 non-cartoon items. In these scales items are in type of four points rating scale, which has two positive and two negative points and do not allow a neutral or mid point response.

Reliability : The Split half-Reliability for each tests and total (60 items) was estimated on a sample of 200 students. The following table shows the reliability coefficients of four attitude instruments and over all test reliability.

Odd-Even Correlation Coefficients

Tests	r
Teachers	0.80.
Learning Process	0.82.
Mathematics	0.79.
Language Arts	0.80.
Total (60 Items)	0.86.

24B (5)

Title of the Instrument : **Vocational Attitude Maturity Scale (V.A.M.S.).**
Authors : Manju Mehta.
Availability : National Psychological Corporation, 4/230, Kacheri Ghat, Agra-282004. (India).
Language : Hindi.
Uses : This test assesses the rate and level of individual's development with respect to career matters, so that help may be given to facilitate vocational maturity of the students who have less vocational maturity. Also useful for XI grade students who are facing problems in making crucial decisions regarding their field of further students.
Level : Students.
Main Features : The test has 20 items in questionnaire format, which are to be answered in 'Yes' or 'No' responses.
Reliability : Kuder-Richardson Formula-20 was applied and the reliability coefficient was found to be 0.89. Internal Consistency estimates were in the 0.70's. The average being 0.74 for Grade VI through XII which are quite near to rtt of 0.89.
Validity : Tetrachoric correlations between the total scores on 20 selected items and the total scores on 100 items pool of preliminary draft was calculated, which was 0.875. Thus it can be said that 20 items scale is as good in discriminating vocationally mature subjects from vocationally immature subjects as 100 item scale and that the scale has construct validity. Factorial validity of the scale was also established by factor analysis of the data of 168 subjects on the 20 selected items was done using principal component analysis method.
Norms : Percentile Norms available.
Time Limit : No time limit should be given for the test. However, most of the students finish it within 10 minutes.
Validity : The validity coefficients, with English version of four Instruments were estimated on a sample of 200 Pupils of secondary classes. The following table shows the validity coefficients of four instruments :

Validity Coefficients

Tests	r
Teachers	0.49
Learning Process	0.51
Mathematics	0.54
Language Arts	0.48

Time Limit : No time limit for this test.

Norms : Percentile norms are available at : Indian Psychological Corporation, Shanti Sadan, Rae Behari Lal Road, Lucknow.

References : *Arlin-Hills Attitude Surveys,* Published by Psychologists & Educators Inc. Jacksonville, Illinois 62650. U.S.A.

24B (6)

Title of the Instrument : **A Scale for Measuring Attitudes Towards Educational Administration (ATEA)**

Author: T.R. Sharma.

Availability : National Psychological Corporation, 4/230, Kacheri Ghat, Agra-4.

Uses : It measures the teacher's attitude towards educational administration.

Main Features : Twenty Statements constituted the scale. Statements at Sr. No. 1,3,4,5,6,10,11,12,13, and 16 are indicating favourable attitudes and the statements at Sr. No. 2, 7, 8, 9, 14, 15, 17, 18, 19, and 20 are indicating non-favourable attitude. Five point scale given against each item.

Reliability : Likert (1967) while describing the method of constructing an attitude scale, has expressed that all statements should consist of expression of desired behaviour and not be statements of fact. Reliability of the scores on the scale was calculated by product-moment method by correlating the scores obtained on 5-point scale for favourable and unfavourable statements. Coefficient of reliability correlation thus calculated was 0.91.

Validity : The discrimination level ranged between 1.76 to 11.1 between two groups of teachers. The validity of the scale was determined by finding out the discrimination level; i.e. the higher scores and the lower scores. Calculation of the C.R. showed that they differed significantly to defend the validity of the scale.

Time Limit : No fixed time.

Norms : No norms available before hand.

References :

1. Bhardwaj, Hari Dutt (1957) : An Investigation into the Inspecting Procedure as visualised by Headmasters in Jullunder Distt. Pb. (unpublished.)
2. Bhatnagar, S.K. (1955) : *An Investigation into the Supervisory Services of Secondary Schools Delhi,* Publication No. 26 NIE, Delhi.

3. Crites, J.O. (1971) : The Maturity of Vocational Attitudes in Adolescence. A.P.G.A. Inquiry Series Number 2. American Personal and Guidance Association 1607 New Hampshire Avenue, N.W. Washington, D.C.
4. Earnest O. Melby (1955) : *Administering Community Education*, Englewood Cliffs, Prentice Hall Inc.
5. Edward, A.L. (1969) : *Techniques of Attitude Scale Construction*, Appleton Century Crofts, Inc.
6. Ghouri, G.M. (Y.N.M.) : An Investigation into the Attitude of Secondary School Teachers Towards the Prevailing Practices in Rajasthan, Rajasthan.
7. Garret.H.E. (1971) : *Statistics in Psychology and Education Vakils*, Feffer and Simons Private Ltd., Bombay.
8. Mehta, M. (1977) : Effect of Discordant and non-Discordant in Formation upon vocational maturity, unpublished Doctoral Dissertation, University of Rajasthan, Jaipur.

Institutional Characteristics

A

25A (1)

Title of the Instrument : **Administrative Practices Rating Scale**.

Purpose : To know the various administrative Practices in the universities.

Author : Virendra Singh.

Languages : English.

Availability : Dr. Virendra Singh, Assistant Professor, Vidya Bhawan Teachers College, Udaipur-313001 (Rajasthan).

Uses : To know the various administrative practices in the universities both in India and abroad.

Level : Persons working in the universities.

Main Features : There are 24 items. It is a five point scale. The areas are Amendments of Act; Relationship between universities and other bodies i.e. Government, UGC, IUB, etc., Relationship with international organisations; University Officials, and their functions; Election of members for different bodies: tenure of different bodies; Decision in the meeting of different bodies; Implementation of decisions; Selection and promotion, various facilities and benefits to members of staff; Admission of students, Students Union and Students Union and Student representation in various bodies.

Reliability and Validity of Data : This is not used.

Time Limit : No time limit.

Norms : There are norms and are available with the author.

References :

1. Singh Virendra : "The Student Bodies in the Universities", *Journal of Higher Education*, Vol. 8 No 2 Autumn, 1982.
2. Singh Virendra : "A Comparative Study of Administration of Selected Universities in India and Abroad:, Udaipur, University of Udaipur-1978 600p, *Bulletin*, Vol. XXX 1982 No. I International Association of Universities, Paris, Feb. 1982.

ADMINISTRATIVE PRACTICES RATING SCALE

Instructions to the Raters. Against each statement written below five alternative responses are given. Instead of reprinting each alternative response against each sub-item, two commas indicating dittos are given just below each of the five alternative responses printed at the top against each item. You are requested kindly to encircle the response or the dittos which best fits the University you are rating.

		In no case	In a few cases	Generally	In most cases	In all cases
(i)	The amendments in the act or statutes of your University are made,	"	"	"	"	"
(a)	Due to political pressure.	"	"	"	"	"
(b)	Because a group of influential persons want it	"	"	"	"	"
(c)	Because the officials of the University desire it.	"	"	"	"	"
(d)	As and when there is a need of the situation.	"	"	"	"	"
(e)	(any other)	"	"	"	"	"

		Not at all influenced	Influenced a little	Influenced generally	Much Influenced	Very much influenced
(ii)	The Government influences the administration of your University					
(a)	in the appointment of teachers and other officials.	"	"	"	"	"
(b)	in the admission of the students,	"	"	"	"	"
(c)	in the framing of courses.	"	"	"	"	"
(d)	in matters of finance i.e. grants-in-aids.	"	"	"	"	"
(e)	in the formulation of policy or plans.	"	"	"	"	"
(f)	(any other).	"	"	"	"	"
(iii)	Your University is influenced by various bodies like U.G.C., I.U.B., etc.	"	"	"	"	"
(a)	because it gets financial help from them	"	"	"	"	"
(b)	in the ex-change of teachers.	"	"	"	"	"
(c)	in the field of maintenance of standard.	"	"	"	"	"

(Contd.)

		Not at all influenced	Influenced a little	Influenced generally	Much Influenced	Very much influenced
(d)	in the recognition of degrees and diplomas	"	"	"	"	"
(e)	(any other)	"	"	"	"	"
(iv)	Your University is influenced by the International organisations,					
(a)	because it gets financial Assistance from	"	"	"	"	"
(b)	in the maintenance of standard.	"	"	"	"	"
(c)	in the recognition of degrees and diplomas.	"	"	"	"	"
(d)	in the field of exchange of ideas.	"	"	"	"	"
(e)	(any other)	"	"	"	"	"

		Never	Occasionally	Normally	Mostly	Always
(v)	Are all the appointment of officials in your University made,					
(a)	due to political pressure ?	"	"	"	"	"
(b)	on the basis of academic record of merit?	"	"	"	"	"
(c)	due to official pressures?	"	"	"	"	"
(d)	on the basis of seniority?	"	"	"	"	"
(e)	(any other factor)	"	"	"	"	"
(vi)	The officials of your University, in administrative matters					
(a)	follow the rules and regulations.	"	"	"	"	"
(b)	are influenced by political pressure.	"	"	"	"	"
(c)	are influenced by the opinion of the junior.	"	"	"	"	"
(d)	are influenced by the opinions of the high officials.	"	"	"	"	"
(e)	use their own judgement?	"	"	"	"	"
(f)	(any other)	"	"	"	"	"
(vii)	The officials of your University in financial matters,					
(a)	follow the rules and regulations.	"	"	"	"	"
(b)	are influenced by political pressure.	"	"	"	"	"
(c)	keep in view the opinion of juniors officials.	"	"	"	"	"
(d)	are influenced by the opinion of the high officials.	"	"	"	"	"
(e)	use their own judgment.	"	"	"	"	"
(f)	(any other)	"	"	"	"	"

(Contd.)

	Never	Occasionally	Normally	Mostly	Always
(viii) The officials of your University in academic matters,					
(a) perform their work according to the rules and regulations.	”	”	”	”	”
(b) are influenced by political pressure.	”	”	”	”	”
(c) are influenced by the opinion of junior officials	”	”	”	”	”
(d) are influenced by the opinion of high officials.	”	”	”	”	”
(e) use their own individual judgment.	”	”	”	”	”
(f) deviate from the rules due to academic reasons.	”	”	”	”	”
(g) (any other)	”	”	”	”	”

	Not at all influenced	Influenced a little	Influenced generally	Much Influenced	Very much influenced
(ix) In dealing with the community the officials,					
(a) are influenced by political pressure.	”	”	”	”	”
(b) are influenced by the opinion of the junior officials.	”	”	”	”	”
(c) are influenced by the opinion the higher officials.	”	”	”	”	”
(d) use their own judgment.					
(e) (any other)	”	”	”	”	”
(x) The relationship of the officials with the bodies like U.G.C., I.U.B. etc.					
(a) is influenced by political pressure.	”	”	”	”	”
(b) is influenced by the opinion of the junior officials.	”	”	”	”	”
(c) is influenced by the opinion of the higher officials.	”	”	”	”	”
(d) is a matter of personal judgement.	”	”	”	”	”
(e) any other factor	”	”	”	”	”
(xi) The relationship of the officials with the Government					
(a) is influenced by political pressure.	”	”	”	”	”
(b) is influenced by the opinion of junior officials.	”	”	”	”	”
(c) is influenced by the opinion of higher officials.	”	”	”	”	”
(d) is a matter of personal judgement.	”	”	”	”	”

(Contd.)

		Not at all influenced	Influenced a little	Influenced generally	Much Influenced	Very much influenced
(e)	(any other factor)	”	”	”	”	”
(xii)	The relationship of the officials with the other University,					
(a)	is influenced by political pressure.	”	”	”	”	”
(b)	is influenced by the opinion of junior officials.	”	”	”	”	”
(c)	is influenced by the opinion of higher officials.	”	”	”	”	”
(d)	is a matter of personal judgement.	”	”	”	”	”
(e)	(any other factor)	”	”	”	”	”

		Never	Occasionally	Normally	Mostly	Always
(xiii)	(a) the officials supervise the work of their juniors personally.	”	”	”	”	”
(b)	the supervision is based on the report of the juniors	”	”	”	”	”
(c)	a separate body does the supervision work.	”	”	”	”	”
(d)	(any other method of supervision).	”	”	”	”	”
(xiv)	The election of the members for different bodies of the University.					
(a)	is politically motivated.	”	”	”	”	”
(b)	is contested on the basis of different group interests.	”	”	”	”	”
(c)	is based on the seniority.	”	”	”	”	”
(d)	is contested by the candidates backed by the authorities.	”	”	”	”	”
(e)	is held strictly in accordance with the rules and regulations.	”	”	”	”	”
(f)	(any other factor)	”	”	”	”	”
(xv)	The tenure of different bodies is,					
(a)	as laid down in the statutes and the act.	”	”	”	”	”
(b)	extended or shortened on political consideration.	”	”	”	”	”
(c)	extended or shortened on the basis of decision taken by the body concerned.	”	”	”	”	”
(d)	extended or shortened because officials want it.	”	”	”	”	”
(e)	extended or shortened due to unavoidable situations	”	”	”	”	”
(f)	(any other factor)	”	”	”	”	”

(Contd.)

	Never	Occas-ionally	Normally	Mostly	Always
(xvi) The decisions in the meetings of the different bodies of your University are					
(a) dictated by the chair.	"	"	"	"	"
(b) are made by a majority vote.	"	"	"	"	"
(c) are taken on political grounds.	"	"	"	"	"
(d) are influenced by the interest of a praticular group	"	"	"	"	"
(e) are taken in accordance with the rules and regulations	"	"	"	"	"
(f) (any other factor)	"	"	"		
(xvii) The implementation of the decisions taken by different bodies of your university is,					
(a) delayed by the authorities.	"	"	"	"	"
(b) put of till they are again considered by the bodies	"	"	"	"	"
(c) based on political consideration.	"	"	"	"	"
(d) not cared by the authorities.	"	"	"	"	"
(e) (any other factor)	"	"	"	"	"
(xviii) The selection of the staff (Teaching & non-teaching) of your University is made on the basis of,					
(a) the academic record of the candidates.	"	"	"	"	"
(b) the seniority.	"	"	"	"	"
(c) the performance at the interview.	"	"	"	"	"
(d) the political push.	"	"	"	"	"
(e) (any other factor)	"	"	"	"	"
(xix) The promotion of the staff (teaching and non-teaching) of your University goes by					
(a) seniority.	"	"	"		"
(b) performance at the interview.	"	"	"	"	"
(c) confidential reports and past record.	"	"	"	"	"
(d) Political pressure.	"	"	"	"	"
(e) (any other factor)	"	"	"	"	"

	In no case	In a few cases	Gener-ally	In most cases	In all cases
(xx) The various facilities are given to a Member of the staff (teaching & non-teaching) of your University.					
(a) by virtue of the post he holds.	"	"	"	"	"
(b) due to favours shown by higher authorities.	"	"	"	"	"

(Contd.)

	In no case	In a few cases	Generally	In most cases	In all cases
(c) due to political backings.	"	"	"	"	"
(d) due to the influence he commands.	"	"	"	"	"
(e) (any other factor).	"	"	"	"	"
(xxi) The benefits are given to the staff of your University.					
(a) in accordance with their rules and regulations.	"	"	"	"	"
(b) by virtue of the post held.	"	"	"	"	"
(c) favours shown by authorities.	"	"	"	"	"
(d) because the person concerned is influential.	"	"	"	"	"
(e) due to political push.	"	"	"	"	"
(f) (any other factor)	"	"	"	"	"
(xxii) The admission of the students to the various course in your University is based on.					
(a) the academic record.	"	"	"	"	"
(b) the performance in the admission test.	"	"	"	"	"
(c) the performance in the interview.	"	"	"	"	"
(d) the political backing	"	"	"	"	"
(e) the reservation of seats.	"	"	"	"	"
(f) (any other factor)	"	"	"	"	"
(xxiii) The students get seat in the students Union of your University.					
(a) due to the political backings.	"	"	"	"	"
(b) because an influential students' group is backing them.	"	"	"	"	"
(c) on merit.	"	"	"	"	"
(d) on the basis of the amount of money spent by the student.	"	"	"	"	"
(e) (any other factor)	"	"	"	"	"
(xxiv) The students are given representation in various bodies of the University.					
(a) in accordance with the rules and regulation.	"	"	"	"	"
(b) due to the political backings.	"	"	"	"	"
(c) students backing.	"	"	"	"	"
(d) on merit.	"	"	"	"	"
(e) whenever the students demand.	"	"	"	"	"
(f) (any other factor)	"	"	"	"	"
(g) no representation is given.	"	"	"	"	"

Signature
Dean Designation
Washburn University of Topka University
School of Law.

25A (2)

Title of the Instrument: **Classroom Climate Scale.**

Purpose : To Measure student's perceptions of the psychological processes going on in the classroom.

Author : Shefali Pandya.

Language : English.

Availability : With the author.

Uses : To describe the classroom climate in secondary schools.

Levels : High School Students.

Main Features : The scale comprises of three dimensions :

1. Relationship Dimension.
2. Personal Development Dimension.
3. System maintenance Dimension. These dimensions have been adopted from the study of classroom Environment by Moos and Tricket. But the items have been constructed by the author.

There are 30 items to measure each dimension. In all the Classroom climate Scale consists of 90 items. It is a four-point Likert-type scale. The four points are : always, frequently, sometimes, never. Items worded positively are scored as : Always-4 ; Frequently-3; Sometimes - 2 ; Never-1. Items worded negatively are scored in the reverse order. The scoring is done in such a manner that higher the score, better is the climate. The scale has some positively worded and some negatively worded items.

Reliability : Reliability of the scale was established by Split-half and test-retest methods. The following are the reliability coefficients:

		Split-Half Cor. Coeff.	Test-retest Cor.Coeff.
1.	Classroom Climate	0.83	0.85
2.	Relationship Dimension	0.82	0.83
3.	Personal Development Dimension	0.80	0.84
4.	System Maintenance Dimension	0.84	0.85

The internal consistency reliability has been established by calculating Dimension total correlations which are as follows:

	Dimension	'r'
1.	Relationship Dimension	0.57
2.	Personal Development Dimension	0.51
3.	System Maintenance	0.49

Validity : The content validity was established by obtaining opinions of experts in the field of education on the items. The discrimination index for each item was calculated. Those items whose discrimination index was more than 0.20 were retained.

Time Limit : 25 to 30 minutes.

Norms : Norms are available with the author.

References :

1. Baxter, B. : *Teacher-Pupil Relationships*. The Macmillan Co. Ltd., New York, 1961.
2. Blair, G. M.; Jones, R.S. and Simpson, R.H.: *Educational Psychology*. The Macmillan Co. Ltd., New York, 1966.
3. Fraser, B.J. *Classroom Environment*, Croom Helm Ltd., U.S.A.,1986.
4. Good, C.V. *Dictionary on Education*, McGraw-Hill Book Co. Ltd., 1959.
5. Good, T.L. and Brophy, J.E. *Psychological Concepts in the Classroom*. Harper and Row, New York, 1974.
6. Laycock, S.R. and Munro, B.C. *Educational Psychology,* Unwin Brothers Ltd., Great Britain, 1972.
7. Skinner, C.E. : Educational Psychology. Prentice Hall Inc. New Delhi, 1968.

CLASSROOM CLIMATE SCALE

Instructions : The form has 20 statements. Please read each statement carefully and then indicate your opinion on each statement by putting (✓) in the space provided beside it. Please put (✓) in only one column for each statement. You can give your opinion according to the following scale: Always, Frequently, Sometimes, Never.

Kindly answer the questions regarding teachers keeping in mind your classteacher.

Thanking you,

Yours sincerely,

Shefali Pandya

		A	F	S	N
1 (i)	My class participates enthusiastically in class activities.				
2 (a)	There is unity in my class.				
3 (ts)	Our teacher gives a chance to each student of my class to talk to him/her.				
4 (ta)	We spend more time discussing activities not connected with the lesson being taught.				
5.(c)	Only the clever students are given importance in my class.				
6 (in)	Our teacher just reads from the book while teaching a lesson in the class.				
7. (o)	Our class is very noisy.				
8. (r)	Each student in my class knows what the rules are.				
9. (tc)	Our teacher insists that rules should be followed.				
10.(i)	Students of my class are disinterested in taking part in the discussions in the class.				
11. (ts)	Our teacher takes personal interest in the students.				
12. (a)	When any student talks in the class, the others are busy doing their own work				
13.(ta)	Getting a certain amount of work done within a given period is insisted upon in my class.				
14.(c)	Leaders in my class are selected according to their abilities rather than their rank in the exams.				
15.(in)	our suggestions on new ways of learning are unwelcome by our teacher.				
.16.	We remain quiet even in the absence of our teacher.				
17.(r)	The rules in my class keep on changing.				
18. (tc)	Our teacher is unable to control our class.				

A F S N

19.(c) if a student in my class wins a prize, others try to show that it is of no value.

20.(o) There are fixed rules which we have to follow in our class.

21. (tc) our teacher listens to us before she gives us punishment.

22. (r) When a new rule is made, it is explained to us why it is made.

23.(in) our teacher uses different teaching aids like charts, models, etc. while teaching a lesson.

24.(c) Students of my class take part in interclass competitions.

25. (ta) Students do very little work in our class.

26.(i) Students of my class go on looking at their watch during a lesson.

27. (a) There are some students in my class with whom nobody talks

28.(ts) I like the behaviour of my teacher.

29.(i) The students of my class show interest in new activities performed in the class.

30.(ts) Our teach discourages us to ask questions in the class.

31. (a) I feel that my class is like a prison.

32 (ta) Our teacher encourages us to read other books relating to the topic and discuss them.

33 (tc) Our teacher has to keep on shouting to make the students quiet.

34 (c) Those who get good results in my class are praised by all.

35.(o) Good discipline is maintained in my class.

36(in) Students of my class show a lack of interest in new method of learning.

37 (r) Teacher's favourite students do not get any punishment for breaking a rule.

A F S N

38 (tc) The moment our teacher enters the class, everybody is quiet.
39 (ta) We are aware of what is taught in the class.
40 (r) Students in my class get punishment without any cause.
41 (c) Students of my class would do anything to get good results in the exams.
42 (o) The discussions in my class end up in confusion.
43 (in) The students of my class give good suggestions for planning the classroom activities in a new way.
44 (rc) Students of my class know that they will be punished if they break a rule.
45 (i) Students of my class enjoy our classroom activities so much that they dislike to remain absent in the school.
46 (ts) our teacher avoids discussing personal information regarding any student with others.
47 (a) Students of my class are happy when one of us is in trouble.
48.(tc) Our teacher loses his/her temper without any reason.
49.(i) It is easy to get a group together for a project in my class.
50.(a) We avoid discussing our classmates faults in the presence of people who do not belong to our class.
51 (ts) Our teacher shows a lack of appreciation for the good work done by us.
52 (c) Competitions help us to gain more knowledge.
53 (ta) Our syllabus remains incomplete at the end of the year.
54 (o) The activities in my class are planned in advance.
55 (in) We find it difficult to understand a lesson if it is taught by a new method.

		A	F	S	N
56 (r)	When we are punished, we know what the punishment is for.				
57 (i)	The students of my class help each other.				
58 (a)	Some of my classmates are left alone during times of trouble.				
59 (ts)	Our teacher forgets the names of the students of my class.				
60 (ta)	Our teacher gives us information outside the textbook.				
61 (c)	Students of my class take defeat sportingly.				
62 (in)	Our teacher uses many method to teaching.				
63 (o)	Teachers of our class say that we are a well-behaved class.				
64 (r)	Innocent students get punished in my class.				
65.(tc)	Our teacher knows what the students in the last row are doing during a lesson.				
66. (i)	In taking decisions, all the students of my class participate.				
67 (ts)	Our teacher spends little time talking to us.				
68 (a)	The students of my class are friendly with each other.				
69 (c)	For different competitions, the same students are selected in my class.				
70 (ta)	Our teacher takes care to see whether all the students in the class have completed the work given to them.				
71.(o)	We are discouraged to question the decisions made by the teacher.				
72 (in)	Students of my class enjoy planning new ways of learning a lesson in the class.				
73 (tc)	We go on talking to each other even in the presence of our teacher.				
74 (r)	We are told clearly what rules we are expected to follows.				

A F S N

75 (c) Students of my class are disinterested in doing better than their classmates.

76 (in) Our teacher comes to the class well-prepared whenever new methods are used for teaching a lesson.

77.(a) Students of my class talk politely with each other.

78 (r) All the students in my class get the same punishment for breaking a rule.

79 (tc) Our teacher allows us to do anything in the class during a lesson so long as we remain quiet.

80 (ta) Plans of work or activities keep on changing in my class.

81 (ts) Our teacher is unfriendly with the students.

82 (a) my class is divided into two or three groups which keep on fighting with each other.

83.(i) In my class, students mix with each other well.

84 (tc) If a rule is broken, our teacher gives punishment quietly without getting angry.

85 (o) Students of my class fool around a lot during a lesson.

86 (ta) In our classroom, we work according to The time-table.

87.(ts) our teacher helps us to find out our belongings which are missing.

88 (a) Students in My class carry tales about other students.

89.(i) In my class students show a lack of interest in what the teacher teaches.

90 (in) Our teacher keeps on giving us the same kind of home work.

Positively worded items 1, 2, 3, 8, 9, 11, 13, 14, 16, 20, 21, 22, 23, 24, 28, 29, 32, 34, 35, 38, 39, 43, 44, 45, 46, 49, 50, 52, 54, 56, 57, 60, 61, 62, 63, 65, 66, 68, 70, 72, 74, 76, 77, 78, 83, 84, 86, 87.

Negatively worded items 4, 5, 6, 7, 10, 12, 15, 17, 18, 19, 25, 26, 27, 30, 31, 33, 36, 37, 40, 41, 42, 47, 48, 51, 53, 55, 58, 59, 64, 67, 69, 71, 73, 75, 79, 80, 81, 82, 85, 88, 89, 90.

Scoring key

	Always	frequently	Sometimes	Never
Positively worded items	4	3	2	1
Negatively worded items	1	2	3	4

B

25B (1)

Title of the Instrument : **School Environment Scale.**

Purpose : To Study the perception of the students regarding various areas of school Environment Disciplinary policy of the school, Discipline among students, Discipline among teachers, Teachers student relation, Inter student relations, Home and School relations, Social activities and their organisations in School, Students interest in social activities, Class-room climate, Teacher's teaching qualities, Academic atmosphere in the school, Student's interest in academic activities, Aesthetic and physical amenities.

Author: Ms. Sarla Jawa.

Languages : Hindi and English.

Availability : Dr. Ms. Sarla Jawa, Department of Psychology, Lady Sriram College for women, Lajpatnagar, New Delhi-110024, India.

Uses : To study the perception of the students regarding various areas of school environments.

Levels : 13 to 18 years of age.

Main Features : It is a self administered 4 points rating scale with 74 items standardized on 400 students.

Reliability : The Split Half reliability was found to be 0.95.

Validity : Validity indices of the different items found by calculating F ratio between responses of 27 per cent highest total scorers and 27 per cent lower total scorers. Construct Validity was computed by finding the correlation between the areas of school environment and total test scores, which was found to be ranging from 0.69 to 0.86.

Time Limit : About 30 minutes. (No time limit.)

Norms : Nil.

References : A Study of creativity and some of its personality and environmental correlates. Unpublished doctoral thesis, University of Delhi, 1975.

25B (2)

Title of the Instrument : **Academic Climate Description Questionnaire (ACDQ.)**

Author : M.L. Shah and Amita Shah.

Availability : Ankur Psychological Agency, 22/481, Indira Nagar, Lucknow-16.

Language : Hindi.

Uses : To measure academic climate of the school environment.

Level : Students of school level.

Main Features : There are 84 statements in the inventory. Each statement has three alternatives from which the subject can choose any one.

Reliability : Split-half method was used and value was found to be 0.85. Two test-retest reliabilities were determined one after an interval of three months and other of six months, and the values were found to be 0.78 & 0.73.

Validity : Content analysis and face validity found.

Norms : Percentile Norms were computed for both boys and girls separately.

References :

1. Anastasi, A.A.(1961) : *Psychological Testing*. New York : Mcmillan Co. pp. 430-32.
2. Austin, A.W. (1962) : An empirical characterization of higher educational Institutions. *Journal of Educational Psychology*, pp. 224-35.
3. Garret, H.E. (1962) : *Statistics in Psychology and Education*, Bombay : Allied Pacific Pvt. Ltd., pp. 336-67.
4. Goyal, R.P. (1980) : Creativity and School Climate: An Exploratory Study, *Journal of Psychological Researches*, 17 (2), 77-80 (IPA, 5 : 144).
5. Sharma, M. L. (1979) *Schools in Context*, Indian Publications, Ambala.

25B (3)

Title of the Instrument : **School Environment Measuring Scale.**

Purpose : To measure Adaptability to School Environment Among Adolescents.

Author : Dr. (Mrs). Sushma Talesara.

Language : Hindi.

Availability : Dr. Sushma Talesara, 172/12, Ashok Nagar, Udaipur-313001. Telephone : 26698.

Uses : The tool can be used by guidance workers and counsellors for diagnosing the adjustment problems of adolescent boys and girls in the school situations.

Levels : 12 to 18 age group.

Main Features : It is a situational test covering four dimensions viz. creative stimulation vs. suppression, cognitive encouragement vs. retribution, permissiveness vs. strict control and reward vs. punishment. Five situations have been included under each dimension and each situation is required to be tackled in one of the five different ways. Scoring is done as per five point scale.

Reliability Data: Test-retest reliability of the scale is 0.94 and Split-half reliability is 0.64.

Validity Data : Concurrent validity is 0.904 and instrinsic validity ranged between 0.54 and 0.73.

Time Limit : 25 Minutes.

Norms : Under preparation.

References : Doctoral Thesis, M.L. Sukhadia University, Udaipur - 1989.

24 B(7) This Scale should be read after page 267

Title of the Instrument : **Vocational Attitude Maturity Scale (V.A.M.S.).**

Author : Manju Mehta.

Availability : National Psychological Corporation, 4/230, Kacheri Ghat, Agra-282004.

Languages : English, Hindi.

Uses : To measure vocational attitude maturity of adolescents.

Main Features : Self administrable, 20 items scale based on Crite's attitude scale of the Vocational Development Inventory (VDI).

Reliability : Reliability Coefficient by Kuder-Richardson Formula 20 = 0.69.

Validity : Construct Validated: Tetracoric correlation between total scores on 100 items pool of preliminary draft and total scores on 20 items selected for final scale was 0.875.

Factor analysis using principle component method and rotation by Kaisar Varimax method extracted eight factors covering 60 per cent of the total variance. These factors were named as :

1. Vocational aspiration level.
2. Influence and money in job choice,
3. Altruism and Passivity in job choice,
4. Lack of job awareness and change in job preferences,
5. Indecisiveness in vocational choice,
6. Vocational understanding
7. Lack of independence
8. Chance factor in vocational choice.

Norms : Percentile norms available.

References :

1. Bajaj, S. (1989) :Effect of vocational maturity, Need for achievement and Psychological adjustment upon vocational indecision. Unpublished masters thesis, University of Rajasthan.
2. Srivastava, K. (1986) : Effect of intelligence and vocational attitude maturity upon vocational unrealism. Unpublished Master's thesis, University of Rajasthan.

THIRD HANDBOOK OF PSYCHOLOGICAL AND SOCIAL INSTRUMENTS

About the Author

Professor D.M. Pestonjee is presently the L&T Chair Professor of Organizational Behaviour at the Indian Institute of Management, Ahmedabad, India. He is a psychologist by training having obtained his M.A. in Psychology with a First Class First and Ph.D. in Industrial Psychology from the Aligarh Muslim University.

He has over three decades of teaching experience and has successfully supervised sixteen Ph.D candidates. He is author/co-author of nine books and over 100 research articles. Among his better known works are : *Second Handbook of Psychological and Social Instruments* (1988), and the celebrated *Stress and Coping — The Indian Experience* (1992).

Professor Pestonjee has been active as a trainer and consultant in non-business sectors like, education and health. He has been Temporary Advisor to WHO, USAID, OXFAM. He was also an Individual Category Elected member of the International Social Service Council of the UNESCO to represent Management Sciences for three terms, 1980-83; 1983-86; 1986-88. He was also a Member of the Executive Committee of the International Sociology Association 1986-90. He served as a Regional Representative of the International Association of Applied Psychology.

He has served on several national bodies like the Indian Council of Social Science Research, the All India Council for Technical Education, and the Indian Council of Medical Research.

His current areas of interest are executive stress, coping and issues related to executive health, job satisfaction and morale.

Concepts in Communication
Informatics & Librarianship-75
General Editor : **S.P. AGRAWAL**

THIRD HANDBOOK OF PSYCHOLOGICAL AND SOCIAL INSTRUMENTS

Volume Two

Edited and Compiled by

Prof. D.M. PESTONJEE
L&T Chair Professor of Organizational Behaviour & Chairman, OB Area
Indian Institute of Management, Ahmedabad

CONCEPT PUBLISHING COMPANY, NEW DELHI - 110059

ISBN 81-7022-652-X (Vol. 1)
ISBN 81-7022-653-8 (Vol. 2)
ISBN 81-7022-654-6 (Set)

First Published 1997
Reprinted 2003

Published and Printed by
Ashok Kumar Mittal
Concept Publishing Company
A/15-16, Commercial Block. Mohan Garden,
NEW DELHI-110059

Phones : 25351460, 25351794
Fax : 091-11-25357103
Email : publishing@conceptpub.com

General Editor's Introduction

Experimental psychologists have made valiant efforts to upgrade psychology to the level of exact sciences like physics, chemistry and biology. They have not been able till now to attain the desired goal. But they have achieved some success in this direction in the form of psychological testing which, by systematic use of tests, strives to quantify the psychological behaviour, abilities, and problems and to make predictions about psychological performance. Through the professionally developed tests we are now able to evaluate human abilities, aptitudes, educational achievements, skills, interests, attitudes, and the personality characteristics. As a matter of fact, the psychological testing accorded a respectability to psychology and revolutionized it by making it 'as a science objectively and quantitatively oriented, in contrast to the earlier orientation of more subjective and philosophical nature.' These psychological tests, which have been recognized as standardised instruments, have proved very much efficacious and have played important role in tackling the problems 'of the mentally retarded, of educating the slow-learning children, of classifying and training military personnel, of selecting and promoting personnel in industry and the government, and of helping maladjusted individuals adjust to the demands of life.'

The present publication, which is the third Handbook in the series of Handbooks on the instruments for measurement of behaviour and standardised in India, attempts to provide reliable and authentic information on the subject. It will prove a great boon to the researchers, teachers of psychology, education and sociology, pyschiatrist, guidance counsellors, personnel administrators and the serious students of psychology. The compilers of this Handbook (as also other two Handbooks brought out earlier) have made tremendous efforts to collect these instruments from various sources and obtain technical details about them from their authors. It is really a creditable job that most of the major instruments have been retrieved and made available to the users at one place.

The present Handbook comprises four parts, namely. Personality, Education, Organisational Behaviour, and Social Phenomena. Each part is divided into sections which include four categories of instruments: Instruments reproduced with information, instruments with technical information only, citations, and adaptations. Instruments dealing with personality dimensions are reported under five sections which are: (i) General, (ii) Adjustment and Problems, (iii) Anxiety, (iv) Self-Concept, and (v) Motivation. In all 95 instruments have been included in this part. Of these, 16 instruments have been reproduced here (14 of them are in the general category) and 15 are adaptations. Only technical information about the remaining 64 instruments has been provided in this part. The instruments pertaining to the second part of the different educational dimensions have also been categorised under five sections: (i) General Instruments, (ii) Student Problems and Adjustment, (iii) Interests and Preferences, (iv) Attitudes, and (v) Institutional Characteristics like climate, etc. In all, there are 64 instruments reported in this area of which 15 have been reproduced here. Technical information about other 47 instruments has been given in this part. The remaining two are adaptations. The instruments dealing with various dimensions of organizational behaviour have been reported under two sections: (i) Industrial Organizations, and (ii) Health Organizations. For instance, these instruments deal with job satisfaction, job motivation, organizational effectiveness, occupational and role stress, participation, role conflicts, and attitudes etc. There are in all 32 instruments listed under this part. Of these, 25 have been reproduced here. Only information has been provided for 6 instruments. The areas covered by the instruments reproduced here include managerial styles, interpersonal needs, motivational aspects in organizations, organizational effectiveness, job satisfaction, managerial behaviour, job anxiety, occupational and role stress, participation, performance rating, general personality of workers, and role conflict etc. The fourth and the last part reports instruments dealing with several social dimensions. These instruments have been categorised under six sections: (i) Values, (ii) Stratification, (iii) Social Distance and Group Attitudes, (iv) Modernization and Social Change, (v) Religion and Morality, and (vi) Other Social Attitudes. In all, 79 instruments have been reported in this part. 52 instruments have been originally reproduced here. Information has been provided for other 22 instruments. 3 are citations and 2 are adaptations.

S.P. AGRAWAL

PREFACE

There is a continual and felt need to have access to instruments for measurement of behaviour and social phenomena. It is precisely two decades now, since the First Handbook by Professors Udai Pareek and T. Venkateshwara Rao was published. This was followed in 1988 by the Second Handbook under the authorship of the present author. We are now presenting the Third Handbook of Psychological and Social Instruments.

In the present volumes, we have 270 entries. Of these, (A) 108 are complete instruments, (B) 140 are instruments with technical information only, (C) 03 citations, and (D) 19 are adaptations. Table is shown below :

Table: Break-Up of All the Instruments Included in the Handbook

Classification	Originals Reproduced	Only Information	Citations	Adaptations	Total
	A	B	C	D	
Personality	16	64	—	15	95
Education	15	47	—	02	64
Organisational Behaviour	25	07	—	—	32
Social Phenomena	52	22	03	02	79
Total	108	140	03	19	270

In preparing a Handbook of this nature, it is necessary to collect materials from various sources. Materials were sifted from back issues of various journals. A comprehensive questionnaire was sent to all Indian Universities (specially Heads/Deans of Faculty of Psychology and Education), Professors and teachers of Psychology, Education, and Sociology, and researchers in the field. In a majority of cases, three to four reminders were required. This delayed our efforts to put together the Handbook. However, we are thankful to all the scholars who provided their valuable materials.

On Using the Handbook

The classification system of the instruments is not based on theoretical distinctions, but it is a pragmatic one reflecting the number of instruments reported. The classification system of the instruments is the same as has been followed in the First Handbook (1974) and also in the Second Handbook of Psychological and Social Instruments (1988). The uniformity of the classification of instruments was maintained as the author wanted to make it easy for those people referring to the new edition, the easy accessibility of new instruments in their respective coding system, and also for those who are referring for the first time, this Handbook would be of extreme help to find out the latest instruments developed.

The coding is based on the following 3 tier classification :

Part indicates the field. The Handbook is divided into four parts:

1. Personality,
2. Education,
3. Organisational Behaviour, and
4. Social Phenomena.

Each Part is further divided into sections. The first numeral of the code number of the instrument indicates the *part* and the second numeral indicates the *section* under that part.

Under each Section, four categories of instruments are included:

A — Instruments reproduced with information,
B — Instruments with technical information only,
C — Citations, and
D — Adaptations.

The category is indicated by the letter codes mentioned above. In each category, the instruments are serially numbered. Thus, in numbering an instrument, the *Part* number occurs first, followed by the *Section* number, and Category (A, B, C, or D explained above) which is followed by serial number of the instrument. For example, 12A10 would indicate that the instrument is in Part 1, i.e., Personality, dealing with Adjustment (Section 2), is reproduced here with information (Category A) and has a serial number 10 in that category. Similarly, 31D2 indicates that the instrument is from Organisational Behaviour (Part 3), dealing with Industrial Organisation (Section 1), is an Indian adaptation (Category D) and has a serial number of 2 under that category.

Two indices are provided at the end of the *Handbook*, namely, instrument index and author index. These may be used by the reader for locating a desired instrument in the *Handbook*.

Preparing the Handbook is a patently time consuming activity which depends on cooperation of several academic collaborators. Thanks should be given to authors and publishers of several tests and instruments whose works are included here.

The project for preparing the Handbook was financed by a research grant from the Indian Council of Social Science Research (ICSSR). The ICSSR deserves the thanks of the whole Social Science community for encouraging and financing not only the present Handbook but also the earlier Handbooks.

The American Psychological Association (APA) has very graciously allowed me to incorporate the "Standards for Educational and Psychological Tests (1974)" in the present Handbook.

Lastly, I would like to thank Ms. Nina Muncherji for her help; I will also like to thank Ms.Havovi J Ginwala for her help in the project and also for having typed the whole Handbook having had to read literally several hundred types of handwritings.

Ahmedabad **D.M. PESTONJEE**

STANDARDS FOR EDUCATIONAL AND PSYCHOLOGICAL TESTS PROVIDED BY THE AMERICAN PSYCHOLOGICAL ASSOCIATION (APA)

Highlights

1. When a test is published or otherwise made available for operational use, it should be accompanied by a manual (or other published or readily available information) that makes every reasonable effort to follow the recommendations of these standards and, in particular the information required to substantiate any claims that have been made for its use.
2. A test manual should describe fully the development of the test: the rationale, specifications followed in writing items or selecting observations, and procedures and results of item analysis or other research.
3. The test and its manual should be revised at appropriate intervals. The time for revision has arrived whenever changing conditions of use or new research data make any statements in the manual incorrect or misleading.
4. The test, the manual, the record forms, and other accompanying material should help users make correct interpretations of the test results and should warn against common misusers.
5. The test manual should state explicitly the purposes and applications for which the test is recommended.
6. The test manual should describe clearly the psychological, educational, or other reasoning underlying the test and nature of the characteristic it is intended to measure.
7. The test manual should identify any special qualifications required to administer the test and to interpret it properly.
8. Evidence of validity and reliability, along with other relevant research data, should be presented in support of any claims being made.
9. Test developers or others offering computer services for test interpretation should provide a manual reporting the rationale and evidence in support of computer-based interpretation of scores.
10. The directions for administration should be presented in the test manual with sufficient clarity and emphasis so that the test user can duplicate the administrative conditions under which the norms and the data on reliability and validity were obtained.

11. Instructions should prepare the examinee for the examination : Sample material, practice use of answer sheets or punch cards, sample questions, etc., should be provided.
12. The procedures for scoring the test should be presented in the test manual with a maximum of detail and clarity to reduce the likelihood of scoring error.
13. Norms should be published in the test manual at the time of release of the test for operational use.
14. Norms presented in the test manual should refer to defined and clearly described populations. These populations should be the groups with whom users of the test will ordinarily wish to compare the persons tested.
15. In reporting norms, test manuals should use percentiles for one or more appropriate reference groups or standard scores for which the basis is clearly set forth; any exceptional type of score or unit should be explained and justified. Measures of central tendency and variability always should be reported.
16. Local norms are more important for many users of tests than are published norms. A test manual should suggest using local norms in such situations.
17. Derived scales used for reporting scores should be carefully described in the test manual to increase the likelihood of accurate interpretation of scores by both the test interpreter and the examinee.
18. If scales are revised, new forms added, or other changes made, the revised test manual should provide tables of equivalence between the new and the old forms. This provision is particularly important in cases where data are recorded on cumulative records.
19. Where it is expected that a test will be used to assess groups rather than individuals (i.e., for schools or programs), normative data based on group summary statistics should be provided.
20. A manual or research report should present the evidence of validity for each type of inference for which use of the test is recommended. If validity for some suggested interpretation has not been investigated, that fact should be made clear.
21. A test user is responsible for marshalling the evidence in support of his claims of validity and reliability. The use of test scores in decision rules should be supported by evidence.
22. All measures of criteria should be described completely and accurately. The manual or research report should comment on the adequacy of a criterion. Whenever feasible, it should draw attention to significant aspects of performance that the criterion measure does not reflect and to irrelevant factors likely to affect it.

23. A criterion measure should itself be studied for evidence of validity and that evidence should be presented in the manual or report.
24. The manual or research report should provide information on the appropriateness of or limits to the generalizability of validity information.
25. The sample employed in a validity study and the conditions under which testing is done should be consistent with recommended test use and should be described sufficiently for the reader to judge its pertinence to his situation.
26. The collection of data for a validity study should follow procedures consistent with the purposes of the study.
27. Any statistical analysis of criterion-related validity should be reported in the manual in a form that enables the reader to determine how much confidence is to be placed in judgments or predictions regarding the individual.
28. A test user should investigate the possibility of bias in tests or in test items. Whenever possible, there should be an investigation of possible differences in criterion-related validity for ethnic, sex, or other subsamples that can be identified when the test is given. The manual or research report should give the results for each subsample separately or report that no differences were found.
29. When a scoring key, the selection of items, or the weighting of tests is based on one sample, the manual should report validity coefficients based on data obtained from one or more independent cross-validation samples. Validity statements should not be based on the original sample.
30. To the extent feasible, a test user who intends to continue employing a test over a long period of time should develop procedures for gathering data for continued research.
31. If test performances is to be interpreted as a representative sample of performance in a universe of situations, the test manual should give a clear definition of the universe represented and describe the procedures followed in the sampling from it.
32. If the author proposes to interpret scores on a test as measuring a theoretical variable (ability, trait, or attitude), his proposed interpretation should be distinguished from interpretations arising on the basis of other theories.
33. The test manual or research report should present evidence of reliability, including estimates of the standard error of measurement, that permits the reader to judge whether scores are sufficiently dependable for the intended uses of the test. If any of the necessary evidence has not been collected, the absence of such information should be noted.
34. The procedures and samples used to determines reliability coefficients

or standard errors of measurement should be described sufficiently to permit a user to judge the applicability of the data reported to the individuals or groups with which he is concerned.

35. Reports of reliability studies should ordinarily be expressed in the test manual in terms of variances of error components, standard errors of measurement, or product moment reliability coefficients. Unfamiliar expressions of data should be clearly described, with references to their development.
36. If two or more forms of a test are published for use with the same examinees, information on means, variances, and characteristics of items in the forms should be reported in the test manual along with the coefficients of correlation among their scores. If necessary evidence is not provided, the test manual should warn the reader against assuming equivalence of scores.
37. Evidence of internal consistency should be reported for any unspeeded test.
38. The test manual should indicate to what extent test scores are stable, that is, how nearly constant the scores are likely to be if a parallel form of a test is administered after time has elapsed. The time interval to be considered depends on the nature of the test and on what interpretation of the test scores is recommended.

Standards for the Use of Tests

1. A test user should have a general knowledge of measurement principles and of the limitations of test interpretations.
2. A test user should know and understand the literature relevant to the tests he uses and the testing problems with which he deals.
3. One who has the responsibility for decisions about individuals or policies that are based on test results should have an understanding of psychological or educational measurement and of validation and other test research.
4. Test users should seek to avoid bias in test selection, administration, and interpretation; they should try to avoid even the appearance of discriminatory practice.
5. Institutional test users should establish procedures for periodic internal review of test use.
6. The choice or development of tests, test batteries, or other assessment procedures should be based on clearly formulated goals and hypotheses.
7. A test user should consider more than one variable for assessment and the assessment of any given variable by more than one method.
8. In choosing an existing test, a test user should relate its history of

research and development to his intended use of the instrument.

9. In general a test user should try to choose or to develop an assessment technique in which "tester-effect" is minimized, or in which reliability of assessment across testers can be assured.
10. Test scores used for selection or other administrative decisions about an individual may not be useful for individual or programme evaluation and vice versa.
11. A test user is expected to follow carefully the standardized procedures described in the manual for administering a test.
12. The test administration is responsible for establishing conditions, consistent with the principle of standardization, that enable each examinee to do his best.
13. A test user is responsible for accuracy in scoring, checking, coding, or recording test results.
14. If specific cutting scores are to be used as a basis for decisions, a test justification, or explanation of the cutting scores adopted.
15. The test user shares with the test developer or distributor a responsibility for maintaining test security.
16. A test score should be interpreted as an estimate of performance under a given set of circumstances. It should not be interpreted as some absolute characteristic of the examinee or as something permanent and generalizable to all circumstances.
17. Test scores should ordinarily be reported only to people who are qualified to interpret them. If scores are reported, they should be accompanied by explanations sufficient for the recipient to interpret them correctly.
18. The test user should recognize that estimates of reliability do not indicate criterion-related validity.
19. A test user should examine carefully the rationale and validity of computer-based interpretations of test scores.
20. In norm-referenced interpretations, a test user should interpret an obtained score with reference to sets of norms appropriate for the individual tested and for the intended use.
21. Any content-referenced interpretation should clearly indicate the domain to which one can generalize.
22. The test user should consider alternative interpretations of a given score.
23. The test user should be able to interpret test performance relative to other measures.
24. A test user should develop procedures for systematically eliminating from data files test-score information that has because of lapse of time, become obsolete.

CONTENTS

VOLUME ONE

PART 1 : PERSONALITY

PART 2 : EDUCATION

VOLUME TWO

PART 3 : ORGANISATIONAL BEHAVIOUR

PART 4 : SOCIAL PHENOMENA

PART THREE

ORGANISATIONAL BEHAVIOUR

INTRODUCTION

In this part of the Handbook, the instruments dealing with organizational behaviour have been reported. These instruments are reported under two sections:

1. Industrial Organizations, and
2. Health Organizations.

The instruments dealing with educational organizations have been reported in the earlier part. The instruments dealing with agricultural practices etc. have been reported in the next part under the section of modernization and social change. The instruments in this part deal with various dimensions of organizational behaviour like job satisfaction, job motivation, organizational effectiveness, occupational and role stress, participation, role conflicts, and attitudes etc. The detailed break-up of the instruments is given in the Table.

Table : Break-Up of Instruments on Organizational Behaviour

Classification	Originals Reproduced	Only Infor-mation	Citations	Adapt-ations	Total
	A	B	C	D	
Industrial Organizations	25	07	—	—	32
Health Organizations	—	—	—	—	—
Total	25	07	—	—	32

Industrial Organizations

There are in all 32 instrument listed under this part. Of these 25 have been reproduced here. Only information has been provided for 7 instruments. The areas covered by the instruments reproduced here include managerial styles, interpersonal needs, motivational aspects in organizations, organizational effectiveness, job satisfaction, managerial behaviour, job anxiety, occupational and role stress, participation, performance rating, general personality of workers, and role conflict etc. The instruments are meant for industrial workers, managers, working women and others who are engaged in some organizations.

Most of the instruments have reported either split-half or test-retest reliability. A few have reported both the reliability coefficients. For some instruments, only split-half reliability coefficients are reported. A number of instruments have reported Cronbach's alpha reliability. The values wherever reported are fairly high. Validity has been reported for all the scales except for two scales where one scale does not report any validity and one instrument reports validity under preparation. Face, construct, content, concurrent and factorial validities are reported for some of the instruments. A few of them have reported only factorial validity. Ratings and biserial coefficient of correlation have also been used to validate some of these instruments.

Norms are not available for most of these instruments. As the norms of the kind of industrial populations are subject to the change according to geography, size of industry and type of industry, these are generally of restricted utility.

Among the instruments reproduced here, most of the instruments deal with various aspects of organizational behaviour and are very useful for researchers, managers, and executives to understand various aspects of organizational behaviour like managerial styles, values, preferences, general belief, locus of control, interpersonal needs, and different motivational aspects in organizations. There are also instruments, which are reproduced here for references and the details can be had from the authors.

There is a scale called Organizational Commitment Instrument (OCI) by C. Balaji which measures the level of commitment in organizations. Reliability coefficient is found by Cronbach's Alpha which was found to be sufficiently high.

There is another scale Personal Efficacy Scale by Ashok Pratap Singh and Patiraj Kumari, which can be used to assess the personal efficacy of the persons employed in blue-collar jobs, white collar jobs, female dominated jobs and of the full-time housewives. Reliability and validly are under preparation for this scale.

There are Organizational Climate Questionnaire, Organizational Stress Questionnaire, Job Satisfaction Questionnaire, and Job Strain Questionnaire by Shailendra Singh. All these scales are mainly useful to measure the overall organizational climate of any institution.

Factors like stress, job-satisfaction, or the diagnosis of job strain may be included in these types of scales. Junior and middle level executives, and the supervisory staff may be given these types of scales to measure their adjustment levels in an organization.

There is another scale by A.K. Srivastava and A. Krishna which is in both the languages English as well as Hindi and is meant for employees of managerial (executive) and supervisory cadres of any organization. It assesses the extent of functional (facilitating or desirable) stresses relating to Organizational or job roles. Five dimensions of job roles, namely, excessive responsibility of others, excessively large work load, making decisions that affects others, perceiving oneself not fully qualified and competent, and strenuous tasks bringing recognition and personal growth. All the items in the test are 'true-keyed' and to be rated on the five-point scale.

There is another scale by A.K. Srivastava and Ranjana Banerjee called the Organizational Effectiveness Index, which assesses the extent of perceived behavioural effectiveness of production and non-production (service) organizations. Eight dimensions of Organizational effectiveness (behavioural), namely, effective and non-effective leadership, inter personal competence, enhanced output, efficient service, employee's commitment, satisfaction and morale, dynamism and adaptability to changes for growth and advancement; conducive organizational climate and immediate and efficient dealing of emergencies and organizational problems are measured by this scale.

Among the other scales reproduced here, 5 are developed by K. Prathap Reddy. Detailed information regarding reliability, validity, norms, or references etc. are not provided for some of the instruments which are available with the author. These instruments deal with various aspects of organizational structure and are very useful for researchers, managers, and executives to understand the structure of an organization. The main uses are to determine the effect of rate of change on organizational structure, measure of actual decentralization, or structure in use, the extent of formalization of an organization, the effect of culture on organizational structure and functioning, as also the extent of decentralization in an organization.

There is one scale which measures personnel policies and practices of an organization, as seen through the eyes of its employees by Baldev R. Sharma. Other scales measure job satisfaction, quality of life of industrial workers, level of job involvement of employees, job motivation, training needs of ICDS project functionaries.

Two scales are by Neelam Mahajan, one to measure the training needs of ICDS project functionaries, and second is the measurement of perceptions of coordination of ICDS project functionaries.

There are 6 instruments for which only information is provided. One adaptation is also included here which is an Indian Adaptation of Career Maturity Inventory (CMII) (Attitude Scale and Competency Test) by John O' Crites and Nirmala Gupta. Adaptation has been made in the Hindi language. Level are the XII standard students of Indian schools.

Health Organizations

No instrument is available which can be included in this section.

Industrial Organizations

A

31A (1)

Title of the Instrument : **Organizational Commitment Instrument (OCI).**
Author : C. Balaji.

Table 1: Correlation of OC with satisfaction with different aspects of employment

No.	Variable	r with OC
1.	Salary	0.30[c]
2.	Promotional opportunity	0.21[b]
3.	Comfortable physical conditions in work place	0.37[c]
4.	Opportunity to participate in making decisions connected with job	0.19[b]
5.	Support and cooperation from superior	0.25[c]
6.	Importance of job in organization	0.37[c]
7.	Perquisities/allowances/other benefits	0.28[c]
8.	Opportunity to use knowledge and skills	0.28[c]
9.	Variety in job	0.32[c]
10.	Opportunity to associate with superiors	0.27[c]
11.	Support and cooperation from subordinates	0.28[c]
12.	Prestige of organization	0.48[c]
13.	Job security	0.26[c]
14.	Opportunity to improve knowledge and skills	0.25[c]
15.	Challenge in job	0.28[c]
16.	Independence/autonomy in job	0.23[b]
17.	Support and cooperation from colleagues	0.29[c]
18.	Status of job as considered by friends/relatives	0.33[c]
19.	Organization in general	0.48[c]

a, b and c denote significance of r at 0.05, 0.01 and 0.001 levels respectively.

ORGANIZATIONAL COMMITMENT QUESTIONNAIRE

1. I am willing to put in a great deal of effort beyond that normally expected in order to help this organization be successful.
2. I talk about this organization to my friends as a great place to work for.
3. I feel very little loyalty to this organization (R).
4. I would accept almost any type of job assignment in order to keep working for this organization.
5. I find that my values and the organization's values are very similar.

6. I am proud to tell others that I am a part of this organization.
7. I could just as well be working for a different organization as long as the type of work was similar (R).
8. This organization really inspires the very best in me in the way of job performances.
9. It would take very little change in my present circumstances to cause me leave this organization (R).
10. I am extremely glad that I chose this organization to work for over others I was considering at the time I joined.
11. There's not too much to be gained by sticking with this organization indefinitely (R).
12. Often, I find it difficult to agree with this organization's policies on important matters relating to its employees (R).
13. I really care about the fate of this organization.
14. For me this is the best of all possible organizations for which to work.
15. Deciding to work for this organization was a definite mistake on my part (R).

Source : Mowday, *et al.,* 1979, p. 228.
Note : Statements with (R) at the end were reverse scored.

31A (2)

Title of the Instrument : **Personal Efficacy Scale.**
Authors : Ashok Pratap Singh and Patiraj Kumari.
Availability : Department of Psychology, Banaras Hindu University, Varanasi - 221 005, U.P.
Languages : English and Hindi.
Uses : It can be used to assess the personal efficacy of the persons employed in blue-collar jobs, white collar jobs, female dominated jobs and of the full-time housewives.
Main features : Five point-scale, 28 items.
Level : Full-time housewives and persons employed in blue-collar jobs, white-collar jobs and female dominated jobs.
Reliability : Under preparation.
Validity : Under preparation.
Time : No time limit.
Norms : Not available.
References : Not available.

PERSONAL EFFICACY SCALE

In this scale there are some questions which are related to you. There are five possible answers of each question below which, brackets are given. According to your opinion, give the right answer by making tick (✓) mark within the bracket.

	Strongly disagree	Dis-agree	Uncer-tain	Agree	Stro-ngly Agree
	1	2	3	4	5
1. I do the most risky work	( )	( )	( )	( )	( )
2. I fix the more difficult goal in my work	( )	( )	( )	( )	( )
3. I like to persist in any work for a long time.	( )	( )	( )	( )	( )
4. I always involve myself in the work.	( )	( )	( )	( )	( )
5. I set success in my work due to my own abilities.	( )	( )	( )	( )	( )
6. I fail due to lack of my efforts.					
7. Others expect that I will be successful.	( )	( )	( )	( )	( )
8. I accept that I am responsible for my failure.	( )	( )	( )	( )	( )
9. I accept that lack of self confidence is the cause of my failure.	( )	( )	( )	( )	( )
10. I accept that lack of expectation and aspiration is the cause of my failure.	( )	( )	( )	( )	( )
11. I have the capability to perform my job properly.	( )	( )	( )	( )	( )
12. I have the ability to do my work without supervision.	( )	( )	( )	( )	( )
13. I have the ability to do the different kinds of job.	( )	( )	( )	( )	( )
14. I do not depend on others for my own work.	( )	( )	( )	( )	( )

(Contd.)

	1	2	3	4	5
15. I have the ability to plan my work in proper way.	( )	( )	( )	( )	( )
16. I have the ability to initiate any new work.	( )	( )	( )	( )	( )
17. I do not feel burdened in my work.	( )	( )	( )	( )	( )
18. I like to do extra works.	( )	( )	( )	( )	( )
19. Usually my work is not completed.	( )	( )	( )	( )	( )
20. I feel boredom in my work.	( )	( )	( )	( )	( )
21. Generally my speed of work is fast.	( )	( )	( )	( )	( )
22. Lack of money is the cause of my failure.	( )	( )	( )	( )	( )
23. Physical fatigue reduces my working capacity.	( )	( )	( )	( )	( )
24. Social cooperation helps me in getting success.	( )	( )	( )	( )	( )
25. When I do not get salary in matching to my ability then my work is affected.	( )	( )	( )	( )	( )
26. I succeed when I get opportunity to increase efficiency.	( )	( )	( )	( )	( )
27. Monotony and lack of freedom are responsible for my failures in the work.	( )	( )	( )	( )	( )
28. Knowledge about the instruments and rules of the company helps in getting success.	( )	( )	( )	( )	( )

31A (3)

Title of the Instrument : **Organizational Climate Questionnaire.**
Author : Shailendra Singh.
Availability : Shri Ram Centre for Industrial Relations and Human Resources, 4E/16, Jhandewalan Extension, New Delhi-110 055
Language : English.
Uses : To measure organizational climate.

Levels : Junior and middle level executives.

Main features : It is a 31 items questionnaire in which each statement is rated on a 5-point scale. In all, 9 dimensions of organization climate are sought to be measured.

Reliability : Standardized alpha reliability is established.

Validity : Content validity established.

Time : Ten minutes.

References : Singh, S., "Organizational stress and executive behaviour." Unpublished Research Monograph, Shri Ram Centre for Industrial Relations and Human Resources, New Delhi, 1989.

ORGANIZATIONAL CLIMATE QUESTIONNAIRE

Following statements describe some characteristics of work organizations. Please read each statement carefully and decide : *To what extent each statement is true in case of your organization.*

1. Means true to almost no extent
2. Means true to a small extent
3. Means true to some extent
4. Means true to a great extent
5. Means true to very great extent

1. Professional Help (a = 72)

(1) Achieving goals a target set or excelling them is the main concern here.

(2) Relevant information is made available to all those who need it and can use such information for achieving high performance.

(3) The main concern of the people here is to help each other develop greater skills for advancement of the organization.

(4) People here have concern for one another and help each other spontaneously when such help is needed.

2. Formalization (a = 84)

(5) Our organization has a rigid set of rules and norms which we are supposed to follow strictly.

(6) Officials and employees are subject to strict systematic discipline and control in the conduct of their official jobs.

(7) People are constantly watched for obeying all the rules pertaining

to their jobs.

(8) Sanctions for violating rules and procedures of the organization are severe.

(9) The job assignments in this organization is clearly defined and logically structured.

(10) Each post has clearly defined sphere of roles in legal sense.

3. Professional Management (α = 80)

(11) Here rewards and promotions are given on the basis of the merit of the candidate.

(12) Those who can achieve results are highly trusted.

(13) Knowledge and expertise are recognised and rewarded here.

(14) The specialists and experts are highly trusted here.

(15) In this organization people are rewarded in proportion to the excellence in their job performance.

(16) The specialists and experts are highly trusted here.

4. Organizational Risk Taking (α = 88)

(17) The organization willingly takes a chance on a good idea.

(18) The organization prefers novel than safe and sure approach

(19) The organization encourages general orientation towards risk taking.

(20) The organization takes some pretty big risks occasionally to keep ahead of the competition.

5. Standardization (α =65)

(21) Most of my normal daily activities in the organization have rules and procedures stating the way I am to perform them.

(22) The maintenance of organizational norms and policies are the main criteria of success.

(23) There are rules and regulations for handling any kind of problem which may arise in making most of the decisions.

6. People Organization (α = 76)

(24) Philosophy of our management emphasizes human factors (how people feel etc.)

(25) Management believes that if the people are happy productivity will take care of itself.

7. Centralization (a = 68)

(26) Employees have to ask their superiors before they do almost anything important.
(27) Even for small matters higher ups are consulted for final answer.

8. Formalized Communication (a = 59)

(28) Any job policy related information is communicated to employees through established channels.
(29) Instructions are issued here by bosses and are expected to be carried out without delay and protest.

9. Welfare Concern (a = 51)

(30) Union management relations are cordial.
(31) Management does every thing to ensure the well-being of the employees.

31A (4)

Title of the Instrument : **Organizational Stress Questionnaire.**
Author : Shailendra Singh.
Availability : Shri Ram Centre for Industrial Relations and Human Resources, 4E/16, Jhandewalan Extension, New Delhi-110 055.
Language : English.
Uses : To measure organizational stress.
Level : Junior and middle level executive and supervisory staff.
Main features : It is a 33 items questionnaire consisting of both positively and negatively keys items in which each statement is rated on a 5-point scale. In all, 10 dimensions of stress is sought to be measured.
Reliability : Standardized alpha reliability is established.
Validity : Content validity established.
Time : Ten minutes.

---

a=Standardzed Alpha reliability.

References : Singh, S., "Organizational stress and executive behaviour." Unpublished Research Monograph, Shri Ram Centre for Industrial Relations & Human Resources, New Delhi, 1989.

ORGANIZATIONAL STRESS QUESTIONNAIRE

Below are given some job and work experiences.

Choosing an appropriate number indicate to what extent they are true in your case.

1. True to almost no extent
2. True to small extent
3. True to some extent
4. True to a great extent
5. True to very great extent

1. Lack of group cohesiveness (α=80)

1. People of my work group are ready to help each other (R).
2. People or my work group get along very well (R).
3. People of my work group stick together very well (R).
4. My subordinates are cooperative (R).

2. Role Conflict (α = 81)

5. I receive an assignment without adequate resources and materials to execute it.
6. I am required to do thing that should be done differently
7. I work with two more groups who work quite differently.
8. I receive incompatible requests from two or more people.
9. I do things that are acceptable to one person not to others.

3. Feeling of Inequality (α = 90)

10. I feel my salary remuneration is fair considering what other people in this firm are paid (R).
11. I feel my salary remuneration is fair considering what other firms in this area pay (R).
12. I feel my fringe benefits are fair considering the fringe benefits provided by other firms in this area (R).

4. Role ambiguity (α = 70)

13. I can predict what others will expect of me tomorrow in my job (R).
14. I am clear what others expect of me on my job (R).
15. On my job, whatever situation arises there are established

procedure for handling it (R).

16. I get enough facts and information to work my best (R).

5. **Role overload (α = 83)**
   17. I don't get enough time to finish my assignments.
   18. I can give better performance if some more time is available to my discretion.
   19. I don't have sufficient number of people to carry out the assignment.
   20. A large proportion of my job is a rush job.
   21. Often I am asked to speed up my job

6. **Lack of supervisory support (α = 83)**
   22. My superior/boss keeps her/ himself informed about the way his or her people think and feel about things (R).
   23. My superior/boss stands up to outsiders for the people he/she supervisors (R).
   24. My superior/boss takes personal interest in those he/she supervisers (R).

7. **Constraints of change and rule regulations (α = 81)**
   25. Policies and regulations limit the alternative solution open to me.
   26. Speed of technical change creates problem in my job.

8. **Job difficulty (α = 63)**
   27. My job assignments are quite difficult
   28. My job assignments are taxing to my abilities

9. **Job requirement-capability mismatch (α = 65)**
   29. I can easily succeed in the present job (R).
   30. My abilities don't fit to the requirement of the job.
   31. My abilities are well matched to requirements of the job (R).

10. **Inadequacy of role authority (α = 79)**
   32. My formal authority provides me with adequate power over the behaviour of my subordinates (R).
   33. I have enough power to discipline the people in my own work group for the not carrying out, the instructions that are given to them (R).

α = Standardized Alpha Reliability; (R) Stands for a reversed coded item.

31A (5) By Shailendra Singh

JOB SATISFACTION QUESTIONNAIRE

(Standardized Alpha Reliability= 0.96)

Please indicate : How satisfied are you with the following by using appropriate rating scale.

1. Means very dissatisfied
2. Means Dissatisfied
3. Means Neutral
4. Means Satisfied
5. Means very satisfied

How satisfied are you with :

(1) Physical work conditions.
(2) The freedom to choose your own method of working.
(3) Your fellow workers.
(4) The recognition you get from good work.
(5) Your immediate boss.
(6) Amount of responsibility you are given.
(7) Opportunities to use your abilities.
(8) Industrial relations with management and workers.
(9) Your rate of pay.
(10) Your chance of promotion.
(11) The way your firm is managed.
(12) The attention paid to suggestions you make.
(13) Your hours of work.
(14) The amount of variety in your job.
(15) Your job security.
(16) Opportunity to help others with personal problems at work.
(17) Chances to learn new things.
(18) Power and prestige in the job.
(19) Opportunity to make decisions.
(20) Opportunity to achieve something worthwhile.

31A (6)

Title of the Instrument : **Job Strain Questionnaire.**

Author : Shailendra Singh.

Availability : Shri Ram Centre for Industrial Relations and Human Resources, 4E/16, Jhandewalan Extension, New Delhi-110 055

Language : English.

Uses : To diagnose level of job strain.

Level : Junior and middle level executive and supervisory staff.

Main features : It is a 14-items questionnaire consisting of both positively and negatively keyed items, in which each statement is rated on a 5-point scale. In all 3 dimensions of job strain is measured.

Reliability : Standardized alpha reliability for Latent Hostility =.83, Depression = .73, Physical strain =.82.

Validity : Content and concurrent validity established. All the three dimensions of job strain, as hypothesized, were significantly and negatively related to job satisfaction.

Time Limit : Five minutes.

References : 1. Singh, S, "Organizational Stress and executive behaviour." Unpublished Research Monograph, Shri Ram Centre for Industrial Relations & Human Resources, New Delhi, 1989.

JOB STRAIN QUESTIONNAIRE

Following statements are related to your reactions the job at work. Choose an appropriate rating describe: How frequently on each of them occur in your case.

1. Means Never 2. Means Rarely 3. Means some times 4. Means Rather often 5. Means Nearly all the time

1. **Latent Hostility (α=83)**
   1. I have to be quite aggressive to survive in my job.
   2. There are times when I would like to be able to tell some one what I think of them.
   3. I feel I should blame them who really deserve it.
   4. I just have to put up with other people's incompetence.
   5. I have found it difficult to keep my temper at work.
2. **Depression (α = 73)**
   6. I find it easy to do things I used to do (R).
   7. My mind is as clear as it used to be (R).
   8. I still enjoy the thing I used to do. (R).
3. **Physical strain (α = 82)**
   9. I have found it difficult keep my temper at work.
   10. I have felt fidgety as a result of my job.

11. My job troubles me.
12. When I think about my job I get high feelings in my chest.
13. i get tired for no reasons.
14. I find myself for no reasons.

α = Standardized Alpha Reliability; (R) stands for a reversed coded item.

31A (7)

Title of the Instrument : **Functional Role Stress Scale.**

Authors : A. K. Srivastava and A. Krishna.

Availability : Department of Psychology, Banaras Hindu University, Varanasi-221 005, UP.

Language : English and Hindi.

Uses : Assess the extent of functional (facilitating or desirable) stresses relating to organizational or job roles.

Level : The scale is meant for employees of managerial (executive) and supervisory cadres.

Main features : The scale comprises of 25 statements (items) relating to 5 dimensions of job role, namely, excessive responsibility; responsibility of others; excessively large work load; making decision that affects others; perceiving oneself not fully qualified and competent; and strenuous tasks bringing recognition and personal growth. All the items are 'true-keyed' and to be rated on the five-point scale.

The selection of item were made on the basis of their significant ($p < .01$) discriminative by their homogenity indices. These indices were obtained by computing Biserial Correlation for each of the items on a sample of 200 employees. The cut-off point for the selection of the item was 0.29.

Reliability : The indices of split-half (odd-even) reliability (N=200) and re-test reliability (N=100) for the scale as a whole were 0.84 and 0.93, respectively.

Validity : To ascertain the concurrent validity of the scale it was administered along with the measures of job involvement and mental health on a sample of 78 employees of managerial and executive cadres. The coefficients of correlation between functional stress and job involvement, and between functional stress and mental health were found to be .257 and .228, respectively.

Time Limit :15 to 20 minutes.

FUNCTIONAL ROLE STRESS SCALE
INSTRUCTIONS

The present Inventory is meant for a psychological investigation. It consists of some statements about your feelings and experiences relating to your job roles and responsibilities. You have to choose and mark any one of the five alternative responses given against the statements to indicate the extent to which you agree with each statement with reference to your own job.

Kindly respond to all the statements. Your responses will be kept confidential.

Thanks

S.No	Particulers	Totally agree	Agree	Moder-ately agree	Dis-agree	Totally dis-agree
1	2	3	4	5	6	7
1.	I am delegated some extra responsibilities in addition to my prescribed ones.	( )	( )	( )	( )	( )
2.	I am, sometimes, required to give explanation for the unsatisfactory performance/ behaviour of my colleagues.	( )	( )	( )	( )	( )
3.	I have often to give extra time in office due to excessive work load.	( )	( )	( )	( )	( )
4.	It sometimes becomes crucial problem for me to deal with the grievances and representations of subordinates.	( )	( )	( )	( )	( )
5.	I am often entrusted the big responsibility of solving crucial/emergent problems of the department/organization.	( )	( )	( )	( )	( )
6.	The extra ordinary job responsibilities I have to bear out facilitate my personal growth.	( )	( )	( )	( )	( )

(Contd.)

1	2	3	4	5	6	7
7.	It becomes sometimes irritating to explain new personnel their work and responsibilities.	( )	( )	( )	( )	( )
8.	A big burden of supervision and control of a number of employees is on me.	( )	( )	( )	( )	( )
9.	I have been loaded with major responsibility of formulation and/or implementation of important policies.	( )	( )	( )	( )	( )
10.	My job responsibilities are beyond my capabilities.	( )	( )	( )	( )	( )
11.	Often it becomes difficult for me to take decisions in the matters of employees' transfers and/or promotions, or in taking action against them.	( )	( )	( )	( )	( )
12.	The crucial tasks I have to often perform help enhancing my self confidence.	( )	( )	( )	( )	( )
13.	I am often imposed with some responsibilities of other departments.	( )	( )	( )	( )	( )
14.	I have to be ultimately responsible for the performance of a number of employees.	( )	( )	( )	( )	( )
15.	I am not able to do justice with my job due to excessive work load.	( )	( )	( )	( )	( )
16.	I sometimes feel that I am not fully capable and competent to bear out my job responsibilities effectively.	( )	( )	( )	( )	( )
17.	It becomes difficult and dubious for me to take decision in crucial matters pertaining to subordinates' services.	( )	( )	( )	( )	( )

(Contd.)

1	2	3	4	5	6	7
18.	I am to often deal with crucial problems faced by the organization, but I am given full credit and recognition for it.	( )	( )	( )	( )	( )
19.	I sometimes feel that I require more experience/ training for efficiently discharging my duties and responsibilities.	( )	( )	( )	( )	( )
20.	A lot of responsibilities of growth and advancement of the department organization is on my shoulders.	( )	( )	( )	( )	( )
21.	The responsibility of professional growth and fate of a number of employees is on my head.	( )	( )	( )	( )	( )
22.	Being quite busy in my job I find it difficult to give sufficient time to my family and friend circle.	( )	( )	( )	( )	( )
23.	My job responsibilities are quite challenging.	( )	( )	( )	( )	( )
24.	It becomes very difficult for me to satisfy everyone in distribution of work and responsibilities.	( )	( )	( )	( )	( )
25.	I have to finish my work hurriedly due to excess of work.	( )	( )	( )	( )	( )

31A (8) by A.K. Srivastava; Ranjana Banerjee

Title of the instrument : **Organizational Effectiveness Index.**

1. The policies and objectives of the organization are elaborated and clearly explained.
2. *Validity data*: Content and Factorial validity are established.
3. *Time required for administering the test* : 45 to 60 minutes.

4. *Norms* : Nil. Not available.
5. *References on the instruments, its development and use* : NIL.

ORGANIZATIONAL EFFECTIVENESS INDEX

1. The policies and objectives of the organization are elaborated and clearly explained. ☐
2. Authorities' fair dealings and encouraging treatments have generated the feeling of security and confidence among the employees here. ☐
3. Employees of all levels here cooperate with each other to achieve the goals of the organization. ☐
4. Efforts are made at each level for maximum utilization of available resources and facilities. ☐
5. Employees feel satisfied here of being a member of well functioning team. ☐
6. The organization quickly adapts to new circumstances. ☐
7. The organization has been able to attract and retain competent persons due to its congenial atmosphere. ☐
8. Organizations' policy of free and frank discussions at every level has been quite effective in easily resolving most of its problems. ☐
9. Functions/jurisdictions of each department/section of the organization are clearly specified. ☐
10. Managerial personnels here make effective and continuous supervision of role enactment of the subordinates. ☐
11. Colonial relationships between management and workers has created conducive work climate in the organization. ☐
12. Efficiency is the key note of the culture of this organization. ☐
13. Attractive benefits (wages) offered to competent and efficient employees has bound them with the organization. ☐
14. The organization is quite dynamic and progressive in its approaches. ☐
15. The organization may be characterized by a relaxed and easy-going work climate. ☐
16. Interdepartmental conflicts are resolved on principles, and in view of larger good of the organization. ☐
17. The organization has an effective communication system with feed-back mechanism. ☐
18. Executives here show enormous drive and enthusiasm in carrying out their job responsibilities. ☐

19. When someone is on a difficult assignment he can usually count on getting assistance from his superiors and/or colleagues. ☐
20. Employees here constantly strive to reach new heights of performance and achievements. ☐
21. Employees of all cadres here are deeply involved in their jobs. ☐
22. Prompt adoption of improved systems and work methods has helped organization achieve greater efficiency. ☐
23. Atmosphere here is quite cordial and people have high concern for one another. ☐
24. In a major crisis employees of the organization bind together and work till the crisis situation is over. ☐
25. Sharply defined and logically structured jobs in the organization facilitate their smooth performance. ☐
26. Supervisory personnel here use their expertise and competence rather than formal authorities in influencing their subordinates. ☐
27. A predominant concern of the organization is to encourage friendly reactions among its employees. ☐
28. The organization is deeply committed to provide high quality products/efficient services to its clients. ☐
29. Employees of the organization on the whole are contended with and committed to their job responsibilities. ☐
30. Innovations in the organization are implemented through highly result-oriented employees. ☐
31. The philosophy of the organization emphasizes the human factors (e.g. employees' feelings, sentiments and aspirations). ☐
32. Most interdepartmental conflicts in the organization arise out of striving for higher achievements. ☐
33. Our productivity does not suffer from lack of proper planning and coordination. ☐
34. The organization makes best use of experts and highly qualified executives in making policies and their implementations. ☐
35. Informal intra and inter-cadre interactions have helped understanding and resolving many problems of industrial relations. ☐
36. The thrust of the organization is on getting results through dedication and participation of its people. ☐

37. Absenteeism rate at every level is markedly low in the organization. ☐
38. System and policies of the organization are continuously reviewed and modified to suit new situations and challenges. ☐
39. Prevailing atmosphere of support and cooperation in the organization attenuates the strains of excessive workload. ☐
40. Employees' demands and grievances are settled taking them in confidence. ☐
41. Effective coordination has resulted in excellent collaborative achievements by the organization as a whole. ☐
42. Management here makes prompt and rigorous implementation of new plans and policies. ☐
43. Cordial relations and feeling of trust among the employees has boosted up their morale. ☐
44. Employees here are provided with necessary information and facilities required for better performance. ☐
45. Employees of the organization get rewards and recognition in proportion to the excellence of their job performance. ☐
46. Management here does not hesitate in making major changes in organizational structure and system for its growth, and advancement. ☐
47. Members of the organization consider the organization's achievements as their personal success.
48. Management's promptness to attend and resolve employees' complaints and problem has abviated many serious consequences. ☐
49. Interdepartmental coordination and control system are so maintained as to make maximum utilization of human resources. ☐
50. Effective leadership in the organization may be given maximum credit for organization's achievements. ☐
51. Good interpersonal relations prevailing in the organization has been helpful in its smooth functioning. ☐
52. Employees are usually required here to complete their assigned tasks within the dead-line fixed for them. ☐
53. Employees' high morale, resulted from 'we-feeling' prevailing here, has helped achieving organizational goals. ☐
54. Leadership here is quite dynamic. It changes its style and approach in accordance with the demands of the situations. ☐

55. The friendly treatment and encouragements employees get from their authorities out weigh the threats and criticisms. ☐
56. Authorities here take prompt and effective actions to resolve the problems faced by the organization. ☐

31A (9)

Title of the Instrument : **A Job Satisfaction Scale.**

Purpose : To measure job satisfaction for use in industrial and banking set up.

Author(s) : B.L. Dubey, K.K. Uppal, S.K. Verma, C.K. Maini.

Language : English.

Availability : Dr. B.L. Dubey, Department of Business Management, Punjab University, Chandigarh-160 014.

Uses : Assess job satisfaction; evaluation of employee welfare schemes; research.

Levels : Individuals/groups. All Educated. (English knowing).

Main features : A 25 item scale on a five point scale, strongly agree to score 0 to 4 item. Total 0 to 100 per subject.

Reliability : Test-retest = 0.64, Split-Half reliability coefficient = 072.

Validity : Independent of age, education, and salary, Moderately and negatively correlated with unstability (-.50) and extraversion (-0.42) but not with other personality variables like psychotism, social desirability, quality of life, depression, etc.

Time Limit : 20-25 minutes.

Norms : Normally distributed.

References : Dubey , B.L.; Uppal, K.K. and Verma, S.K. (1989). Further validation of a job satisfaction Scale. *Indian Psychological Review*, 34.

JOB SATISFACTION SCALE

Age :........................... Education ....

No. of dependents : ....

Marital status: .... Rural/Urban : ....

Service Experience : ....

Salary : .... Date : ....

Name of Organisation : ....

Type of work : ....

Instructions : Kindly go through each item with five alternatives and tick (✓) the most appropriate one only.

		Strongly agree	Agree	Undecided	Dis-agree	Strongly dis-agree
1	2	3	4	5	6	7
1.	I have been getting promotion as per my qualification and experience	....	....	....	....	....
2.	I have full confidence in the management of this organization	....	....	....	....	....
3.	Favouritism does not have any role to play in this organization.	....	....	....	....	....
4.	On the whole, I am satisfied with the general supervision in my department.	....	....	....	....	....
5.	Working conditions in this organization are satisfactory.	....	....	....	....	....
6.	I think this organization treats its employees better than any other organization.	....	....	....	....	....
7.	My supervisor keeps me informed about all policies/happenings of the organization.	....	....	....	....	....
8.	I feel that I have opportunity to present my problems, to the management.	....	....	....	....	....
9.	My present job is as per my ability/qualification and experience.	....	....	....	....	....

(Contd.)

1 2	3	4	5	6	7
10. My supervisor behaves properly with me.	......	......	......	......	......
11. I feel proud of working in this organization.	......	......	......	......	......
12. Comparing the salary for similar jobs in other organizations I feel my pay is better.	......	......	......	......	......
13. As per work requirement, my pay is fair.	......	......	......	......	......
14. My supervisor takes into account my wishes as well as work done.	......	......	......	......	......
15. My organization adopts best methods of work as early as possible.	......	......	......	......	......
16. My job has helped me to learn some skills.	......	......	......	......	......
17. I feel that my job is reasonably secure as long as I do good work.	......	......	......	......	......
18. Promotions are made on merit in this organization.	......	......	......	......	......
19. I usually feel fresh at the end of the day's work.	......	......	......	......	......
20. My pay is enough for providing necessary things in my life.	......	......	......	......	......
21. There is high team spirit in the work group.	......	......	......	......	......
22. I am satisfied with welfare facilities (Medical, etc.) provided by the organization.	......	......	......	......	......
23. On the whole, I feel I have good prospects of advancement in my job.	......	......	......	......	......

(Contd.)

1	2	3	4	5	6	7
24.	I do not like to do this job but circumstances force me.	....	....	....	....	....
25.	If I get similar job in any other organization I would like to quit this job.	....	....	....	....	....

31A(10) and 31A(11)

Title of the Instrument : **1. Job Satisfaction Determinants Delineation Scale. 2. Job Satisfaction Measurement Scale.**

Purpose : 1. To delineate the determinants of job satisfaction, 2. To measure the level of job satisfaction.

Authors : Satinder Pal Kaur and Amarjit Singh

Languages : Punjabi and English.

Availability : Unpublished M.Sc. Thesis, Punjab Agricultural University, Ludhiana.

Uses : To delineate the determinants and to measure the level of job satisfaction of *Gram Sevikas*.

Levels : Gram Sevikas.

Main Features : Likert type scale, Five point continuum 30 items in each scale.

Reliability : Reliability coefficient was determined by the Spearman Brown formula.

Sr. No.	Name of the scale	Reliability Coefficient
1.	Scale to delineate the determinants of job satisfaction.	0.98
2.	Scale to measure the level of job satisfaction.	0.98

Validity : Instrinsic validity was calculated by taking the square root of reliability coefficient and it came out to be 0.99.

Time Limit : 30 minutes.

Norms : Scale given by Wanus and Lawler (1972) with little modifications was employed to delineate the determinants of job satisfaction and to measure the level of job satisfaction. Some statements from the job satisfaction inventory developed by Indireson (1980) were added to the scale in consultation with the advisory committee members.

Scoring Procedure

Category	Score
Very much important/satisfied	5
Important/satisfied	4
Cannot say	3
Not important/satisfied	2
Not at all important/satisfied	1

References :
1. Guilford, J.P. (1954) : *Psychometeric Methods.* Bombay, Tata McGraw Hill p. 350.
2. Indiresan, J. (1980) : "Perception of Leadership Style and Satisfaction of different need areas," *Ind. Journal of Social Work*, Vol. XII No.1, pp 27-18.
3. Wanous, J.P. and E.L. Lawler III (1972): "Measurement and meaning of job satisfaction" *Journal of Applied Psychology*. Vol. 56, No.2 pp. 95-105.

JOB SATISFACTION DETERMINANTS' DELINEATION SCALE

How important to you are tnese characteristic or qualities from the point of view of job of *Gram-Sevika* please tick (✓) in the appropriate column.

S.No.	Job Facets	Not at all impor-tant	Not Impor-tant	Can not say	Import-ant	Very much impor-tant
		1	2	3	4	5
1.	Self esteem or respect from your colleagues	....	....	....	....	....
2.	Prestige of job inside department	....	....	....	....	....
3.	Prestige of job outside of department	....	....	....	....	....
4.	Opportunity for professional growth	....	....	....	....	....
5.	Opportunity for promotion	....	....	....	....	....

(Contd.)

	1	2	3	4	5
6. Opportunity of job outside department	......	......	......	......	......
7. Pay for job	......	......	......	......	......
8. Amount of close supervision	......	......	......	......	......
9. Opportunity for close friendship	......	......	......	......	......
10. Opportunity to help others	......	......	......	......	......
11. Feeling of Job security	......	......	......	......	......
12. Opportunity to complete work	......	......	......	......	......
13. Feeling of accomplishment	......	......	......	......	......
14. Chance to do a whole piece of work	......	......	......	......	......
15. Opportunity to get to know others	......	......	......	......	......
16. Opportunity to do challenging job	......	......	......	......	......
17. Opportunity to do many things	......	......	......	......	......
18. Liking for the nature of the work	......	......	......	......	......
19. Variety on the job	......	......	......	......	......
20. Comforts of physical work conditions (place of work, transportation, light etc.)	......	......	......	......	......
21. Technical facilities to do the job	......	......	......	......	......
22. The fringe benefits (house ing, medical, provident fund etc.)	......	......	......	......	......
23. Opportunity for independent thought	......	......	......	......	......
24. Freedom of job	......	......	......	......	......
25. Opportunity to participate in decision-making	......	......	......	......	......

(Contd.)

	1	2	3	4	5
26. Opportunity for feedback on performance	....	....	....	....	....
27. Use of your talents	....	....	....	....	....
28. Feeling that know when do job well	....	....	....	....	....
29. Help from the administration in doing job	....	....	....	....	....
30. Fairness of authority	....	....	....	....	....

JOB SATISFACTION MEASUREMENT SCALE

How satisfied are you with these aspects of your job? Please tick (✓) mark in the appropriate column.

S.No.	Job Facets	Not at all satis-fied	Not satis-fied	Can not say	Satis-fied	Very much satis-fied
		1	2	3	4	5
1.	Self esteem or respect	....	....	....	....	....
2.	Prestige of Job inside department	....	....	....	....	....
3.	Prestige of job outside department	....	....	....	....	....
4.	Opportunity for professional growth	....	....	....	....	....
5.	Opportunity for promotion	....	....	....	....	....
6.	Opportunity of job outside department	....	....	....	....	....
7.	Pay for job	....	....	....	....	....
8.	Amount of close supervision	....	....	....	....	....
9.	Opportunity for close friendship	....	....	....	....	....
10.	Opportunity to help others	....	....	....	....	....
11.	Feeling of job security	....	....	....	....	....
12	Opportunity to complete work	....	....	....	....	....

(Contd.)

	1	2	3	4	5
13. Feeling of accomplishment	....	....	....	....	....
14. Chance to do a whole piece of work	....	....	....	....	....
15. Opportunity to get to know others	....	....	....	....	....
16. Opportunity to do challenging job	....	....	....	....	....
17. Opportunity to do many things	....	....	....	....	....
18. Liking for the nature of the work	....	....	....	....	....
19. Variety on the job	....	....	....	....	....
20. Comforts of physical working conditions (place of work, transportation, light etc.)	....	....	....	....	....
21. Technical facilities to do the job	....	....	....	....	....
22. The fringe benefits (house ing, medical, provident fund etc.)	....	....	....	....	....
23. Opportunity for independent thought	....	....	....	....	....
24. Freedom on job	....	....	....	....	....
25. Opportunity to participate in decision-making	....	....	....	....	....
26. Opportunity for feedback on performance	....	....	....	....	....
27. Use of your talents	....	....	....	....	....
28. Feeling that know when do job well	....	....	....	....	....
29. Help from the administration in doing job	....	....	....	....	....
30. Fairness of authority	....	....	....	....	....

31A (12)

Title of the Instrument :**Rate of Organizational Change.**
Purpose : For measuring the extent of change in various aspects of an

organization.

Authors : K. Prathap Reddy.

Language : English.

Availability : K. Prathap Reddy, Assoc. Professor, NAARM, Rajendranagar, Hyderabad-500 030.

Uses : To determine the effect of rate of change on organizational structure.

Levels : Senior managers.

Main features :

Reliability : Has high reliability.

Validity : Has Face validity.

Time Limit : 5 minutes

Norms : Available with the author.

References : Was used by the author in his FPM Thesis on "Influence of Organizational Structure," submitted to I.I.M. Ahmedabad.

RATE OF ORGANIZATIONAL CHANGE

During the last 10 years, have any major changes taken place in the organization's

		Yes/No	If Yes, details
(a)	Ownership	....	....
(b)	Products	....	....
(c)	Site	....	....
(d)	Organizational Structure	....	....
(e)	Organization's Policy/Policies	....	....

A 'Yes' response was scored '2' and a 'no' response '0'. Thus the score ranged from 0 to 10. This was divided by the logarithm of organization's age to obtain the final square on rate of change.

31A (13)

Title of the Instrument : **Authority Utilization.**

Purpose : For measuring the extent of delegated authority.

Authors : K. Prathap Reddy.

Language : English.

Availability : K. Reddy, Assoc. Professor, NAARM, Rajendranagar, Hyderabad-500 030.

Uses : As a measure of actual decentralization, or structure in use.

Levels : First line supervisor level.

Main features : Rating Scale.

Reliability : Operating Marketing decisions=0.83, Production Decisions =0.85, Manufacturing Supervision and Target Setting Decisions=0.65, Technology Decisions=Not Applicable.

Validity : Has high face validity.

Time Limit : 10 minutes.

Norms : Available with the author.

References :Was used by the author in his FPM Thesis on "Influence of Organizational Culture on Organizational Structure," submitted to IIM, Ahmedabad.

AUTHORITY UTILIZATION

A. The following items were used for measuring authority utilization in marketing decisions.

Q. Chief executives generally delegate a certain amount of power to the people lower down in the organization's hierarchy. In some cases, however, people may exercise more power than what is actually delegated to them. In some other cases, it may be the other way round.

We would like to know how formally delegated authority and the authority actually exercised differ for the following types of decisions in your organization. The delegation of authority could be to the individuals or to the groups (e.g., committees). Please indicate your choice by circling the appropriate number. If you are working in a division, please respond to these statements with reference to your division.

* If no power is delegated for a particular decision, write 'NA' against that statement.

1. For development of marketing strategy of a new product or major changes in the marketing strategy of existing products.

Formally delegated authority exceeds the authority actually used by the person/ committee	Both are same 1 2 1 0 1 2	Authority actually exercised by the person/committee exceeds the formally delegated authority

2. For pricing of new products or significant price changes in the existing products.

Formally delegated authority exceeds the authority actually used by the person/ committee	Both are same 1 2 1 0 1 2	Authority actually exercised by the person/committee exceeds the formally delegated authority

3. Terms for negotiating with the customer.

Formally delegated authority exceeds the authority actually used by the person/ committee	Both are same 1 2 1 0 1 2	Authority actually exercised by the person/committee exceeds the formally delegated authority

4. For determining annual sales targets.

Formally delegated authority exceeds the authority actually used by the person/ committee	Both are same 1 2 1 0 1 2	Authority actually exercised by the person/committee exceeds the formally delegated authority

5. Any comments you would like to make:

The responses on the left were scored negatively, while those on the right were scored positively. The mid-point was scored as Zero. Items 3 and 4, which related to operating marketing decision, were called "authority utilization in operating marketing decisions" (OMD). Items 1 and 2 related to non-routine marketing decisions like planning for introduction of new products in the market, and making substantial changes in the resisting marketing strategy. This was called "authority utilization in new product marketing decisions" (NPMD).

B. The following items were used for measuring authority utilization in production decisions.

Q. Chief executives generally delegate a certain amount of power to the people lower down in the organization's hierarchy. In some cases, however, people may exercise more power than what is actually delegated to them. In some other cases, it may be the other way round.

We would like to know how formally delegated authority and the authority actually exercised differ for the following types of decisions in your organization. The delegation of authority could be to the individuals or to the groups (e.g., committees). Please indicate your choice by circling the appropriate number. If you are working in a division, please respond to these statements with reference to your division.

*If no power is delegated for a particular decision, write 'NA" against that statement.

1. For rescheduling or altering the manufacturing plan resulting from machine breakdowns, non-availability of inputs etc.

Formally delegated	Both are same	Authority actually
authority exceeds	1	exercised by the
the authority actually	2 1 0 1 2	person/committee
used by the person/		exceeds the formally
committee		delegated authority

2. For development of a new product or service.

Formally delegated	Both are same	Authority actually
authority exceeds	1	exercised by the
the authority actually	2 1 0 1 2	person/committee
used by the person/		exceeds the formally
committee		delegated authority

3. For use of overtime and/or additional machinery.

Formally delegated	Both are same	Authority actually
authority exceeds	1	exercised by the
the authority actually	2 1 0 1 2	person/committee
used by the person/		exceeds the formally
committee		delegated authority

4. For determining delivery dates, or prioritizing orders.

Formally delegated	Both are same	Authority actually
authority exceeds	1	exercised by the
the authority actually	2 1 0 1 2	person/committee
used by the person/		exceeds the formally
committee		delegated authority

5. Type of capital equipment to be purchased.

Formally delegated	Both are same	Authority actually
authority exceeds	1	exercised by the
the authority actually	2 1 0 1 2	person/committee
used by the person/		exceeds the formally
committee		delegated authority

6. For procurement of critical inputs at short notice, probably overlooking the normal purchase procedures.

Formally delegated	Both are same	Authority actually
authority exceeds	1	exercised by the
the authority actually	2 1 0 1 2	person/committee
used by the person/		exceeds the formally

committee		delegated authority

7. For maintaining discipline of the subordinates.

Formally delegated authority exceeds the authority actually used by the person/ committee	Both are same 1 2 1 0 1 2	Authority actually exercised by the person/committee exceeds the formally delegated authority

8. For determining the annual production targets.

Formally delegated authority exceeds the authority actually used by the person/ committee	Both are same 1 2 1 0 1 2	Authority actually exercised by the person/committee exceeds the formally delegated authority

9. Any comments you would like to make:

Items 1, 2, 3, 4, and 6 were related to routine production decisions and it was called 'authority utilization in production decisions' (PD). Items 7 and 8, were together called 'authority utilization in manufacturing supervision and target setting decision' (MSTSD). Item 5 was called authority utilization in technology decisions (TD).

31A (14)

Title of the Instrument : **Formalization of Personnel Rules.**
Purpose : For measuring the extent of formalization of an organization.
Authors : K. Prathap Reddy.
Language : English.
Availability : K. Prathap Reddy, Assoc. Professor, NAARM, Rajendranagar, Hyderabad.
Uses : As at 31A (13).
Levels : First line supervisor level.
Main features : Summated rating scale.
Reliability : Existence of Personnel Rules : 0.96., Implementation of Personnel Rules : 0.95.
Validity : Has high face validity.
Time Limit : 10 minutes.
Norms : Available with the author.
References : Was used by the author in his FPM thesis on "Influence of Organizational Culture on Organizational Structure," submitted to IIM, Ahmedabad.

FORMALIZATION OF PERSONNEL RULES

Formalization is the extent to which rules, procedures, instructions, and communication are written down.

The following items are used for measuring formalization.

Q. We would like to know whether you have formalized (written) rules and practices in your organization/division (if you are working in a division) for the following personnel functions. If they exist, please indicate to what extent these are strictly adhered to. Please indicate your choice by circling the appropriate number.

If any statement is not relevant to your organization/division, please write 'NA' against that first statement. Similarly, if your answer to the first statement is '1' or 'NA', please write 'NA' against the second statement.

1. Formal rules for inviting and screening the applications for recruitment of *direct workers*.

(i)	Complete absence of formal rules and procedures	1 2 3 4 5	Very detailed rules and procedures exist
(ii)	They are never followed	1 2 3 4 5	They are very strictly followed

2. Formal rules for inviting and screening the applications for recruitment of *supervisory and managerial personnel.*

(i)	Complete absence of formal rules and procedures	1 2 3 4 5	Very detailed rules and procedures exist
(ii)	They are never followed	1 2 3 4 5	They are very strictly followed

3. Formal rules for conducting tests and interviews for recruitment of *direct workers*.

(i)	Complete absence of formal rules and procedures	1 2 3 4 5	Very detailed rules and procedures exist
(ii)	They are never followed	1 2 3 4 5	They are very strictly followed

4. Formal rules for conducting tests and interviews for recruitment of *supervisory and managerial personnel*.

(i)	Complete absence of formal rules and procedures	1 2 3 4 5	Very detailed rules and procedures exist

(ii) They are never followed	1 2 3 4 5	They are very strictly followed

5. Criterial for selection and appointment of *direct workers*.

(i) No formal rules exist	1 2 3 4 5	Elaborate criteria exist
(ii) They are never followed	1 2 3 4 5	They are very strictly followed

6. Criteria for selection and appointment of *supervisory and managerial personnel*.

(i) No formal rules exist	1 2 3 4 5	Elaborate criteria exist
(ii) They are never followed	1 2 3 4 5	They are very strictly followed

7. Formal assessment procedures for promotion of *direct workers*.

(i) Complete absence of formal rules and procedures	1 2 3 4 5	Very detailed rules and procedures exist
(ii) They are never followed	1 2 3 4 5	They are very strictly followed

8. Formal assessment procedures for promotion of *supervisory and managerial personnel*.

(i) Complete absence of formal rules and procedures	1 2 3 4 5	Very detailed rules and procedures exist
(ii) They are never followed	1 2 3 4 5	They are very strictly followed

9. Formal assessment procedures for salary and wage review (i.e. granting increments, etc.) of *direct workers*.

(i) Complete absence of formal rules and procedures	1 2 3 4 5	Very detailed rules and procedures exist
(ii) They are never followed	1 2 3 4 5	They are very strictly followed

10. Formal assessment procedures for salary and wage review of *supervisory and managerial personnel*.

(i) Complete absence of formal rules and procedures	1 2 3 4 5	Very detailed rules and procedures exist
(ii) They are never followed	1 2 3 4 5	They are very strictly followed

11. Formal procedures for handling grievances.

(i)	Complete absence of formal rules and procedures	1 2 3 4 5	Very detailed rules and procedures exist
(ii)	They are never followed	1 2 3 4 5	They are very strictly followed

12. Formal procedures for sponsoring individuals for internal as well as external (outside the organization) training programmes.

(i)	Complete absence of formal rules and procedures	1 2 3 4 5	Very detailed rules and procedures exist
(ii)	They are never followed	1 2 3 4 5	They are very strictly followed

13. Formal procedures for job rotation.

(i)	Complete absence of formal rules and procedures	1 2 3 4 5	Very detailed rules and procedures exist
(ii)	They are never followed	1 2 3 4 5	They are very strictly followed

14. Formal procedures for annual performance appraisal.

(i)	Complete absence of formal rules and procedures	1 2 3 4 5	Very detailed rules and procedures exist
(ii)	They are never followed	1 2 3 4 5	They are very strictly followed

15. Formal rules for determining eligibility, and for sanctioning perks like house building loans, car allowance, etc.

(i)	Complete absence of formal rules and procedures	1 2 3 4 5	Very detailed rules and procedures exist
(ii)	They are never followed	1 2 3 4 5	They are very strictly followed

The scores on existence of personnel rules (formalization) and their implementation are treated separately.

31A (15)

Title of the Instrument : **Organizational Culture.**
Purpose : For measuring the culture of an organization.
Authors : K. Prathap Reddy.
Language : English.

Availability : Dr. K. Prathap Reddy, Assoc. Professor, NAARM, Rajendranagar, Hyderabad-500 030.

Uses : To determine the effect of culture on organizational structure and functioning.

Levels : All levels.

Main features : Summated rating scale.

Reliability : Dependency norms : 0.84, Power-orientedness norm : 0.79,. Others : Not applicable.

Validity : Has high face validity.

Time Limit : 10 minutes.

Norms : Available with the author.

References :Was used by the author in his FPM Thesis on "Influence of Organizational Culture on Organizational Structure," Submitted to IIM, Ahmedabad

ORGANIZATIONAL CULTURE

Dependency Norms

The following items were used for measuring norms of dependency.

1. Subordinates here expect detailed guidance from their bosses to correct or prevent them making mistakes.

Strongly disagree 1 2 3 4 5 Strongly agree

2. Decisions are mostly made at the top and communicated downwards, and people generally prefer this.

Strongly disagree 1 2 3 4 5 Strongly agree

3. Loyalty is rewarded more than anything else in this organization.

Strongly disagree 1 2 3 4 5 Strongly agree

4. Superiors here strongly prefer that their subordinates ask them for instructions and suggestions before initiating a task.

Strongly disagree 1 2 3 4 5 Strongly agree

5. People here usually refer even simple problems to their superiors and look for solutions from them.

Strongly disagree 1 2 3 4 5 Strongly agree

The scores on all these items were aggregated and mean was calculated to arrive at the final score. It ranged from 1 to 5, a higher score indicating higher dependency level.

Norms of Power-Orientedness

Three items were used to measure this variable. These items were derived from factor analysis. The scores of all the three items were aggregated after reversing the score on item 2, and averaged to arrive at the final score. It ranged from 1 to 5, a higher score indicated higher level of power-orientedness.

1. Only a few people are treated well by the top management and they are quite influential.

Strongly disagree 1 2 3 4 5 Strongly agree

2. High value is put here on both the superior and subordinate trusting each other.

Strongly disagree 1 2 3 4 5 Strongly agree

3. When there are conflicts or disagreements, those who are stronger force their point of view on those who are weaker.

Strongly disagree 1 2 3 4 5 Strongly agree

Bureaucratic Norms

This variable was operationalized by a single item.

1. People here are mainly concerned about following laid down rules and procedures.

Strongly disagree 1 2 3 4 5 Strongly agree

The score on this scale ranges from 1 to 5, a higher score indicating existence of higher level of bureaucratic norms.

Close Supervision Norms

This was measured by the following item.

1. Supervision here is usually meant to check mistakes and employees prefer this.

Strongly disagree 1 2 3 4 5 Strongly agree

Norms of Centralized Risk Taking

This scale consisted of a single item. The item was:

1. Before initiating innovations or changes, managers here have to go to their bosses for approval and guidance.

Strongly disagree 1 2 3 4 5 Strongly agree

A higher score on this scale indicates that the organization is characterized by greater centralized risk-taking culture.

31A (16)

Title of the Instrument : **Formal Decentralization.**

Purpose : For measuring the extent of decentralization in an organization.

Authors : K. Prathap Reddy.

Language : English.

Availability : Dr. K. Prathap Reddy, Assoc. Professor NAARM, Rajendranagar, Hyderabad-500 030.

Uses : As at 31A (13).

Levels : First line supervisors onwards.

Main features : 20 items.

Reliability : Decision Recommendation Level : 0.98, Decision Approval level : 0.98.

Validity : Has high face validity.

Time Limit : 12 minutes.

Norms : Available with the author.

References : Was used by the author in his FPM Thesis on "Influence of Organizational Culture on Organizational Structure," submitted to IIM, Ahmedabad.

FORMAL DECENTRALIZATION

Decentralization is the extent to which the locus of decision-making authority is delegated to lower levels of hierarchy.

The actual questions asked for measuring *decentralization* are given below.

Q. We are interested to know who makes certain kinds of decisions in your organization. In Column 1, please indicate the designation of the person/committee (if it is a committee, please specify its composition) that examines various alternatives, estimates costs and benefits and takes a decision, even though the formal approval for such decision may have to be obtained from higher level.

In Column 2, please indicate the designation of person/committee (if it is a committee, please specify its composition) that formally *approves* the decision so that action can be properly initiated.

	Designation of the person/committee members who take the decision (Col.1)	Designation of the person/committee members who formally approve the decision (Col.2)
1	2	3
1. Determining marketing strategy for a new product.		
2. Major changes in the marketing strategy of an existing product		
3. Determining delivery dates or prioritizing orders		
4. Determining terms for negotiating with the customer		
5. Decisions concerning special terms of sales that can be offered to the customer		
6. Determining annual sales targets for each product		
7. Decision to offer or not to offer a quotation, where necessary		
8. Decision to supply an alternate product/ item to the customer		
9. Pricing of new products and/or significant changes in the pricing of existing products		
10. Other marketing decisions (please specify)		
11. Determining the annual production targets for each product		

(Contd.)

1	2	3
12. Changes in manufacturing plan (e.g. rescheduling) resulting from machine breakdowns, non-availability of inputs, etc.		
13. Procurement of critical inputs at short notice, probably overlooking normal purchase procedures		
14. Fixing norms/standards for inventory levels		
15. Development of a new product or service		
16. Use of overtime		
17. Type of capital equipment to be purchased		
18. Allocation of machinery and people to different products		
19. Discontinuing production of an existing product		
20. Plant layout and alterations in the existing plant layout		
21. Decisions regarding subcontracting, or machinery, or use of additional manpower		
22. Any comments you would like to make :		

The data under each column were treated separately, the first column representing decentralization in terms of decision recommendation level, and the second column in terms of decision approval level. The data were first converted into hierarchical levels based on organization chart. They were then converted into an equivalent score of X, the largest number of hierarchical levels found in any organization included in the sample.

31A (17)

Title of the Instrument : **Organizational Climate Questionnaire.**

Purpose : To measure personnel policies and practices of an organization, as seen through the eyes of its employees.

Authors : Baldev R. Sharma.

Language : English.

Availability : Shri Ram Centre for Industrial Relations and Human Resources, 4E/ 16, Jhandewalan Extension, New Delhi-110 055.

Uses : To measure organizational climate (OC).

Levels : First-line Supervisors (but with slight change it can be used for junior/middle managers also).

Main features : It is a 27 item questionnaire in which each statement is rated on a 4 point scale. In all 9 dimensions of OC are sought to be measured.

Reliability : Given.

Validity : Concurrent validity was established. All 9 dimensions of OC, as hypothesized, were positively and significantly related to supervisory-management relations.

Time Limit : 15-20 minutes.

Norms : Baldev R. Sharma, Not by Bread Alone : A Study of Organizational Climate and Employer-Employee Relations in India. New Delhi: Shri Ram Centre for Industrial Relations and Human Resources, 1987.

References : Given in the manual.

ORGANIZATIONAL CLIMATE QUESTIONNAIRE

Organizational Characteristics	How Far True in the Case of Supervisors?			
	Not at all (0)	A little (1)	A good deal (2)	Very much (3)
1. Employees in this company have many opportunities for advancement.				
2. There is a sound grievance-handling procedure here that tells employees what to do if they have a grievance.				

(Contd.)

	(0)	(1)	(2)	(3)
3. Salaries, allowances and perquisites of employees in this company are attractive considering their job responsibilities.				
4. Through regular meetings and joint forums, employees here are actively involved in solving day-to-day problems.				
5. Employees belonging to different categories and departments are treated impartially by the management of this company.				
6. In this company, good work is always recognised by the management.				
7. This company provides safe working conditions to its employees.				
8. This company provides adequate training facilities to its employees.				
9. The management of this company provides adequate welfare facilities to employees at the work place.				
10. This company plans on a regular basis for career development of its employees.				
11. The management of this company is always sympathetic in dealing with employee problems.				
12. Considering qualification and skills, salaries, allowances and perquisites of employees of this company are attractive.				
13. Employees here are represented in various committees for joint decision-making.				

(Contd.)

	(0)	(1)	(2)	(3)
14. This company recruits people after objective assessment of the merits of each case.				
15. Employees who contribute to the company's productivity and efficiency and invariably appreciated here.				
16. This company provides attractive retirement benefits to its employees.				
17. The employees of this company are regularly sent for various training courses and conferences.				
18. This company provides adequate welfare facilities and amenities to its employees and their families.				
19. The employees of this company have many opportunities to grow.				
20. The management here is always ready to look into the grievances and complaints of the employees.				
21. Salaries, allowances and perquisites in this company compare favourably with those prevailing in other companies.				
22. Before taking any important decision, the management here always consults the employees.				
23. Service rules and policies are consistently followed in this company in dealing with personnel matters.				
24. Hard work is invariably recognised and appreciated in this company.				

(Contd.)

	(0)	(1)	(2)	(3)
25. This company provides adequate job security to its employees.				
26. This company provides adequate general and technical education to its employees.				
27. The welfare facilities provided by this company compare favourably with those provided by other companies.				

31A (18)

Title of the Instrument : **Job-Satisfaction Questionnaire.**
Purpose : To measure job satisfaction.
Authors : Hardeo Ojha
Language : Hindi
Availability : Dr. Hardeo Ojha, Department of Psychology, Bhagalpur University, Bhagalpur-812007
Uses : To measure job satisfaction
Levels : Factory workers and office employees of all ages mentioned in published paper.
Time Limit : No time limit.

JOB SATISFACTION QUESTIONNAIRE

Instructions

Given below are some questions related to your job. Against every question there are two alternative answers 'Yes' and 'No'. Please read each question carefully and encircle any of the two answers which is applicable in your case. Kindly reply to each question unhesitatingly.

Question	*Answers*	
1. Are you satisfied with your salary?	Yes	No
2. Do you like your job-environment?	Yes	No
3. Do family problems create hindrances in your job?	Yes	No
4. Are your suggestions for improvement in work accepted?	Yes	No
5. Are you anxious about your future in your job?	Yes	No

	Question	*Answers*	
6.	Do you have tense relation with your senior officers?	Yes	No
7.	Are the behaviour of your officers favourable to you?	Yes	No
8.	Don't you like to stay even for a moment after working hour is over?	Yes	No
9.	Do you get social recognition for your job?	Yes	No
10.	Are you satisfied with the rules of appointment and promotion in your job?	Yes	No
11.	Has your working place any unfavourable effect upon your health?	Yes	No
12.	Are you interrupted even when you perform your duty sincerely?	Yes	No
13.	Do you feel that your future is safe due to your job?	Yes	No
14.	Do superior officers appreciate your suggestions?	Yes	No
15.	If on certain occasions your work load increases do you have objections?	Yes	No
16.	Are your abilities fully utilized in your present job?	Yes	No
17.	Do you have such feelings that you may be removed from job any moment?	Yes	No
18.	Do you feel novelty in your work?	Yes	No
19.	Do you sometimes feel that you should give up your job?	Yes	No
20.	Do your officers become harsh whenever you commit mistakes in your work?	Yes	No
21.	Is your present work interesting to you?	Yes	No
22.	Are you able to strengthen your social position by remaining in your present job?	Yes	No
23.	Is there conflict between your coworkers?	Yes	No
24.	Have you opted for this job out of compulsions?	Yes	No
25.	If you are assigned the job of others in addition to your own do you perform it happily?	Yes	No
26.	Do you become disinterested in work if there is delay in getting advance?	Yes	No
27.	Do you get any reward for improvement in work?	Yes	No
28.	Do you feel that your job is inferior in comparison to other jobs?	Yes	No

Question	*Answers*
29. Are you able to realize your ambitions by your job?	Yes No
30. If for certain specific reason you do not reach to your working place in time would you get rebuff?	Yes No
31. Do your fellow-workers help each other in work?	Yes No
32. Do you think that you could have got better salary and recognition in other jobs in comparison to your present one?	Yes No

31A (19)

Title of the Instrument : **A Quality of Life Scale for Industrial Workers.**

Purpose : To measure quality of life of industrial workers.

Authors : B.L. Dubey, Dwivedi, P.|Verma, S.K.; Department of Business Management, Punjab University, Chandigarh.

Language : English.

Availability : Scale is published in The Creative Psychologist, 1988, Also available with Dr. B.L. Dubey.

Uses : To measure quality of life of industrial workers.

Levels : Educated sample.

Main features : 24 item scale on a five point format.

Reliability : Test-retest reliability coefficient=0.58, Split-Half reliability coefficient = 0.87; Internal Consistency (E 1/3 value) of items satisfactory.

Validity : Correlation with other tests. Insignificant correlations with emotional instability, extraversion, social desirability, job satisfaction, age, education, salary.

Time Limit : 8-10 minutes.

Norms : On 323 industrial workers.

References :Dubey, B.L.; Dwivedi, P. and Verma, S.K. (1988) : Construction and standardization of a quality of life scale for use with industrial workers in India. *Creative Psychologist*, 1(1) 75-83.

QUALITY OF LIFE SCALE FOR INDUSTRIAL WORKERS

Age .... Education....................................... Sex ....
Occupation .... Organisation ....
Private Sector/Pub. Sector/Any other ....
Total income per month ....

Instruction: Kindly go through each item with 5 alternatives and tick (✓) one alternative only

1	I am happy with my Present assignment	Very Much	Quite Much	To some extent	Very little	Not at all
2	Problems in my life are	Very Much	Quite Much	Not Much	Very little	Not at all
3	My social interaction are	Very Much	Quite Much	Not Much	Very little	Not at all
4	My interest in life is	Very Much	Quite Much	Not Much	Very little	Not at all
5	I am dependent (financially) upon others	Very Much	Quite Much	Not Much	Very little	Not at all
6	I have been happy in my life	Very Much	Quite Much	Not Much	Very little	Not at all
7	A am happy with Present political system	Very Much	Quite Much	Not Much	Very little	Not at all
8	I feel my existence in this world is meaningful	Strongly agree	Agree	Undec-ided	Dis-agree	Stro-ngly dis-agree
9	What I have is enough for me	Strongly agree	Agree	Undec-ided	Dis-agree	Stro-ngly dis-agree
10	As a whole my needs are	Very much satis-fied	Satis-fied	Satis-fied to some extent	Dis-sati-sfied	Very much dis-safied
11	My relations with my family member are	Very good	Quite good	Normal	Poor	Very poor
12	My relations with others are	Very good	Quite good	Mediocre	Poor	Very poor

13	My relations with my life partner are	Very good	Quite good	Normal	Poor	Very poor
14	My level of aspir ations is	Very high	Quite high	Average	Low	Very low
15	My social prestige is	Very high	Quite high	Average	Low	Very low
16	As a whole my achieve-ment in life is	Very high	Quite high	Average	Low	Very low
17	I have peace of mind	Always	Often	Occas-ionally	Sel-dom	Never
18	I spare time for my hobbies	Always	Often	Occas-ionally	Sel-dom	Never
19	I feel secure	Always	Often	Occas-ionally	Sel-dom	Never
20	I manage time to know new things	Always	Often	Occas-ionally	Sel-dom	Never
21	I have been lucky in my life	Always	Often	Occas-ionally	Sel-dom	Never
22	As a whole, I keep good health	Always	Often	Occas-ionally	Sel-dom	Never
23	I feel inferior	Always	Often	Occas-ionally	Sel-dom	Never
24	As a whole, I feel happy	Always	Often	Occas-ionally	Sel-dom	Never

31A (20)

Title of the Instrument : **Job Satisfaction Questionnaire.**
Purpose : Measure dimension of Job satisfaction.
Author(s) : N.K. Chadha, Department of Psychology, Delhi University, Delhi.
Language : English.
Availability : N.K. Chadha, Department of Psychology, Delhi University, Delhi.
Uses : Measures Job satisfaction.
Levels : Workers and supervisors.
Main features : Five point scale, 97 items.
Reliability and Validity : Given.
Time Limit : 30 minutes.
Norms : Not available.

References :Used in M.A. and M.Phil. dissertation.

JOB SATISFACTION QUESTIONNAIRE

Name : N.K. Chandha, Vinod Sahni, Shubda Handoo
Age
Designation
Qualification

Instructions

There are as set of questions in this booklet which you are required to answer. You should tickmark (✓) **any one** of the five response category of Strongly Agree (SA), Agree (A), Undecided (U), Disagree (D), Strongly Disagree (SD) which suits you the best. Kindly respond to each item. All responses will be kept confidential.

	Response Category				
	SA 1	A 2	U 3	D 4	SD 5
1. I often feel that my employer will not terminate me if I commit a mistake.					
2. My job is more varied and less monotonous.					
3. In the workings of my organisation my opinion/ participation is considered					
4. I feel badly if I do not perform well on my job.					
5. I have various venues open for refreshing my knowledge in my field.					
6. I have often felt that at our organisation we have infrequent promotions.					
7. The respect and regards that people shown on me is because of the job I hold.					
8. Fringe benefits in my organisation are fantastic.					

(Contd.)

	1	2	3	4	5
9. While working together people discuss with each other and listen to each other in my organisation					
10. The most important thing that happen to me are involved with my job.					
11. The head of my organisation is just the right person for the seat					
12. My present job demands a high degree of accuracy.					
13. Drinking water facilities are satisfactory and usually provided at work place.					
14. I will quit the present job if I am offered another at a higher pay.					
15. My organization provides good housing facilities to its employees.					
16. I have never felt at ease in the present job as the ways of doing things are rapidly changing.					
17. I have faced a situation when an undeserving candidate was promoted.					
18. Recreational facilities are negligible in my organisation.					
19. I like and respect my colleagues.					
20. I have substantial discretion in scheduling the work and determining the procedures in carrying out work.					

(Contd.)

	1	2	3	4	5
21. Since I have joined this organisation I have hardly had time to fulfil my various desires due to time constraints.					
22. I have to work very hard here if I am to keep my job secure.					
23. The activities of my superiors are governed with self-interest.					
24. I am contented with the increments that the orgnisation grants us.					
25. I have control over the pace of my work.					
26. Present job gives me a tremendous sence of accomplishment.					
27. I am confident that when the time comes I will be promoted i.e. on the basis of seniority.					
28. Present job requires use of different talents which are present in me.					
29. I feel that my contribution to the organisation is worth while.					
30. Canteen and catering facilities are available at appropriate time.					
31. I like to go on learning as much as possible about my work.					
32. Role expectations in my organisation are ambigous.					
33. I often feel that in my organisation promotions are based on individual calibre.					

(Contd.)

	1	2	3	4	5
34. Compared to the nature of work salary scales here are very poor.					
35. Each employee here is assigned has specific place.					
36. I seldom watch the clock when I am at office as time passes smoothly.					
37. Taking up this job involves no risk as it guarantee fair amount of security.					
38. I spend quite a lot of my work time in making personal telephone calls.					
39. Things are clearly planned before taking action in my organisation.					
40. I have the liberty to carry on my job without any obstacle.					
41. My excellent performance is accompanied with a pat on my back.					
42. When Monday morning comes I think longingly of being able to lie in a hospital with a broken leg.					
43. Major satisfaction in my life comes from my job.					
44. I obtain direct and clear information about the effectiveness of my performance.					
45. I often find myself at a disadvantage while working due to lack of technical information.					
46. Noise pollution is kept under control here.					
47. It would take a sizable raise in pay to get me accept a different job.					
48. I often complete work just for the leck of it.					

(Contd.)

	1	2	3	4	5
49. I often day dream about having a better position in the same kind of job.					
50. I would advise my child to take up the same kind of work as mine if he had the ability and temperament to do so.					
51. I seldom talk about problems pertaining to work with my co-worker.					
52. My superiors think that I am unable of doing a good job.					
53. I feel blue when something regarding my job goes wrong.					
54. I do a job from beginning to end with a visible outcome.					
55. I have been absent from work for long vacation in the past year.					
56. We have no influence in decision concerning out welfare.					
57. During monsoons my room becomes damp and moist.					
58. Sense of aimlessness and apathy among top managers precludes any attempt to give firm goals to my organisations.					
59. I would be happy to do the same job even if I were paid one-third less.					
60. Job I feel is a whole way of life.					
61. I don't want to be at the mercy of events, I have to master and control all the things affecting me.					

(Contd.)

	1	2	3	4	5
62. Rules and policies are effectively enforced in my organisation.					
63. Our superiors give us all kind of support at work in my organisation.					
64. At slack times I commit mistakes in my work as my room-is not well lighted.					
65. My work has big patches of boredom.					
66. As far as company at work is concerned I am like a square peg in a round hole.					
67. Reality does not offer satisfaction, interactions with other will fail so it is safer to remain distant here.					
68. If I am to leave this job. I would miss the work here. the most.					
69. Our relationship with superiors are very cordial.					
70. If I leave this job I would miss its money the most.					
71. Pay scales here are in accordance with seniority.					
72. I really perform better when I am trying to beat others.					
73. If I an caught in a conflict between home and job my choice always would be home.					
74. My job has a substantial impact on the life/work of other people.					
75. I joined this job because it seemed just the right thing for me.					

(Contd.)

	1	2	3	4	5
76. I joined the present job because it was all I could find at that point of time.					
77. I often feel responsibility should be shared in my organisation.					
78. I feel that job is only way to make enough money to keep one self alive.					
79. There is an effective body to handle grievances here.					
80. In my organisation there are others who to an extent, are depending on me to succeed.					
81. When my 'Boss' throws his temper tantrums at me I feel like going on a strike to set him right.					
82. We often face problems because there is crowding in our rooms-we are too many people in a room.					
83. I am advised on improvement methods in my organisation while working.					
84. Monetary rewards are contingent on performance here, this is what I like about my organisation					
85. Emphasis is placed on quality of performance at my work place.					
86. Concentration on work is a tough task as various noises (working typist, constantly ringing telephones etc.) are very distracting.					
87. Lack of charm and sympathy is one problem with my superiors.					

(Contd.)

	1	2	3	4	5
88. I keep my personal life strictly separate from my work (check with your partner on this).					
89. There is a body which provides feedback to subordinates.					
90. The whole frantic irrational scramble to beat others (professionally) is present in my organisation.					
91. At slack times I get vague pains when I am at work.					
92. I am well rewarded for my efforts by my organisation.					
93. I would take a day off from my work just to have fun.					
94. If I won or suddenly inherited a large sum of money, I would take up some kind of work that I have always.					
95. I often feel that my job is more than I aspired for.					
96. I feel that competition is vital to a successful career.					
97. Employee turnover in our organisation is very low as the company plans and policies are adequate.					

31A (21)

Title of the Instrument : **Job Involvement Scale.**

Purpose : To assess the level of job involvement of employees.

Author(s) : Ashok Pratap Singh.

Language(s) : English and Hindi.

Availability : Department of Psychology, Banaras Hindu University, Varanasi - 221005.

Uses : It can be used to assess the degree of job involvement of employees of any category or job.

Levels : Workers, Supervisors, and managerial class of any industry.

Main Features : There are 54 items in this scale. Each statement of the scale has four response alternatives, namely strongly agree, agree, disagree, and strongly disagree. The items of the scale were framed in such a way that they can be used for measuring the degree of involvement of all subjects irrespective of the nature of their work, organization, and machines and tools they use.

Reliability : The Reliability of the scale was computed by the Cronbach's alpha coefficient technique and it was found to be 0.83.

Validity : The index of homogeneity and internal validity of the scale were determined by computing the point biserial coefficient of correlation (rpb=.40) to ascertain how the scores on the individual items, ranging form 1 to 4 contribute to total score. The scores on job involvement scale of Lodahl and Kejner (1965) was used as one of the validation criteria for this scale. The coefficient correlation between the two tests was found to be.93.

Time limit : No time limit.

Norms : Use available from Dr. Ashok Pratap Singh.

References :

1. Nath, K. (1988) : "Organizational Climate, role stress and locus of control in job involvement among banking personnel". Unpublished Ph. D. thesis, Department of Psychology, Banaras Hindu University, Varanasi.
2. Singh, M.P. (1989) : "A study of values and styles of coping as related to outcome variables in public and private enterprises." Unpublished Ph. D. Thesis, Department of Psychology, Banaras Hindu University, Varanasi.

JOB INVOLVEMENT SCALE

1. I do not want to engage myself in the work after the working hours.
2. I feel relaxed after the working hours.
3. I feel pity when there is no work to do.
4. I feel boredom when I do not have any work to do.
5. I am fully committed to my job.
6. To do work is the best source of recreation for me.
7. When the work problem is not solved then I continue to think about that in the home also.

8. Sometimes it is difficult for me to have sleep when I think about the job.
9. Sometimes I cut my lunch break period to complete my job.
10. I prepare myself at home to accomplish the work in a better way
11. I spend my leisure time in job related activities.
12. I get disappointed when my work is not completed.
13. I keep myself engaged in the work without thinking about the happenings with me.
14. I become anxious when the work is not completed.
15. I think about the work at the time of doing it.
16. I leave other important things for my work.
17. In the holidays also I think that my work is not being done.
18. I usually look at the watch for knowing about the time to stop the work.
19. I complete my work even if it takes more than alloted time without any extra salary.
20. How good a man is, can be understood by his quality of work.
21. I get maximum satisfaction from my work.
22. My time flies at the work.
23. The important events of my life are related to my work.
24. I feel frustrated on my failures at the work.
25. There are other important work to me than the present one.
26. Work is every thing for me.
27. Probably I will be continuing on my job even if I have no need of money.
28. Mostly I like to stay at home in comparison to coming for the work.
29. My work is the most important part of my life.
30. I keep myself involved in my work.
31. I escape from taking extra work and responsibility other than the alloted work.
32. In the past I had more interest in my work than the present.
33. There are other things important than this work.
34. Sometimes I would like to blame myself for my faults at work.
35. I do not stay overtime even if some work is left incomplete
36. I find boredom in my job.
37. I do not think about the work at the time of returning back to home from work.
38. I have chosen suitable job for myself.
39. More money can be earned from some other job.
40. I work only for the money.

41. I am unable to complete my work.
42. I do not think about the job on the holidays.
43. My work is not comfortable.
44. I stop doing my work after the working hours is over.
45. I will not advise for doing this work to my any close relatives.
46. I do not get disappointed after being unsuccessful.
47. My work is so good that I do not get fatigued even after doing it for longer times.
48. I find any work burdensome.
49. I try to do more than the supervisor expect from me.
50. In spite of several problems I try to compete my work.
51. I try to complete the allotted work even if it takes more time and energy.
52. I try to do my work with full honesty and sincerity.
53. I take any damage to the mine as my own.
54. I feel happiness in completing my work.

31A (22)

Title of the Instrument : **Job Motivation Scale (Revised.)**

Purpose : For measiring job motivation.

Authors : S. Sultan Akhtar and Manju.

Languages : English and Hindi.

Availability : Prof. S. Sultan Akhtar, Department of Psychology, Aligarh Muslim University, Aligarh.

Uses : For research and classification.

Levels : Employees of all levels.

Main Features : It is a five point Likert type of scale, it consists of 20 items divided into extrinsic and intrinsic factors.

Reliability : rll = .91 (N= 100).

Validity : Newly introduced items were correlated with the old ones and the values ranged between .34 to .44.

Time Limit : No time limit.

Norms : Norms were calculated on 100 samples.

References :

1. Akhtar , S.S. & Nizami, M.A. (1987) : Factor Analytical Study of Job Motivation of different work Groups. Paper presented at the 24th Annual Conference of Indian Academy of Applied Psychology. Waltair.
2. Akhtar, S.S. & Bhargava, Y (1974) : Job Motivational Factors Under different Organizational

Climates. Proceedings of the 18th International Congress of Applied Psychology. Montreal, (Canada.).

JOB MOTIVATION SCALE

The purpose of the present investigation is to study the needs and aspirations of people working in various capacities in India. The success of the study would entirely depend on your honest and frank responses.

You are not required to reveal your identity and your response would be treated in strict confidence.

We are confident that you would cooperate wholeheartedly and help us in achieving our objective.

Prof. S. Sultan Akhtar and Manju
Department of Psychology,
Aligarh Muslim University,
Aligarh.

The following statements pertain to your working situation. Please read carefully and indicate the extent to which you find them satisfying. Each statement is to be evaluated as suggested below.

Against each statement a bracket has been provided :

If you are very much satisfied then put (5) within the bracket.

If you are satisfied then put (4) within the bracket

If you are slightly satisfied then put (3) within the bracket

If you are dissatisfied then put (2) within the bracket

If you are very much dissatisfied then put (1) within the bracket

In this manner each statement is to be evaluated from 1 to 5

S.No	Items	Response
1.	To complete a job successfully.	( )
2.	To be singled out for praise.	( )
3.	To like the actual task involved in getting the job done.	( )
4.	To gain responsibility for own or others working in a job.	( )
5.	To change status through promotion.	( )
6.	To be happy with one's earnings.	( )
7.	Change in a job which could lead to further growth.	( )

(Contd.)

S.No	Items	Response
8.	To experience satisfying social interactions with one's subordinate.	( )
9.	To obtain social status through job.	( )
10.	To have greater autonomy for work scheduling.	( )
11.	To experience satisfying social interaction with one's boss.	( )
12.	To experience satisfying social interactions with one's co-workers.	( )
13.	To have competent supervisors.	( )
14.	To be in an organization (institution) with good policies and administrative procedures.	( )
15.	To be given more responsibility in the job.	( )
16.	To have good physical surroundings on the job.	( )
17.	To have one's personal life affected for good, by occurrences on the job.	( )
18.	To have objective indications of security, (such as job tenure and company stability.	( )
19.	To have housing facilities.	( )
20.	To have more opportunities for promotion of efficient employees.	( )
21.	To get transportation facilities.	( )
22.	To have health suitable for the job.	( )
23.	To like leave policies.	( )
24.	To have opportunities for recreations.	( )
25.	Experiencing no feeling for casteism on the job.	( )
26.	To get medical facilities.	( )
27.	To have mobility with regard to work.	( )
28.	To participate in decision making processes.	( )

31A (23)

Title of the Instrument : **Training Needs Quotient.**
Purpose : To measure the training needs of ICDS Project functionaries.
Author : Neelam Mahajan.
Languages : English.
Availability : Central Library IARI, New Delhi.
Uses : It can be used to ascertain training needs of project level functionaries of Integrated Child Development Services Scheme.
Levels : (a) Child Development Project Officers, Mukhaya Sevikas, and Anganwadi Workers.

Main Features : A fairly comprehensive and exhaustive training need inventory list comprising of 33 training items was prepared and arranged along a five point Likert type training needs continuum scale items were selected on the basis of course content outlined by NIPCCD for various ICDS functionaries.

Reliability : Not calculated.

Validity : Scale items were selected on the basis of course contempt outlined by NIPCCD for various ICDS Functionaries after discussion with various personnel and their trainers.

References :

1. Sharma, S. N. and Singh Y.P. (1970) : "A Study of the selected factors affecting the training needs of animal husbandry, Extension Officers in Punjab" *Indian Journal of Ext. Edu.* VI: (1-2) pp. 24-33.
2. Ministry of Social and Women's Welfare, Govt, of India "Compilation of Guidelines and instructions regarding the scheme of ICDS and functional literacy for adult women" New Delhi 1982.

TRAINING NEEDS QUOTIENT

	Not at all needed	Needed a little	Some what needed	Very much needed	Absolute must for training
1	2	3	4	5	6
(a) Objectives, importance and working of the ICDS project organization and roles of functionaries at various levels ?	1	2	3	4	5
(b) Methodology of community surveys and identification of potential beneficiaries ?	1	2	3	4	5
(c) Office procedures and maintenance of relevant records, registers and accounts ?	1	2	3	4	5
(d) Techniques of communicating effectively with potential women and children beneficiaries as well as community leaders ?	1	2	3	4	5
(e) Basic concepts in interpersonal relations?	1	2	3	4	5

(Contd.)

1	2	3	4	5	6
(f) Organizing and exploiting the potential of demonstrations, exhibitions. field trips, field days and campaigns for improved nutrition and health practices?	1	2	3	4	5
(g) Organizing and using Youth clubs, Mahila Mandals and Charcha Mandals (discussion groups) for spread of sound nutrition and health pracitices?	1	2	3	4	5
(h) Knowledge of factors which affect the adoption or rejection of nutrition and health practices by beneficiaries : Cultural, Economic, Social, Situational and Psychological Factors?	1	2	3	4	5
(i) Use of audio-visual aids and equipment?	1	2	3	4	5
(j) Ante-natal and post-natal care of mothers?	1	2	3	4	5
(k) Growth and development stages of a healthy child ?	1	2	3	4	5
(l) Principles of treatment of common illnesses afflicting children?	1	2	3	4	5
(m) Identification and immediate management of 'at risk" children?	1	2	3	4	5
(n) Assessment of age, evaluation of nutritional and health status of a child and use of simple tools and equipment for the same?	1	2	3	4	5
(o) Common vaccines, their storage and immunization schedules?	1	2	3	4	5
(p) Health, personal hygiene, environmental sanitation and control for communicable diseases ?	1	2	3	4	5
(q) Family planning and fertility control methods?	1	2	3	4	5
(r) Functional literacy for women and mothers?	1	2	3	4	5

(Contd.)

1	2	3	4	5	6
(s) Knowledge of women crafts and counselling principles ?	1	2	3	4	5
(t) Non-formal education for pre-school children?	1	2	3	4	5
(u) Making of toys and simple educational aids from local materials for learning of crafts by pre-school children?	1	2	3	4	5
(v) Planning and food preparation for suplementary nutrition?	1	2	3	4	5
(w) Knowledge of Modern Nutrition Technology:	1	2	3	4	5
1. Principles of balanced diet?	1	2	3	4	5
2. Nutritive value of commonly available foods and nutritional requirements for various members of a family?	1	2	3	4	5
3. Cheap nutritious diets and meal planning from locally available foods?	1	2	3	4	5
4. Improved cooking practices?	1	2	3	4	5
5. Storage and preservation of foods ?	1	2	3	4	5
6. Antenatal and Postnatal maternal nutrition?	1	2	3	4	5
7. Infant feeding?	1	2	3	4	5
8. Weaning foods?	1	2	3	4	5
9. Nutrition for the pre-school children?	1	2	3	4	5
10. Therapeutic nutrition?	1	2	3	4	5
11. Malnutrition and nutrition deficiency diseases?	1	2	3	4	5

31 A (24)

Title of the Instrument : **Perception of Coordination Scale.**

Purpose : To measure the perceptions of Coordination of ICDS project functionaries.

Author : Neelam Mahajan.

Languages : English.

Availability : Central Library IARI, New Delhi.

Uses : It can be used to determine the perceptions of coordination of ICDS project functionaries.

Levels : ICDS Project functionaries viz Child Development Project Officers, Mukhya Sevikas and Anganwadi Workers.

Main Features : Items with poor discriminating value were rejected. For this purpose mean and variance of response to each individual items was evaluated by finding the value of t-ratio. Statements in the item pool were rank ordered according to their t-values. Items for which t is statistically insignificant (using single tail test) are left out thus finally selecting 15 items.

Reliability : Cronbach given in Guilford and Fruchter (1978) was calculated to test the reliability of scale computed value of Cronbach being 0.70.

Validity : The content validity of the scale was ensured from 20 judges who were experts in ICDS scheme and scientists from Agricultural Extension field possessing knowledge of ICDS. The intrinsic Validity of the scale was determined by internal consistency indices like Cronbach and factor analysis.

Time Limit : 20 minutes.

Norms : Not applicable.

References : 1. Guilford and Fruchter (1978).

SCALE TO MEASURE PERCEPTIONS OF COORDINATION OF ICDS PROJECT FUNCTIONARIES.

AN = Almost never =1
OC = Occasionally =2
OF = Often =3
VF = Very often =4
AA = Almost always =5

S.No	Statement	*AN*	*OC*	*OF*	*VF*	*AA*
1.	Information is timely passed on to right person in the organization for appropriate action.	1	2	3	4	5
2.	The work assignments are usually well planned.	1	2	3	4	5
3.	Functionaries exchange their opinions and ideas freely.	1	2	3	4	5
4.	Problems arising out of coordination of activities of the functionaries of various components of the project are not well handled.	1	2	3	4	5

(Contd.)

S.No	Statement	*AN*	*OC*	*OF*	*VF*	*AA*
5.	People often plan their activities together and coordinate their efforts.	1	2	3	4	5
6.	Functionaries prefer to work as a team most of the time.	1	2	3	4	5
7.	Functionaries receive the needed cooperation from other agencies/ departments by maintaining linkages with them.	1	2	3	4	5
8.	There is mutual mistrust among the personnel of the organization.	1	2	3	4	5
9.	Clearcut instructions are usually received from colleagues on how to complete the job successfully.	1	2	3	4	5
10.	Time, energy and sometimes money is unnecessarily wasted in extending help to other functionaries or in seeking cooperation from them.	1	2	3	4	5
11.	Work situation in the organization prohibits employees to perform satisfactorily.	1	2	3	4	5
12.	The supervisor allows considerable flexibility to the subordinates so that they can perform their jobs well.	1	2	3	4	5
13.	Abilities, knowledge and experiences of functionaries are not being utilized properly in the organization.	1	2	3	4	5
14.	Many conflicts are left unresolved in the organization.	1	2	3	4	5
15.	The supervisor gives enough authority and responsibility to the subordinates in performing their job.	1	2	3	4	5

31A (25)

Title of the Instrument : **Inter Personal Trust Scale (IPTS).**

Author : S.C. Gupta and Vinita Mathur.

Availability : HCM Rajasthan State Institute of Public Administration, Jaipur.

Level : General population.

Uses : The instrument is meant for training purposes. The participants can examine their inter-personal trust—orientation with the help of IPTS. Also may be used for research as well as for many other purposes.

Main Features : This scale is designed to measure the inter personal trust orientation. It consists of one item for each stage of Assumption—Perception—behaviour—Feedback cycle of five types of need-oriented human interactions.

Reliability : The split half reliability of the scale was found to be 0.91 which is significant at 0.01 level.

Validity : Correlation Coefficients found were as follows : (N=166)

1. Telling 0.18*
2. Selling = – 0.02
3. Participating = – 0.07
4. Delegating = –0.08
5. Leadership effectiveness = –0.17*

Time Limit: No time Limit.

Norms : In the manual.

---

* = $p < 0.05$

IPTS

This questionnaire is designed to know about your experiences while interacting with people in general. Please read the statements given below and give your responses by writing 1,2,3 or 4 where;

1 Means "totally disagree"
2 means " somewhat agree"
3 means "agree to a large extent" and
4 means " totally agree"

1. Most of the people do not do what they say.
2. If you expose your weaknesses before others, you are in for trouble.
3. Nobody is my friend or enemy in this world.
4. People seem to be in search of opportunities to belittle and degrade me.
5. Most of the people do not feel happy when they see others flourishing.
6. If you have high expectations from people you will be disappointed.
7. I am a lot more cautious while dealing with strangers.
8. I have a feeling that most of the people don't understand me.

9. Most of the people don't think positively about others,
10. There is so much competition in this world that people will not hesitate in stepping on your toes to go ahead.
11. Neither do I like to seek obligation from others, nor do I like others patronising me.
12. Whenever I relied on people I was deceived.
13. Most of the people show frindliness only when they have some self-interest.
14. Unless you show people your power, they underestimate you.
15. I always try to achieve better than others.
16. People have generally taken advantage of my goodness,
17. Most of the people are not what they pretend to be.
18. If you share your sorrows with people you will only be ridiculed.
19. I know how to retort back when somebody blames me.
20. People seem to be in a habit of opposing even the best of my intentions.

Scale 31 A (26) Printed on page 615

B

31B (1)

Title of the Instrument : **Employees Motivation Schedule.**

Author : A.K.Srivastava.

Languages : Hindi

Availability : Manovaignanik Parikchan Samsthan, UH B-28, Sanjay Nagar Colony, Chowkaghat, Varanasi.

Uses : To test the level of motivation in Employees.

Levels : Employees working in various Production and non-production organizations.

Main Features : This scale consists of 70 items (10 for each area) relating to certain mentioned needs being manifested in work (job). All the items are "true keyed" and are to be responded on a four point scale i.e., always,/mostly/seldom/never.

Reliability : The following table records the reliability coefficients of the seven sub-scales of the schedule :

Sub-scales	Serial No of the items	Split-Half (N=200)	Retest(N=95)
1.	1-10	.82	.86
2.	11-20	.79	.84
3.	21-30	.74	.84
4.	31-40	.77	.81
5.	41-50	.81	.83
6.	51-60	79	.84
7.	61-70	.72	.79

Validity : The following table shows Validity results :

Work Motivation	Job Involvement (N=101)	Role Stress (N=200)
1. Personal growth	.78	-.65
2. Achievement	.73	-.57
3. Self Control	.65	-.50
4. Monterey gain	.55	-.32
5 Non-financial gains	.53	-.31
6. Social affliction	.67	-.39
7. Self actualization	.53	-.38
8. The whole scale	.83	-.51

Time Limit : No fixed time.

Norms : Scoring norms are available.

31B (2)

Title of the Instrument : **Job Satisfaction, Scale.**

Authors : M/s. National Psychological Corporation, Kacheri Ghat, Agra-4.

Languages : English.

Uses : Satisfaction-Dissatisfaction can be measured for any category of worker, on job intrinsic and job-extrinsic factors.

Levels : All categories of workers.

Main Features : It consists of 30 items. Items are rated on a five point scale. The scale has both positive and negative items.

Reliability : Test-retest reliability = .98.

Validity : The scale compares favourably with Muthayya's job-satisfaction questionnaire giving a validity coefficient of .743.

Moreover the satisfaction measures obtained on the scale have a close resemblance to the ratings given to the employees on a 3 point scale. The coefficient of correlation was .812.

Time Limit : No time limit.

Norms : Provided in the manual.

31B (3)

Title of the Instrument : **The Occupational Stress Index.**

Authors : A.K. Srivastava and A.P. Singh.

Availability : M/s. Manovaigyanic Parikshan Sansthan, Sanjay Nagar Conoly, Varanasi.

Languages : Hindi.

Uses : To measure the extent of stress perceived by employees arising from various constituents and conditions of their jobs.

Level : Employees of all levels in industries or non-production organisations.

Main Features : The scale consists of 48 items, each to be rated on a five point scale. Out of 46 items, 28 are true keyed and rest 18 are 'false keyed'. The items relate to almost all relevant components of the job life which cause stress.

Reliability : Split-half=.93, Cronbach's Alpha-Coefficient for the scale as a whole =.90.

Validity : Validity of the O.S.I. was determined by Computing coefficients of correlation between the scales on the O.S.I. and the various measures of job attitudes and job behaviour.

Time Limit : No time Limit.

Norms : Norms are provided in the manual.

31B (4)

Title of the Instrument : **Role-Conflict (R-C) Scale.**

Author : A.K. Pandey.

Availability : M/s. Manovaigyanik Parikchhan Sansthan, UHD-28, Sanjay Nagar Colony. Chowkaghat, Varanasi.

Language : Hindi.

Uses : To measure role-conflict in large groups, for research, survey purposes, for comparison of populations working in organizations and to increase production, etc.

Level : For group administration as well as for individual testing of

Indian sample.

Main Features : It's self-administering inventory with 30 items. Items are rated on a 5 point scale.

Reliability : Split-Half = .79; Test- retest + .87.

Validity : Criterion-related validity=.81.

Time Limit : No time limit, takes normally 30 minutes.

Norms : Percentile norms are provided in the manual.

References : Provided in the manual.

31B (5)

Title of the Instrument : **PGI Job Satisfaction Scale (Revised.)**

Purpose : To measure job satisfaction.

Authors : A.C. Moudgil, S.K. Verma, Kuldip Kaur, Kulwant Kaur. (1988).

Language : Hindi.

Availability : Scale is published in Personality study and Group Behaviour, 1988, Vol.8, No. 2, pp. 69-75. Or from the authors.).

Uses : To measure job satisfaction.

Levels : Educated subjects.

Main Features : 20 item scale on a five point format, range of scores = 0 to 80.

Reliability : Test-retest reliability = 0.81, Internal consistency of items (E 1/3 Value.).

Validity : Correlation with other tests.

Time Limit : 10 to 15 minutes.

Norms: Available.

References : 1. Moudgil, A.C.: Verma, S.K. Kaur, Kuldip and Kaur, Kulwant (1988) : PGI Job Satisfaction Scale (revised form). *Personality Study and Group Behaviour*. 8(2) 69-75.

31B (6)

Title of the Instrument : **Work Motivation Questionnaire (WMQ).**

Author : K.G. Agarwal.

Availability : M/s. National Psychological Corporation,4/230, Kacheri Ghat, Agra-4.

Languages : English and Hindi.

Uses : To measure work motivation and satisfaction of the employees of different strata in any industry of organization.

Level : Managers and blue collar employees.

Main Features : It consists of 26 Likert type items with 5 alternatives answers, one of which is required to be checked.

Reliability : Split half reliability established = .99. Summated scoring is done by assigning 5 to the most positive responses and 1 to the extreme negative response.

Validity : Face validity, Item validity, and factorial validity established.

Time Limit : No prescribed time limit.

Norms : NIL.

31B (7)

Title of the Instrument : **Leadership Effectiveness Dimension Scale.**

Author(s) :•Asha Hingar and Sangeeta Sharma.

Availability : Dr. Asha Hingar, 329, Himmat Nagar, Tonk Road, Jaipur-302018.

Languages : English.

Uses : To measure the various dimensions of leadership effectiveness and leadership styles of white collar employees, in private and public organisations.

Main Features : 30 item scale consisting of six leadership effectiveness dimensions, Emotional Stabilizer (ES); Team Builder (TB), Performance Orientor (PO); Potential Extractor (PE); Socially Intelligent (SI); Value Inculcator (VI). It is rated on a five point scale, as, always, usually; some-times; rarely; never. Higher score indicates higher leadership effectiveness.

Score ranges form 30-150.

Reliability : Split half reliability with odd and even method is 0.69.

Validity : Construct validity is 0.49.

References :

1. Hinger, Asha (1981) : "Psychometric Study of Leadership styles." M. Phil Dissertation : University of Rajasthan.
2. Hingar, Asha (1984) : "Psychometric Verification of Leadership Styles." *Indian Management*, Sept. Vol. XXIII, Nor 9.
3. Baheti, Smita (1994), Leadership Effectiveness : A Conceptual Study. MA Dissertation : University of Rajasthan.

PART FOUR

SOCIAL PHENOMENA

INTRODUCTION

This part of the Handbook reports instruments dealing with several social dimensions. The instruments are reported under six sections :

1. Values,
2. Stratification,
3. Social Distance and Group Attitudes,
4. Modernization and Social Change,
5. Religion and Morality, and
6. Other Social Attitudes.

The classification is based on the consideration of a number of instruments forming into a distinct category rather than on any theoretical basis. For example, the instruments reported under social distance and group attitudes modernization and social change, religion and morality and other social attitudes are by and large, the instruments which deal with social attitudes. The section of modernization and social change includes a few specific dimensions like family planning, agricultural innovations, social and cultural modernization scales. Although sufficient number of these instruments are available and may be grouped separately, but these have been grouped under modernization and social change to avoid any specific-issue based classification. The instruments on other social attitudes include several dimensions of social issues like attitudes towards governmental family planning, mentally retarded, alienation, political awareness, socio-political attitudes, national integration, parent-child relations and social support etc. In a way, most of the miscellaneous categories of instruments dealing with social phenomena and social issues have been included in this section.

In all, 79 instruments have been reported in this part of the Handbook. 52 instruments have been originally reproduced here. Information has been provided for other 22 instruments. Three are citations and 2 are adaptations. The detailed break-up of the instruments is given in the Table on the next page.

Table : Details of the Instruments Related to Social Phenomena

Classification	Originals Reproduced	Only Information	Citations	Adaptations	Total
Values	03	02	—	—	05
Stratification	02	01	—	—	03
Social Distance and Group Attitudes	01	—	—	—	01
Modernization and Social Change	12	04	01	—	17
Religion and Morality	—	03	—	01	04
Other Social Attitudes	34	12	02	01	49
Total	52	22	03	02	79

Values

The instruments in this section cover value dimensions like achievement values, values dominating life style etc. Only 5 instruments have been reported in this section. Three original instruments have been reproduced and there are 2 instruments where only information is provided. Out of the 5 instruments, one scale measures the attitudes or the values towards family planning. The scale is available both in English as well as in Hindi. This scale is mainly useful for finding out the values of unmarried youth in the age range 18-28 years. The scale has internal consistency check, and test of significance was applied for 45 pairs. This scale does not carry any validity coefficients nor has any norms been developed.

The other scale is called Value Orientation Scale which is developed by N.S. Chauhan, N. Singh and others. It is meant for adolescents and adults and measures the Value dimensions like Cosmopolitanism/localism, Fatalism/Scienticism, Venturesomeness/non-venturesomeness, Traditionism/progressiveism, Autocratism/Democratism, and Empathy/Non-empathy. This scale is also available in both the languages i.e., in Hindi and English.

Reliability Correlation coefficients have been found for each of the above value dimensions and they were found to be consistently high.

There is another scale Career and Family Values Scale by Sadhna Tanwar and Kulwinder Singh which meaures female values in family and career contexts. Test is ideal for college going females. Split-Half reliability has been found out for this scale, and the coefficients of correlation have been found to be consistently high. Known contrasted group method has been chosen to find out the validity of the scale. Norms have also been found out on a sample of 1000 college females. Percentile norms and stanine equivalents are provided.

There are two instruments where only information has been provided. One instrument is the P.G.I Achievement Value Index by D.K. Menon and others, which may be used for the measurement of achievement values in educated as well as uneducated classes of people. The scale is in Hindi. Test-retest, and underscore reliabilities have been found out by ratings method. Construct validity has been found out by correlating the tests with other tests.

There is another instrument which measures guilt feelings after vasectomy by M.B. Paliwal. The scale which is available in Hindi can assess feelings of guilt in industrial workers after vasectomy. Reliability coefficient for this test was found to be sufficiently high. High content validity was found. No norms have been provided.

No citations as well as adaptations have been reported in this section. Instruments in this section are very few and do not cover any specific sector. Some specific scales are needed for specific professions like teaching, management, engineering, social work, medicines etc., as these professions require some specific value-dimensions.

Stratification

The instruments dealing with the socio-economic status are reported in this section. There are only 3 instruments available of which 2 are original and reproduced here in full. Information about other one is reported. These instruments are generally to be administered on adult population for information about the parental income, material possessions, education etc. of the family members.

The first to be reproduced here is Kalliath SES Inventory by R.P Kalliath. The test is in English and it measures the socio-economic status of urban literate population. There are several criteria which the test measures like types of family, type of accommodation, facilities and services available at home, articles and gadgets possessed, total monthly income, literacy level of parents, spouse, etc. The test has high reliability coefficients. Test-retest as well as the parallel form reliability has been found out. Content validity of the test has been established.

There is another scale called Scale for Assessing Middle Class Housing Conditions (MCHCS) by S.R. Mahajani and Asha Nimkar which assesses the housing conditions of middle class families. The test was devised for home scientists, housewives, architects, and also town planners.

The scale has test-retest and split-half reliability coefficients which were found to be very high. Content validity was found out. No norms are available for this test.

There is another scale which also assesses socio-economic status of urban subjects. It has also reported fairly high reliability and validity.

Social Distance and Group Attitudes

This section includes information about the instrument dealing with social distance, discrimination and sociometric choices. Only one instrument has been reported in this section which is reproduced here.

Community Participation Index by Neelam Mahajan has been used to determine the level of community participation in ICDS project organizations. The scale is in English, and it is an 11 item Likert type five-point scale. No reliability, validity or norms have been reported.

Instruments dealing with other social problems like communal and racial conflicts etc., are very much lacking. We need to have more instruments on these themes as social scientists in general believe that psychologists have not contributed their might to larger social and national issues.

Modernization and Social Change

There are in all 17 instruments listed under this title of which 12 have been originally reproduced here. Information is provided for other 4 instruments. One is a citation, and no adaptation has been reported. These instruments deal with several indications of modernization and social change, like attitudes, towards social and cultural modernization, family planning, awareness of congruence, differential perceptions of adopters and non-adopters, level of farm mechanization, and women's social freedom etc.

Among the instruments reproduced here, 4 are scales measuring attitudes towards modernization of farmers, knowledge and retention of literate rural farm women, and opinion of rural women towards smokeless *chulha*, kitchen gardening and animal husbandry practices.

These 4 instruments are mainly devised for farmers and modernization in the agricultural technology.

The first instrument is by B.S. Bhatia which measures knowledge of Punjab farmers. The scale is in English as well as in Punjabi languages. The instrument is mainly for research and assessment of extension project.

The second instrument Knowledge and Retention Test of Literate Rural Farm Women by Rajinder Kaur and Dr. B.S. Hansra is also in English and Punjabi. This scale can be used to determine the retention of nutritional knowledge gained by the literate rural women. There is another scale, Opinion Scale by Rajinder Kaur and Ranjit Singh available in English and Hindi. The scale has been devised to find out the opinion of the rural women towards smokeless chulha, kitchen gardening and animal husbandry practices. Here, there are three scales (separate scale for each practice) for measuring the rural women's opinion.

Scale by R.K. Samanta called Management Orientation Scale can be used to measure the management (Planning, Production, and Marketing) orientation of farmers. 18 items are distributed in three categories. There is another scale called Modernization Attitude Scale by B.M. Mathur, which measures the attitudes of adults towards various facets of modernization. The scale is available in Hindi as well as English.

There is one scale by Neelam Mahajan which has been devised to determine the Nutrition and Health Education among child development project officers, mukhya sevikas, and angadwadi workers. There is also a rating scale for studying some aspects of social change.

There is a scale by N.S Chauhan and others which measures cultural conformity and cultural rebellion for adolescents, and adults.

All the scales have reported sufficiently high reliability coefficients as well as validity coefficients. Most of the scales have reported either split-half or test-retest reliability. One test has reported Kuder-Richardson reliability coefficient computed from analysis of response from 370 respondents. The values wherever reported are fairly high. Validity has been reported for all the instruments except for one instrument. Content validity, intrinsic validity, internal consistency are the more common types of validity coefficients mentioned.

Information is provided for other 4 instruments developed by U.D. Pandey. One instrument measures the need for achievement; there is one which measures tendency of over dependency, and two are for those who are in the field of agriculture.

Split-half reliability has been reported for all the 4 scales, and validity has been reported in one scale. There is one scale by B.A. Parikh and others on Family Planning, which can be used on parents, students, as well as couples.

Other scales measure the differential perceptions of adopters and non-adopters, the levels of modernity of the relationships between and among parents and children, the knowledge of rural youth leaders, and the adult education's achievements. All these instruments have reported fairly high reliability and validity data.

On the whole, the instruments reported in this section deal with important aspects of social issues and sufficient attention has been paid to the standardization of most of these scales.

Religion and Morality

There are four instruments reported under this section. No original instrument is available which may be reproduced here.

Information is provided for 3 instruments. One instrument is an adaptation, while no instruments have been cited. There are two instruments, The Extrinsic Religious Belief Scale and The Intrinsic Religious Belief Scale, by U.D. Pandey which measures the extrinsic as well as the intrinsic aspects of religious beliefs of Hindu faith. Split half reliability as well as validity have been mentioned for the second instrument.

There is a scale called Attitude Towards Religion by B.A. Parikh and others. There is one adaptation. This is an adaptation of Kohlberg's Moral Judgement Test for Indian children by Jayanthi Sunderasan and others for children aged 10+ years. The scale may be used to ascertain the developmental stage at which the child is with reference to moral judgement. The test consists of two forms : Form A and Form B. Inter scorer reliability was found out to be consistently high.

This is one area where more instruments on various other aspects are very much needed.

Other Social Attitudes

In this section 49 instruments have been included. The instruments relate to social phenomena other than those reported earlier. Out of 49 instruments. 34 have been reproduced here. Information is given for 12 and 2 are cited and one is an adaptation. The areas covered by these instruments include general attitude of people, attitudes towards governmental family planning programme, alienation, relationships, political attitudes and awareness, life satisfaction, national integration, and social support etc. As the variety of dimensions indicates, instruments in social research are concerned with a variety of areas relevant to the emerging needs of the society.

There is a scale by S. Sultan Akhtar and Priti Vadra available in English and Hindi which measures stress emanating from social and family situations. It is a Likert type, 5-point self rating scale reporting fairly high reliability and validity. The other instruments reproduced here measure sibling-relationships, alienation, political efficacy, socio-political attitudes, and political awareness.

Among the other instruments reported here, there are a few scales on parental attitudes towards their child, home environment scale, attitudes towards drinking alcohol, attitudes of youths towards narcotic drugs, attitudes towards women, working women, problem checklist for working women, parent-child relationships, a law scale, scales on mother-child relationships, population issues, social issues, style of living, influence of parents in choice of certain items by the students, family relationships etc. All these different scales have reported fairly high standardization data.

One instrument is as adaptation. The scale is a Bengali Adaptation of Moos's Menstrual Distress questionnaire. Satisfactory reliability and validity for the adaptation are reported.

There are several other social phenomena on which scales and instruments need to be developed even though the present scales are satisfactory. There are areas of specific significance like group conflict, work alienation, social commitment, poverty, power and social deprivation etc. which need to be explored in detail.

Values

A

41A (1)

Title of the Instrument : **Value System Scale.**

Purpose : The scale was prepared and standardized for doctoral work in psychology.

Author : R.D. Sharma.

Languages : English and Hindi.

Availability : Dr. R.D. Sharma, Project Officer, Department of Adult, Continuing Education, and Extension, Garhwal University, Srinagar (Gwl.) Pin : 244 174.

Uses : This scale is found suitable for measuring attitudes towards family planning.

Level : Unmarried youth in the age range of 18-28 years.

Main Features : Ten statements were arranged on the basis of Thurstone's (19279,19276) Law of Comparative Judgement Case V in the form of a Scale by combining them in all possible pairs and so the number of pairs came to be 45.

Reliability : Internal consistency check and Test of significance were applied for 45 pairs. The absolute average discrepancy is 0.68 and Chi-square Value for test of significance is 34.96 for 36 d.f. Therefore, the scale values of the ten statements are tenable.

Validity : Nil.

Time Limit : No time limit but it generally takes 15-20 minutes.

Norms : Nil.

References : Similar statements have already been used and found suitable for measuring attitude towards family planning in India and abroad (Carolina Population Centre Monographs, August, 1960).

VALUE SYSTEM SCALE

Sex :	Male Female	Occupation	Service Study

Below are given some pairs of the statements concerning marriage. Each statement is important but you have to compare to judge which statement is more important out of each pair. You have to make a cross (X) in the square given against the statement which you think more important. Remember, you have to make a cross (X) on statement only. There are no right or wrong answers : your answers will be kept confidential and will be used for research work only.

Example : You would like to accept family planning in your married life because :

You may provide more facilities to your children ☐
You may become free from mental tension ☐

Though both statements are important in the above example but after comparison it has made a cross (X) against one of them.

You should like to accept family planning in your married life because:

Wife may find time to work out side. ☐
Time may be saved for recreation. ☐

Care to individual child may be given, ☐
Wife may maintain her health and beauty. ☐

Number of birth may be reduced. ☐
Care to individual child may be given. ☐

Time for recreation may be saved. ☐
Number of birth may be reduced. ☐

Money be saved for old age. ☐
Wife may maintain her health and beauty ☐

Money be saved for children's education. ☐
Fear of pregnancy to wife be eliminated. ☐

Number of birth may be reduced. ☐
Peace in the home be maintained ☐

Money be saved for old age. ☐
Number of birth may be reduced. ☐

Wife may maintain her health & beauty ☐
Time for recreation may be saved. ☐

Wife may maintain health & beauty. ☐
Number of birth may be reduced. ☐

Fear of pregnancy to wife be eliminated. ☐
Care to individual child may be given, ☐

Number of birth may be reduced. ☐
Time for recreation may be saved. ☐

Wife may maintain health & beauty ☐
Money be saved for children's education ☐

Money be saved for children's education. ☐
Number of birth may be reduced. ☐

Number of births may be reduced. ☐
Living standard may be raised. ☐

Wife may maintain health & beauty. ☐
Peace in the home be maintained. ☐

Money be saved for old age. ☐
Living standard may be raised ☐

Living standard may be raised ☐
Fear of pregnancy to wife be eliminated. ☐

Money be saved for old age. ☐
Peace in the home may be maintained. ☐

Wife may maintain health & beauty. ☐
Fear of pregnancy to wife be eliminated. ☐

Care to individual child may be given, ☐
Time for recreation may be saved. ☐

Wife may find time to work outside. ☐
Fear of pregnancy to wife be eliminated. ☐

Wife may maintain her health & beauty ☐
Living standard may be raised ☐

Money be saved for children's education ☐
Time for recreation may be saved. ☐

Money be saved for children's education ☐
Peace in the home may be maintained ☐

Care to individual child may be given, ☐
Money be saved for old age. ☐

Living standard may be raised ☐
Time for recreation may be saved. ☐

Wife may find time to work out side. ☐
Money be saved for children's education ☐

Care to individual child may be given, ☐
Living standard may be raised ☐

Wife may find time to work out side. ☐
Living standard may be raised ☐

Money be saved for children's education. ☐
Living standard may be raised ☐

Fear of pregnancy to wife be eliminated. ☐
Number of birth may be reduced. ☐

Money be saved for old age. ☐
Money be saved for children's education. ☐

Money be saved for old age. ☐
Fear of pregnancy to wife be eliminated. ☐

Care to individual child may be given, ☐
Wife may find time to work outside. ☐

Time for recreation may be saved. ☐
Fear of pregnancy to wife be eliminated ☐

Peace in the home may be maintained ☐
Fear of pregnancy to wife be eliminated ☐

Money be saved for old age. ☐
Time for recreation may be saved. ☐

Wife may find time to work outside. ☐
Money be saved for old age. ☐

Wife may find time to work outside. ☐
Peace in the home may be maintained ☐

Time for recreation may be saved. ☐
Peace in the home may be maintained ☐

Peace in the home may be maintained ☐
Living standard may be raised ☐

Wife may find time to work outside. ☐
Wife may maintain her health and beauty ☐

Care to individual child may be given, ☐
Money be saved for old age. ☐

Care to individual child may be given, ☐

Peace in the home may be maintained ☐

41A (2)

Title of the Instrument : **Value Orientation Scale.**
Purpose : Measurement of value orientation.
Author(s) : Chauhan, N.S., N. Singh, S. Arora, R. Bhardwaj, and M. Mathur.
Languages : Hindi and English.
Availability : MAPA Meerut, D- 69, Shastrinagar, Meerut.
Uses : See manual.
Levels : Adolescents, Adults.
Main Features : Self anchoring technique, sex areas, types of scores.
Reliability : The coefficient of reliability for the six value-orientations are given below:

	Value / Dimensions	Symbols	Rel. Coef.
1.	Cosmoplitanism/localism	C-L	0.65
2.	Fatalism/Scienticism	F-S	0.69
3.	Venturesomeness/non-venturesomeness	V-N	0.55
4.	Traditionism/Progressivism	T-P	0.76
5.	Autocratism/Democratism	A-D	0.87
6.	Empathy/Non-empathy	E-N	0.50

Validity : Not determined.
Time Limit : No time limit.
Norms : Available in the manual. Rural, Urban, and Caste Norms available.
References :

1. Aberle ; A.; Cohen, A., Levy, M. and Sutton, F : "The Functional prerequisite of a society" *Ethics* LX, 1950, 100-111.
2. Allport, G.W. : *Personality*. New York, 1957.
3. Allport, G.W. & Vernon, P.E: *A Study of Values*, Boston, 1931.
4. Aurora, S. : A comparative study of 16 P.F. of Deviants and non-Deviants of Higher Secondary School Going Boys.(Ph.D Thesis submitted to Agra Univ.) 1980.

5. Ayer, A.J. : On the analysis of Moral Judgements. *Horizon* (London), XX, 1949, no. 117, pp. 175-176.

VALUE ORIENTATION SCALE

(CL)

Ram and Dileep, despite being radically different in nature and behaviour, were food friends.

Dileep used to meet everybody with an open mind, used to talk and mix with them. His friend circle included not only the people of the village but many people of the city, even some belonging to the foreign countries. He used to mix with all these. Dileep used to look a city man despite living in the village.

Ram, too, used to meet freely and used to mix with them. His friend circle was small and was limited to the village alone. He was a complete worshipper of his family. He, living in the village, was totally a member of the village.

Dileep
11
10
9
8
7
6
5
4
3
2
1

Had it been possible to put mixing behaviour according to its extensity, on the ladder rung, the top and bottom rungs mights have been received by Dileep and Ram, respectively.

* On which rung of the ladder, would you like to put your friendly behaviour for the present (Tick it).

1 2 3 4 5 6 7 8 9 10 11

* On which rung of the ladder, could you place your friendly behaviour five years back from now? (Tick it).

1 2 3 4 5 6 7 8 9 10 11

* On which rung of the ladder, could you place your friendly behaviour five years ahead from now? (Tick it).

1 2 3 4 5 6 7 8 9 10 11

(FS)

Ram had a complete faith in religious traditions. He self contended mind used to dislike exploitation of opportunities and head-breaking efforts. None can check what is lotted and nor can get what is not lotted New experiments in farming. as such, had no fascinations for him.

Dileep was completely enamoured by the new scientific discoveries. What not the science can do? Fate too can be reversed.

What to speak of farming, welfare, wealth, even like can be enhanced by taking help of science. Desirable change can be brought in all.

If possibility of change had been placed on the rung of the Ledder, the top and bottom rungs might have been awarded to Dileep and Ram, respectively.

Dileep
11
10
9
8
7
6
5
4
3
2
1

* On which rung of the Ladder, would you like to put your possibility of change to day? (Tick it).
1 2 3 4 5 6 7 8 9 10 11.

* On which rung of the Ladder could you place your possibility of change, five years back from now? (Tick it).
1 2 3 4 5 6 7 8 9 10 11.

* On which rung of the Ladder, will you like to place your possibility of change, five years ahead from now? (Tick it).
1 2 3 4 5 6 7 8 9 10 11.

(VN)

New experiments, whether in farming or in any area, involve a risk in the beginning. Land, money and labour, all are put on risk, fruits are available or not is a consideration of the future. Even then, Dileep was ahead of all in such activities. Putting life on a risk is essential for great success. Dileep was extremely venturesome.

Ram took this venturesomeness senseless. Following the determined way was alone desirable according to him. He did not have any intoxication for doing new actions. His contended mind never liked to put the old familiar course at risk for the 'news' one.

Dileep
11
10
9
8
7
6
5
4
3
2
1

Had it been possible to put this "risking behaviour" on the Ladder, the top and bottom rungs, might have been given to Dileep and Ram, respectively.

* On which rung of the Ladder, would you like to put you 'risk taking behaviour', to day? (Tick) it).

1 2 3 4 5 6 7 8 9 10 11.

* On which rung of the Ladder, could you place you 'risk taking behaviour', five years back from now? (Tick it).

1 2 3 4 5 6 7 8 9 10 11.

* On which rung of the Ladder, will you like to place your 'risk taking behaviour', five years ahead from now? (Tick it).

1 2 3 4 5 6 7 8 9 10 11.

(TP)

Values and customs coming down from ancestors were highly important in the life of Ram. Life is for values and not for the stomach. New experiments of farming, poultry and piggery were meant for satiation of hunger, are also active to promote it. A hungry life that follows old tradition is better. Ram was proud of his traditions.

Old traditions for Dileep, were for time gone by. They were not for the day. He had a great liking for new means of production. This enhances richness of life. He was completely a man of the new times and had no hitch in running a Piggery even.

Dileep
11
10
9
8
7
6
5
4
3
2
1

Had it been possible to put on the Ladder, the extensity between traditions and progressiveness, the top and bottom rungs high have been given to Dileep and Ram, respectively.

* On which rung of the Ladder, would you like to put your extensity of behaviour today? (Tick it).

1 2 3 4 5 6 7 8 9 10 11.

* On which rung of the ladder, could you place your extensity of behaviour, five years back from now? (Tick it)

1 2 3 4 5 6 7 8 9 10 11.

* On which rung of the Ladder, will you like to place your extensity of behaviour, five years ahead from now? (Tick it).

1 2 3 4 5 6 7 8 9 10 11.

(AD)

It is not easy to take decision for new actions and new policies. The opinions, mostly used in decisions, come from the family, friends and the majority of people. There are but a few strong and stable people who resort to self-decisions. Whatever the conscience says is the best. Ram was such a person who used to take decision himself. he did not give to or received opinion from others. Dileep's style was that of a friend. His best liking was to take decision collectively. His extended friendship network was of a good avail. Had it been possible to put on the Ladder the decision process from 'One to many' top and bottom rungs might have been given to Dileep and Ram, respectively.

Dileep
11
10
9
8
7
6
5
4
3
2
1

* On which rung of the Ladder, would you like to put your decision process, today? (Tick it).
1 2 3 4 5 6 7 8 9 10 11.

* On which rung of the Ladder, could you place your decision process five years back from now? (Tick it).
1 2 3 4 5 6 7 8 9 10 11.

* On which rung of the Ladder, will you like to place your decision process five years ahead from now? (Tick it).
1 2 3 4 5 6 7 8 9 10 11.

EN

Personality and one's nature possess both stability and flexibility. People of rigid nature and personality do not like to do 'each and every action. They do those actions for which they are meant. The nature and personality of Ram were of a rigid variety. He had a liking only for farming. He could not do other occupational tasks.

There was an unique flexibility and empathy in the nature and personality of Dileep. He could do new occupations well like farming.

Had it been possible to place on the Ladder the potentiality from 'rigid to empathy', the top and bottom rungs might have been given to Dileep and Ram, respectively.

Dileep
11
10
9
8
7
6
5
4
3
2
1

* On which rung of the Ladder, would you like to put your potentiality of flexibility, today? (Tick it).

1 2 3 4 5 6 7 8 9 10 11.

* On which rung of the Ladder, could place your potentiality of flexibility, five years back from now ? (Tick it).

1 2 3 4 5 6 7 8 9 10 11.

* On which rung of the Ladder, will you like to place your potentiality of flexibility, five years ahead from now? (Tick It).

1 2 3 4 5 6 7 8 9 10 11.

41 A (3)

Title of the Instrument : **Career and Family Values Scale for College Females.**

Purpose : Measures female values in family and career contexts.

Author : Sadhna Tanwar and Kulwinder Singh.

Language : English.

Availability : MAPA (Meerut) D-69 Shastrinagar, Meerut.

Uses : Research in career and family values.

Levels : College going females.

Main Features : Five point Rating Scale, 40 items.

Reliability : Split-half reliability, The coefficients of correlation between two halves of the scale for career and family values came out to be= 0.86 and 0.84 respectively which are significant at 0.01 level. The Test-Retest reliability coefficients of correlation between first and second administrations for Career and Family Values Scale on College females were computed. The co-efficients of correlation for career and family values on two administrations came out to be 0.95 and 0.96 respectively, significant 0.01 level.

Validity : Known Contrasted group method was taken as an external criterion for measuring the validity of the scale.

Time Limit : No time limit is fixed for completing the test. However, an individual usually takes 20-30 minutes in responding to 40 items in the scale.

Norms : Norms for the Career and Family Values Scale have been prepared on a sample of 1000 college females. Percentile norms and stanine equivalents are provided separately for career and family values.

References :

1. Albrecht, S. L., H.M. Bahr and B.A. Chadwick. "Changing Family and Sex Roles : An Assessment of Age Differences." *Journal of Marriage and the Family*, 1979, 41 (1), 41-50.

2. Anastasi, A. *Psychological Testing*. Fourth Edition. New York : Macmillan Publishing Co. Inc. 1976.
3. Astin, H. "A Profile of the Women in Continuing Education." In H. Astin (Ed.) *Some Action of Her Own : The Adult Women and Higher Education*. Lexington, Mass: Lezington Books, 1976.
4. Bardwick, J. *Psychology of Women : A Study of Bio-Cultural Conflicts*. New York : Harper and Row, 1971.
5. Bem, S.L. "Beyond Androgyny : Some prescriptions a Liberated sexual Identity." In J. Sherman, and F. Denmark (Eds.), *Psychology of Women : Future Directions of Research*. New York: Psychological Dimensions, 1978.
6. Bernard, J. "Change and Stability in Sex-Role Norms and Behaviour."*Journal of Social Issues*, 1976, 32 (3), 207-223.

Statement	(5) Highly Agree	(4) Some-what Agree	(3) Uncer-tain	(2) Some what Dis-agree	(1) Highly Dis-agree
(1) Having a family is more important to me than having a career.	...	...	...	...	...
(2) Having children is important for me but more important is to have some area of work apart from family in which I can find personal fulfilment.	...	...	...	...	...
(3) I can't picture a fully satisfying life without a career of my own.	...	...	...	...	...
(4) For me, it would be more important to help my husband in his career than to have a career of my own.	...	...	...	...	...

(Contd.)

Statement	(5)	(4)	(3)	(2)	(1)
(5) Working women do not suffer from the complexes of inferiority.	...	...	...	...	...
(6) There is not much use for me to plan ahead my career as I give greater importance to my family life.	...	...	...	...	...
(7) I feel that the responsibilities of a family are so great that a career cannot be taken up.	...	...	...	...	...
(8) Working women have real knowledge of handling things.	...	...	...	...	...
(9) In general working women are more fulfilled and satisfied than the housewives.	...	...	...	...	...
(10) Mother's career is hindrance in the way of proper upbringing of the children.	...	...	...	...	...
(11) A Working Mother can establish a much happier and more secure relationship with her children than the mother who does not work.	...	...	...	...	...
(12) Women with job have many more chances of progressing in life than the women with no jobs.	...	...	...	...	...
(13) Women should be concerned with their household duties rather than with their career.	...	...	...	...	...
(14) A woman should make long range plans for her career in the same way as a man does for his.	...	...	...	...	...

(Contd.)

Statement	(5)	(4)	(3)	(2)	(1)
(15) Unless it is absolutely necessary. Women should restrict their activities and interests to home.	...	...	...	...	...
(16) Women are made to make homes.	...	...	...	...	...
(17) Women should be able to follow any vocation or profession they wish, even if it violates the tradition.	...	...	...	...	...
(18) I would not like to neglect my family life for the sake of my career.	...	...	...	...	...
(19) Working women feel confident that they can do any outside work more efficiently as compared to the women who are confined to home life only.	...	...	...	...	...
(20) Today a woman should realize that taking up a career is more important than being merely a housewife.	...	...	...	...	...
(21) A working woman cannot possibly be as good a mother as the one who stays at home.	...	...	...	...	...
(22) Working women are capable of competing with men in fields of social cultural and professional realms.	...	...	...	...	...
(23) A woman is most secure and safe at home only.	...	...	...	...	...
(24) A life divided between house and office comes in the way of family's happiness.	...	...	...	...	...

(Contd.)

Statement	(5)	(4)	(3)	(2)	(1)
(25) Women today think that life without a career is not worth living.	...	...	...	...	...
(26) A woman who takes up a career is incompetent to run a home.	...	...	...	...	...
(27) Women are as capable as men in making successful careers.	...	...	...	...	...
(28) Today career plays an important role in the woman's life.	...	...	...	...	...
(29) A good housewife pays greater importance to family life than to a career.	...	...	...	...	...
(30) Although women hold many important jobs their proper place is in the homes.	...	...	...	...	...
(31) By taking up a job a woman can achieve as much as a man.	...	...	...	...	...
(32) A woman's most important task in life should be taking care of her family.	...	...	...	...	...
(33) A woman should have exactly the same job opportunities as a man has.	...	...	...	...	...
(34) Working women are conscious of their rights and duties.	...	...	...	...	...
(35) Woman should be concerned with their duties of child rearing and home care rather than with their careers.	...	...	...	...	...

(Contd.)

Statement	(5)	(4)	(3)	(2)	(1)
(36) I would give up my job if I feel it is interfering with my family life.	...	...	...	...	...
(37) A working woman has more respect in the society than a woman at home.	...	...	...	...	...
(38) Working women feel that they are on an equal footing with men.	...	...	...	...	...
(39) Women should never let outside career interfere with their domestic duties.	...	...	...	...	...
(40) As working woman's loyalities always remain torn between home and office they are liable to face crisis of adjustment.	...	...	...	...	...

B

41B (1)

Title of the Instrument : **P.G.I. Achievement Value Index.**

Purpose : To Assess Achievement Value Orientation.

Author(s) : D.K. Menon , N.N. Wig, S.K. Verma.

Language : Hindi.

Availability : Rupa Psychological Centre, B19/60B, Deoriabir, Bhelupur, Varanasi-221010.

Uses : Measurement of Achievement Value Orientation.

Levels : All Educational levels (Orally to uneducated.)

Main Features : Eight items on a 3 point scale.

Reliability : Test-retest = 0.862, Interscorer = 0.984.

Validity : With Psychiatrists ratings = 0.736, Construct Validity (Correlations with other Tests).

Time Limit : 5-7 minutes.

Norms: On Normals, Family Planning Study subjects, Mothers of normals, mentally retarded and emotionally disturbed children.

References :
1. Menon, D.K. (1981) : A Psychological Study of acceptors and resisters of contraceptives. Unpublished Ph.D thesis in Clinical Psychology, PGI, Chandigarh.
2. Kohli, A. (1986).: Mother's estimation of the intellectual ability of her child, Unpublished Ph.D. thesis in Clinical Psychology, PGI. Chandingarh.

41B (2)

Title of the Instrument : **Test to Measure Guilt Feelings after Vasectomy.**

Purpose : To measure feeling after vasectomy.

Author: M.B. Paliwal.

Language : Hindi.

Availability : Population Center, Indira Nagar, Lucknow.

Uses : Educators of Strategy Planners can assess the feelings after vasectomy.

Levels : Industrial workers.

Main Features : A Sentence completion test containing 20 items.

Reliability : Reliability content validity.

Time Limit : 15 minutes.

Norms : Nil.

References : Amonker, R.G. (1976) : Grother, S.R. (1977); Balakrishna, S. (1974); Paliwal, M.B. (1976).

42A (1)

Title of the Instrument : **Kalliath SES Inventory.**

Purpose : To measure the socio-economic status of individuals.

Author : R.P. Kalliath.

Language : English.

Availability : The test is available with the author at the Department of Education, University of Bombay, Kalina Campus, Bombay-400098.

Uses : The inventory is a useful tool to appraise the social standing or social position of an individual.

Levels : Urban literate population.

Main Features : The inventory assesses the socio-economic status of individuals on the following criteria: Type of family, number of members in the family, type of accommodation, facilities and services available at home, articles and gadgets possessed, total monthly income, literacy level of parents/spouses, occupation of parents/spouses, exposure to media, library and club membership interaction among members on social, economic and political issues. The inventory consists of nine items each of which has subcategories. The scoring Key furnishes details of the method of scoring.

Reliability : The test-retest reliability and the parallel form reliability with Jogwar's SES inventory have been established.

1. Test-retest reliability coefficient = 0.96.
2. Parallel form reliability coefficient = 0.76.

Validity : The content validity of the inventory has been established.

Time Limit : The approximate time required to answer this SES inventory is 15 minutes.

Norms : The scores are interpreted in terms of the low, middle, and upper SES strata.

References : The Kalliath SES Inventory is a tool developed by the author for the purpose of collecting relevant data for her Ph.D. Thesis in Education submitted to the Bombay University.

KALLIATH SES INVENTORY

1. A. My family is a 1. Nuclear/Single Family
2. Joint family
3. Extended family with two or more members besides parents and children.

   b. There are in all (3^2) (4^2) (5^1) (6^1) (7^0 /more^0) members in my family.

   c. 1. I have (1) (2) (3) (4)(0/No) elder brothers.
   2. I have (1) (2) (3) (4) (0/No) younger brothers.
   3. I have (1) (2) (3) (4) (0/No) elder sisters.
   4. I have (1) (2) (3) (4) (0/No) younger sisters.

   2. a. I live in 1. 4 own/rented bungalow/staff quarters bungalow
   2. 3 Ownership/rented/company flat
   3. 2 paying guest accommodation/ rented room
   4. 1 chawl
   5. any other (specify)

   b. My house has 1. 1 one room only
   2. 2 one room and kitchen
   3. 2 rooms and kitchen
   4. 4 three rooms and kitchen
   5. 5 more than three rooms and kitchen

   c. We have 1.1 a common toilet for all persons living in the adjoining flats.
   2. 2 one toilet in the house.
   3. 3 bath and toilet attached to each bed room.

   d. We have 1. 0 no servant
   2. 1 a servant to clean utensils only
   3. 2 a servant to wash clothes only
   4. 3 a servant to clean utensils and clothes
   5. 4 a servant for all the house work except cooking
   6. 5 A servant for all the house work including cooking
   7. 1 a cook
   8. 1 an ayah
   9. 1 a driver
   10. 1 a gardener (not employed by the society)
   11. 1 a watchman (not employed by the society)

3. We posses the following articles

(a) 1.1 Bicycle	(b). 1. Kerosene Stove
2.1 Moped	2. Primus
3.2 Scooter	3.2 Electric stove

4. 2 Motor cycle
5.3 Own car
6.3 Company car
7.4 Foreign car
8. any other (specify

4.2 Gas stove
5. 3 Cooking range
6. 2 Mixer/ blender/grinder
7.2 Oven
8.3 Refrigerator
9.3 Washing Machine

(c) 1.1 Radio
2. 1 Record player
3. 1 Cassette player
4. 2 Radio cassette player
5. 2 Walkman
6. 2 Stereo system
7. 2 Television (black & white)
8. 3 Colour Television
9. 2 Vacuum cleaner

(d) 1.3 V.C.P./V.C.R.
2. 1 Camera
3. 3 Movie camera
4. 3 Movie Projector
5. 2 Video games
6. 2 Telephone
7. 2 Air cooler
8. 3 Air conditioner

(e) Our dining room furniture includes
1. 1 dining table (not in the kitchen)
2. 1 six or more chairs
3. 1 side board

(f) Our drawing room furniture includes
1.2 Sofa
2.1 Centre table
3.1 Coffee table
4.2 Wall unit/side board

(g) Our bedroom furniture includes
1.1 two or more cots/beds
2.1 cupboard/wall unit/almirah
3.1 dressing table

4 The total family income (i.e. income of all earning members including self)

1. 1 less than Rs. 1000 month
2. 2 more than Rs. 1000 less than Rs. 2,000.

3. 3 More than Rs. 2,000 less than Rs. 3,000.
4. 4 more than Rs. 3.000 less than Rs. 4,000.
5. 5 more than Rs. 4,000 less than Rs. 5,000.
6. 6 more than Rs. 5,000 less than Rs. 6,000.
7. 7 above Rs. 6,000.

5. (a) Educational level of my father/husband
1. 0 Illiterate
2. 1 Only primary education
3. 2 S.S.C.
4. 3 Intermediate
5. 4 B.A./B.Sc./B. Com./B.Ed./L.L.B
6. 5 M.A,/M.Sc./M.Com./M.Ed./L.L.B.
7. 6 M.B.B.S,/B.E./B.Tech./C.A./M.B.A.
8. 8 M.D./M.S./Ph.D.
9. Any other
(b) Educational level of my mother/wife
1. 0 Illiterate
2. 1 Only primary education
3. 2 S.S.C.
4. 3 Intermediate
5. 4 B.A./B.Sc./B. Com./B.Ed./L.L.B
6. 5 M.A,/M.Sc./M.Com./M.Ed./L.L.M.
7. 6 M.B.B.S,/B.E./B.Tech./C.A./M.B.A.
8. 7 M.D./M.S./Ph.D.
9. Any other

6. (a) Occupation of my father/husband/guardian
1.1 Daily wage earner
2. Job with monthly salary 2.1 Non-Professional
3. 4 Self employed business. 3.1 Professional
4. 5 Self employed professional
5. 6 Unemployed
(d) My mother/wife is employed as ______________

7. (a) My family subscribes to newspapers.
1.Yes 1 2.0 no.
(b) Name them. 1 each
(c) My family subscribes to magazines.
1. 1 Yes 2. 0 No.
(d) Name them. 1 each

8. (a) My family has library membership.
1. 1 Yes 2. 0 No

(b) We read the following kind of books.
1. 1 comics/stories/fiction
2. 1 film magazines
3. 2 sport magazines
4. 3 news magazines/journals

(c) My family has a club/association membership.
1.1 Yes 2.0 no

(d) Name the club/association

9. (a) We listen to radio news, talks. Discussions
1. 3 Always
2. 2 Frequently
3. 1 Sometimes
4. 0 Never

(b) We watch T.V. news and discussions
1. 3 Always
2. 2 Frequent
3. 1 Sometimes
4. 0 Never

(c) My family members visit art exhibitions/dramas/plays/dance music recitals
1. 3 Always
2. 2 Frequent
3. 1 Sometimes
4. 0 Never

(d) Discussions are held among family members on current political economic and social issues
1. 3 Always
2. 2 Frequently
3. 1 Sometimes
4. 0 Never

42A (2)

Title of the Instrument : **Scale for Assessing Middle Class Housing Conditions. (MCHCS).**
Purpose : To assess housing conditions of middle class families.
Authors : S. R. Mahajani, Asha Nimkar.
Language : English.
Availability : Senior Author.
Uses : To assess housing conditions of middle class families.

Levels : Home scientists, Housewives, Architects, Town Planners.

Main Features : Scale has been used to assess housing conditions of middle class families-having an income of Rs. 601 to Rs. 3000 per month, from rural and urban areas of Akola district in Vidarbha region.

Main Features of the scale are as follows :

1. No. of items-40
2. Dimensions-5
3. Technique Scale-Five points (Highly agreed, Agreed, Neutral, Disagreed, and highly disagreed).

Reliability : Development of scale was tested through content validity which ensured collection and selection of items representing universe of content of respondents perception of middle class Housing Conditions.

Time Limit : 40 to 60 minutes.

Norms : Not yet available.

References : Mahajani, S.R. (1985) : A Study of Housing conditions In Rented and Owned Houses of middle class Families. In Urban and Rural Area of Akola District, Ph.D. Thesis, Nagpur University, Nagpur.

A SCALE TO ASSESS THE HOUSING CONDITION OF MIDDLE CLASS FAMILIES OF RURAL AND URBAN AREAS

(Some statements regarding various aspects of the housing condition of middle class families are given below. Please read them carefully and properly record your response in the given columns to evaluate housing condition of your house).

S.No.	Statements	Proportion of agreement				
		Highly agreed	Agreed	Neutral	Disagreed	Agreed
1	2	3	4	5	6	7
(I)	**Situational aspect**					
1.	It would be beneficial to have educational institutions situated near the house to reduce the conveyance charges.					

(Contd.)

1	2	3	4	5	6	7
2.	For the all-round development of all the members of the family, house should be situated near the playground, garden and library.					
3.	From multi-dimensional point of view, a theatre situated near the house is advantageous.					
4.	The house situated near railway station and bus-stand, saves energy, time and money.					
5.	The house situated near post office and bank causes convenience.					
6.	In daily life to satisfy the imperative necessities, market should be near the house.					
7.	The importance of hospital being near the house is realised in emergency.					
8.	In view of the limited number of family members in service, office near the house should not be insisted.					
9.	Due to the singular role of security in mental stability, house must be placed securely.					
(II) Physical aspect						
1.	In consideration of the limited resources of a middle class person, the total area of the plot should be easy to afford					
2.	The arrangement of rooms in the house based on the architectural principle of					

(Contd.)

1	2	3	4	5	6	7
	circulation helps every work to be done easily and quickly.					
3.	Built-up area in the house should fulfil individual need for space.					
4.	The number and size of rooms in the house should be according to the requirements of the family life cycle.					
5.	To enhance the utility and beauty of the house, its doors and windows should be of appropriate size					
6.	The unsound and old-fashioned outer form of the house creates a sense of depression in the atmosphere of the house.					
7.	The important contribution of the fencing in the security of the house cannot be denied.					
*8.	When energy and time necessary for looking after the yard is taken into account, the advantage of yard is felt to be negligible.					
9.	Due to the lack of particular type of space in the house, the idea of rearing domestic animals cannot be implemented.					
10.	A separate and proper arrangement of vehicles in the house is beneficial for keeping them in order.					

(Contd.)

1	2	3	4	5	6	7
	(III) Material aspect					
1.	Taking into consideration the number and size of rooms in the house, multipurpose furniture is beneficial to middle class people.					
2.	Improper arrangement of furniture in room becomes a hindrance by lessening the utility of the room.					
3.	Built-in arrangements in the house prove beneficial for making up the lack of storage arrangement.					
4.	Use of folding furniture in different rooms leaves more open space for use in the house.					
5.	Storage in the house has acquired a special place and hence, if in the construction of the house preference is given to the necessity of storage, the simplicity and spaciousness is repeatedly experienced.					
	(IV) Hygienic aspect					
1.	To keep cleanliness in the house, ample and continuous water supply acquires a necessary and important place.					
2.	Efficiency of family members mostly depends upon the arrangement of natural and artificial light in the rooms.					
3.	Ample and free air circulation in the house helps to make the atmosphere healthy and vigorous.					

(Contd.)

1	2	3	4	5	6	7
4.	For keeping health each house must have independent bathroom and lavatory.					
5.	An improper drainage system is an invitation to various diseases.					
6.	A proper disposal of waste material through an independent and social system avoids the growth of mosquitoes and flies.					
7.	Healthy atmosphere around the house greatly contributes to the creation of healthy, generation.					
8.	Separate washing area for vessels and clothes help in keeping the house clean.					
(V) Psychological aspect : Satisfaction						
1.	Our own house is a great ambition in human life, especially in a middle class family and what a great satisfaction is constituted in its realisation.					
2.	If our likes and dislikes, actions and thoughts are not reflected through the medium of the house, a sense of futility is created in life.					
3.	In the realisation of our aim, ideal house becomes one of the good instruments.					
4.	Loving and well-wishing neighbours prove instrumental in increasing the satisfaction in the house.					

(Contd.)

1	2	3	4	5	6	7
5.	To get cooperation from our neighbours in critical situations, it is desirable to have cordial relations with them.					
6.	Locality of the house, number and size of rooms according to the taste and need, definitely increase the happiness of the members of the family.					
7.	In consideration of the problems faced in the construction of the house and in its maintenance in future, rented house seems to be preferable.					
8.	Let the house be anywhere and of any type, it's a great happiness and pleasure to live in our own house.					

* Negative statement

B

42B (1)

Title of the Instrument : **A Socio Economic Scale for Urban Subjects.**
Purpose : to assess socio-economic status of urban subjects objectively.
Author(s) : S.C. Gupta and B.B. Sethi.
Languages : English.
Availability : Test not published.
Uses : The identification of change prone in teachers would facilitate restructuring of the higher educational institutions in ways that would adapt them to environmental pressures.
Levels : Higher Education.
Main Features : Likert type of scale (5 point scale.) with 28 items.

Reliability : Test-retest reliability = 0.83.

Validity : Validity by inter correlations between the 4 dimension of change proneness and open mindedness, Liberalism, cosmopolitan, and future orientation and item analysis.

Time Limit : 25 to 30 minutes.

Norms : Not required.

References : Not yet used.

Social Distance and Group Attitudes

A

43A (1) by Neelam Mahajan

Scale to Measure Community Participation Index in Anganwadi Activities

	Extent of Community Participation in AW activities					
	Not appli-cable	Not at all	Seldom	Some, times	Often	Very often
(a) Local women helping in cooking and feeding of children or in preparing snacks etc.?	0	1	2	3	4	5
(b) Contributions of the community in terms of:						
1. Fuel?	0	1	2	3	4	5
2. Food?	0	1	2	3	4	5
3. Utensils or other equipment?	0	1	2	3	4	5
4. Cash donations?	0	1	2	3	4	5
(c) Guidance and help in pre-school and functional literacy activities from:						
1. Primary school teachers?	0	1	2	3	4	5
2. Middle school teacher?	0	1	2	3	4	5
3. Headmaster?	0	1	2	3	4	5
(d) Help from school girls in tending of AW children?	0	1	2	3	4	5
(e) Hello in ensuring attendance of beneficiaries by:						
1. Collecting and bringing AW children to the centre?	0	1	2	3	4	5
2. Bringing ladies to the centres?	0	1	2	3	4	5

Modernization and Social Change

A

44A (1)

Title of the Instrument : **A Test to Measure Knowledge of Punjab Farmers about Agricultural Engineering Technology.**

Purpose : For doctorate level dissertation in the discipline of Extension Education.

Author : B.S. Bhatia.

Language(s) : English and Punjabi.

Availability : B.S. Bhatia, Department of Farm Power and Machinery, Punjab Agricultural University, Ludhiana-141004.

Uses : For research and assessment of extension project.

Levels : Farmers at the individual level.

Main Features : A procedure consisting of six steps was followed for the construction of the test. The terminal group technique and Findley's 'D' Statistic were used for standardization of the test having 18-items.

Reliability : Reliability coefficient of the test determined through split-half technique was 0.967. As the test covered content areas and process objectives and each item underwent item analysis, it was considered valid in terms of content validity also.

Time Limit : 7 to 10 minutes.

Norms : Norms are given in the author's book 'Adoption of Farm mechanization in a Developing Economy published in 1990 by Daya Publishing Houes, Delhi.

References : Given.

A TEST TO MEASURE KNOWLEDGE OF PANJAB FARMERS ABOUT AGRICULTURAL ENGINEERING TECHNOLOGY

What do the following symbols/terms indicate.

a. (Symbol A) marked on a thresher drum (R/W)

b. Kilowatt (R/W)

Identify the farm machines through the photographs shown to you (R/W)

c. (Photograph A) (R/W)

d. (Photograph B) (R/W)

e. Hoeing in wheat can be done in standing position by using________ (R/W)

f. What equipment will you use for breaking the hard crust formed due to rainfall immediately after sowing ? (R/W)

g. Name any two devices that can be used on a syndicator thresher for safety against accidents.
(i)_______ (R/W)
(ii)— (R/W)

h. Which part of disc harrow requires frequent greasing? (R/W)

i. Name the equipment to which the part shown to you belongs:
(Part A) (R/W)
(Part B) (R/W)

j. The most important thing that ensures safe storage of grains in metallic bin is that it is:
(i) Made of tick sheet (R/W)
(ii) Tightly covered (R/W)
(iii) Air tight (R/W)

k. A chain is to—, as belt is to pulley. (R/W)

l. You are required to increase the number of revolutions of your irrigation pump operated by an electric motor. How will you do that? (R/W)

m. Of the followings, which layout of the field will require minimum time for ploughing:
(i) Rectangular field
(ii) Square field
(iii) An irregular field (R/W)

n. One difference between animals and the field machines is that weather has no adverse effect on machines.

o. Why is the flywheel used in diesel engines ? (R/W)

p. Late harvesting by combine results in:
(i) More poor used
(ii) Frequent choking
(iii) More shattering losses (R/W)

44A (2)

Title of the Instrument : **Knowledge and Retention Test of Literate Rural Farm Women.**

Purpose : To study the gain and retention of nutritional knowledge gained by the members of the ladies *Charcha mandals*.

Author : Rajinder Kaur, and B.S. Hansra.

Languages : Punjabi and English.

Availability : M.Sc Thesis of Rajinder Kaur, Manchanda Central Library, Punjab Agricultural University, Ludhiana, Punjab.

Uses : It can be used to determine the retention of nutritional knowledge gained by the literate rural women.

Levels : For literate rural women.

Main Features : The item difficulty index and discriminating index was worked out. Only those items were retained which fell in 24.00 to 78.00 difficulty range and 0.28 to 0.75 item discrimination index. Out of 30 items fifteen were true false items and fifteen were multiple choice items. One score was assigned to correct answers and zero to the incorrect answer.

Reliability : Reliability coefficient was found to be 0.91.

Validity : Content validity was found out.

Time Limit : Part A= 15 minutes. Part B = 15 minutes.

Norms : N.A.

References : Bloom, B.S. (1969). Taxonomy of Educational Objectives, Longman Green and Co. New York.

TEST TO KNOWLEDGE AND RETENTION TEST OF LITERATE RURAL FARM WOMEN

Knowledge Test Part-1

The statements are given as below. Please Mark (✓) against the correct statement and mark (x) against the wrong-statement in the space given.

1. Every child is healthy at birth. ( )
2. Indian diet is usually deficient in carbohydrates ( )
3. The major sources of protein are milk, pulses, flesh & eggs ( )
4. We get carbohydrates from cereals and potatoes. ( )
5. North Indian diet is imbalance. ( )
6. People in the South normally eat rice and dal ( )

8. The major source of protein in India is milk, curd and whey (*lassi*) ( )
9. It is not required to include various sources of protein in our diet. ( )
10. We get fat from rice and potato ( )
11. People in Punjab usually take milk in the evening ( )
12. The groundnut flour is commonly used for eating these days. ( )
13. We can prepare enormous tasty foods from groundnuts. ( )
14. With the help of science. We can extract maximum proteins from groundnuts. ( )
15. Groundnuts should be properly washed before Making the flour from it. ( )

Retention Part-2

Given below are the questions. Each question has one correct answer. Please tick mark (✓) the most correct answer out of the given answers for each questions.

1. If a person does not get balanced diet then the following different health hazards can developed in the body:
   (a) Physical hazards ____
   (b) Mental hazards ____
   (c) Physical and mental hazards ____
2. The diet required for keeping the body healthy
   (a) Non-Vegetarian diet ____
   (b) Balanced diet ____
   (c) Expensive diet ____
3. The function of protein in our body is.
   (a) Protein helps in the building of body ____
   (b) Protein provides the immunity to fight against diseases ____
   (c) Protein helps in making the bones of the body strong ____
4. We get maximum vitamins and minerals from the foods
   (a) Vegetable and fruits ____
   (b) Cereals and pulses ____
   (c) Milk and milk products ____
5. The various needed nutrients required for keeping the body healthy are:
   (a) Milk, curd, eggs, flesh and fish ____
   (b) Protein carbohydrates, fat, vitamins and minerals ____
   (c) Cereals, pulses, fruits and vegetables ____

6. The food contains maximum protein is:
   (a) Sorghum ——
   (b) Barley ——
   (c) Groundnuts ——
7. The groundnut flour can be made more nutritious by:
   (a) Mixing maize flour in groundnut flour ——
   (b) Mixing gram flour and other nutrients in groundnut flour ——
   (c) Mixing barley flour in groundnut flour ——
8. For healthy nation, it is necessary that:
   (a) Children should be fat ——
   (b) Children should be healthy ——
   (c) Children should be more ——
9. In a vegetarian country like India, the main source of protein is:
   (a) Pulses ——
   (b) Fruits ——
   (c) Vegetables ——
10. These days, the type of machines used for grinding the groundnuts are:
    (a) Automatic machines ——
    (b) Manual machines ——
    (c) Automatic and manual machines
11. Previously after extracting the oil from groundnuts, the groundnut cakes has been used as :
    (a) Groundnut cakes were thrown ——
    (b) Groundnut cakes were given to animals ——
    (c) Groundnut cakes were used for manure ——
12. These days, with the help of science, after extracting the oil from groundnuts, the groundnut cake has been used for human being as it contains
    (a) Vitamins ——
    (b) Carbohydrates ——
    (c) Proteins ——
13. While doing physical work our energy get wasted. The nutrients provide energy to our body are:
    (a) Fats ——
    (b) Minerals ——
    (c) Water ——
14. The nutrients provide our body immunity to fight against diseases are:

(a) Fats ——
(b) Vitamins ——
(c) Carbohydrates ——

15. We get maximum fats from the foods:
(a) Sorghum and barley ——
(b) Ghee and oil ——
(c) Fruits and vegetables ——

44A (3)

Title of the Instrument : **Opinion Scales.**

Purpose : To study the opinion of the rural women towards Dhauladhar Chulha (Smokeless Chullah) kitchen gardening and animal husbandry.

Author(s) : Rajinder Kaur and Ranjit Singh.

Languages : Hindi and English.

Availability : From the Authors, Communication Centre, Punjab Agricultural University, Ludhiana, Punjab.

Uses : It can be used to study the opinion of the rural women about smokeless chulha, kitchen gardening and animal husbandry practices.

Levels : For all rural women.

Main Features : Three scales (separate scale for each practice) for measuring the rural women's opinion towards smokeless chulha, kitchen gardening and animal husbandry practices were constructed. Initially, 20 items were collected. The preliminary scales were distributed to 20 experts from each field to seek their opinions about suitability of each item for inclusion in the scales. The mean score for each item was worked out and only those items were retained whose mean score was 6 or above six on the whole 30 items (10 from each) were selected. The format and wording of the statements were also improved as per the suggestions of the experts. Finally, each scale consisted of 10 statements (5 positive and 5 negative). The responses of the respondents were recorded on a three point scale. The normalized scoring procedure used.

Reliability : The test-retest method was employed. 0.80 reliability coefficient was found for smokeless chulha, 0.91 for kitchen gardening, and 0.78 for animal husbandry practices.

Validity : The content validity of the initially constructed instruments was determined with the help of experts. The intrinsic validity of the three opinion scales were also determined which came to be 0.94 for smokeless chulha, 0.95 for kitchen gardening and 0.88 for animal husbandry practices.

Time Limit : Total time required was 30 minutes, 10 minutes, for each scale.

Norms : N.A.

References : Given in the manual.

SCALE TO MEASURE THE OPINIONS OF RURAL WOMEN

Please give your opinions toward Dhauladhar *chulha,* kitchen gardening and animal husbandry practices in respect of the items listed below by placing tick mark [✓] in an appropriate column against each item.

Sr. No.	Practice/Item	Agree	Undecided	Disagree
1	2	3	4	5
	I. Dhauladhar Chulha			
1.	Traditional chulha is better than a Dhauladhar chulha	....	....	....
2.	It is more comfortable to cook on Dhauladhar *chulha*	....	....	....
3.	Consumption of fuel is more in Dhauladhar *chulha*	....	....	....
4.	Dhauladhar *chulha* saves cooking time	....	....	....
5.	Maintenance is not very much important in Dhauladhar *chulha*	....	....	....
6.	Dhauladhar *chulha* is difficult to maintain than traditional chulha	....	....	....
7.	Dhauladhar *chulha* is difficult to use than traditional *chulha*	....	....	....
8.	There is no wastage of heat in Dhauladhar *chulha*	....	....	....
9.	Dhauladhar *chulha* prevents eye and lung diseases caused by smoke	....	....	....

(Contd.)

1	2	3	4	5
10.	Dhauladhar *chulha* training camps are helpful in the use and maintenance of Dhauladhar *chulha*	....	....	....
II Kitchen gardening				
1.	Kitchen gardening provides fresh vegetables for the family	....	....	....
2.	Kitchen gardening develops the habit of doing productive work in the family	....	....	....
3.	Kitchen gardening is not an economic activity	....	....	....
4.	Kitchen gardening does not contribute in the conservation of environment.	....	....	....
5.	Vegetables are necessary to keep the man healthy	....	....	....
6.	Fresh vegetables from kitchen gardening are more nutritive	....	....	....
7.	Kitchen gardening is to make proper utilization of house yard	....	....	....
8.	It is difficult to get small packs of insecticides and pesticides	....	....	....
9.	Kitchen gardening is merely a wastage of time	....	....	....
10.	Kitchen gardening is a good source for spending spare time or leisure time	....	....	....
III. Animal Husbandry Practices				
1.	Crossbred cow is better than a local cow as far as milk yield is concerned	....	....	....
2.	The right time for natural or artificial insemination of cow is not very important	....	....	....

(Contd.)

1	2	3	4	5
3.	Cross breeding of animals is not essential for increasing milk production.	....	....	....
4.	Family income can be raised by rearing cross bred animals	....	....	....
5.	Inferior bulls should not be used for cross breeding of cows	....	....	....
6.	Only healthy animals produce more and hygienic milk	....	....	....
7.	Special ration is not necessary for the pregnant cow	....	....	....
8.	Vaccination is not essential for protecting animals against contagious diseases	....	....	....
9.	Cleanliness is not essential for producing clean milk from the animals	....	....	....
10.	Unproductive animals should not be sent to Gosadan.	....	....	....

44A (4)

Title of the Instrument : **Management Orientation Scale.**

Purpose : To measure the management (Planning, Production and Marketing) orientation of farmers.

Authors : R. K. Samanta.

Language : English.

Availability : Who shall repay Agri. Loans? by G.L. Ray and R.K. Samanta 1981. Calcutta, 12 Bikshau, 33 Chittaranjan Avenue.

Uses : Researchers, Bankers concerned to Agricultural credit.

Levels : Farmers.

Main Features : Likert type, 18 items in 3 categories (6 each)-planning, Production, and marketing.

Reliability : Item collection, judging rating scoring were done using Likert type scores 4 as suggested by Edward (1969). No separate reliability or validity were conducted.

Time Limit : One month.

Norms : Yes, from undersigned.

References : No. of studies on Agri Credit and Farmers behaviour of ISRI, New Delhi, BCKV, Kalyani, (WB), UAS, (Bangalore), have done it.

MANAGEMENT ORIENTATION SCALE

Sl. No.	Statements	Strongly agree	Agree	Disagree	Strongly disagree
1	2	3	4	5	6
A.	**Planning Orientation**				
(i)	Each year one should think afresh about the crops to be cultivated in each type of land.				
(ii)	It is not necessary to make prior decision about the variety of crop to be cultivated.				
(iii)	The amount of seeds, fertiliser and plant protection chemicals needed for raising a crop should be assessed before cultivation.				
(iv)	It is not necessary to think ahead of the cost involved in raising a crop.				
(v)	One need not consult an agricultural expert for crop planning.				
(vi)	It is possible to increase the yield through farm production plan.				
B.	**Production Orientation**				
(i)	Timely planting of a crop ensures good yield.				
(ii)	One should use as much fertiliser as he likes.				
(iii)	Determining fertiliser does by soil testing saves money.				
(iv)	Seed rate should be given as recom mended by the specialists.				
(v)	For timely weed control one should even use suitable herbicides.				
(vi)	With low water rates one should use as much irrigation water available.				

(Contd.)

1 2	3	4	5	6
C. Marketing Orientation				
(i) Market news is not so useful to a farmer.				
(ii) A farmer can get good price by grading his produce.				
(iii) Warehouses can help the farmer to get better price of his produce.				
(iv) One should sell his produce to the nearest market irrespective of price.				
(v) One should purchase his inputs from the shop, where his other relatives purchase.				
(vi) One should grow those crops which have more market demand.				

44A (5)

Title of the Instrument : **Modernization Attitude Scale.**

Purpose : To study attitudes of adults towards various facets of modernization.

Authors : B.M. Mathur.

Language(s) : Hindi and English.

Availability : Dr. B.M. Mathur, Psycho-Tech F-23, Civil Lines, Bhilwara (Raj.) 311001.

Uses : Can be used for studying attitudes of adults towards modernization.

Levels : Adults.

Main features : Items-35; Aspects studied five, viz., Social mobility, Position of women, Family Planning, Marriage and Religion and Superstition; Developed on the lines of Thurston Scale; Items reduced to seven.

Reliability : Test-retest reliabilities range from 0.85 to 0.90.

Validity : Content validity judged by thirty judges.

Time Limit : Fifteen minutes.

Norms : Norms are available with the author.

References : Tool used in Ph.D. thesis by the author-now being used also on adult learners in the state of Rajasthan.

MODERNIZATION ATTITUDE SCALE

Name ....
Age .... Sex ....
Occupation ....
Religion and Cast ....(ST/SC/Others)
Centre ....

Direction

In this list some sentences representing some beliefs related to social life are given. You must certainly offer with the statements similar to your own behalfs. You are required to tick (✓) mark the statements agreeing with you beliefs. Leave the remaining sentences unmarked.

Scores Obtained

S.No.	Area	Scores
1.	SM	
2.	PW	
3.	FP	
4.	MR	
5.	R.S.	

1. Social Mobility

1. It is better not to aspire for the high positions like that of governor as we cannot even dream to achieve them.
2. Untouchability is an obstacle in progress and must be eliminated.
3. If there is a Brahman and a Harijan as candidates for a post, the former must be selected even if he is inferior.
4. It is proper to have reservation in jobs for scheduled castes and tribes because this provides them chance to progress.
5. If he has ability, a person belonging to scheduled caste can get a high position/post.
6. Children must be told that economic prosperity makes life comfortable and efforts should be made for it.
7. A man of low caste does not go on a high post because of his inferior bringing up/rearing.

2. Position of Women

1. The present status of women in India is satisfactory.
2. When the married life becomes unbearable to a woman, she is free to be free from this bond.
3. Giving jobs to women amounts to inefficiency in work.
4. Women are intellectually inferior to men and hence they must not claim equality with men.
5. Since times immemorial women have been source of energy and hence new opportunities, should be provided to them.
6. Women must get equal right in property.
7. The education upto secondary level is enough for women.

3. Family Planning

1. Whether one is rich or poor, one's planned family of two or three children is ideal.
2. May be family planning has some advantages, and therefore there is no harm in adopting it.
3. Since the number of children in small family is less, it leads to low family income.
4. Family planning does not conform with the cultural traditions of our country.
5. Children are the gift of God and man's interference in this matter is undesirable.
6. The concept of small family is generally accepted and therefore family planning must be encouraged.
7. In comparison with big families, better provision of food, and education can be made in small families

4. Marriage

1. Intercaste marriage is useful in society and must be encouraged.
2. The love ,marriage is better because in arranged marriage the expenditure is generally unbearable for parents.
3. The old people frown at the idea of selection of life mate by myself and must, therefore, he discouraged.
4. The individuals and societies propagation of the inter-caste marriage must be boycotted.
5. The freedom to select one's own life mate may lead to both good and bad results.

6. The co-educational institutions should be closed so that intercaste marriages may not take place.
7. Young boys and girls must be given enough freedom so that they may choose their spouses from different castes.

5. Religion and Superstition

1. It is better to consult a doctor rather that an exorcist or *fakir.*
2. The religious rites which are approved on the criteria of science must be accepted and the rest discarded.
3. Those who do good deeds go to heaven and those who do bad deeds for to hell.
4. Every event of man's life is predetermined by fate.
5. However important work it may be, the journey must be cancelled if a cat crosses the path or anybody sneezes.
6. It does not matter whether one goes to a place of worship (Temple church, gurudwara) or not.
7. There is no greater religion than helping other.

44A (6)

Title of the Instrument : **Development of Change Proneness Scale.**
Purpose : To determine the readiness or willingness of the individual and also to accept new ideas and change.
Authors : Prathibha Sood and Shalini Bhogle.
Language : English.
Availability : Test not published.
Uses : The identification of change proneness in teachers would facilitate restructuring of the higher educational institutions in ways that would adapt them to environmental pressure.
Levels : Higher Education.
Main features : Likert type of scale (5 point scale with 28 items.)
Reliability : Test-retest reliability = 0.83.
Validity : Validity by inter correlations between the 4 dimensions of change proneness and item analysis open mindedness, Liberalism, cosmopolitanism, Future orientation.
Time Limit : 25-30 minutes.
Norms : Not required.
References : Not yet used.

DEVELOPMENT OF CHANGE PRONENESS SCALE

Section-I

Instruction

Below are given statements that relate to your personal beliefs and way of living. Please read each statement carefully and decide to what extent you agree with each statement. Kindly rate your choice and put the appropriate letter in the box provided.

Category No. A is strongly agree
" B is agree
" C is undecided
" D is disagree
" E is strongly disagree.

This information will be used for my research study and will be kept confidential. Your cooperation will be very helpful.

☐ 1. The best government is democracy run by the most intelligent people.

☐ 2. Voting rights should be given only to people with formal education.

☐ 3. The educational planners in the fifties were wise enough not to bring about frequent changes.

☐ 4. Most of the ideas which get printed now-days are not worth the paper they are printed on.

☐ 5. Nationalism in the modern world is a force which works against peace.

☐ 6. Studying for one self is much better than attending workshops and seminars.

☐ 7. Freedom of speech is necessary but not for all.

☐ 8. Childhood is the happiest period in life.

☐ 9. The social customs which are part of culture should be adhered to, even if not properly explained.

☐ 10. Changing a job after a certain age does not help the person significantly.

☐ 11. When a person associates with a number of organizations for exchange of ideas, it creates disturbance in his commitment of work.

☐ 12. The way to enjoy life now is to be able to see the present in the light of the future.

☐ 13. Poverty could be almost done away with if we made certain basic changes in our social and economic system.

☐ 14. The past seems to have greater influence on people than the future.

☐ 15. Inter-caste marriages are desirable.

Section-II

There is a little variation to the meaning assigned to the categories A, B, C, D, and E in this part.

Category A denotes Very true of me and my beliefs
" B " Some what true of me and my beliefs
" C " Not sure about it
" D " Unlike me and my beliefs.
" E " Absolutely unlike me and my beliefs.

☐ 16 I feel uneasy when I try out something new.

☐ 17. Often I spend much time thinking about the good times I have had in the past.

☐ 18. Any Cultural Programme which is interesting irrespective of its elegance draws my attention.

☐ 19. I seem to be continually growing and changing.

☐ 20. I do not reject the viewpoint of my opponents but give thought to it even if they say nothing which has any truth.

☐ 21. I wish life were the way it was ten years ago.

☐ 22. I feel happy in the company of my close associates.

☐ 23. One should cancel his plans if he finds that the chances of success are very little.

☐ 24. Most of my plans for the future are not well thought out.

☐ 25. I prefer to live in cities with a particular culture rather than in cosmopolitan cities.

☐ 26. I enjoy the company of a mixed group having different backgrounds (Ethnic, Religious, Lingual etc.) to a company exclusively of a similar background.

☐ 27. I like to attend dramas/dances typical of my home state.

☐ 28. My principles of life tend to be different from those of my age.

44A (7)

Title of the Instrument : **Home Modernity Scale (HMS).**

Purpose : To measure the levels of modernity of the relationship between and among parents and children.

Author(s) : R.P. Kalliath and G.J. Kerawalla.

Language : English.

Availability : The test is available with the authors in the Department of Education, University of Bombay, Kalina Campus, Bombay - 400098.

Uses : To Measure the modernity levels of the : 1. Parent relationship, 2. Parent-child relationship, 3. Sibling relationship.

Levels : High school and college students with an urban background.

Main features : The HMS is an attitude scale which comprises three sub-scales. Part A measures the modernity level of parent-parent relationship and has 60 items. Part B measures the level of modernity of the parent child relationships and it contains 48 items. Part C measures the degree of modernity of the sibling relationships and composes 46 items. The Scale is to be answered on a four point response system where the alternatives are Always, Frequently, Sometimes, and Never. The scale measures the modernity levels of the home relationships with reference to five indices of modernity, namely individualism, achievement orientation, equalitaranism, secularism and openness.

Reliability : The test-Retest reliability split-half reliability and inter correlations among the subscales and inter correlations among the subscales and subscales to total scale are determined.

	Test-retest Corr. Coeff.	Split-Half Corr. Coeff.
MPPR	0.82	0.78
MPCR	0.89	0.79
MSR	0.84	0.71

Subscale to Total scale correlation.

	MPPR	MPCR	MSR
Individualism	0.36	0.29	0.76
Egalitarianism	0.72	0.32	0.72
Secularism	0.72	0.44	0.84
Openness	0.64	0.52	0.69
Achievement Orientation	0.22	0.09	0.64

Significance at 0.01 level r =0.085

(all the corr.coeffs. are significant at 0.01)

Validity : The content validity of the scales is established by obtaining the approval of 8 experts in the field of Education and Sociology.

Time Limit : 35 minutes.

Scoring:

	A	F	S	N
Positive items are scored	3	2	1	0
Negative items are scored	0	1	2	3

Norms : The norms are available in the form of percentile and standard scores.

References :

1. Morrison, S. (1971) : *Schools and Socialisation*, Great Britain : C Nicholls and Co. Ltd.
2. Anderson, G.A. (1961) : "A Skeptical note on education and mobilty" In A H Halrey (Ed)., *Economy and Society*, N.Y.: The Free Press of Gleucor.
3. Inkeles, A. (1966) : "The modernization of man." In M. Weiner (ed) *Modernization : The Dynamics of Growth*. New York : Basic books.
4. The HMS is an attitude scale which was developed and used for data collection for a Ph.D. study in Education on Individual Modernity submitted to the University of Bombay.

Home Modernity Scale
Do not Make any Mark on this Booklet
Separate Answer Sheet is Provided

Instructions

This is a scale to measure one's general home background. The scale is composed of three sub-scales. Part A is on parental Modernity. Part B measures the modernity of Parent Child Relationship and Part C is on the modernity of sibling Relationships. In Part A there are 60 items, In Part B, 48 items and in Part C 46.

Against each statement are given responses such as Always (A), Frequently (F) Sometimes (S) and Never (N). Please read each statement carefully and put a cross in the box corresponding to your choice.

For example if for a certain item your choice is sometimes then on the answer sheet against that item number put a cross in the third box.

Item No. 5	A	F	S	N
	☐	☐	☐	☐

This is not a test and there are no right or wrong answers. Hence do not feel hesitant to give an honest answer. Please do not leave any item unanswered.

The information obtained will be treated as confidential.

Part A

	A	F	S	N
1. My father tells my mother which political candidate to vote for.				
2. Major decisions in the family are taken by my father alone.				
3. My mother would be upset if there was any change in my father's office timing.				
4. My mother insists on my father accompanying her to religious ceremonies.				
5. My father encourages my mother to take important decisions.				
6. My mother needs my father's permission before going out with her friends.				
7. My mother encourages my father to offer prayers and performs religious ceremonies to success in his career/ business.				
8. My father gets upset when my mother disagrees with him.				
9. My mother tries to defend my father even when she knows that he is wrong.				
10. Before buying an expensive item for the house (T.V., refrigerator etc.) my father consults my mother.				
11. My father discourages my mother from observing ritualistic fasts on religious occasions.				
12. My mother gets angry if my father tries to explain the reason behind certain religious practices and rituals.				
13. In all matters my mother follows the advice of my father.				
14. My father helps my mother with house work.				
15. My mother decides independently her mode of dress.				

	A	F	S	N
16. My mother gets angry when my father criticises her brother/father for their high handed behaviour.				
17. My parents understand each other.				
18. My mother is a source of comfort to my father when he is deperessed/in trouble.				
19. My father would be hurt if my mother earned more than him.				
20. My mother had no option in the choice of her husband.				
21. My father's career was chosen for him by his parents.				
22. My father grumbles that he has to stay back after office hours and complete some urgent work.				
23. My father would tip a clerk in order to get some work done soon.				
24. My father approves of our family making friends with those who belong to a different community.				
25. If my father were to select a telephone operator, all other things being equal, he would choose a blind candidate.				
26. My father blames career women for the increasing unemployment in the country				
27. My father thinks that house-work is a waste of time for man.				
28. My father seek the advice of a pundit/ spiritual leader before taking any major decision.				
29. Before deciding on which political candidate to vote for, my father weighs his merits and demerits.				
30. My father gives expensive presents to his boss.				
31. When faced with a setback in his work my father blames it on destiny/fate.				
32. My father would prefer to vote for a candidate who belongs to our own religion.				

A F S N

33. My father tries to learn the latest developments in his field of work.
34. My mother is upset if her weekly horoscope is unpleasant.
35. My mother thinks that intercaste marriages pollute the uppercastes.
36. My mother is a fervent follower of a particular *guru*/godman.
37. My mother would be shocked if she heard of widows remarrying.
38. My mother would be shocked if any of her children wanted a divorce.
39. My mother fasts during an eclipse.
40. My mother wears a sacred cord on her person.
41. According to my mother a woman's ultimate fulfilment is in marriage rather than a career.
42. My mother encourages my maid servant to send her daughter to school.
43. My mother performs ritual because they have been practised for generations.
44. My mother advises our maid servant to limit the size of her family.
45. My mother believes that a woman's career is an important as a man's.
46. My parents would object if their son married a girl from a lower caste.
47. My parents are in favour of family planning.
48. If their daughter wanted to pursue a career and live independently, my parents would object to it.
49. When fixing a marriage my parents consider it important that horoscopes match.
50. My parents would disapprove of their son becoming a professional dancer.
51. My parents would think low for a woman who has divorced her husband.

A F S N

52. My parents would approve of their daughter marrying someone very much younger than her.
53. Boys in our family are sent to more expensive schools than girls.
54. My parents would prefer their son to marry a fair complexioned girl.
55. If my parents were to take paying guests, they would hesitate to choose one who belong to a different community.
56. My parents are prepared to pay a large dowry in order to get a good husband for their daughter.
57. My parents are more concerned with the academic achievements of the sons in the family than the daughters.
58. My parents feel that success depends more on hard work and planning and less on luck and contacts.
59. My parents find/make the best of opportunities to improve their qualifications.
60. My parents take loan from friends.

Part B

A F S N

1. If I buy a new magazines, my farther shows interest in reading it.
2. My father dislike my moving with friends who belong to a lower caste.
3. I feel uneasy in the presence of my father.
4. If I am pulled up by the college authorities for misbehaviour my father tries to see that I am not punished.
5. When I am seriously ill my mother offer special prayer for my recovery.
6. My mother would object to her daughter going out for a movie with boys.
7. I think I am my mother's favourite child.

A F S N

8. My mother understands my point of view.
9. My mother gets upset when I try to argue with her.
10. My mother forbids me to make journeys on certain days of the week.
11. My mother gets angry when I criticised her for being rude to the maid servant.
12. My parents expect me to obey them unquestioningly.
13. My parents take interest in my studies.
14. At home I freely discuses my problems with my parents.
15. My parents would object to my taking up a job outside Bombay.
16. My parents are aware of the grades I got in my examination.
17. I am forced by my parents to attend the religious ceremonies in the house.
18. My parents scold me in front of my friends.
19. Before fixing a family outing my parents ask my opinion.
20. My parents encourage me to take expensive gifts for my teacher to ensure good results.
21. My parents approve of their children mixing with the opposite sex.
22. In order to get good marks in the examination, my parents make me visit certain places of worship.
23. My parents believe me when I speak the truth.
24. My parents have made me aware of the financial position of the family.
25. My suggestions to change the eating habits are welcomed by my parents.
26. My parents urge me to achieve more.
27. Before buying me a present my parents ask me what I would like to have.
28. I am given freedom to do what I want.

A F S N

29. My parents have left it to me to follow or not to follow any religious belief.
30. My parents tell me that my family background is more important than my educational qualifications in getting a job.
31. I am expected to follow unquestioningly the rules of the family.
32. If I openly speak out my view on matter like marriage or family planning, my parents get angry with me.
33. My parents would discourage me from taking admission in a University outside Bombay which offered a course of my interest.
34. In expecting me to obey a decision my parents take care to explain the reason.
35. My parents treat all their children equally.
36. My parents insists on my wearing a sacred cord/talisman/medal.
37. I am expected to observe the food taboos of our community.
38. My parents object if I make friends with foreign students.
39. I am free to have friends of my own choice.
40. My parents discuss with me the various career opportunities.
41. My siblings (brother, sisters) complain that I get preferential treatment from my parents.
42. My parents urge me to be systematic in my studies.
43. My parents encourage me to think independently.
44. My parents are of opinion that they are the best judges in the choice of my life-partner.
45. My parents advise me to start some new work on an auspicious day.

A F S N

46. My parents would be shocked if I took up painting our neighbour's house during the vacation to earn some pocket-money.
47. My parents encourage me to examine the reasons behind accepted practices.
48. My parents are displeased when I break old practices and customs.

Part-C

A F S N

1. My brothers/sisters presume that my likes and dislikes are similar to their own.
2. If I do not go to the temple/church/mosque/gurudwara my brothers/sisters scold me.
3. My brothers/sisters criticize me for having friends among the opposite sex.
4. My brothers/sisters tell me that I need not follow all the food restrictions practised in the family.
5. According to my brothers/sisters going late to one's place of work is a big offense.
6. X any Y are given special training for space orbiting. Between the two only Y is chosen to accomplish the task. My brothers/sisters say that it is because Y is the luckier of the two.
7. My brothers/sisters remind me of my special lucky days.
8. My brothers/sisters criticize me for bringing home friends who belong to a lower caste.
9. My brothers/sisters tell me that I can get good marks if my teacher belongs to our own religious community.
10. If I adopt any new hair style my brothers/sisters make fun of me.

A F S N

11. According to my brothers/sisters the best way to avert calamities is to take God's name.
12. If I buy a new product in the market my brothers/sisters scold me for wasting money.
13. My brothers/sisters ridicule my hobbies.
14. The youngest child in the family escapes all punishment.
15. When I am not well-prepared for an examination my brothers/sisters promise to pray for me.
16. My brothers/sisters defend me against my friends even when I am at fault.
17. My brothers/sisters would entrust me with an important task.
18. According to my brothers/sisters godmen have special power.
19. My brothers/sisters do not give any importance to my opinion.
20. My brothers/sisters boss over me.
21. My brothers/sisters wear a religious medal/talisman.
22. My brothers/sisters would approve of my choosing a life partner from a different community.
23. Before deciding on how to spend the holidays my brothers/sisters consult me.
24. When buying a present for my parents my brothers/sisters and I contribute equally.
25. My brothers/sisters advise me to work systematically right from the start of the year.
26. If I win a prize at a competition my brothers/sisters feel jealous of me.

A F S N

27. My brothers/sisters encourage me to have friends irrespective of their communities.
28. If I fail in an examination my brothers/sisters console me saying that it is fate.
29. My brothers/sisters hurry through a piece of work because they do not get time to complete it.
30. If I join a club without consulting my brothers/sisters they find fault with my choice.
31. My brothers/sisters tell me to accept what they say unquestioningly.
32. My brothers/sisters blame me for their mistakes.
33. When I ask my brothers/sisters to clarify some issue in my studies they try to explain it to me thoroughly.
34. My brothers/sisters tell me that to get on well in life one needs a "god-father".
35. My brothers/sisters advise me to leave the choice of my life partner to the elders.
36. At home my brothers/sisters leave all the menial work to me.
37. My brothers/sisters try to understand my problems.
38. My brothers/sisters remark that girls get good marks because they are girls.
39. My brothers/sisters tell me that to get good marks I should follow their study habits.
40. If I damaged my brothers/sisters property unintentionally they shout at me.

	A	F	S	N
41. If my friend let me down when I needed his help, my brothers/sisters tell me that I should teach him a lesson.				
42. My brothers/sisters believe that boys in the house should be given better facilities to study than girls.				
43. My brothers/sisters get angry with me if I criticize them when they did something wrong.				
44. According to my brothers/sisters a girl's career is as important as a boy's.				
45. My brothers/sisters resent the idea of working under a woman.				
46. My brothers/sisters would expect me to accept their suggestions in choosing a course of study.				

Key

	A	F	S	N
Positive Items	3	2	1	0
Negative items	0	1	2	3

14. Three items from each of the subscales are listed below. The author of the third Handbook of Psychological and Social Instruments is authorised to reproduce these items in the Handbook.

Part A. 1. My father encourages my mother to take important decisions.

2. My mother decides independently her mode of dress.

3. My father helps my mother with house work.

Part B. 1. My mother understands my point of view.

2. My parent take interest in my studies.

3. My parents encourage me to think independently.

Part C 1. If I adopt a new hair style my brother/sister makes fun of me.

2. My brother/sister redicules my hobbies.

3. My brother/sister blames me for their mistakes.

44A (8)

Title of the Instrument :**Rating Scale for Studying Some Aspects of Social Change.**

Purpose : To study adults' beliefs and ideas towards some aspects of social change.

Authors : B.M. Mathur.

Languages : Hindi and English.

Availability : Dr. B.M. Mathur, Principal N.D.V. Women's Teachers Training College, Mahila Ashram, Bhilwara.

Uses : Can be used for studying the beliefs and ideas of adult learners towards a few aspects representing social change.

Levels : Adult learners.

Main features : Items Thirty-Five for each aspect, namely, Social Participation, Social Awareness, Environmental Awareness, and Scientific outlook; Items arranged on three point rating scale.

Reliability : Test-retest reliabilities range from 0.84 to 0.92.

Validity : Content validity judged by twenty experts; biserial correlations above +0.35 for items.

Time Limit : Fifteen minutes.

Validity : Norms available with the author.

References : Tool used in the Ph.D. thesis by the author now being used on Adult learners in Rajasthan.

RATING SCALE FOR STUDYING SOME ASPECTS OF SOCIAL CHANGE

Name ____

Age ______________________ Sex ______________________

Occupation ____

Religion and Caste ______________________________(SC/ST/others)

Centre ____

Direction

In this list certain acts are given which many people are unable to perform in the prevailing circumstances and some consider it proper to perform. There are others who do not know as to what should be done in this circumstances.

You are required to read each sentence and indicate whether you agree with them or not. If you disagree please encircle the word 'Disagree' and if you agree, then make a circle around the word agree'. In case you are not in a position to take decision about any statement, then encircle the word 'Undecided'.

Scores Obtained

S.No.	Areas	Scores
1.	S A	
2.	S P	
3.	P A	
4.	E A	
5.	S O	

Group A

1. No hesitation in giving contribution for the help of handicapped and destitute — D U A SA
2. Taking part in Shramdan and other programmes organized by adult education Centre — D U A SP
3. Organizing/Uniting for the struggle to achieve one's constitutional rights — D U A PA
4. Supporting the laws against the factories discharging effluents in the river/lake — D U A EA
5. Confronting/Examining different Aspects of the advice given by anybody before accepting. — D U A SO

Group B

6. Being prepared to use bio gas or solar cooker, if available in place of cowding or firewood. — D U A EA
7. Joining Yuvak Mandal/Mahila Mandal as its active member

8. Supporting the adoption of new techniques for increasing production in farm/factory D U A SO
9. Always prepared to share griefs and joys of others D U A SA
10. Voting for only the suitable and sincere candidate in election without considering the caste factor D U A PA

Group C

11. Taking caution against possible hazard while using an electric equipment D U A PA
12. Being eager to receive invitation for social functions D U A SP
13. Demanding strict rules for prevention of poisonous gases D U A EA
14. Being fearless in offering constructive criticism of any person political party of government D U A PA
15. Being prepared to mix up with everybody in the neighborhood without any religions consideration D U A SA

Group D

16. Imparting the information received at the Adult Education Centre to others in the village/Colony. D U A SP
17. Advising the friends and neighbourers not to use alcohol and other narcotics D U A SA
18. Being prepared to exercise of vote rightly in any circumstance D U A PA
19. Being prepared to plant more trees for improvement of environment D U A EA
20. Guarding one's opinion through critical/Logical thinking D U A SO

Group E

21. Keeping oneself informed about the activities and service to nation being rendered by different political parties D U A PA
22. Supporting strict punishment for prevention of hunting the wild animals. D U A EA
23. Having affectionate relations with relatives and neighbours D U A SA
24. Thoroughly considering the advantages and disadvantages before buying any article for home D U A SO
25. Being prepared to participate in community games and cultural programmes D U A SP

Group F

26. Offering voluntary services in fairs and other such programmes D U A SP
27. Regarding it proper to do anything independently rather than following the traditional pattern D U A SO
28. Not besitating in severely criticizing a person who fells green trees D U A EA
29. Setting aside personal interests in performing duties towards the nation D U A PA
30. Gladly accepting invitation to attend collective and ideal marriages D U A SA

44A (9)

Title of the Instrument :**Cultural Determination Scale.**
Purpose : Measures cultural conformity and cultural rebellion.
Authors : Chauhan, N.S.; Sharma, A.D.; Bhandari, R.L.; Sharma, Uma.
Language : Hindi (English version attached).
Availability : MAPA (Meerut.) D-69, Shastrinagar, Meerut.
Uses : Attitude research.

Levels : Adolescents, Adults,

Main features : Seven point rating scale ; 40 items.

Reliability : The reliability of the scale has been determined by the test-retest method. The coefficient of reliability has been 0.74 (Mean=129.92 and SD=16.40) for the original scale. The revised scale's reliability coefficient was found to be=0.81.

Validity : The coefficient of validity of the revised scale has been determined with ratings of neighbours which was found to be = 0.63.

Time Limit : No time limit for this test.

Norms : Norms are available in the manual.

References :

1. English, H.B. and A.V. English. A *Comprehensive Dictionary of Psychological and Psychoanalytical Terms*. London, Longmans & Coscen, 1958.
2. Haviland, William, A. *Anthropology*, New York, Holt & Rhinehart. 1974.
3. Sharma, A.D. A study of Impact and Interactions of Cultural Determinism, Religious frustration of the Varsity going students of Aligarh Town. Ph.D. Thesis (Psy.) Agra University, 1979.
4. Singh, V. Culture Stratum, Cultural Determinism and Economic Status as correlates of Important Attitudes in High Caste and Scheduled Caste adults of Meerut.
5. Linton, R. *The Study of Man*. An Introduction. New York Appleton-Century croft 1936,1964.
6. Swartz, M.J. *et al. Anthropology : Perspective and Humanity* New York, Wiley, 1976.
7. Tyler, E.B. *Primitive Culture : Researches into the Development of Mythology, Philosophy, Religion and Language, Art and Customs*. London, J. Murray.

CULTURAL DETERMINATION SCALE

English Version

Name : ____________________ Age: ____________________

Religion: ____________________Caste (if Hindu):

Education : ____________________ Address: ____________________

Instructions

How far do you agree to every statement? The magnitude of agreement for this is divided into seven parts from 'much' to 'less'. You can put your agreement easily somewhere in these seven sections. Caution is to be taken of this fact that your agreement must be well weighted and be an expression of your own liking. As such,

* Make a cautious selection of columns given in answers.
* Go through each statement cautiously.
* Understand the meaning of the statement properly.
* Do not leave any statement without giving answer.
* Do not give more than one answer to be a statement.
* You will like the statements. Express your choice openly.
* Express your answer by making a tick (✓).

How far do you agree?	Abso-utely	Very Much	Much	Ordina-rily	Less	Very Less	Disagree Absolutely
	1	2	3	4	5	6	7
1. Man is to behave according to religious beliefs.							
2. To obey every order of elders is essential.							
3. Man likes to lead life in accordance with family traditions.							
4. It is essential to help poor and helpless.							
5. Participation in social ceremonies has importance.							
6. One derives pleasure in entertaining the guest.							
7. Like to keep wife and children in a joint family.							
8. Keeping a fast is necessary on main religious occasions.							
9. Earning money only through labour and honesty appears decent.							
10. Imparting of modern education to women is essential.							
11. Women should live in veil or Burka.							

(Contd.)

	1	2	3	4	5	6	7
12. Demanding of rights similar to those of man by women is right.							
13. Going out of home for service by women is wrong.							
14. Not taking divorce despite mutual dissatisfaction in husband and wife is right.							
15. Implementation of family planning is undesirable.							
16. Religious education be imparted to children right from the beginning.							
17. Religion alone can make a man like God.							
18. Making a marriage according to religious rites is good.							
19. Getting tied in marriage bonds is essential for every man and woman.							
20. Marriage in ones own caste and religion is ones liking.							
21. It is a wish that people of the same religion may live in the neighbourhood.							
22. One's parents may be disregarded in love-marriage.							
23. The widow should enter into remarriage.							
24. Taking dowry in marriage is desirable.							
25. Administration of wine in marriage is wrong.							
26. It is good to see reading boys and girls in the school.							
27. Dancing by girls in clubs and hotels is obnoxious.							
28. Keeping friendship by girls with boys and roaming with them is improper.							
29. Taking part by girls in games like hockey and cricket is fair.							
30. Proceeding for pilgrimage or *Haj* is essential.							

(Contd.)

		1	2	3	4	5	6	7
31.	Renunciation of ones pleasure for the -good of others is palatable.							
32.	Naming of children be done only according to one's religious traditions.							
33.	Participation in religious prayers in a temple of a mosque is pleasing.							
34.	No auspicious time be seen before initiating a new action.							
35.	Habitation in foreign countries of those going there for higher education, is undesirable.							
36.	A teacher should be religious minded.							
37.	Girls should always depend upon the father, the brother, the husband and the son.							
38.	Smoking in the school campus by teachers or students is undesirable.							
39.	Organising religious conferences in colleges or universities is essential.							
40.	Returning to one's own country after earning money in foreign country is desirable.							

44A (10)

Title of the Instrument : **A Scale to Measure the Differential Perceptions of Adopters and Non-Adopters.**

Purpose : To measure the evaluative perceptions of adopters and non-adopters towards a new practice.

Authors : B. Krishnamurty, *et al.*

Language : English and Kannada.

Availability : Chairman, Dept. of Post-Graduate Studies and Research in Psychology, Gulbarga University, Gulbarga 585106.

Uses : To identify the perceptual barriers which might be responsible for negative attitudes towards the new/proposed practices/

innovations.

Levels : Any practitioner or a potential practitioner of the proposed practice.

Main features : There are three main dimensions and each dimension is subdivided into four sub-dimensions as follows: Dimensions:

1. Practicability : A new Skills, B Marketability, C. Supplies, D. Resourcefulness for inputs for adopters.

2. Productivity : a. Improvement in income, b. utilisation of the locally existing resources, c. Interaction with existing practices, D. Risk-involvement.

3. *Mobility* : a. Temporal latitude of Acceptance, b. Relation to other Agricultural practices, c. Improvement in social status, d. Relation to the living standard. Further each of the sub dimensions is spread on a Likert type five point scale.

Reliability : Split-half (odd Vs. even items reliability of 0.79 achieved.

Validity : Content validity and construct validity are established.

Time Limit : : About 40 to 50 minutes including obtaining personal data.

Norms : Not Applicable.

References :

1. Bose, S.P. (1961) : Characteristics of farmers who adopt agricultural practices in Indian villages. *Rural Sociology*, 26 : 138-145.
2. Cronback, L.J. and Meehl, E.P. (1967) : Construct validity in psychological test, Payne, D.A. and McMorris, R.F. (eds.), *Educational and Psychological Measurement*, Blaisdell Publishing Co., Toronto, pp. 94-104.

· It has also been used by a few Ph. D. Students, but the references are not readily available. The others may have also been used.

A SCALE TO MEASURE THE DIFFERENTIAL PERCEPTIONS OF ADOPTERS AND NON-ADOPTERS

A. Background information of the respondent:

1. Name of the respondent:
2. Name of the village:
3. Name of the taluk:
4. Name of the district:
5. Whether living in a joint family of divided:
6. Age of farmer:

7. Education of farmer:
8. Land holdings:
   Dry
   Wet
   Garden
   Total
9. Annual income:
10. Adopter or non-adopter:
11. New practices adopted (in the case of adopter):
(i)
(ii)
(iii)
(iv)

B. Evaluative Perception Scale

The specified practice of idea:

Dimension-I: Practicability

1. *New Skills*
(a) the learning of no difficult skills
(b) some easily learnable modifications in the existing-skills
(c) not known.
(d) the earning of a few difficult skills
(e) the learning of many difficult skills

2. *Marketability*
The produce of the specified practice would be:
(a) most easily marketable
(b) marketable
(c) uncertain
(d) marketable with some difficultly
(e) marketable with utmost difficulty

3. *Supplies*
The supplies for the adoption for the specified practice could be:
(a) obtained most easily
(b) obtained easily
(c) uncertain
(d) obtained with some difficulty
(e) obtained with utmost difficulty

4 *Resourcefulness for inputs for the adoption of the practice*
The resources could be mobilized to enable me to command the

inputs for the adoption of specified practice:
(a) most easily
(b) easily
(c) not sure
(d) with some difficulty
(e) with utmost difficulty

Dimension - II : Productivity

1. *Improvement in income*
The adoption of the specified practice would result in:
(a) Immediate improvement in income
(b) improvement in income in reasonable period of time
(c) uncertain improvement in income
(d) improvement in income in future
(e) improvement in income in remote future
2. *Utlisation of the locally existing resources*
The adoption of the specified practice:
(a) would make an effective use of many of the existing resources
(b) would make an effective use of some of the existing resources
(c) not known
(d) would make ineffective some of the existing resources
(e) would make ineffective many of the existing resources
3. *Interaction with the existing practices*
The adoption of the specified practice affects the existing practices:
(a) most favourably
(b) favourably
(c) not known
(d) unfavourably
(e) most unfavourably
4. *Risk involvement*
The adoption of the specified practice:
(a) definitely involves no risk
(b) seems to involve no risk
(c) not sure
(d) seems to invove some risk
(e) definitely involves a great degree of risk

Dimension-III : Motivtiy

1. *Temporal latitude of acceptance*
   The qualities of the specified practice should make it eligible for:
   (a) immediate acceptance
   (b) acceptance in the immediate future
   (c) not sure
   (d) acceptance after some lapse of time
   (e) acceptance in the remote future
2. *Relation to other agricultural practices*
   The adoption of the specified practice would"
   (a) develop all the other agricultural practices
   (b) develop some of the agricultural practices
   (c) develop or hinder-not known
   (d) hinder the development of some of the other agricultural practices
   (e) hinder the development of all the other agricultural practices
3. *Improvement in social status*
   The adoption of the specified practice would:
   (a) definitely improve the social status of the individual
   (b) perhaps improve the social status of the individual
   (c) improve or bring down-not known
   (d) perhaps not improve the social status
   (e) definitely not improve the social status
4. *Relation to the living standard*
   The adoption of the specified practice would:
   (a) definitely result in improving the living standard
   (b) Perhaps result in improving the living standard
   (c) not sure
   (d) perhaps not result in improving the living standard
   (e) definitely not result in improving the living standard

44A (11) by Neelam Mahajan

Scale to Measure Nutrition and Health Education Knowledge Index

S.N.	Statements	True	False
1.	A person can enjoy good nutrition and health only if he can afford to purchase		

S.N.	Statements	True	False
	costly foods as meat, fish, cheese grapes, and almonds etc.	1	2
2.	Well mashed solid supplements (like banana, boiled potato, or vegetable) can safely be incorporated into a child's diet when he is 6 months old.	1	2
3.	Children in low income groups are often undernourished since they consume relatively less food due to faulty child feeding practice and food prejudices of their mothers.	1	2
4.	When a child has diarrhoea his stomach should be given rest since intake of food to fluids only increases the quanfity of stools passed by him.	1	2
5.	It is a good practice to cook vegetables and rice in covered pans in just enough water.	1	2
6.	Defecating in the open is quite a natural way of life and no harm should be caused to any one.	1	2
7.	Green vegetables carrots mangoes and musk melon etc. are good for eyesight.	1	2
8.	Consumption of meat, eggs and other fleshy foods is the only way of ensuring protein requirements of the body. It should therefore be encouraged disregarding cultural sentiments of the people.	1	2
9.	Normally cooked vegetables and pulses (without spices) can be introduced onto a child's diet at the age of 9 months.	1	2
10.	Pregnant women should not consume protein-rich foods in order to avoid complications in child-birth (delivery).	1	2
11.	Food should normally be cooked on simmering to moderate heat since high heat results in loss of nutrients, and deterioration in the quality of food.	1	2
12.	Lactating women need to consume more fats and oils to minerals their health.	1	2

S.N.	Statements	True	False
13.	Balanced nutritional requirements can as well be met be consuming cheap local seasonal foods that are available throughout the year	1	2
14.	Fruit of vegetable juice should not be given to 3 month old infants as it causes digestive disorders.	1	2
15.	Intake of fruits and vegetables provide us essential vitamins and minerals required for our body.	1	2
16.	Vegetables should be cut very fine, soaked in water and washed, both before and after cutting.	1	2
17.	Infants can be given soup (tari, without spices) when they are 4 months old,	1	2
18.	There is no harm if the food gets overcooked while drying off the excess water.	1	2
19.	When cooking rice and vegetables the excess water should not be drained off as it results in loss of nutrients like vitamins etc.	1	2
20.	Milk is a perfect diet and as long as the child is taking milk he need not be given solid (weaning) foods.	1	2
21.	It is a good practice to disinfect drinking water by simple means (decantation, adding alum etc.) and even boil it, especially during rainy season.	1	2
22.	Anemia among children and women form low income groups can be Prevented by dispensing iron and folic acid tablets taken orally.	1	2
23.	Colostrum (first milk secreted by mother after delivery) should not be given to the baby.	1	2
24.	A patient's diet should not be reduced since his energy requirements are increased due to illness.	1	2
25.	Eating dal-rice of dal-chapati combination is more nutritious than eating dal or cereals alone.	1	2
26.	Protein quality of a mixed dal is no better than that of a single dal.	1	2
27.	Infants should normally be breast-fed unless a trained health worker doctor recommends bottle feeding.	1	2

S.N.	Statements	True	False
28.	Pregnant and lactating women need at least to eat more of what they normally eat, if they cannot buy mild etc. to meet additional energy and nutrient requirements.	1	2
29.	Vaccination is painful and makes the child weak and sick.	1	2
30.	Breast milk protects the young child from diseases.	1	2
31.	Sprouted dals are not only difficult to digest, they are less nutritious than commonly cooked dals.	1	2
32.	Regular check up of pregnant women at the PHC or by ANM would ensure safe and trouble free delivery because growth of foetus can be monitored and suitable precautions can be taken well in time for any likely complications.	1	2
33.	Going to the PHC for health check up is a waste of time for the nursing mother and rear child.	1	2
34.	Care should be taken to see that the child does not play in dirt and filth.	1	2
35.	Weighing a child can bring bad omen and the child would fall sick.	1	2

44A (12) by G.S. Saini and R. Reddy

Knowledge test

This test consits of 25 items. This will measure the knowledge level of rural youth club members about the different activities undertaken by them.

Scoring Procedure

The rural youth club members to whom the test is to be administered are required to give their response against each item i.e. they should put mark against yes or no or against one of the alternative suggested in some selected items. Each correct answer will be awarded one mark and incorrect will get zero mark. In this way a member will have the maximum of 25 marks and minimum zero marks. The range between 0 to 25 can be divided into three parts i.e. low score range, medium score range and high score range. The placement of youth club members in these categories will indicate their level of knowledge pertaining to club activities.

Time

The youth club members may be given maximum 20 minutes to complete this test. This test should be administered to each individual member. No consultation or copy shall be allowed while administering the test. Items constituting the final knowledge test.

(a) *Put tick against yes or no*

1. Turnip radish and carrot need no fertilizers and manure — Yes No
2. The best time for transplanting onion is in the month of December — Yes No
3. Do you think that turnip, radish and spinach require more spray of pesticides than other vegetables ? — Yes No
4. Spinach and fenugreek are rich in iron and calcium — Yes No
5. The germs causing navelill enter through the navel cord. — Yes No
6. Pre-baiting of rats is done to avoid bait shyness — Yes No
7. Rat eradication campaign in the fields should be undertaken when the crops are tall. — Yes No
8. Public lavatories in the villages can be very much helpful in maintaining village cleanliness — Yes No
9. Instead of telling others the Yuv Dal members shoul follow the campaign of village cleanliness promptly — Yes No

10. Villages cannot be kept clean unless heaps of dung are removed from village surroundings — Yes No
11. Months of July and December are best for doing the cleanliness work in the villages — Yes No

(b) *Put tick against correct answer*

12. How many crops of brinjal can be taken in a year?
    (a) 1. crop
    (b) 2. crops
    (c) 3. crops
    (d) 4. crops
13. Indicate the sowing time of radish
    (a) February to March
    (b) May to June
    (c) August to September
    (d) November to December
14. Bhindi/pea/brinjal/radish spinach is grown through nursery raising
15. Which of the following insecticides is the most safe to spray on the vegetables? Malthion/Rogor
16. Which of the following varieties is of tomato/
    (a) Early Kumari
    (b) Punjab Sunehri
    (c) Punjab Chhuhars
17. Which of the fo;lowing varieties is of musk melon?
    (a) Punjab Kesari
    (b) Punjab Sunehri
    (c) Punjab Chhuhara
18. Seed rate of brinjal per acre is
    (a) 50 to 100 gm
    (b) 150 to 200 gm

(c) 300 to 400 gm
(d) 500 to 600 gm

19. The colostrum (first milk of the dam (mother) is rich in antibodies and Vitamin A/ carbohydrates
20. Feeding the calf with excess of milk may cause diarrhoea/ pneumonia
21. During the winter, the young calves should be kept warm and dry, to avoid chills and pheumonia/worms
22. How much quantity of milk must be fed daily to the calves during the first two weeks of life?
    (a) 1 kg
    (b) 2 kg
    (c) 3 kg
23. For how many days should the rats be fed by poison bait continuously?
    (a) 2 to 3 days
    (b) 3 to 4 days
    (c) 6 to 7 days
24. Groundnut oil/kerosene oil is used to stop the breeding of mosquitoes in the stagnam water ponds.

(c) *Fill in the Blank*

25. Rat causes damage not only to the food and material but also to ________. (Life)

The correct answer is indicated by putting tick (✓) against each item of the knowledge test.

B

44B (1)

Title of the Instrument : **Agricultural Innovativeness Scale.**
Authors : U.D. Pandey.
Availability : The Author, DIPR, Ministry of Defence, Delhi.
Language : English.
Uses : Measures the attitude of cultivators for the adoption of innovation in the agricultural field.
Levels : Those who are in the field of agriculture.
Main features : There are 17 items in a five point Likert type of scale. The mean, median SD skewness and deviation score (XL) are 59.56, 63.97, 14.14, -.95, and 82.89.
Reliability : The Split Half reliability was found to be = 0.85.
Validity : 80 per cent agreement of the judges opinion.

44B (2)

Title of the Instrument : **The Social Innovativeness Scale.**
Authors : U.D. Pandey.
Availability : The Authors DIPR, Ministry of Defence, Delhi.
Language : English.
Uses : Measures the attitudes of cultivators for the adoption of social innovation.
Levels : Those who are in the field of agriculture.
Main features : There are 17 items in a 5 point Likert type of scale.
Reliability : The reliability coefficient was found to be 0.88.

44B (3)

Title of the Instrument : **The Dependence Proneness Scale.**
Author : U.D. Pandey.
Availability : DIPR, Ministry of Defence, Delhi.
Language : English.
Uses : Measures the tendency of overdependency.
Levels : Those who are in the field of agriculture.
Main features : This is a 20 point Likert type 5 point scale.
Reliability : The reliability was found to be 0.89. (Split half).

44B (4)

Title of the Instrument : **Achievement Motivation Scale.**
Author : U.D.Pandey.
Availability : DIPR, Ministry of Defence, Delhi.
Uses : Measures the need for achievement.
Main features : It is a Likert type 5 point scale.
Reliability : The split-half reliability was found to be 0.52.

All these scales should be read after page 449

C

44C (1)

Title of the Instrument : **Adult Education Achievement Test**
Authors : Vidyavati Malliya, K.C. Malliya and L.N. Dubey.
Availability : National Psychological Corporation, 4/230, Kacheri Ghat, Agra, Agra-4.
Language : Hindi.
Uses : To test the adult education's achievements.
Main Features : It is in Hindi, has 75 items and these items are divided into 5 categories of 1. Language, 2. Maths, 3. Local and Social Knowledge and 5. General Knowledge. Each category has 15 questions.
Levels : Those who come for adult education for measuring their achievements in different fields.
Reliability : Table 1.

		Sample	Language	Maths	Civics and Social	Political	Gen. Know.
Men	—	356	0.61	0.69	0.68	0.60	0.80
Women	—	200	0.69	0.61	0.62	0.65	0.78

Table 2.

Language	Maths	Civic & Social	Politics	Gen. Know
0.60	0.78	0.70	0.69	0.80

Validity : Not available or found.
Norms : Available.
Time Limit : One hour.

B

Religion and Morality

45B (1)

Title of the Instrument : **The Extrinsic Religious Belief Scale.**
Authors : U.D. Pandey.
Availability : DIPR, Ministry of Defence, Delhi.
Language(s) : English and Hindi.
Uses : To measure the extrinsic aspects of religious beliefs of Hindus.
Levels : Hindu people.
Main features : It is a Likert type 5 point scale. The subjects have to judge whether the statements are right or wrong.
Reliability : Not mentioned.

45B (2)

Title of the Instrument : **The Intrinsic Religious Belief Scale.**
Authors and Availability : U.D. Pandey, DIPR, Ministry of Defence, Delhi.
Language : English.
Uses : To measures the intrinsic beliefs of Hindu religion.
Levels : People belonging to the Hindu faith.
Main features : There are 15 items of the scale and each item has two alternatives : 1. Measures intrinsic aspects. the mean, median and S.D. skewness and deviation score are 11.54, 13.54. 3.86 –1.44 and 50.70 respectively.
Reliability : Split half reliability was found to be = 0.79.
Validity : 80 per cent agreement among the judges.

45B (3)

Title of the Instrument : **Attitude Towards Religion.**

Authors : B.A. Parikh and Others.

Availability : Department of Psychology, M.T.B. Arts College, Surat-395001.

Language : English.

Uses : To measure the attitude of people towards religion.

Levels : Students of college or any other level.

Main features : The inventory consists of 20 statements. The statements concern various aspects of religion. There is a 6-point scale and so the range of score will be from 20 to 120.

45D (1)

Title of the Instrument : **Adapted Kohlberb's Moral Judgement Test (for Indian Children).**

Authors : Jayanthi Sunderasan, Kunjan Saxena, and Shobha Soalapurkar. Guide : T.S. Saraswathi.

Availability : Department of Human Development and Family Studies, M.S. University of Baroda, Baroda-390002.

Language : English.

Uses : It may be used to ascertain the developmental stage at which the child is with reference to moral judgement prior to planning any stimulation programme or activities for promoting the same.

Levels : Children aged 10+ years.

Main features : The test consists of two forms: Form A and Form B. Each form has three story situations, each of which poses a hypothetical moral dilemma, in which acts of obedience to laws and rules or commands conflict with the needs or welfare of other persons. Forms A and B have been equated so that they can be used as alternate forms.

Reliability : Inter scorer Reliability was found out on the moral maturity scores was found out to be 0.88.

Validity : Factor analysis of the data yielded a 'g' factor score of 0.44; when issue 4 which posed problems the factor rose to 0.50.

Norms : Given in the manual.

References : Given in the manual.

Other Social Attitudes

A

46A (1)

Title of the Instrument : **Social and Family Role Stress Scale (SFRS= Scale).**

Purpose: To measure stress emanating from social and family situation.

Authors : S. Sultan Akhtar and Priti Vadra.

Language(s) : English and Hindi.

Availability : Prof. S. Sultan Akhtar, Department to Psychology, A.M.U., Aligarh-202002.

Uses : No tool exists for the measurement of extra organisational Stressors. The present one will be of great use for delineating outside the organizational factors and for classifying people under stress. Its uses are—for research and classification.

Levels : All levels of employees working in an organization.

Main features : It is a Likert type, 5-point self Rating Scale. It consists of 25 items covering social and family areas.

Reliability : Split-half reliability found by Spearman-Brown formula is 0.81.

Validity : Item—total and inter—item correlations were computed which ranged between 0.27 to 0.58. Varimax Rotation technique was also applied to extract the factors which ranged between 0.37 to 0.82.

Time Limit : There is no time limit but the respondents are required to work as quickly as possible and on an average the administration times is 15-20 minutes.

Norms : SD norms are available. (From the authors.)

References : Its uses are for identifying outside the work sources of stress.

1. Akhtar, S.S., Vadra, P. (1989) : Social and Family Aspects of Role Stress—Developement of a Scale. Paper to be presented in the 26th IAAP Conference to be held in Calcutta (March 1989.)
2. Akhtar, S.S., Vadra, P. (1988) : Social and Family Aspects of Role Stress–(Sent for Publication in Psychological Reports.).

SOCIAL & FAMILY ROLE STRESS SCALE

Please read carefully each statement and rate them from 1 to 5 as suggested below :

If you find yourself in total agreement with the statement put 5 in the bracket,

If you agree put 4 in the bracket,

If undecided put 3 in the bracket.

If you disagree put 2 in the bracket and,

If you find yourself in total disagreement then put I in the bracket.

1. The members of my family think that I should have opted for some other job. ( )
2. My spouses/family reminds me that my job does not carry much social prestige. ( )
3. It is distressing to know that people consider my job to be inadequate for the expression of my talents. ( )
4. My family members often remind me that this job is not fit for me. ( )
5. The members of my family often complain that I am under-paid. ( )
6. My family members complain that the job activities do not allowed sufficient time for recreation. ( )
7. My family members try to impress upon me that I cannot achieve the objectives of my life through the present job. ( )
8. Often I undergo mental tension at home due to my job. ( )
9. The members of my family get irritated when I do pending work in home. ( )
10. Hard working people frequently appreciate the role that I play. ( )
11. I often realize that my job-related responsibilities lead to the negligence of the studies of my children. ( )
12. I am often accused that I do not share the home responsibilities as I should do. ( )
13. I feel distressed to hear that I could have earned more if I would have selected some other job. ( )
14. The family members complain that my health is deteriorating due to work overload. ( )
15. I feel embarrassed by the comments of my family that I do not have the courage to get ahead. ( )
16. I do not talk about my professional colleagues at home because my family members consider them to be untrustworthy. ( )
17. I cannot invite my family colleagues at home because my family does not like them. ( )
18. The tension associated with my work role may be reduced if the members of my family happen to know my organizational duties and functions. ( )

19. Differences between me and my family members pertaining to my work often lead to a difficult situation. ( )
20. I do not entertain the recommendations of my near and dear ones for certain favours pertaining to my job and for that I have to suffer mental agony. ( )
21. The challenging nature of my job is not appreciated by my family members. ( )
22. My family members have an aversion towards my acceptance of more work-related responsibilities. ( )
23. My family contributes immensely to my progress. ( )
24. My desire to complete the pending work at home often creates a conflicting situation. ( )
25. In order to give due importance to my family I have to forego career development opportunities. ( )

46A (2)

Title of the Instrument :**Life Change Measure.**

Purpose : To assess the Life Stress caused by major Life changes. This is done in two ways : 1. In terms of Life Change Units (LCU) and 2. In terms of self-ratings of experienced life events.

Authors : Bhaskar R. Shejwal.

Language : English.

Availability : Dr. B.R. Shejwal, Department of Psychology, University of Poona, Pune-411007.

Levels : Adults.

Main features : The LCU's have been developed by using the magnitude Estimation technique on a large sample (N=402) from Poona City. The LCM is a list of 42 Life events. The experienced events reported by subject could be scored for the degree of stress in terms of LCU and/or self-ratings given by subject.

Reliability : The test-retest reliability of stress measurement in terms of LCU was found to be 0.73.

Time Limit : Fifteen to twenty minutes.

Norms : The LCU units are available from the author. The norms in terms of self-ratings are not prepared yet.

References :
1. Shejwal, B.R. (1984) : A study of life stress and some of its personality correlates. Ph. D. thesis submitted to the University of Poona.
2. Shejwal, B.R. & Palsane, M.N. (1986) : Locus of

control: A personality correlate in Life events stress *Psychological Studies*, 31-2, 177-181

LIFE CHANGE MEASURE

Name .... Male/Female ....
Age .... Education .... Married/Unmarried ....
Religion .... Occupation .... Income ....

Directions

Events which take place in one's life, bring disturbances in one's routine. In such situations one has to make some changes in life to maintain equilibrium. Listed below are several events, which occur in people's lives. Your have to read each event and indicate when during the last two years it occurred in your life, if at all it has occurred. This period has been divided thus: from today to '6 months ago',6-12 months ago''1 to 1½ years ago', '1=1/2 to 2 years ago'. Place a tick mark (✓) under the appropriate column for the time of occurrence of an event.

Next, consider the extent to which the said event had a positive or negative impact on you. If the event had a very good impact on you. The tick mark (✓) + 3; if it had a very bad impact then mark-3. if the event had no impact then mark "0" (zero) Bad impact is shown by –1 to-3, good impact is shown by +1 to + 3, and '0' (zero) indicates no impact whatsoever. Some events may have had some good and some bad impact: in such a case indicate both for the event, accordingly.

		6 months	6-12 months	1-1½ years	1½-2 years	– 3 extremely - ve	– 2 moderately - ve	– 1 somewhat - ve	0 No impact	+1 Slightly +ve	+2 Moderately +ve	+3 Extremely +ve
No.	Event	1	2	3	4	5	6	7	8	9	10	11
1.	Marriage											
2.	Trouble with the boss											
3.	Detention in jail/ Institution.											

(Contd.)

No.	Event	1	2	3	4	5	6	7	8	9	10	11
4.	Death of spouse.											
5.	Major change in sleeping habits (a bit more or a lot less sleep, or change in time).											
6.	Death of a close family member.											
7.	Foreclosure on a mortgage or loan.											
8.	Death of close friend											
9.	Minor violations of the law (e.g. disturbing Peace, entry in a prohibited area)											
10.	Pregnancy (of wife of close relatives)											
11.	Major change in health of a family member											
12.	Major change in nature of a family member											
13.	Sexual difficulties											
14.	In-law trouble.											
15.	Major change in financial state (a lot worse off or a lot better off)											
16.	Gaining a new family member (through birth or old person moving in etc.)											
17.	Change in residence.											
18.	Son/daughter leaving home (due to marriage, education etc.)											
19.	Marital separation from mate											
20.	Change in temple activities											
21.	Marital reconciliation with mate											

(Contd.)

No.	Event	1	2	3	4	5	6	7	8	9	10	11
22.	Being fired from job/work											
23.	Divorce											
24.	Changing to a different line of work											
25.	Arguments with spouse (due to child rearing, personal habits)											
26.	Major change in responsibilities at work (due to transfer, demotion.)											
27.	Wife beginning/ceasing work outside the home											
28.	Major change in working hours or conditions											
29.	Change in type and amount of recreation											
30.	Major personal injury of illness											
31.	Major business readjustment (merger, reorganization, bankruptcy etc.)											
32.	Change in social activities (clubs, movies, visits, etc.)											
33.	Change in living conditions (building a new home, remodelling etc.).											
34.	Trouble with neighbour											
35.	Retirement from job											
36.	Unemployment											
37.	Daugthter's marriage											
38.	Becoming broken-hearted											
39.	Loss of limb in an accident											
40.	Trouble with colleagues/ friends											
41.	To lose a case in the court											
42.	Serious illness of a friend.											

Besides above events if you have experienced some other events, please report them as above.

46A (3)

Title of the Instrument : **Perceived Parental Perception Inventory (PPPI).**

Authors : Kusum K. Bhatt, Reader, Department of Psychology, Gujarat University.

Purpose : This inventory has been prepared to measure the perceived parental perception of a child. Every child believes that he is liked, disliked, approved, or criticised by his parents. This perception creates some emotional set up in the mind of the child which can influence his self-perception as well as his social-cultual interaction. In this inventory, the S is to be asked what be thinks about his progress, his appearance, etc. The response given by the child will show whether the child feels his parents are satisfied or dissatisfied.

Language(s) : Gujarati and English.

Availability : Dr. Kusum K. Bhatt, 30, Govt. Housing Society, Navrangpura-380009.

Uses : 1. It measures the family adjustment of a child.

2. It measures the difference between mother and father as their behaviour is perceived by the child.

3. It also measures how far parental perception is correlated, whether mother or father is having a positive impact on personality of the child as measured through child perception.

Levels : : It is applicable to 8 to 16 years old Gujarati medium school going children.

Main features : The inventory consists of six areas of personality. In each area a specific No. of items are given against which the S is required to answer what he thinks his father's and mother's opinion about his particular trait are. Eg : Satisfactory/Non- satisfactory/ cannot say.

My height

Mother

Father

S has to answer one category for father and one category for mother.

The area covered and the No. of items in each are as follows:-

Physical Appearance	26
Family life	09
School life	14
Nature and Personality traits	37
Social behaviour	21
Additional items	11

S is required to tick mark only one category for father and one for mother. Opinion for both may or may not be the same.

Weightage is given as follows :

a. Satisfactory +1.
b. Non- satisfactory -1.
c. Cannot say 0.

After final total is done, Scores are calculated as A+B+C.

Reliability : Retest- reliability of the test was calculated. It is 0.76.

Observational validity of the test was established by expert opinion and interview technique while establishing the final items.

From the scores obtained, children who were regarded as having family trouble and those coming from healthy families were compared.

t is 0.47 significant at 0.01 level for a sample of 40 subjects.

Time Limit : There is no time limit for the inventory but normal subjects can complete it within 25-30 minutes.

Norms : Available in the manual.

References :

1. Allport, G.W (1937) : *Personality Psychological Interpretation*. Holt, Rhinchart and Winston, New York.
2. Allport, G.W. (1943) : The Ego in Contemporary Psychology. *Psychological Review*, New York.
3. Jersild, A.T. (1952) : The Search of Self. Teacher's College Columbia University, New York.
4. Mehta, P.H. (1968) : The self concept of Bright, Underachieving male High School students, Delhi, N.C.E.R.T.
5. Thompson, G.G. (1965) : *Child Psychology*, Times of India Press, Bombay.
6. Watson, R.I. (1959) : *Psychology of the Child*, John Wiley & Sons Inc. New York.
7. Wiley, R.C. (1961) : *The Self Concept*. Lincoln University of Nebraska Press.

PERCEIVED PARENTAL PERCEPTION INVENTORY (F & M)

This is the English translation of the Perceived Parental Perception Inventory (PPPI), originally prepared in Gujarati. Here, the items are classified into the following areas:

1. Physical Appearance
2. Family Relations

3. School Life
4. Personality Traits
5. Social Behaviour
6. Additional IItems

Before introducing each area, the original instructions are repeated to reinforce the modified response pattern where the Ss is to respond separately for his mother and father.

Name in Full: ______________________________
School: ______________________________
Grade: ______________ Division: __________ Sex: ______

Instructions

Here before you, is a list of items describing your personality. Against each item there are two main divisions; one is for your mother and the other one is for your father. Both of these divisions are classified into three categories; Satisfied (S), Not Satisfied (NS), and Don't Know (DK). Your task is to present separately the views of your father and mother as perceived by you about the items presented here, e.g. take the first item 'Your Height'

		S	NS	DK
Your	M			
Height	F			

First try to think how your mother feels about it, and then put 'X' in the appropriate cell against M. Then try to think about your father how feels about your height and pur 'X' in the appropriate cell against F. In this way finish the whole list carefully and completely.

Section I
Physical Appearance

Following items are about your Physical Appearance. Against each item, there are three alternatives in the divisions representing your mother and your father separately. Please put 'X' in the cell you find most applicable in each case

No.	Items		S	NS	DK
1.	Your Height	M			
		F			
2.	Your Weight	M			
		F			
3.	Your Appearance	M			
		F			
4.	Your Facial Beauty	M			
		F			
5.	Your Smile	M			
		F			
6.	Your Cheeks	M			
		F			
7.	Your Forehead	M			
		F			
8.	Your Eyes	M			
		F			
9.	Your Eyebrows	M			
		F			
10.	The Shape of Your Ear	M			
		F			
11.	The Shape of Your Nose	M			
		F			
12.	Your Lips	M			
		F			
13.	Your Teeth	M			
		F			
14.	Your Hands	M			
		F			
15.	Your Fingers	M			
		F			
16.	Your Nails	M			
		F			
17.	Your Legs	M			
		F			
18.	Your Gait	M			
		F			
19.	Your Voice	M			
		F			

(Contd.)

No.	Items		Categories		
			S	NS	DK
20.	Your Health	M			
		F			
21.	No. of your dresses	M			
		F			
22.	Satisfaction from your	M			
	Fashionable clothes	F			
23.	Cleanliness of your clothes	M			
		F			
24.	Importance given by you	M			
	to fashions	F			
25.	Your opinion about your	M			
	financial position	F			

Section II
Family Relations

Following items are selected from your day-to-day family life. Read them carefully and then show how your father and mother would react about you in each case by putting the 'X' mark in the appropriate cell.

No.	Items		Categories		
			S	NS	DK
1.	Your Respect Towards your	M			
	family	F			
2.	Your care taken by your	M			
	mother	F			
3.	Your care taken by your	M			
	father	F			
4.	Your behaviour towards	M			
	your mother	F			
5.	Your behaviour towards	M			
	your father	F			
6.	Your attitude towards the	M			
	efficiency of your siblings	F			
7.	Your affection for your	M			
	siblings	F			
8.	Satisfaction you get from	M			
	your family	F			
9.	Your position in your family	M			
		F			

Section III
School Life

Following items present certain situations from your school life. Here also you have to show how your father and mother would react to them regarding your reaction in each case and put the 'X' mark in the appropriate cell.

No.	Items		Categories		
			S	NS	DK
1.	Your attitude towards your school life	M F			
2.	Your attitude towards your studies	M F			
3.	Satisfaction you get from your teachers	M F			
4.	Satisfaction you get from your class room progress	M F			
5.	Your academic position among other students	M F			
6.	Your participation in class room debates	M F			
7.	Your confidence to speak before your class	M F			
8.	Academic facilities you get from your family	M F			
9.	Your regularity in your home work	M F			
10.	Insight to tap the correct source for study difficulties	M F			
11.	Capacity to understand the class room teaching	M F			
12.	Your Attitude Toward your Annual Exams.	M F			
13.	Your confidence to come First in your class	M F			
14.	Your capacity to solve your academic difficulties independently	M F			

Section IV
Personality Traits

Following items show your personality traits. Read them carefully and try to judge what your father and mother think about you in connection with those traits. Show their judgement separately by putting the 'X' mark in the appropriate cell.

No.	Items		S	NS	DK
1.	Memory of prices	M			
		F			
2.	Memory of Names and Faces	M			
		F			
3.	Intellectual problem solving capacity	M			
		F			
4.	Correct imagination in Detective stories	M			
		F			
5.	Curiosity to know more over and above school subjects	M			
		F			
6.	Enthusiasm to learn new things	M			
		F			
7.	Witticism	M			
		F			
8.	Clarity in thought presentation	M			
		F			
9.	Attitude toward the utility of truthfulness	M			
		F			
10.	Attitude toward unclaimed articles	M			
		F			
11.	Clarity in the monetary transaction	M			
		F			
12.	Honesty in the monetary transaction	M			
		F			
13.	Attitude to the difference of opinion with the elders	M			
		F			
14.	Your patience	M			
		F			
15.	Your ambition to be great	M			
		F			

(Contd.)

No.	Items		Categories		
			S	NS	DK
16.	Attitude toward those who direct your attention to your mistakes	M F			
17.	Compromising tendency	M F			
18.	Power to pursue your studies depute temptations	M F			
19.	Your attitude to a situation where you have not been deliberately invited by your friend	M F			
20.	Your fitness to stick to a decision once taken	M F			
21.	Determination to complete a task once undertaken in spite of difficulties	M F			
22.	Capacity to undertake family responsibilities in the absence of parents	M F			
23.	Your readiness to understand the real cause when your parents disappoint you	M F			
24.	Capacity to resolve dilemma	M F			
25.	Capacity to understand the seriousness of various tasks and act accordingly	M F			
26.	Capacity to joke	M F			
27.	Control over anger	M F			
28.	Frankness	M F			
29.	Attitude towards stories with happy ending	M F			
30.	Attitude towards weakminded people	M F			

(Contd.)

No.	Items		Categories		
			S	NS	DK
31.	Fearlessness	M			
		F			
32.	Courage to face unexpected question at examination	M			
		F			
33.	Your behaviour at the time of frustration of long cherished hope	M			
		F			
34.	Habit of Nail biting	M			
		F			
35.	Proportion of sleep disturbing dreams	M			
		F			
36.	Reaction to darkness	M			
		F			

Section V
Social Behaviour

Following items show specific situation in your social life.. Try to visualize what your parents think about you in connection with each one of them and show their responses separately by putting the 'X' Mark in the appropriate cell.

No.	Items		Categories		
			S	NS	DK
1.	Capacity to participate in the organization of picnics or social gatherings	M			
		F			
2.	Your patience in explaining any subject through discussion and clarification	M			
		F			
3.	Other peoples willingness to work in co-operation with you	M			
		F			
4.	Capacity to make other people work as you desire	M			
		F			

(Contd.)

No.	Items		Categories		
			S	NS	DK
5.	Capacity to co-operate with others.	M F			
6.	Your behaviour towards unfamiliar guests	M F			
7.	Capacity to mix freely in your friends circle	M F			
8.	Attitude towards pessimists	M F			
9.	Capacity to pardon the insult done by others	M F			
10.	Tendency to insulting others	M F			
11.	Aloofness	M F			
12.	Capacity to adjust to new social environment	M F			
13.	Tendency to compromise in quarrels with your friends	M F			
14.	Ability to judge people before forming friendship	M F			
15.	Capacity to give correct advice to your friends	M F			
16.	Degree of suspiciousness in your temperament	M F			
17.	Willingness to help your friends in trouble	M F			
18.	Satisfaction you get from your friends	M F			
19.	Your behaviour towards the opposite sex	M F			
20.	Behaviour of the opposite sex towards you	M F			
21.	Attitude towards the moral faults of your friends	M F			

Section VI
Additional Items

In this section are presented certain items about your views and attitudes towards the life in general. Here also you have to show what your parents think about you and present their views separately by putting the 'X' mark in the appropriate cell.

No.	Items		Categories		
			S	NS	DK
1.	Knowledge about the sexual relations of man and woman	M F			
2.	Your ideas about marriage	M F			
3.	Capacity to organize finances	M F			
4.	Capacity to help your family financially	M F			
5.	Clarity about future profession	M F			
6.	Correct information about the political situation	M F			
7.	Behaviour towards the scheduled caste people	M F			
8.	Attitude towards the caste system	M F			
9.	Attitude towards the richer class	M F			
10.	Attitude towards your financial condition	M F			
11.	Your self satisfaction.	M F			

46A (4)

Title of the Instrument : **Scale to Measure Attitude of ICDS Project Functionaries Towards Integrated Child Development Services Scheme.**

Purpose : To measure the attitude of ICDS project level functionaries towards ICDS scheme.

Author : Neelam Mahajan.

Language : English.

Availability : Central Library, Indian Agricultural Research Institute, New Delhi.

Uses : It can be used to determine the attitude of ICDS Project functionaries towards Integrated Child Development Services Scheme.

Levels : Project level functionaries of ICDS Scheme viz. Child Development Project Officer, Mukhya Sevika, Anganwadi Worker.

Main Features : Likert Scaling technique is used. Poor items were eliminated. For this purpose mean and variance of response to each individual statement is evaluated by finding the value of t-ratio. Statements in the item pool are ordered according to their t-values. Items for which it is statistically insignificant (using single tail test) are left out. Finally 12 items were selected.

Reliability : Cronbach Alpha given in Guilford and Fruchhter (1978) was calculated for 370 respondents Computed value of Cronbach Alpha being 0.70.

Validity : The content validity of the scale was ensured from 20 judges who were experts in ICDS Scheme (Functionaries engaged in operation of ICDS Scheme and Scientists from Division of Agricultural Extension possessing knowledge of ICDS scheme. The intrinsic validity of the scale was determined by internal consistency intrinsic validity of the scale was determined by internal consistency indices like Cronbach Alpha.

Time Limit : 15 minutes.

Norms : N.A.

References :

1. Guilford J.P and Fruchter, Benjamin (1978) : *Fundamentals of Statistics on Psychology and Education*. Mcgraw Hill Kogkusha Ltd.
2. Edward, A.L. (1957) : *Techniques of Attitude Scale Construction*, USA Appleton Century Crofts Inc.

SCALE TO MEASURE ATTITUDE OF ICDS PROJECT FUNCTIONARIES TOWARDS ICDS SCHEMES

SA = Strongly agree with the statement = 1
A = Tend to agree with the statement = 2
U = Undecided. Neither agree nor disagree = 3

D = Tend to disagree with the statement = 4
SD = Strongly disagree with the statement = 5

S.No.	Statement	SA	A	U	D	SD
1.	With the start of an ICDS project the infant mortality rate would go down considerably in the area.	1	2	3	4	5
2.	People talk about the ICDS scheme but actually not much work is being done.	1	2	3	4	5
3.	ICDS would in no way help improve the nutritional status of children in the 0-6 age group.	1	2	3	4	5
4.	ICDS would accentuate rather than moderate regional inequalities and social disparities.	1	2	3	4	5
5.	ICDS would improve women's knowledge regarding nutrition.	1	2	3	4	5
6.	ICDS would help inculcate good nutritional habits among children.	1	2	3	4	5
7.	Adequate referral services are not available to women and children through ICDS.	1	2	3	4	5
8.	Functional literacy classes for women hardly serve any useful purpose.	1	2	3	4	5
9.	It is only because of ICDS that women and children would be able to avail of medicines for common ailments and immunization against terrible diseases.	1	2	3	4	5
10.	The training programmes for ICDS functionaries is a waste of time.	1	2	3	4	5
11.	ICDS is doing quite a good job in bringing about socio-economic changes in the rural, tribal and urban slum areas.	1	2	3	4	5
12.	ICDS would create more problems instead of solving them.	1	2	3	4	5

46A (5)

Title of the Instrument : **Sex Differentiation Scale.**
Purpose : To assess the level of Sex differentiation in family.
Author(s) : Ashok Pratap Singh and Patiraj Kumari.
Language(s) : Hindi and English.
Availability : Department of Psychology, Banaras Hindu University, Varanasi-221005.
Uses : It can be used to assess the level of sex differentiation along families.
Levels : Family member
Main Features : Five point scale, 19 items.
Reliability : Under preparation.
Validity : Under preparation.
Time Limit : No time limit.
Norms : Not available
References : Not available.

SEX DIFFERENTATION SCALE

In this scale there are some questions related to you and your family. Five probable answers of each question are given below. According to your opinion give the right answer by making tick (✓) mark within the bracket.

	Strongly disagree	Disagree	Uncertain	Agree	Strongly agree
	1	2	3	4	5
1. In my family more attention is paid to the comfort of boys than the girls.	( )	( )	( )	( )	( )
2. In my family boys health is considered to be more important than the girls from the childhood.	( )	( )	( )	( )	( )
3. In my family boys are brought up more nicely than the girls.	( )	( )	( )	( )	( )

(Contd.)

	1	2	3	4	5
4. In my family high education for the girls is not considered to be genuine.	( )	( )	( )	( )	( )
5. Ladies do not get full freedom in my family.	( )	( )	( )	( )	( )
6. Ladies are not permitted to do any outdoor job in my family.	( )	( )	( )	( )	( )
7. Boys get more love and affection than the girls in my family	( )	( )	( )	( )	( )
8. Males are encouraged to do competitive and courageous work in my family.	( )	( )	( )	( )	( )
9. Members of family think that girls' efficiency in the homework is their biggest achievement.	( )	( )	( )	( )	( )
10. Female's cooperation is not taken to provide the means for living in my family.	( )	( )	( )	( )	( )
11. Ladies think that only males are responsible for earning in my family.	( )	( )	( )	( )	( )
12. Ladies consider that coking, washing, cleaning and other houseworks are their main duties in my family.	( )	( )	( )	( )	( )
13. Working ladies are not considered to be respectful in my family.	( )	( )	( )	( )	( )
14. The oldest lady of my family gives the suggestions at the time of emergency in the family.	( )	( )	( )	( )	( )
15. Mostly the ladies want to be fully dependent on male members in my family	( )	( )	( )	( )	( )

(Contd.)

	1	2	3	4	5
16. Male members are expected to provide proper standard of living to the family.	()	()	()	()	()
17. Ladies feel mental and physical torture in doing outdoor jobs due to the division of labour on the basis of sex.	()	()	()	()	()
18. Boys are free to choose their life partners.	()	()	()	()	()
19. The male members take final decision for the marriage of the girls.	()	()	()	()	()

46A (6)

Title of the Instrument : **Marital-Role Preference Scale.**

Purpose : This scale was modified and standardized for Doctoral work in Psychology.

Authors : R.D. Sharma.

Availability Dr. R.D Sharma Project Officer Department of Adult, Continuing Education and Extension, Garhwal University, Srinagar (Garhwal) Pin 246 174.

Language(s) : English and Hindi..

Uses : This scale is to determine the role Preference of Young men and Women as husbands or wives in their married life.

Levels : Unmarried youth in the age range 18-28 years.

Main Features : Likert's (1932) Sigma deviation method was used to measure marriage attitude. The subjects had to answer on a five-point scale. Following Likert's method items which showed a favourable attitude were treated as positive responses. Items which showed an unfavorable attitude were taken as negative responses. There are 23 items in the scale.

Reliability : The reliability of the Scale was determined by the split-half method. Based on the analysis of responses. The split-half reliability of the scale is 0.80.

Validity : Nil.

Time Limit : No time limit but generally it takes 10-20 minutes.

Norms : Nil.

References : This scale was originally developed by Jacobson (1952) and modified by Arkoff *et al.* (1963) and Gardiner (1968). The modified form of this scale was used in a comparative study of Thailand, India and United States by Gardiner, Singh and D. Orazio. (1974).

MARITAL ROLE PREFERENCE SCALE

Sex: Female ☐ Male ☐

Occupation: Study ☐ Service ☐

Below are given some statements. Read these statements carefully. There are five categories given against each statement strongly agree (S.A.) Agree (A), Undecided (UD), Disagree (D), Strongly Disagree (S.D.). You have to make a circle (o) around one of them, which indicates your inner feeling.

There are no right or wrong answers: We are interested in knowing how you really feel for the statements. Your answers will be kept confidential and will be used for research work only.

Statement Categories

Example: Wife should be free to go out at night by herself

(S.A.) A UD D S.D.

In the above example S.A. has encircled, it shows strongly agreeness with this statement.

S.No.	*Statements*	*Categories*				
1.	The husband should decide whether to not to have children.	S.A.	A	UD	D	S.D.
2.	The husband should help with the housework	S.A.	A	UD	D	S.D.
3.	The wife should take her husband's religion as hers.	S.A.	A	UD	D	S.D.
4.	The husband should help take care of children.	S.A.	A	UD	D	S.D.
5.	If the husband insists, the wife should quit a needed job.	S.A.	A	UD	D	S.D.
6.	The husband should help wash dishes	S.A.	A	UD	D	S.D.
7.	Wives are too independent these days.	S.A.	A	UD	D	S.D.

(Contd.)

S.No.	*Statements*	*Categories*				
8.	If the husband wants children the wife should agree.	S.A.	A	UD	D	A.D.
9.	The husband should decide how to spend any extra money.	S.A.	A	UD	D	A.D.
10.	Husbands should be more strict with their wives.	S.A.	A	UD	D	A.D.
11.	A married women should not work outside the home.	S.A.	A	UD	D	A.D.
12.	What a husband does in his spare time is his business.	S.A.	A	UD	D	A.D
13.	The husband should decide where to live.	S.A.	A	UD	D	A.D.
14.	Woman's place is in the home.	S.A.	A	UD	D	A.D.
15.	The wife should fit her life to her husband's.	S.A.	A	UD	D	A.D.
16.	The wife should mend and sew the family's clothes.	S.A.	A	UD	D	A.D.
17.	The husband's wishes should be first in most things.	S.A.	A	UD	D	S.D.
18.	Marriage is the best career for a women.	S.A.	A	UD	D	S.D.
19.	The husband should be the boss in the family	S.A.	A	UD	D	S.D.
20.	Marriage should be a full time job for the wife.	S.A.	A	UD	D	S.D.
21.	If the husband is running around with another woman, his wife should be patient until he comes to his senses.	S.A.	A	UD	D	S.D.
22.	A wife should let her husband decide most things.	S.A.	A	UD	D	S.D.
23.	Almost all money matters should be decided by the husband.	S.A.	A	UD	D	S.D.

46A (7)

Title of the Instrument : **An Inventory for Juvenile Delinquency.**

Author(s) : I.A. Khan, A.A.Khan, and M.M. Husain.

Availability : Department of Psychology, AMU., Aligarh, *Indian Journal of Criminology*, Vol. 10. No. 1, Jan 1982.

Language(s) : English.

Uses : To assess delinquency in India.

Levels : Institutionalized as well as high school students/delinquents.

Main Features : There are 50 items. Each item is to be answered in yes/no whatever is applicable to the subjects. The direction of the response is indicative of delinquency.

Reliability : Split-Half reliability of the test was determined which yielded a coefficient of 0.91. (Others in the manual) Ranges from 0.85 to 0.92.).

Validity : When two groups were compared the validation was found to be 0.89 to 0.91.

Norms : Available in the manual.

Time Limit : No time limit.

References :

1. Banks, C.; Malaney, E., and Willcock, H.D. (1975): Public attitude to crime and the penal system. *British Journal of Criminology*, 15, 228-40.
2. Carroll, R.M., Pine, S.M.; Cline, C.J. & Kleinhans, B.R. (1974) : Judged seriousness of water-gate-related crimes. *Journal of Psychology*, LXXXVI. 235-39.

46A (8)

Title of the Instrument : **Social Maturity Scale.**

Authors : Pratiksha H. Raval.

Availability : The Yoga Education Centre, 3, Pratapkunj Society, Wasana, Ahmedabad-7.

Language : English.

Uses : Assesses the individual differences among the group of individual with desired variables. Allows us to know the differences in level as well as in the rate of development in social behaviour. Helps parents in drawing the chart of growth and maturation of particular child. Helps to obtain maturational history of the individuals. Influence of any social variables upon the social maturity can be studied by this scale, such as race, nationality, caste, sub-caste, socio-economic levels, etc.

Levels : Children under the age of 10 years.

Main Features : 170 items are grouped under the 12 categories (mentioned in the manual) on the basis of relevant theoretical dimensions. Each item is defined conceptually as well as behaviourally.

Reliability : Test-retest reliability after the interval of one month was found to 0.99. After one year interval reliability was found to be 0.96.

Validity : Content validity as well as construct validity were emphasized.

Norms : Available in the manual.

Time Limit : No time limit.

46A (9)

Title of the Instrument : **Attitude of Medical Practitioners.**

Purpose : Attitude of Medical Practitioners.

Authors : B.K. Man Mohan Singh.

Language : English.

Availability : Dr. B.K. Man Mohan Singh, Lecturer, Department of Psychology, Osmania University, Hyderabad- 500007.

Uses : Medical practitioners attitude towards children, parents, self and medical profession.

Levels : Medical Practitioners/Students of Medicine.

Main Features : Likert's Summated rating Techniques 5 item each for children, Self and Profession 27 item for profession.

Reliability : Test-retest Method Children, 0.803 Self 0.937 Parents 0.620 Profession 0.602-Overall 0.677.

Validity : Point Biserial Correlation with two categorically distinct groups of those who are satisfied and those who are not is 0.3342.

Time Limit : 20 Minutes.

Norms : Not available.

References : "Occupational Heredity", Unpublished Ph.D. thesis, Department of Psychology, Osmania University, Hyderabad-500007.

Kindly put a check (✓) mark at the appropriate and applicable alternative/s. Please strike out the alternative/s not applicable.

Attitudes Towards Parents

1. In general Doctors do not choose medical profession because of the influence of their parents

(1) Strongly Agree (2) Agree (3) Uncertain
(4) Disagree (5) Strongly disagree

2. I do owe my greatest obligation to my parents/father /mother for selecting my profession.
(1) Strongly Agree (2) Agree (3) Uncertain
(4) Disagree (5) Strongly disagree
3. I do believe that my parents/father/mother are/is the most admirable person/s I have known.
(1) Strongly Agree (2) Agree (3) Uncertain
(4) Disagree (5) Strongly disagree
4. The students whose parents were doctors in general enjoy privileges and were favourites of the staff at the medical college.
(1) Strongly Agree (2) Agree (3) Uncertain
(4) Disagree (5) Strongly disagree
5. The students whose parents were doctors in general enjoy privileges and were favourites of the staff at the hospital while they were under training.
(1) Strongly Agree (2) Agree (3) Uncertain
(4) Disagree (5) Strongly disagree

Kindly put a check (/) mark at the appropriate and applicable alternative/s. Please strike out the alternative/s not applicable.

Attitude Towards Children

1. Doctors should encourage their children to take up medicine
(1) Strongly Agree (2) Agree (3) Uncertain
(4) Disagree (5) Strongly disagree
2. Doctor parents normally encourage their children to take up the role of a doctor while playing.
(1) Strongly Agree (2) Agree (3) Uncertain
(4) Disagree (5) Strongly disagree
3. There should be a specific percentage of seats reserved in medical colleges for children whose parents are doctors.
(1) Strongly Agree (2) Agree (3) Uncertain
(4) Disagree (5) Strongly disagree
4. A doctor encourages his children to take up medicine because the income is good.
(1) Strongly Agree (2) Agree (3) Uncertain
(4) Disagree (5) Strongly disagree

5. A doctor encourages his children to take up medicine because it is a noble profession.
   (1) Strongly Agree (2) Agree (3) Uncertain
   (4) Disagree (5) Strongly disagree

Kindly put a check (/) mark at the appropriate and applicable alternative/s. Please strike out the alternative/s not applicable.

Attitudes Towards Self

1. I am self made man/woman
   (1) Strongly Agree (2) Agree (3) Uncertain
   (4) Disagree (5) Strongly disagree
2. In my own esteem I have been able to accomplish fairly much
   (1) Strongly Agree (2) Agree (3) Uncertain
   (4) Disagree (5) Strongly disagree
3. In my colleagues' esteem I have been able to accomplish fairly much
   (1) Strongly Agree (2) Agree (3) Uncertain
   (4) Disagree (5) Strongly disagree
4. Doctors in general have a feeling of being accepted by others in their profession.
   (1) Strongly Agree (2) Agree (3) Uncertain
   (4) Disagree (5) Strongly disagree
5. A challenging situation brings the best out of me.
   (1) Strongly Agree (2) Agree (3) Uncêrtain
   (4) Disagree (5) Strongly disagree

Kindly put a check (/) mark at the appropriate and applicable alternative/s. Please strike out the alternative/s not applicable.

Attitudes Towards Profession

1. It should be possible to reduce the duration of medical education without sacrificing quality
   (1) Strongly Agree (2) Agree (3) Uncertain
   (4) Disagree (5) Strongly disagree
2. Refresher courses and conferences tend to have very limited value in society like ours
   (1) Strongly Agree (2) Agree (3) Uncertain
   (4) Disagree (5) Strongle disagree

3. Patients tend to take advantage of a doctor's goodness
   (1) Strongly Agree (2) Agree (3) Uncertain
   (4) Disagree (5) Strongle disagree
4. Advances in medical diagnosis have deprived the doctor of challenges.
   (1) Strongly Agree (2) Agree (3) Uncertain
   (4) Disagree (5) Strongle disagree
5. Discovery of strong drug have tended to reduce the doctor to a pharmacist
   (1) Strongly Agree (2) Agree (3) Uncertain
   (4) Disagree (5) Strongly disagree
6. People do not respect the doctors as they did in earlier days
   (1) Strongly Agree (2) Agree (3) Uncertain
   (4) Disagree (5) Strongly disagree
7. After a few years, there is every possibility of a doctors life becoming monotonous and routine in the present day world.
   (1) Strongly Agree (2) Agree (3) Uncertain
   (4) Disagree (5) Strongly disagree
8. These days people have more faith in drugs than in doctors.
   (1) Strongly Agree (2) Agree (3) Uncertain
   (4) Disagree (5) Strongly disagree
9. Patient's gratitude compensates for the doctor's adverse working conditions
   (1) Strongly Agree (2) Agree (3) Uncertain
   (4) Disagree (5) Strongly disagree
10. Doctors are no better or no worse than any other group of comparable, educated and trained professionals.
   (1) Strongly Agree (2) Agree (3) Uncertain
   (4) Disagree (5) Strongly disagree
11. Doctors can maintain their status only when they are well paid
   (1) Strongly Agree (2) Agree (3) Uncertain
   (4) Disagree (5) Strongly disagree
12. The mental picture of doctors as self-sacrificing is changing fast
   (1) Strongly Agree (2) Agree (3) Uncertain
   (4) Disagree (5) Strongly disagree
13. In general people consider doctors as having special merits not possessed by others
   (1) Strongly Agree (2) Agree (3) Uncertain
   (4) Disagree (5) Strongly disagree
14. Medical graduates are opting for jobs not connected with medicine

because the medical profession has ceased to be satisfying.
(1) Strongly Agree (2) Agree (3) Uncertain
(4) Disagree (5) Strongly disagree

15. By dint of hardwork alone can a doctor establish himself
(1) Strongly Agree (2) Agree (3) Uncertain
(4) Disagree (5) Strongly disagree

16. Successful doctors are not necessarily the best professionally
(1) Strongly Agree (2) Agree (3) Uncertain
(4) Disagree (5) Strongly disagree

17. No matter how hard the doctor tries ultimately fate prevails
(1) Strongly Agree (2) Agree (3) Uncertain
(4) Disagree (5) Strongly disagree

18. Death is brought about not only by disease but also by sins
(1) Strongly Agree (2) Agree (3) Uncertain
(4) Disagree (5) Strongly disagree

19. Very often competent doctors do not come to be regarded as successfull
(1) Strongly Agree (2) Agree (3) Uncertain
(4) Disagree (5) Strongly disagree

20. The real skill of a doctor depends on his ability to help the patient cure himself
(1) Strongly Agree (2) Agree (3) Uncertain
(4) Disagree (5) Strongly disagree

21. Some times grand mothers prescription are as good as sophisticated medical prescriptions
(1) Strongly Agree (2) Agree (3) Uncertain
(4) Disagree (5) Strongly disagree

22. In many instances modern doctors are not very much ahead of his ancient colleagues
(1) Strongly Agree (2) Agree (3) Uncertain
(4) Disagree (5) Strongly disagree

23. While treating a patient remuneration is generally farthest from a doctor's mind
(1) Strongly Agree (2) Agree (3) Uncertain
(4) Disagree (5) Strongle disagree

24. Very few doctors weigh side-effects before administering the medicine
(1) Strongly Agree (2) Agree (3) Uncertain
(4) Disagree (5) Strongly disagree

25. The family members like parents, children, wife etc. have social

standing a social prestige just because they happened to be related to the doctor

(1) Strongly Agree (2) Agree (3) Uncertain
(4) Disagree (5) Strongly disagree

26. It is better to end the misery of those who are terminally ill and suffer intensely

(1) Strongly Agree (2) Agree (3) Uncertain
(4) Disagree (5) Strongly disagree

27. Doctors do feel guilty whenever they fail to save a life.

(1) Strongly Agree (2) Agree (3) Uncertain
(4) Disagree (5) Strongly disagree

46A (10)

Title of the Instrument : **Maternal/Parental Attitude Towards their Child (age 3-6 years.).**

Purpose : To assess the parental attitudes in an interview form.

Author : Shalini Bhogle.

Languages : English can be transferred into a regional language in an interview setting.

Availability : The scale is not published so I may not be able to send copies and other details to every person who asks for it.

Uses : Can be used by Clinicians, Paediatricians, Educationists, Psychologists, Researchers.

Levels : For parents living with their children: Norms and healthy born (3 to 6 years.)

Main Features : Content analysis of response to each item against standard sketches of eight types of attitudes given. The mother and father are interviewed independently and scoring is done separately. Each parent is labelled according to the predominant attitude based on the score.

Reliability : +.90 is the test-retest reliability coefficient.

Validity : +0.85 judges rating for the sketches prepared and enclosed in the manual.

Time Limit : 15-20 minutes.

Norms : Available.

References : NIL.

PARENTAL ATTITUDE INVENTORY (MOTHER AND FATHER)

Mother-Father

1. Your child declares one day in the morning that he will not go to the school that day, when asked he coolly says he has stomach pain.
2. You had visited one of your rich friends. There your child behaves in an awkward manner making you feel embarrassed.
3. Your elder child has put sand in the ear of the baby.
4. (a) You have heard your child using slang language.
   (b) Your child has addressed you in slang language in front of others.
5. Your neighbour comes and complains that your child has beaten up his small child.
6. Examinations are approaching very near and your child is totally indifferent about studies and plays the whole day.
7. Your child has pricked the baby with a pin stating that he is a doctor and is giving injection to the baby.
8. Your child is playing with a match-box, he is burning the sticks oblivious of the surroundings.
9. Your child is running high fever. It is hot outside and/or (it is raining) you have warned your child to stay in bed but still you find that he is playing outside.
10. (a) One day you find a five rupee note in your child's pocket you know that you never gave it to him.
    (b) One day you find a one rupee note in your child's pocket which you never gave it to him.
11. Your child often comes from the school complaining that he has lost something and today he has lost the complete bag with the tiffin box in it.

Father

1. Your child is repeatedly meddling with radio/T.V.
2. You come home from the office one day to find some of your important papers have been spoiled by your child.
3. (a) Your friends have come to discuss something urgent, your child comes and sits on your lap and refuses to go.

(b) You are talking with an important person, your child comes and starts speaking in the middle.

4. Your are extremely tired and want to take rest. Your child starts crying loudly.
5. (a) Your friend has forgotten his cigarette packet in your house, Next day you find your child secretly smoking it.

   (b) You see your child secretely smoking the half burnt *bidi*.
6. You are going for some urgent work on your Scooter/Cycle. Your child pursues you to take him for a round.
7. Your have taken your child to the market, there he sees one particular toy which is costly and demands to have it immediately (you are not having enough money at that time).
8. Your wife has (served) prepared tea/coffee for you and your friend. your child is not allowed to drink it as he is small. After the friend goes you see your child drinking the remaining portion of the coffee from the cup to your friend.
9. (a) Your child has lost his new costly pen/present.

   (b) Your child has lost his new chappels.

Mother

1. You are busy finishing some urgent work and your child is repeatedly asking you to give him something to eat, you know that the child is not hungry.
2. You want to go out shopping and do not want to take your child with you though the child is pestering to come with you.
3. (a) You are extremely tired, your child persuades you to give a toy which you have kept aside.

   (b) You are extremely tired and resting but your child does not let you rest by making noise.
4. It is summer and you have stored some drinking water for the whole day your child has dipped his dirty hand in it.
5. You are in the kitchen and you have asked your child to take care of the baby. After some time you hear the baby crying, when asked, the child says "I did not do anything, we were just playing".
6. (a) You are going for a wedding, your child who is playing outside, comes and clings to you with his dirty hands spoiling your saree.

   (b) You are getting ready for a party, your child who is playing outside comes and clings to you with his dirty hands spoiling your saree.

7. A new building construction is going on near your house. You have warned your child not to go there and play. But inspite of your telling he goes and comes back badly hurt.
8. (a) You have made your child's favourite dish on his birthday but he says that he does not want to eat it.
   (b) You have made *kheer* on a festival day because everybody in your home likes, but your child refuses to eat it.
9. (a) Some guests are coming for dinner. You have prepared the sweet-dish and kept it aside. In the evening you find that your child has consumed a major portion of it.
   (b) Your husband had bought 'mithai' for all of you, but your child has eaten it away.

46A (11)

Title of the Instrument : **Home Environment Scale.**

Purpose : To study the Perception of Children regarding various areas of Home Environment-Personal freedom, Critical, Social isolation, Acceptance, Understanding, Severity of Discipline, Emotional stability in disciplinary action, Neglecting, Rapport with parents, Rapport with siblings, socio-economic image, Interparental relations, General Satisfaction.

Authors : Sarla Jawa.

Language(s) : Hindi and English.

Availability : Dr. Ms. Sarla Jawa, Department of Psychology, Lady Shriram College for Women, Lajpatnagar, New Delhi-24.

Uses : To study the Perception of Adolescents regarding various areas of home environments.

Levels : 13 to 18 years of age.

Main Features : It is self administered 5 point scale with 74 items. Standardized on 400 adolescents.

Reliability : The Split-Half reliability was found to be 0.88.

Validity : Validity indices of the different items found by calculating F ratio between responses of 27 per cent highest total scores and 27 per cent lower total scorers.

Time Limit : About 30 minutes. (No time limit).

Norms : NIL.

References : A Study of creativity and some of its personality and environmental Correlates. Unpublished doctoral thesis. University of Delhi, Delhi.

HOME ENVIRONMENT SCALE

(Translation only)

Name of the Student ____________ Class ____________ Section ___

School ____

Purpose

The home atmosphere of each individual differed from one another. We are interested in knowing how the perception of the individual affects his development. The achievement of this purpose depends on your cooperation. How you feel about your home atmosphere, can be best revealed by you only. We hope. you will give us your honest opinion about your home atmosphere. We assure you that your answers will be kept confidential and will be used for research purpose only. Please give your judgment honestly.

Instructions

Some statement regarding home atmosphere are given in this booklet. Corresponding to such statement some alternative answers are given. Please read such statement and its possible answer carefully, put a tick mark (x) in the box ( ) corresponding to your answer that best describes your home atmosphere

Example:

	Always	Very often	Some times	Sel- dom	Never
I feel my parents are conservative	( )	( )	(x)	( )	( )

It means that I feel it some times that my parents are conservative.

	Always	Very often	Some times	Sel- dom	Never
1. I feel that my parents donot let me take decision even when I can take them.	( )	( )	( )	( )	( )
2. I feel that my parents do not give me an opportunity to expreses my ideas.	( )	( )	( )	( )	( )

(Contd.)

	Always	Very often	Some times	Sel-dom	Never
3. My parents interfere in my personal matters.	( )	( )	( )	( )	( )
4. My house appears to me like a prison.	( )	( )	( )	( )	( )
5. I feel that my parents behave forwards me as if I am a child.	( )	( )	( )	( )	( )
6. I feel that even when I am right my parents do not agree with me.	( )	( )	( )	( )	( )
7. My parents criticise my way of dressing up.	( )	( )	( )	( )	( )
8. My parents keep a close watch over me.	( )	( )	( )	( )	( )
9. I am criticized for every little thing.	( )	( )	( )	( )	( )
10. My parents criticise me in front of my brothers and sisters.	( )	( )	( )	( )	( )
11. My parents criticize me in front of my friends.	( )	( )	( )	( )	( )
12. My family members always try to find fault in me.	( )	( )	( )	( )	( )
13. I feel the parents do not approve of my friends visiting me at home.	( )	( )	( )	( )	( )
14. I feel that my parents hold very orthodox view.	( )	( )	( )	( )	( )
15. I feel that my friends are not welcomed at home.	( )	( )	( )	( )	( )
16. I feel that my parents are not cordial.	( )	( )	( )	( )	( )
17. I feel that I am a burden on my parents.	( )	( )	( )	( )	( )
18. I feel that no one likes me at home.	( )	( )	( )	( )	( )

(Contd.)

	Always	Very often	Some times	Sel- dom	Never
19. I feel that my parents show favouritism towards some children.	( )	( )	( )	( )	( )
20. I feel that my being at home does not in any way make my parents happy.	( )	( )	( )	( )	( )
21. I feel that my parents love me very little.	( )	( )	( )	( )	( )
22. I feel that my parents give my brothers and sisters what they ask for, but not to me	( )	( )	( )	( )	( )
23. I feel that my parents do not try understand my feelings.	( )	( )	( )	( )	( )
24. I feel that cannot behave as my parents expect me to do.	( )	( )	( )	( )	( )
25. My parents behave in such a way that I do not know as to what will annoy them.	( )	( )	( )	( )	( )
26. Because of differences of opinions, there is always tension between me and my parents,	( )	( )	( )	( )	( )
27. When I tell my parents something in trust, they make fun of me.	( )	( )	( )	( )	( )
28. I feel that my parents have such expectations from me that I cannot fulfil.	( )	( )	( )	( )	( )
29. I just cannot understand what kind of behavior my parents expect from me.	( )	( )	( )	( )	( )

(Contd.)

	Always	Very often	Some times	Sal- dom	Never
30. I feel. I cannot get along with my parents.	( )	( )	( )	( )	( )
31. My parents want whatever they say should be done accordingly and immediately.	( )	( )	( )	( )	( )
32. I feel that my parents punish too severely.	( )	( )	( )	( )	( )
33. My parents are of the opinion that children should do whatever they say without any arguments.	( )	( )	( )	( )	( )
34. My parents scold or beat me on small matter.	( )	( )	( )	( )	( )
35. When I make mistake my parents scold me on all my earlier mistakes too.	( )	( )	( )	( )	( )
36. When my parents are annoyed with one child they scold all the others too.	( )	( )	( )	( )	( )
37. My parents worry me by repeating my faults over and over again	( )	( )	( )	( )	( )
38. When my parents are unhappy over something they take it out on others.	( )	( )	( )	( )	( )
39. I feel that my parents do not care for my likes and dislikes.	( )	( )	( )	( )	( )

(Contd.)

	Always	Very often	Some times	Sel-dom	Never
40. I feel that my opinion is not asked for in domestics matters.	( )	( )	( )	( )	( )
41. I feel that in no matter am I encouraged by people at home.	( )	( )	( )	( )	( )
42. I feel that my parents do not pay any attention to me.	( )	( )	( )	( )	( )
43. I feel that in taking decisions on matters relating to the home my parents do not take into account my interests and needs,	( )	( )	( )	( )	( )
44. I feel that my parents are not interested in either my success or failures.	( )	( )	( )	( )	( )
45. I feel reluctant to talk of my experiences either my parents.	( )	( )	( )	( )	( )
46. I feel hesitent to talk to my parents.	( )	( )	( )	( )	( )
47. I feel reluctant to talk of my parental matters to my parents	( )	( )	( )	( )	( )
48. I do not want to be with my parents much.	( )	( )	( )	( )	( )
49. I cannot talk unhesitantly about my problems to my parents.	( )	( )	( )	( )	( )
50. I feel that my parents are not very frank with me.	( )	( )	( )	( )	( )
51. I do not get along well with my brothers and sisters.	( )	( )	( )	( )	( )

(Contd.)

	Always	Very often	Some times	Sel-dom	Never
52. My brothers and sisters boss over me.	( )	( )	( )	( )	( )
53. I feel that my brothers and sisters do not like me.	( )	( )	( )	( )	( )
54. My brothers and sisters do not care for me.	( )	( )	( )	( )	( )
55. My brothers and sisters keep quarreling with me.	( )	( )	( )	( )	( )
56. My brothers and sisters keep worrying me	( )	( )	( )	( )	( )
57. I do not like my brothers and sisters.	( )	( )	( )	( )	( )
58. I feel that my brothers and sisters do not love me.	( )	( )	( )	( )	( )
59. I feel that there is not so much place at home where I can sit with my friends.	( )	( )	( )	( )	( )
60. I often feel that my house is situated in an unclean locality.	( )	( )	( )	( )	( )
61. I feel that we are financially hard up at home.	( )	( )	( )	( )	( )
62. I sometime feel that there is no place at home where I can study.	( )	( )	( )	( )	( )
63. I feel that there are no modern pieces (of furniture, electrical gadgets etc) in my house.	( )	( )	( )	( )	( )

(Contd.)

	Always	Very often	Some times	Sel- dom	Never
64. I feel that my parents are less wealthy as compared to the parents of my friends.	( )	( )	( )	( )	( )
65. I feel that it would have been better if my parents had not got married to each other.	( )	( )	( )	( )	( )
66. I feel that my father feels happy when my mother is not at home.	( )	( )	( )	( )	( )
67. I feel that my father bosses too much over my mother	( )	( )	( )	( )	( )
68. I feel that the relations between my parents are restrained.	( )	( )	( )	( )	( )
69. I feel that my mother feels happy when my father is not at home.	( )	( )	( )	( )	( )
70. I feel that my mother bosses over my father.					
71. There are quarrels over trivial matters at home.	( )	( )	( )	( )	( )
72. I feel alien in my house.	( )	( )	( )	( )	( )
73. I feel that there is certain tension in the atmosphere at home.	( )	( )	( )	( )	( )
74. I feel that my friends are more satisfied with their parents than I am.	( )	( )	( )	( )	( )

(Contd.)

46A (12)

Title of the Instrument : **A Scale to Measure Attitude Towards Drinking Alcohol.**

Purpose : To measure attitude of youths towards drinking alcohol.

Authors : B.R. Bhadra and P.R. Girija.

Language : English.

Availability : Department of Psychology, University of Agricultural Sciences Hebbal, Bangalore-560024.

Uses : To identify youths attitude towards drinking alcohol in order to introduce preventive and remedial measures wherever necessary.

Levels : College students.

Main Features : Likert's Scaling technique was used. The scale consists of 34 statements with five rating points.

Reliability : Split-Half reliability coefficient is 0.84. Test-retest reliability coefficient is 0.74.

Validity : Validity coefficient between attitude and belief ranges from 0.28 to 0.38, Construct validity coefficient between attitude and using behaviour is 0.51.

Time Limit : About 30 minutes.

Norms : Not available.

References :

a. Girija, P.R. and Bhadra, B.R. (1983) : A Scale to measure attitude towards drinking alcohol. *Asian Journal of Psychology and Education*, Vol. 11, No. 1. 40-48.

b. Bhadra B.R. and Girija, P.R. (1981) : Attitude, Belief and Behaviour towards alcohol use. *In Current Research in Drug Abuse in India.* Ed.D. Mohan, H.S. Sethi and E. Tongue. 198-203.

A SCALE TO MEASURE ATTITUDE TOWARDS DRINKING ALCOHOL.

	Strongly agree	Agree	Undecided	Disagree	Strongly disagree
1	2	3	4	5	6
1. Alcohol drinking is a public issue that affects every one.	—	—	—	—	—
2. Alcohol leads to domestic unhappiness	—	—	—	—	—

(Contd.)

1	2	3	4	5	6
3. Alcohol helps to gain many friends.	—	—	—	—	—
4. Drinking alcohol is like gambling.	—	—	—	—	—
5. Alcohol increases efficiency	—	—	—	—	—
6. Alcohol helps to mix with others freely	—	—	—	—	—
7. Drinking leads to bankruptcy	—	—	—	—	—
8. Drinking alcohol is an indication of maladjustment.	—	—	—	—	—
9. Alcohol is necessary to celebrate happy occasions.	—	—	—	—	—
10. Alcohol helps to forget sorrows.	—	—	—	—	—
11. Money spent on alcohol is a waste.	—	—	—	—	—
12. Alcohol is necessary to remove mental restraints	—	—	—	—	—
13. Alcohol helps to establish contact with people in power	—	—	—	—	—
14. Alcohol consumer is a burden on society.	—	—	—	—	—
15. Alcohol helps to improve complexion.	—	—	—	—	—
16. Drinking alcohol is like playing with fire.	—	—	—	—	—
17. Drinking hampers thinking.	—	—	—	—	—
18. Alcohol is necessary for excitement.	—	—	—	—	—
19. It is a pleasure to keep company with the people who drink alcohol.	—	—	—	—	—

(Contd.)

1	2	3	4	5	6
20. Drinking alcohol helps to build one's confidence.	—	—	—	—	—
21. Alcohol leads to immortality	—	—	—	—	—
22. Alcohol is necessary for an individual to face challenging situations.	—	—	—	—	—
23. Alcohol is necessary to put on weight.	—	—	—	—	—
24. Matrimonial alliance is undesirable with the family of alcohol consumers.	—	—	—	—	—
25. Alcohol consumers should not be allowed to participate in social functions.	—	—	—	—	—
26. Drinking is a bad act.	—	—	—	—	—
27. Alcohol consumers should be severely punished.	—	—	—	—	—
28. Weak minded people drink alcohol.	—	—	—	—	—
29. Alcohol is not as injurious to health as one thinks.	—	—	—	—	—
30. Alcohol should be allowed during religious functions.	—	—	—	—	—
31. Alcohol should be served as a social drink like Torino, Coca-cola etc.	—	—	—	—	—
32. Drinking alcohol is a symbol of social status.	—	—	—	—	—

1	2	3	4	5	6
33. Alcohol drinking should be prohibited	—	—	—	—	—
34. Alcohol is necessary for hard working people.	—	—	—	—	—

Scoring : Responses are scored by assigning values 1, 2, 3, 4 and 5 for strongly agree, agree undecided, disagree and strongly disagree respectively for pro-alcoholic statements and the rerverse set of numerical values are assigned for anti-alcoholic statements.

46A (13)

Title of the Instrument : **A Scale to Measure Attitude of Youths Towards Narcotic Drugs.**

Purpose : A Scale to measure attitude of youths towards narcotic drugs.

Authors : B.R. Bhadra and P.R. Girija.

Language : English.

Availability : Department of Psychology, University of Agricultural Sciences, Hebbal, Bangalore-560024.

Uses : To identify individuals of pro-narcotic and antinarcotic attitudes and to help them wherever necessary.

Levels : College Students.

Main Features : The scale was constructed using Likert's scaling technique, and it consists of 18 statements with five rating points.

Reliability : Split-half reliability coefficient is 0.53.

Validity : Construct validity was worked out by using biserial correlation between attitude scores and drug using behaviour, and it ranges from 0.22 to 0.45.

Time Limit : About 20 minutes.

Norms : Not available.

References : Girija, P.R. and Bhadra, B.R. (1977) : Attitude towards narcotic drugs. *Asian Journal of Psychology and Education*. Vol. 2, No. 3, 31-36.

A SCALE TO MEASURE ATTITUDE TOWARDS NARCOTICS

	Strongly agree	Agree	Undecided	Disagree	Strongly disagree
(a) Dependence on narcotic drugs reveals a basic defect in ones character	—	—	—	—	—
(b) Dependence on narcotic drugs is basically as immoral as stealing	—	—	—	—	—
(c) Dependence on narcotic drugs hurts none but the consumer himself	—	—	—	—	—
(d) As an ideal policy, I support the prohibition of all narcotic drugs.	—	—	—	—	—
(e) Youngsters are also human and cannot abstain from narcotic drugs.	—	—	—	—	—
(f) Dependence on narcotic drugs is harmful to health, but sometimes necessary in the modern world.	—	—	—	—	—
(g) Dependence on narcotic drugs is merely playing a game.	—	—	—	—	—
(h) If one could get rid of his difficulties by depending on narcotic drugs, that should be the thing to do.	—	—	—	—	—
(i) A little consumption of narcotic drugs (apart from health reasons) may be permissible.	—	—	—	—	—

(Contd.)

	Strongly agree	Agree	Undecided	Disagree	Strongly disagree
(j) In order to promote friendly relationship, one may have to take it occasionally.	—	—	—	—	—
(k) I have nothing but contempt for addicts.	—	—	—	—	—
(l) Dependence on narcotic drugs is the only way to keep one awake.	—	—	—	—	—
(m) A narcotic is usually lazy.	—	—	—	—	—
(n) A narcotic is simply a parasite.	—	—	—	—	—
(o) Narcotic drugs are necessary to celebrate happiness or sorrow.	—	—	—	—	—
(p) Narcotic drugs are necessary during religious ceremonies.	—	—	—	—	—
(q) Narcotics are responsible for social disorder.	—	—	—	—	—
(r) People should not show too much concern to narcotics.	—	—	—	—	—

Scoring : Responses are scored by assigning values 1, 2, 3, 4 and 5, for strongly agree, agree, undecided, disagree and strongly disagree respectively for pro-narcotic statements and the reverse set of numerical values are assigned to anti-narcotic statements.

46A (14)

Title of the Instrument : **A Scale to Measure Attitude Towards Women.**
Purpose : To measure attitudes of youths towards women.
Authors : B.R. Bhadra and P.R. Girija.
Language : English.
Availability : Department of Psychology, University of Agricultural

Sciences, Hebbal, Bangalore-560024.

Availability : To assess youths attitude towards women.

Levels : College students.

Main Features : Scale contains 25 statements with five rating points. Likert's summated rating scale was used in constructing the scale.

Reliability : Split-half and odd-even reliabilities coefficients were 0.81 and 0.81 respectively.

Validity : Nil.

Time Limit : About 25 minutes.

Norms : Not available.

References : B.R. Bhadra and P.R. Girija (1976) : A Scale for the measurement of attitudes towards women. *Asian Journal of Psychology and Education*, Vol.1, No.2, 41-44.

A SCALE TO MEASURE ATTITUDE TOWARDS WOMEN

	Strongly favourable	Favourable	Undecided	Unfavourable	Strongly unfavourable
1	2	3	4	5	6
1. Women should be encouraged to participate in politics.	—	—	—	—	
2. Employed women create social disorders	—	—	—	—	—
3. Unmarried woman is a liability to the family.	—	—	—	—	
4. Women should have equal rights over property.	—	—	—		
5. Women should be encouraged to participate in social organisations.	—	—	—	—	
6. Man should be the leader and women the followers.	—	—	—	—	—

(Contd.)

1	2	3	4	5	6
7. Educated women tends to neglect her responsibilities.	—	—	—	—	—
8. Women should be given equal opportunities in any type of employment.	—	—	—	—	—
9. Women should be encouraged to participate in games.	—	—	—	—	—
10. Women should be respected like men	—	—	—	—	—
11. Women cannot adapt to new situations as men do.	—	—	—	—	—
12. Women should be encouraged to contribute towards the economic welfare of the family.	—	—	—	—	—
13. Women are as intelligent as men.	—	—	—	—	—
14. Earning women do not enjoy a high social status in society.	—	—	—	—	—
15. Women should be given equal opportunities.	—	—	—	—	—
16. Women are most suited for domestic duties.	—	—	—	—	—
17. Women should not be treated as 'Beasts of burden.	—	—	—	—	—
18. Women should be paid equally for the same type of work as men do.	—	—	—	—	—
19. Illiterate women are better house-wives.	—	—	—	—	—

(Contd.)

1	2	3	4	5	6
20. Parents should give equal opportunities while educating their daughters and sons.	—	—	—	—	—
21. Widows should be encouraged to remarrv just as widows do.	—	—	—	—	—
22. Women can protect the nation like man.	—	—	—	—	—
23. Women are more traditional minded than men.	—	—	—	—	—
24. Women should be free to choose their husbands.	—	—	—	—	—
25. Women are a hindrance to modernisation.	—	—	—	—	—

The response are scored by assigning the values 5, 4, 3, 2 and 1 for strongly favourable, favourable, undecided, unfavourable and strongly unfavourable for positive statements and the reverse set of numerical values are assigned to the negative statements.

46A (15)

Title of the Instrument : **P.G.I. Yoga Attitude Scale.**

Purpose : To assess attitude towards yoga.

Authors : Poonam Grover, S.K. Verma, Dwarka Pershad, and V.K. Varma (Dept. of Psychiatry, PGI, Chandigarh.)

Language(s) : English and Hindi.

Availability : Rupa Psychological Centre, B19/60B, Deoriabir, Bhelupur, Varanasi-221010.

Uses : To study attitude towards Yoga and also evaluation of Yoga therapy.

Levels : All educational levels (orally to illiterates,)

Main Features : 16 items, on a Five-point Likert type scale.

Reliability : Test-retest= 0.809.
Split-Half = 0.859.

Validity : Concurrent validity (0.73 with Kaivalyadham Yoga Attitude Scale.) Concept validity (Comparison of yoga vs. non yoga group, and Comparison of yoga scores before and after yoga.)

Time Limit: 5-10 minutes.

Norms : Four Non-Yoga groups and 4 yoga groups from PGI Chandigarh and Pune.

References : Grover, P.; Verma, S.K.; Pershad, D., and Varma, V.K. (1988), *Manual for PGI Yoga Attitude Scale*. Rupa Psychological Centre, Varanasi.

Further matter of the scale 46A (15) is given on page 618

46A (16)

Title of the Instrument : Socio-Genic Need Satisfaction Scale.

Purpose : Measure satisfaction of socio genic needs.

Authors : Chauhan, N.S.; U. Dhar; Y Singh.

Language(s) : Hindi and English.

Availability : MAPA, D-69, Shastrinagar, Meerut.

Uses : Measures Parent-child relationships.

Levels : Adolescents.

Main Features : 5 point rating scale. 46 items.

Reliability :

Table 1

Area	Children	Adolescents	Adult	Senescents
Acceptance	0.74	0.83	0.87	0.72
Cooperation	0.64	0.69	0.67	0.59
Identification	0.72	0.61	0.65	0.59
Dominance	0.52	0.55	0.63	0.51
Rejection	0.42	0.46	0.54	0.72
Isolation	0.81	0.74	0.63	0.61
Differentiation	0.49	0.59	0.48	0.67
Submission	0.64	0.72	0.72	0.66

Validity : Cofficients of validity for children, Adolescents, Adults and Senescent with reference to the eight areas.

Areas	Children	adolescents	Adult	Senescents
Acceptance	0.61	0.72	0.68	0.58
Cooperation	0.72	0.58	0.62	0.48
Identification	0.53	0.52	0.48	0.44
Dominance	0.44	0.41	0.52	0.42

(Contd.)

Areas	Children	adolescents	Adult	Senescents
Rejection	0.48	0.50	0.46	0.40
Isolation	0.64	0.56	0.52	0.62
Differentiation	0.52	0.62	0.57	0.72
Submission	0.49	0.46	0.48	0.70

Time Limit : Unlimited.
Norms : Available in the manual.
References : Nil.

SOCIOGENIC NEED SATISFACTIONS SCALE

	Very much	Much	Ordinary	Less	Very less	Not at all
1. All co-operate with me.	—	—	—	—	—	—
2. They see me a sinner.	—	—	—	—	—	—
3. All love me	—	—	—	—	—	—
4. I submit to them in no time.	—	—	—	—	—	—
5. I like tolerant people.	—	—	—	—	—	—
6. People keep a distance from me.	—	—	—	—	—	—
7. I can lend a defeat to any in any task.	—	—	—	—	—	—
8. Usually I differ from others.	—	—	—	—	—	—
9. All are available at my disposal.	—	—	—	—	—	—
10. Often, they hate me.	—	—	—	—	—	—
11. They have a liking for me.	—	—	—	—	—	—
12. Often, I lay confidence in people.	—	—	—	—	—	—
13. I took help from model people to complete good tasks.	—	—	—	—	—	—
14. I keep away from people despite being in their midst.	—	—	—	—	—	—
15. Often, I do not care for others.	—	—	—	—	—	—
16. Comparatively, I am quick in getting liberal.	—	—	—	—	—	—
17. Readily, I co-operate with others.	—	—	—	—	—	—
18. My entry in their houses is seen as undesirable	—	—	—	—	—	—

(Contd.)

	Very much	Much	Ordi- nary	Less	Very less	Not at all
19. They honoured me by taking me their part and parcel.	—	—	—	—	—	—
20. People make use of me in completion of tasks.	—	—	—	—	—	—
21. I love people with a soft corner for them.	—	—	—	—	—	—
22. Often, I sit lonely.	—	—	—	—	—	—
23. They are afraid of me.	—	—	—	—	—	—
24. I am greater sufferer thank others.	—	—	—	—	-	—
25. My achievements are due to help from others.	—	—	—	—	—	—
26. They take me as condemned.	—	—	—	—	—	—
27. They are pleased with my behaviour.	—	—	—	—	—	—
28. People hold me for my mistakes.	—	—	—	—	—	—
29. I adhered to religion in thoughts and actions.	—	—	—	—	—	—
30. I feel suffocated in getting mixed with others.	—	—	—	—	—	—
31. I remain hard to them.	—	—	—	—	—	—
32. Comparatively. I give in alms to few beggers only.	—	—	—	—	—	—
33. My friends have assisted me a lot.	—	—	—	—	—	—
34. They speak ill of me.	—	—	—	—	—	—
35. Others respect me so often.	—	—	—	—	—	—
36. Often, I follow their decisions.	—	—	—	—	—	—
37. Tears of sufferers induced me to weep.	—	—	—	—	—	—
38. Usually, I work isolatedly.	—	—	—	—	—	—
39. I befooled them easily.	—	—	—	—	—	—
40. I take more time to rub off heart burning.	—	—	—	—	—	—

46A (17)

Title of the Instrument : **Scale to Measure Attitudes Towards Working Women. (Revised).**

Purpose : To measure the Attitudes Towards Working Women

Authors : Prof.S. Sultan Akhtar & Sangeeta Sharma.

Language(s) : English and Hindi.

Availability : S. Sultan Akhtar, Dept. of Psychology, Aligarh Muslim University, Aligarh.

Uses : For Research and Classification.

Levels : College and University. Students.

Main Features : It is 3 point Likert Type Scale, it consists of 22 Items, in Five areas viz. Public Social Relation, Family and Home, Work and Efficiency and Employment.

Reliability : rll=0.68. (N= 100).

Validity : The items were selected on the basis of Varimax Analysis which exists between 0.25 to 0.76.

Time Limit : No time limit.

Norms : SD Norms Calculated on 100 samples.

Reference : Akhtar, S.S; Pestonjee, D.M., (1966) : Attitudes Toward Working Women, the *Indian Journal of Social Work*, Vol. XXX (No.1.).

SCALE TO MEASURE ATTITUDES TOWARDS WORKING WOMEN

You are requested to express your 'Agreement' or 'Disagreement with each of the statement given below. There are no 'right' or 'wrong' answers.

1. If you find yourself in agreement with the statement then write 'A' within the bracket.
2. If you disagree with the statement then write "L" within the bracket.
3. If you are undecided then write only 'U'.

1. Women was made by God to be a custodian of home and not a wage earner. ( )
2. Working women are generally smart. ( )
3. By encouraging women to work national development may be achieved. ( )
4. Often working women are instrumental in developing good image of organization. ( )
5. Marital discontent may be due to the working life. ( )

6. Working women exploit the situation to their advantage. ( )
7. Working women are found to be suspicious by nature. ( )
8. Working women is more apt to impress others than a non-working women. ( )
9. Working women generally develop superiority complex. ( )
10. Working women are sociable by nature. ( )
11. Working women who have children. feel guilty of neglecting them. ( )
12. Biological make-up of women restricts their employment opportunities. ( )
13. Working women are usually more cheerful and temperamentally pleasant than non-working women. ( )
14. Working women do not enjoy as much prestige in our society as do the non-working women. ( )
15. Women are generally more suitable for sales division. ( )
16. Women should take up jobs to improve their family finances. ( )
17. It is not possible for women to work with full devotion. ( )
18. Family quarrels may be checked by encouraging women to take up employment. ( )
19. Women from respectable family should not seek employment. ( )
20. Working women usually prove to be good house wife. ( )
21. Women are ambitious to be easily satisfied with their jobs. ( )
22. Working women enthusiastically participate in welfare programmes. ( )

46A (18)

Title of the Instrument : **Interpersonal Trust Scale.**
Purpose : Seven dimensions of Interpersonal trust.
Authors : N.K. Chadda.
Language : English.
Availability : Dr. N.K. Chadda, Department of Psychology, Delhi University, Delhi-ll0007.
Uses : For research and diagnosis.
Levels : 18-21 years.
Main Features : Five point scale, 48 items.
Reliability : Reliability Coefficients :

Dimensions	Confi-dence	Reli-ance	Faith	Credi-bility	Secu-rity	Confi-denti ality	Commu-nicab-ility
	I	II	III	IV	V	VI	VII
Split-Half	0.92	0.90	0.94	0.91	0.98	0.89	0.92
Retest	0.91	0.91	0.92	0.90	0.96	0.86	0.88

Overall split-half reliability coefficient = 0.93

Overall test-retest reliability coefficient=0.86

Validity : Face validity of the test is confirmed by the agreement of the ten judges who found the items of the test valid.

Cross validity:

	Confi-dence	Reli-ance	Faith	Credi-bility	Secu-rity	Confi den	Comm-unica-bility
	0.86	0.82	0.74	0.75	0.78	0.91	0.92

Overall cross-validity coefficient=0.75

N=150 was used for split-half reliability.

N=50 was used for test-retest reliability.

N= 126 was used for cross validation in each group.

Time Limit : 25 minutes.

Norms : Available with the author.

References : Nil.

INTERPERSONAL TRUST SCALE

1.	'Practice what your preach' is sincerely adhered to by most idealist.	SA	A	U	D	SD
2.	Most parents can be relied upon to carry out their threats of punishment.	SA	A	U	D	SD
3.	Most salesmen are honest in describing their product.	SA	A	U	D	SD
4.	Most people have the courage of their convictions.	SA	A	U	D	SD
5.	Most experts can be relied upon to tell the truth about the limits of their knowledge	SA	A	U	D	SD
6.	Most students in school would not cheat even if they were sure of getting away with it.	SA	A	U	D	SD

7. Most people will not humiliate you in public. SA A U D SD
8. A person will believe his best friend's excuse for not having kept their date. SA A U D SD
9. Most officials elected publicly are really sincere in their campaign promises. SA A U D SD
10. It is hard to get objective accounts to public events even through the media. SA A U D SD
11. The common man is sincerely concerned about the problems of others.
12. A person when tells the truth is more of a friend than one who indulges in flattery. SA A U D SD
13. Most people do not concern themselves with other people's private matters. SA A U D SD
14. It is wise to believe in the 'essential goodness of man'. SA A U D SD
15. Panents can usually be relied upon to keep their promises. SA A U D SD
16. One has to be alert in these competitive times or some one may take advantage of you. SA A U D SD
17. Most candidates can resist the temptation of peaking into the examiners to feller when the examiner is suddenly called out of the room. SA A U D SD
18. Friends can be relied upon not to cause embarrassment by revealing private matters. SA A U D SD
19. Most people follow the motto, 'Do unto others as you would have them do unto you. SA A U D SD
20. We can all get unbiased treatment at the judiciary. SA A U D SD
21. At the time of financial need, relatives can be relied upon to help. SA A U D SD

22. An average person will strictly adhere by his opinion if he thinks he is right even when others disagree.	SA	A	U	D	SD
23. Business men are more important than poets and writers for the society.	SA	A	U	D	SD
24. Officials working in the Ministry of Defence can be relied upon not to reveal the defence strategies.	SA	A	U	D	SD
25. People usually tell the truth, even when they know that they are better off by lying.	SA	A	U	D	SD
26. Most doctors can be relied upon to diagnose effectively.	SA	A	U	D	SD
27. One is better off being cautious in dealing with strangers until they have provided evidence that they are trust worthy.	SA	A	U	D	SD
28. The use of postal box numbers through newspapers is a sure way of maintaining one's anonymity.	SA	A	U	D	SD
29. Most people are basically good and kind	SA	A	U	D	SD
30. All political parties can be called upon for their cooperation towards a national cause.	SA	A	U	D	SD
31. Most people do all work because of self-interest.	SA	A	U	D	SD
32. Family planning propaganda is beneficial to the country.	SA	A	U	D	SD
33. The members on an interview board do not reveal information to any candidate whom they may know personally.	SA	A	U	D	SD
34. Most people prefer working in government enterprises as it provides pension benefits in old age.	SA	A	U	D	SD

35. Most people are brave.	SA	A	U	D	SD
36. Most people will act as 'good Samaritans' if given the opportunity.	SA	A	U	D	SD
37. Listening to others with genuine interest encourages others to express themselves more freely.	SA	A	U	D	SD
38. Psychologists can be relied upon to keep their cases confidential.	SA	A	U	D	SD
39. Even the most hardened and vicious criminal has a spark of decency within him.	SA	A	U	D	SD
40. One can rely upon people with a sense of responsibility.	SA	A	U	D	SD
41. Most people will stop and help a person whose car has broken down.	SA	A	U	D	SD
42. Discussion of personal matters are generally kept out of one's professional relationships.	SA	A	U	D	SD
43. Most people will do something for others only if it is beneficial to themselves also.	SA	A	U	D	SD
44. For most, honesty is the best policy, only because they are afraid of getting caught.	SA	A	U	D	SD
45. One should never confide in others as it makes matters worse for him.	SA	A	U	D	SD
46. Only few people adhere to the ethical standards regarding honesty and morality, which most people claim to possess.	SA	A	U	D	SD
47. Intelligence bureaus employ only those persons whom they can rely upon.	SA	A	U	D	SD
48. Most Catholics do not go for confession because they feel that they cannot rely on the priest.	SA	A	U	D	SD

46A (19)

Title of the Instrument : **Problem Checklist for Working Women**

Purpose : To know the personal, familial and occupational problems of working women.

Authors : Vishwa Vijaya Singh.

Language : English.

Availability : Dr. Mrs. Vishwa Vijaya Singh, Vidya Bhawan Udaipur, Rajasthan-313001.

Uses : To know the different problems of married working women in four Professions i.e. Teaching, Medical, Clerical and Administration.

Levels : Married working women.

Main Features : There are 79 items. There are three areas. They are Personal Social Problems, Familial Problems and Occupational Problems.

Reliability : Test-retest method with interval of one month. Pearson Product Moment Correlation Formula was used. Reliability = 0.89.

Validity : The scores of Problem Checklist for working women and the scores of Family Adjustment Inventory for working women (developed by the author) were used for validity by using Pearson product Moment Correlation Method. Validity =0.57.

Time Limit : No time limit.

Norms : There are norms, available with the author.

PROBLEM CHECKLIST FOR WORKING WOMEN

5	
6	
7	
8	
9	

1. I feel tired due to dual roles.
   Agree/Disagree/Undecided
2. I sometimes feel restless due to over burden
   Agree/Disagree/Undecided
3. I am easily misunderstood.
   Agree/Disagree/Undecided
4. Life seems to be drudgery (dull) for me because I have to share responsibilities at home and in the job Agree/Disagree/Undecided
5. I do not get time for entertainment.
   Agree/Disagree/Undecided

10	
11	
12	
13	
14	
15	
16	
17	
18	
19	
20	
21	
22	
23	
24	
25	
26	
27	

6. I do not have any interest in any domestic work due to strains of job. Agree/Disagree/Undecided
7. I sometimes become confused to decide the priorities of my responsibilities between job and home. Agree/Disagree/Undecided
8. I face problems of interpersonal relationships at home. Agree/Disagree/Undecided
9. I do not have any freedom to take my own decisions even with regard to my personal life. Agree/Disagree/Undecided
10. I am not allowed to spend my own earned money the way I feel like spending. Agree/Disagree/Undecided
11. I have tensions in life due to my job. Agree/Disagree/Undecided
12. I get easily irritated due to overwork. Agree/Disagree/Undecided
13. I face inner conflict due to two major responsibilities. Agree/Disagree/Undecided
14 I feel guilty conscious for not performing my domestic role properly. Agree/Disagree/Undecided
15. I feel disturbed when any member of my family is ill and I have to go to my job. Agree/Disagree/Undecided
16. I feel boredom on holidays. Agree/Disagree/Undecided
17. I feel I have no time to look after my own health. Agree/Disagree/Undecided
18. I do not get sufficient time for rest. Agree/Disagree/Undecided
19. I am unable to take part in social gathering due to my job. Agree/Disagree/Undecided
20. I am unable to attend the social ceremonies i.e. marriages etc. Agree/Disagree/Undecided
21. I am unable to attend the guests properly due to my job. Agree/Disagree/Undecided
22. Being in job, I am unable to maintain proper relations with my relatives. Agree/Disagree/Undecided
23. I am unable to help in the difficulties of others. Agree/Disagree/Undecided

28 24. I have to face jealousies of others due to our better standard of living Agree/Disagree/Undecided

29 25. I have to face idle gossip and suspicion of others because I am working. Agree/Disagree/Undecided

30 26. I have to face social criticism on account of working with male colleagues. Agree/Disagree/Undecided

27. The traditional Indian society does not consider a
31 working women respectable. Agree/Disagree/Undecided

32 28. I am not able to perform all domestic responsibilities. Agree/Disagree/Undecided

33 29. I do not get servants to help in domestic work. Agree/Disagree/Undecided

34 30. I do not get much help from my children in domestic work. Agree/Disagree/Undecided

35 31. I do not get sufficient time to look after my children properly. Agree/Disagree/Undecided

36 32. I have tension in absence of appropriate arrangements for looking after my children. Agree/Disagree/Undecided

37 33. I have to leave young children at home in the care of untrained and unreliable maid servant. Agree/Disagree/Undecided

38 34. I have to leave my infant child with grand parents neighbours and other relatives. Agree/Disagree/Undecided

39 35. I do not get enough time to give full motherly affection to my children due to remaining overbusy with my job. Agree/Disagree/Undecided

40 36. I do not get enough time to teach my children proper behaviour. Agree/Disagree/Undecided

37. I do not get enough time to pay attention towards
41 the habit formation of my children. Agree/Disagree/Undecided

42 38. I do not get enough time for the all round development of my children. Agree/Disagree/Undecided

43 39. I do not get enough time to help my children in home works and studies. Agree/Disagree/Undecided

44 40. I do not get time to see the teachers of my children about their progress. Agree/Disagree/Undecided

45 41. I do not get much time to look after my children about their illness. Agree/Disagree/Undecided

46 42. Due to my dual responsibilities l am unable to serve meals in time. Agree/Disagree/Undecided

47 43. I am unable to attend the nutritional needs of the members of my family. Agree/Disagree/Undecided

48 44. I have to waste a lot of time and energy in preparing typical Indian dishes. Agree/Disagree/Undecided

49 45. I do not get sufficient time to purchase domestic things. Agree/Disagree/Undecided

50 46. I can not pay attention to the elders in the joint family. Agree/Disagree/Undecided

51 47. The members of my family have too many expectations from me. Agree/Disagree/Undecided

52 48. I have tension in my marital life being in job. Agree/Disagree/Undecided

53 49. I receive very little help from my husband in carrying out household chores. Agree/Disagree/Undecided

54 50. My expenditure has increased due to my job inspite of increase in family income. Agree/Disagree/Undecided

55 51. I feel I do not receive attention respect and consideration I should from my husband. Agree/Disagree/Undecided

56 52. I do not get affection and sympathy I deserve from my in laws. Agree/Disagree/Undecided

57 53. Members of my family do not approve of my job. Agree/Disagree/Undecided

58 54. I cannot do full justice to my work as I have too much work to do. Agree/Disagree/Undecided

59 55. I have to take frequent leave for domestic purpose thus affecting my job responsibilities. Agree/Disagree/Undecided

60 56. I feel that working women have to take maternity and other leave which comes in the way of promotion and progress in the job. Agree/Disagree/Undecided

61 57. I sometimes get late for my job due to domestic responsibilities. Agree/Disagree/Undecided

62	
63	
64	
65	
66	
67	
68	
69	
70	
71	
72	
73	
74	
75	
76	
77	
78	

58. I have a difficulty of conveyance for reaching the place of work. Agree/Disagree/Undecided
59. I have to waste my time at bus stops. Agree/Disagree/Undecided
60. I some time reach late due to long distance between my home and place of work. Agree/Disagree/Undecided
61. I have to go out on tours thereby creating problems at home. Agree/Disagree/Undecided
62. I feel tense in the presence of male colleagues. Agree/Disagree/Undecided
63. I have to face certain difficult situation while working with male colleagues. Agree/Disagree/Undecided
64. Due to rotation with male colleagues in the job there is a change of misunderstanding and sometimes even leading to strained relations with husband or other members of the family. Agree/Disagree/Undecided
65. Working women are suspected and even accused of having relation with male colleagues. Agree/Disagree/Undecided
66. I am sometimes confused as to what should be my actual conduct with my male colleagues. Agree/Disagree/Undecided
67. Many times I have to face uncivilised or indecent behaviour of the people on the job and in the society. Agree/Disagree/Undecided
68. I feel that working women are prone to exploitation from their male counterparts in the job. Agree/Disagree/Undecided
69. I feel the males do not recognise my worth. Agree/Disagree/Undecided
70. I have not been given promotions to responsible positions simply because I am a woman. Agree/Disagree/Undecided
71. Some jobs are exclusive monopoly of males. Agree/Disagree/Undecided
72. Facility of creches (public nursery of infants) is not available. Agree/Disagree/Undecided
73. I sometimes have to remain away from my family due to my transfer. Agree/Disagree/Undecided

79	
80	
81	
82	
83	
84	

74. I had to forgo promotions or better placement for the sake of my family. Agree/Disagree/Undecided
75. I may have to drop my own job when my husband is transferred or moves to another place.
Agree/Disagree/Undecided
76. Problem in my job affect my mental peace.
Agree/Disagree/Undecided
77. My job requirements are very difficult and tedious.
Agree/Disagree/Undecided
78. I face difficulty when I have to do night duty.
Agree/Disagree/Undecided
79. I have difficult time with my male subordinates.
Agree/Disagree/Undecided

SCORE

Areas	A	B	C	D	E	Total Score
Areas						

46A (20)

Title of the Instrument : **Parent Child Relationship Scale.**

Purpose : To measure characteristic behaviour of father and mother as experienced by their children on ten dimensions.

Author : Nalini Rao.

Language(s) : English/Hindi/Kannada.

Availability "Parent Child Relationship Scale" 1988.
[Complete set with manual, scale protocol, and scoring sheet.] Available with : National Psychological Corporation, Bhargava Bhawan, 4/230, Kacheri Ghat, Agra-282 400 India. [Kannada Scale available with the author.]

Uses : 1. The data available on the items of the scale can be grouped with fairly universal scale dimensions of children experience of family interaction with the two parent factor.

2. Data on ten dimensions of parent behaviour can be obtained on bother father and mother separately.

3. It is found credible to use each of the ten sub-scales independently in studies where any of the specific parental behavioural dimension is being examined.

4. The scale has been found to be very useful and effective both as product and presage variable in the analysis of problems involving social, psychological and school factors.

Levels : Upper primary and secondary school children.

Main Features : (A) 100 items of the scale are grouped into ten sub-scales with ten items in each of the sub-scale measuring protecting, symbolic punishment, Rejection, Object Punishment Demanding, Indifferent, Symbolic Reward, loving, Object Reward and Neglect behaviour.

(B) Scores on Father and mother can be obtained on separate forms, on a five point rating scale.

(C) One of the built in advantage is that the behavioural dimensions of the scale are so oriented, the items render itself to be scored without reversing the order of weights for negative behavioural dimensions of the scale.

Reliability : Test-retest reliability coefficient on 94 students over a five week interval ranged from 0.770 to 0.871 of father form and from 0.772 to 0.873 on mother form.

Validity : 1. Face validity was established by way of reassigning items to predetermined dimensions by judges.

2. Construct validity established by correlating the scores on PCR scales with the scores of 93 secondary school students on Bronfenbrenner Parent behaviour Questionnaire ['r' ranged from 0.289 to 0.578.].

PCR scores of 122 secondary school students were also correlated with 5 dimensions of Indian Adaptation of CRPBI. ['r' ranged from 0.328 to 0.457].

3. Concurrent validity established on the three parallel forms in Hindi, English and Kannada; coefficient of correlation on the two parent forms ranged from 0.688 to 0.812.

Time Limit : No time limit.

Norms : No.

Development of the Instrument : A total sample of 1106 students in the age group 12-18 years from standards 7 to 12 was used for standardizing the scale.

References : "A Study of the Socio-psychological correlates of social development of high school children in grades VIII, IX & X in some high schools of Bangalore city". Doctoral Dissertation in Education Bangalore University, 1978.

PARENT CHILD RELATIONSHIP SCALE

Please give the following information:
(1) Name: ____________________
(2) Age ______________ (3) Sex : ______________
(4) Class in which you are studying: ______________

Dear Friend:

A number of statements are given below, which describe different ways that fathers and mothers act towards their children. Read each statement carefully and think how well it describes the behaviour of your father and mother towards you. Apply them to *your father* and answer all the statements; then apply them to *your mother* and answer them once again. Write your responses in the columns under "father" and "mother" for each statement. If the behaviour is found—

"Always" - mark '5' in the column.
If you see it "many times" mark '4' in the column
If you see it "Sometimes" mark '3' in the column
If you see it " rarely" mark '2' in the column
If it occurs " Very rarely" Mark '1' in the column

Study the example given below:

My Father		My Mother
2	1. Lets me off easily when I do wrong	4
4	2. Shows interest in my school work	3

Now answer the statements:

Always = 5, Many times = 4, Sometimes = 3, Rarely = 2 Very Rarely = 1

My Father		My Mother
	1. is ready to help me all the time	
	2. complains about me when I do not listen to him/her	
	3. lets me know I am not wanted	
	4. takes away my play things when I am bad	
	5. does not tolerate even my small misbehaviour	
	6. does not ask me how I spent the money given to me	
	7. encourages me to keep up my work	

8. is really interested in my affairs
9. takes me out to cinema or other places as a reward
10. Keeps forgetting important things he/she is supposed to do for me
11. carefully protects me from accidents
12. puts me to shame when I misbehave
13 refuses to involve in my problems and troubles
14. slaps or hits me for my bad behaviour
15. makes it clear that he/she is the boss in the house.
16. has set very few rules for me
17. compares me favourably with other children when I do well
18. makes me feel wanted and needed.
19. Gives me more freedom as a reward
20. is too busy to answer my questions
21. (a) cannot think of punishing me
    (b) wants to know all that happened to me to make sure I am safe
22. scolds me when I am bad
23. does not spend much time with me
24. cuts down my pocket money as punishment
25. presses me to do better than others in everything.
26. lets me escape easily when I do some small wrongs
27. tells me he/she is proud of me
28. talks to me in a warm and affectionate way
29. buys me sweets, dress of story book as reward
30. does not bother to know what I am doing in school
31. comes to my help when I am teased or hit by other children
32. punishes me by not looking at me or talking to me when I do wrong
33. does not want me to bring friends home

34. will not let me play when I am bad
35. commands how I should spend my free time
36. is not aware what I am doing in school
37. treats me as if I am a grown up, responsible person when I behave well
38. comforts me when I am scared or upset
39. allows me to stay with friends for longer time as a reward
40. does not care whether I get and eat right kind of food
41. does not want me to play outside when I am not well, for fear I might get sick
42. shows I am not loved any more
43. dislikes my interests and hobbies
44. hits or beats me as punishment
45. instructs me to behave properly even in front of others.
46. (a) lets me do whatever I like after school
    (b) lets me dress in anyway I like
47. praises me before my playmates
48. willingly helps me in my work whenever I go to him/her
49. rewards me by letting me not to do some of the regular duties in the house
50. behaves as if I am not existing there
51. takes my side when I am opposed by somebody
52. talks about my bad behaviour before my playmates when I misbehave
53. knowingly and wantingly hurts my feelings
54. gives me extra work as punishment
55. pushes me to do well in school
56. (a) does not check on me
    (b) does not object when I am late for meal
57. shows more affection when I am good
58. takes my point of view and encourages me to say it
59. gets me/makes me my favourite food as a reward.

60. pays attention only to silence me when I worry him/her
61. is anxious when I am away and till I come home
62. frightens or threatens me when I do wrong
63. makes fun of me and taunts me
64. punishes me by pushing me out of the room
65. does not allow me to question about his/her ways
66. does not question about me going out or coming home
67. gives me special attention as a reward
68. allows me to do things I thought were important even if it were troublesome to him/her
69. lets me go out with friends as reward
70. does not care who my friends are
71. keeps me away from situations that might be unpleasant to me
72. tells me he/she was ashamed of me when I misbehave
73. finds fault with me even when I am good
74. takes away my books and play things as a punishment
75. wants to have complete control over me
76. allows me to stay away from school whenever I want
77. says nice things about me when I am good
78. encourages me to bring friends home and treats them well.
79. rewards me by giving me extra money or increasing my pocket money
80. leaves me alone for myself when I am in trouble
81. feels bad to refuse me anything I ask
82. compares me with other children and tells me I am bad, when I misbehave
83. does not want me to be with him/her when he/she is in the company of their friends

84. punishes me by being more strict with me
85. expects me to obey him/her without a second word
86. lets me off when I do not obey rules
87. makes me feel happy and proud when I did something nice
88. teaches me things I want to learn
89. hugs me and pats me when I am good
90. does not know what my needs are
91. worries about my health
92. strongly warns me about the harmful results when I do wrong
93. does not want my company
94. punishes me by not taking me to cinema or their places that I had been promised
95. strictly enforces rules to keep the house clean
96. does not check on whether I did my home work
97. praises me to others
98. enjoys listening to my experiences
99. gives me surprise gifts as reward
100. does not care whether I have some nice clothes/things as other children]

46A (21)

Title of the Instrument : **Our Attitudes.**
Purpose : Scales six types of attitudes.
Authors : Chauhan N.S.; L. Singh; S. Arora; R.L. Bhardwaj; M. Mathur; Yogendra Chauhan.
Language(s) : Hindi and English.
Availability : MAPA (Meerut), D-69, Shastrinagar, Meerut.
Uses : Measures the attitudes, six types of attitude scales.
Levels : Adolescents, Adults, Senesants.
Main Features : Thurstone's Technique, 150 items for six attitude areas and each attitude has 25 items. Social change, Social distance, Liberalism, Nationalism, Social Revolution, and Untouchability.

Reliability : Split-half reliability coefficient was found to be:

1. Nationalism r = 0.92
2. Liberalism r = 0.88
3. Social Change r = 0.71
4. Revolutionism r = 74
5. Social Distance r = 0.81
6. Untouchability r = 0.91

Validity : (Against ratings of neighbours)

1. Nationalism r = 0.62
2. Liberalism r = 0.82
3. Social Change r = 58
4. Revolutionism r = 0.61
5. Social Distance r = 0.72
6. Untouchability r = 0.74

Time Limit : Unlimited.

Norms : Given.

References :

1. Allport, G.W. : *Personality : A Psychological Interpretation*. New York, 1937.
2. Aurora, S. : Comparative Study of Personality Factors of Deviants and Non-Deviants. Unpubl. Ph.D. Thesis, 1981 (Agra University).
3. Chauhan, N.S.: Culture Stratum, Value-Orientations, Personality Factors and Sex as Correlates of Attitudes to Social Change and Social Change and Social Distance. Unpubli. Monograph, 1981.
4. Chauhan, N.S. and Singh, S.: Attitude Scale (Hamare Drishtikona) Psychology Department, Agra College, Agra, 1972.
5. Deutch, Karl : *Social Mobilization and Political Science Review*, 55, 1961.
6. Edwards, A.L. : *Techniques of Attitude Scale Construction*. Bombay, 1969.
7. Eisenstadt, S.N.: *Modernization : Protest and Change*. Prentice-Hall of India, New Delhi, 1969.
8. English, H.B. and English, A : *A Comprehensive Dictionary of Psychological and Psychoanalytical Terms*. Longmans-Green, 1958.
9. Eysenck, H.J. (ed.) : *Encyclopedia of Psychology*. Fontana, 1975.
10. Jasoda, M. and Warren, N. (eds.): *Attitudes : Selected Readings*, Penguin, 1966.

11. La Piere, R.T.: *Social Change*. Mcgraw-Hill, New York, 1965.
12. Long, L. and Mehta, P. (Eds.) : *The First Mental Measurement Handbook for India*. N.C.E.R.T., New Delhi, 1966.
13. McGuigan F.J. : *Methodology of Experimental Psychology*. Prentice-Hall of India, New Delhi, 1969.
14. Moore, W.E.: *Social Change*. Prentice-Hall of India. New Delhi, 1965.
15. Parsons, T.: *The Social System*. Free Press Glencoe Illinois, 1959.
16. Parsons, T. and Shils, E. (Eds). *General Theory of Action*, Harward University Press, Camb. Man. 1954.
17. Sherif, M. and Cantril, H.: The Psychology of Attitudes. *American Psychological Review*. 52, 1945.
18. Srinivas, M.N.: Seshaiah, S. and Parathsarathy, V.S.: *Dimensions of Social Change in India*. Allied, Bombay, 1978.
19. Thakkar, K.K.: The Problem of Casteism and Untouchability, *Indian Jr. of Soc. Work*, 1956.
20. Thurston, L.L. and Chave, E.J. : *The Measurement of Attitudes*, University of Chicago Press, Chicago, 1929.

OUR ATTITUDES

---

* Tick in the bracket (/) of those actions in the "Answer sheet' that you do or like to do.

** Leave those actions that you do not do or do not like to do.

---

1. To be in staunch opposition of communalism.
2. Not accepting the ancient Varna-organisation.
3. Giving financial support at the time of daughter's marriage of a helpless person like a widow.
4. Tendering resignation when compelled to do anti-national act.
5. Putting revolutionary ideas before others.
6. Dining together with an individual of any religion or community.
7. Taking a bath after getting the shadow of a Jatav or a Harijan.
8. Supporting love-marriage.

9. Spreading the poison of communalism, regionalism.
10. Treating a distressed person like rejected persons.
11. Helping others without thinking for caste and status.
12. To be in favour of not letting women going out of home.
13. Being effortful for the abolition of sub-castes.
14. Opposing all kinds of inequalities.
15. Undergoing pains for the service of others.
16. Seeing the national integration as supreme.
17. Not showing hitch for working against traditions.
18. Going to and dining in marriage-celebrations of Harijans.
19. Taking even the shadow of an untouchable, as a crime.
20. Breaking away with old ideology, work system and tradition.
21. Doing anti-national activities for one's family.
22. Giving a harsh reply with indifference without realising the need of the person.
23. Remaining in favour of not giving service to people of Scheduled caste in one's work-centre.
24. Organising the forces rising against those who break social customs and traditions.
25. Putting proposals in meetings for anti-dowry policies in marriages.
26. Not participating in marriages of low caste people.
27. Keeping in readiness for help of others always.
28. Seeing the whole nation as one's family.
29. Getting ready to marry a girl of one's own caste.
30. Keeping in favour of sitting with Harijans, in dinners.
31. Not in favour of giving high education to girls.
32. Dishonouring people below one's own caste.
33. Feeling pleased in distress and dishonour of others.
34. Trying to provide service only to one's kiths and kins.
35. Keeping oneself a staunch traditionist.
36. Not taking water from the hand of an untouchable.
37. To be ready for eradication of bad practices.
38. To permit ones children, without discrimination to play with children of low castes.
39. Tolerating difficulties in execution of one's duties.
40. Putting strong opposition against regionalism.
41. Not getting ready to bow before traditions.
42. Sitting with people of every religion and community.
43. Going to celebration of people of low castes.
44. Motivating the feeling of revolution in the youth.

45. Giving importance to the specific section on the basis of religious inclinations and language.
46. Never helping people at the time of distress.
47. Not to marry in castes lower than one's own.
48. Pleading for and following ancient traditional thoughts.
49. Dining with interest whether served by people of any caste or community.
50. Writing articles in newspapers against people taking dowry.
51. Becoming a staunch nationalist.
52. Trying one's best to remain loyal to one's master.
53. Not liking the interaction and mixing of ones family women with ladies of low castes.
54. Extending new thoughts to people.
55. Understanding the possibility of uplift of society in execution and following of customs and traditions alone.
56. Mixing with people of each caste and religion.
57. Giving maximum of mental torture to ones dependents and servants.
58. Becoming member of the group in power only for the interest of one's family.
59. Keeping links with all such institution that stand for customs and traditions.
60. Taking bath on being touched by untouchables.
61. Helping the flood-victims.
62. Propagating for national solidarity.
63. Behaving against one's caste traditions.
64. Dining only at the places of high caste people.
65. Getting membership of institutions that strive against old bad practices.
66. Going to the Harijan habitation for eradication of sorrow and distress of people.
67. Not marrying with people of untouchables.
68. Pleading for imparting of high education to women.
69. To be highly critical of those eradicating inequality.
70. According to high status in society to Brahmins in all probabilities.
71. Giving priority to ones caste and religion in education and job.
72. Getting ready to quarrel with others for cheap things.
73. Tolerating decently the behaviour of others done in excited conditions.

74. Being a strong opposition to those who talk on the basis of caste-religion and state.
75. Having no faith in social formalities.
76. Believing the Varna-System as a God-act.
77. Doing a strong opposition of the Varna-system.
78. Keeping no discrimination against Harijans.
79. Not taking food or water touched by an untouchable in the hotel.
80. Taking a vow to become a revolutionary.
81. Not allowing a Shudra to sit on ones coach.
82. Favouring girls not to get education with boys.
83. Giving priority to one's own caste in casting of votes.
84. Criticizing people on all matters.
85. Giving financial support to diseased.
86. Giving a fair appointment to the worker without discrimination of caste, religion and state.
87. Keep talking after accepting the welfare of Harijan as a great need.
88. Not allowing to lift leaf-dishes to anybody while giving a dinner at ones house.
89. Having a liking only for straight forward forthright talks.
90. Not keeping any hitch in meeting and coming into contact with people of low castes.
91. Maintaining the behaviour of untouchability with Harijans.
92. Not in favour of imparting much education to girls.
93. Keeping different behaviour with different people.
94. Doing the Dead-Feast or *Shraddha*.
95. Standing for opportunistic ideology.
96. Thinking only the welfare of ones own or the family.
97. Not minding the untouchables.
98. Keeping ready to die to keep ones word.
99. Sharing in every body's pleasure and sorrow.
100. Not to follow old traditions and customs.
101. Becoming member of institutions that regard the whole nation as one.
102. Doing all things with a liberal mind and heart.
103. Not attending to poor people.
104. Doing nothing in the name of the national interest.
105. Keeping faith in religious actions.
106. Keeping contacts only with people higher than ones own caste.

107. Keeping no faith at all in the tradition of Purdah.
108. Sitting on the coach of untouchables.
109. Influencing others through a sweet language.
110. Loving each person of the nation.
111. Keeping active in cutting of celebrations of rites.
112. Providing equal seats to women of every caste and religion in one's marriage celebrations.
113. Holding as just the limited rights of women in society
114. Habilitating Harijans in own neighbourhood.
115. Seeing the untouchable as worthy of 'no touch'
116. Taking interest in completion of traditionistic acts.
117. Taking people of all castes and religion, as brothers.
118. Continuing to accomplish traditionistic activities.
119. Making efforts for the uplift of one's relations alone.
120. Remaining true in speech and behaviour.
121. Making no objection in cleaning of ones kitchen by a sweeper.
122. Making staunch opposition to exploitation current in religion and education.
123. Not accepting discrimination of caste and creed.
124. Bringing about a change in old ideologies through peaceful means.
125. Becoming respectable for the nation through one actions.
126. Keeping sweet relations with people in vicinity.
127. Beating and rejecting the poor coming for alms and education.
128. Supporting people doing adulteration, black marketing and espionage.
129. Following the traditionistic and customs of dining.
130. Giving proper treatment to people of low Varna than one's own.
131. Organising labourers against the capitalists.
132. Not dining with the untouchables.
133. Shaking hands with the sweeper without any hitch.
134. Having full faith in traditions and customs.
135. Taking part in all social functions of each caste and religion.
136. Getting ready to construct a progressive society.
137. Accepting citizens of the nation as equal.
138. Giving help to every poor.
139. Keeping indifferent to people of the neighbourhood.
140. Keeping identical faith in each religion.
141. Reforming the habitats of the poor.
142. Giving a good thrashing to ones child on playing with people of low castes.

143. Being a staunch supporter of the caste system.
144. Eradicating untouchability.
145. Taking forced labour from untouchables.
146. Marrying a Harijan girl despite being a Brahmin.
147. Creating a revolution in society against caste and creed.
148. Bringing about a slow change in backward traditions and customs.
149. Renunciating ones individual interests for society and the nation.
150. Keeping beds and utensils more than one's need for helping others.

46A (22)

Title of the Instrument : **Attitudes Towards Women Scale.**

Purpose : To measure attitudes towards women, their role and status vis-a-vis men, traditional versus egalitarian orientation towards sex-roles.

Authors : Nandini Diwan.

Language(s) : English. Translation into Marathi and Standardization Planned in the future.

Uses : Longitudinal and Across-sectional studies, group comparisons, measuring effectiveness of specially designed awareness and consciousness-raising programmes.

Levels : Anyone above 16 years of age and familiar with English.

Main Features : It is a Likert-type scale (5 point scale : 1 =Strongly disagree, and 5= strongly agree) with 36 items.

Reliability : Split-Half reliability coefficient (Spearman Brown formula)= 0.83.

Validity : Detailed analysis not yet done, Four female judges—all lecturers in Psychology-were consulted independently during the preparation of the scale and their suggestions were taken into account. Each judge evaluated the scale as having adequate face and content validity. The test author met 80 participants and gave them feedback about their ATWS scores (in the pilot study 80 subjects were involved.) Each of them reported that the score reflect their real attitudes.

Time Limit : About 15 minutes may be required.

Norms : Norms are based on scores of 200 males and 200 females. The range of possible scores=36 to 180, with higher scores indicating more favourable and egalitarian attitudes. 16 items (marked '+') are worded in such a way that agreement with them reflects favourable attitudes: remaining 20 items are negatively worded (marked'—') and these items scores should be reversed when finding out the total score on 36 items.

Males *Frequency Distribution*

Scores	*Frequencies*
160-169	1
150-159	5
140-149	13
130-139	34
120-129	55
110-119	50
100-109	31
90-99	10
80-89	01
	N=200

Males :
Mean=121.15
Median=120.95
S.D.= 14.21
Percentiles:
P10 = 102.40
P20 = 108.85
P30 = 113.10
P40 = 117.10
P60 = 124.59
P70 = 128.23
P80 = 133.32
P90 = 139.21

Females :
Mean = 135.55
Median = 135.38
S.D. = 12.94

(Contd.)

ATWS Scores	*Frequencies*
160-169	05
150-159	26
140-149	41
130-139	68
120-129	36
110-119	21
100-109	03

Percentiles:
P10 = 117.60
P20 = 123.94
P30 = 129.50
P40 = 131.26
P60 = 138.32
P70 = 142.43
P80 = 147.30
P90 = 153.73

Mean score of females is significantly higher than the mean score of males.

References : The 20-item FEM scale was used as the main base of this ATWS. A few items were taken from the AWS (Attitudes Towards Women Scale) by Spence and Helmreich. These were modified to make their meaning easily understandable by Indians or to make the wording positive from negative (16 out of 20 items in FEM scale are negatively phrased and thus, a 'response set' may influence the score). Some items were retained in their original form. In addition to these items, 7 items were developed by the author were included-these pertained to current Indian Women's issues, like attitudes toward single/barren women, widows, female foeticide and infantile etc.

References :

1. Smith, E.R., Ferree, M.M & Miller, F.D. A Short Scale of Attitudes Toward Feminism. *Representative Research in Social Psychology*, 1975, 6, 51-56.
2. Spence, J.T., Helmreich R. & Stapp, J. : A Short Version of the Attitudes Toward Women Scale. *Bulletin of Psychometric Society*, 1973, 2 (4), 219-220.

ATTITUDES TOWARDS WOMEN SCALE

Please Read The Instructions Carefully:-

Fill in the required details :-

Name :

Age : Sex: Date:

Class: College:

Address & Phone No. :

Here is a list of statements. You have to read each one carefully and indicate how much you agree or disagree with it, on a scale ranging from 1 to 5. If you *Strongly Disagree* with a statement write the number '1' in front of it. If you *Disagree* with it, write the number '2' in front of it. If you *neither agree nor disagree* with a statement, i.e. if you are neutral to it, choose the number '3'.

In case you *Agree* with a statement, write the number '4' in front of it, and if you *Strongly Agree* with a statement, write the number '5' in front of it.

1	2	3	4	5
Strongly Disagree	Disagree	Neutral	Agree	Strongly Agree

Now, if you have understood the above instructions clearly, start reading the statements one by one and indicate appropriate number. There is no time limit, but try to go as fast as you can. Do not omit any item and please think seriously about each statement before responding to it. There are no 'right' or 'wrong' answers. Your responses will be kept strictly confidential. So, please answer truthfully, according to what you honestly feel. As far as possible, do not choose the number '3' i.e. the neutral response.

+ 1) Women have the right to compete with men in every sphere of activity.

– 2) As the head of the household, the father should have final authority over his children.

– 3) The unmarried mother is morally a greater failure than the unmarried father.

– 4) A woman who refuses to give up her job to move with her husband would be to blame if the marriage broke up.

– 5) A woman who refuses to bear children has failed in her duty to her husband.

+ 6) Women should be permitted to hold political offices that involve great responsibility.

+ 7) Every woman should not be expected to change her name when she marries.

+ 8) Whether or not they realize it, most women are exploited by men.

–9) Only women who are frustrated and unattractive join the women's Liberation Movement.

–10) A working woman who sends her six month old baby to a day-care centre is a bad mother.

–11) A woman to be truly womanly should gracefully accept chivalrous attentions from men.

+12) It is absurd to regard obedience as a wifely virtue.

–13) A good wife is one who clings sweetly to her husband in order to please him.

–14) Realistically speaking, most progress so far has been made by men and we can expect it to continue that way.

–15) One should never trust a woman's account of another woman.

+16) It is desirable that women be appointed to police forces with the same duties as men.

–17) Women are basically more unpredictable than men.

–18) It is all right for women to work, but men will always be the basic bread winners.

–19) A woman has the right to go to the same places or have the same freedom of action as a man.

–20) Swearing and abusing generally sound much worse coming from a woman.

–21) Some equality in marriage is a good thing, but by and large the husband ought to have the making say in family matters.

+22) People should be employed and promoted strictly on the basis of ability, regardless of sex.

+23) A woman who has a job she enjoys is likely to be a better wife and mother, because she has an interest and some fulfilment outside the home.

–24) A married man should be paid more than a woman for performing the same job.

–25) Generally speaking, women think less clearly than men.

+26) It is wrong to believe that only simple and dull domestic chores can be performed by women.

+27) A woman should feel as free as a man to propose marriage.

–28) Women should worry less about their rights and more about becoming good mothers.

–29) The life of a woman who is unmarried or has no children is unhappy and incomplete.
–30) As widowhood is a very unhappy experience, most women would prefer death to widowhood.
–31) Women are always dependent on men, first as daughters, then as wives and then as mothers.
+32) Marriage should not be considered as an essential and the most important event in every woman's life.
+33) Parents should give all the privileges and freedom to a daughter that they give to a son.
+34) The birth of a boy should not be considered as a happier event than the birth of a girl.
+35) Women should assume their rightful place in business and all the professions along with men.
+36) The practice of female infanticide or medically terminating pregnancy if the sex of the foetus is found to be female is totally wrong and should be abolished.

46A (23)

Title of the Instrument : **Scale to Measure Attitude Towards Agriculture as a Profession.**

Purpose : To measure the attitude of under-graduate students of B.Sc. Agriculture towards agriculture as a profession.

Authors : Inderjit Chawla and A.N. Shukla.

Language : English.

Availability : Central Library, PAU Ludhiana (Pb.).

Uses : It can be used to determine the attitude of under-graduate students towards agriculture as a profession and as an occupation.

Levels : Undergraduate students of B.Sc. Agriculture class.

Main Features : For the purpose of item analysis of the statements, Edward's HL test (1957) was applied. The calculated value of 't' equal to 2.00 or above. It was found that only 19 statements had value 2.00 and above. Thus these 19 statements were finally selected for measuring the attitude of the respondents, towards agriculture as a profession.

Reliability : The reliability of the attitude scale with split-half and analysis of variance came to be 0.67 and 0.89 respectively.

Validity : The content validity of the scale was ensured from 20 judges who were experts in the field of agriculture. The intrinsic validity of the scale was determined by taking square root of the reliability coefficient.

Time Limit : 20 minutes.

Norms : N.A.

References :

1. Edward, A.L. (1955) : *Techniques of Attitude Scale-Construction*, New York, Appleton, p-149.
2. Guilford, J.P. (1954) : *Psychometric Methods*, Tata McGraw Hills, p-373.

SCALE TO MEASURE ATTITUDES TOWARDS AGRICULTURE AS A PROFESSION

Here are some statements concerning the attitude towards agriculture as a profession. Please indicate your response by putting a (✓) mark against each statement in an appropriate column with which you are in agreement. The abbreviation used in the scale stands for.

SA — Strongly Agree
A — Agree
UD — Undecided
D — Disagree
SD — Strongly Disagree.

Sr. No.	Statement	Response category SA	A	UD	D	SD
1.	I like it because it commands high respect in public.					
2.	I like agricultural profession because one has to work for only fixed period of time in a day.					
3.	I like agricultural profession as it develops the ability to work in groups.					
4.	I like it as it requires less hard work.					
5.	I like agricultural profession as it develops awareness about the surrounding environment.					
6.	I like it because it is easy.					
7.	I like it as one develops a sense of responsibility					

(Contd.)

Sr. No.	Statement	SA	A	UD	D	SD
8.	I like this profession as one gets at least a fixed salary every month.					
9.	I like agricultural profession as it has more advantages than monetary benefits					
10.	I like it as there are more chances of promotion.					
11.	I do not like it as I do not enjoy to interacting with the rural people.					
12.	I do not like it as it creates botheration for the whole time					
13.	I do not like this profession as the independency of one's life is lost.					
14.	I do not like it as he has to sit continuously for very hours.					
15.	I do not favour it as it is a boring work.					
16.	I do not prefer agricultural profession as one has to obey the order of his boss.					
17.	I do not like it as it does not suit my nature.					
18.	I feel that it could not be satisfying for me to spend my whole life in the office					
19.	I do not prefer it as one has to work under pressure.					

46A (24)

Title of the Instrument : **Interview Schedule for Mothers : Socialization of Children And Adolescent Girls From an Ecological Perspective.**

Authors : Guide : R.S. Saraswathi, R. Misra, S. Kapadia, R.Dutta and Meera Gore.

Availability : Department of Human Development and Family Studies, M.S. University of Baroda, Baroda-390002.

Language : English.

Uses : This test may be used to obtain basic data on socialization practices and attitude and to identify aspects in child specialization requiring intervention and also for planning related intervention strategies and programmes, particularly those related to improving the status of women.

Levels : Adolescents girls and mothers.

Main Features : This is an open ended, and unstructured interview schedule which consists of questions of 10 different aspects featuring the Home environment.

Reliability : Inter-interviewer reliability has been established. Consensus has been 100%.

Validity : No validity indices have been reported.

Norms : Given

References :

1. Dutta, R. (1983) : Socialization in an impoverished agricultural community : An ecological perspective. Unpublished master's dissertation, M.S. University of Baroda, Baroda.

INTERVIEW SCHEDULE FOR MOTHERS

I. Children : Preferred number and sex

1. How many children do you think one should have?
2. Who decides about the number and timing/spacing of children?
3. Do you think having a son is a must? Why?
4. Do you think man and women are equal? Or are men more intelligent than women? Why do you think so?
5. Can a woman live alone or do you think she is dependent on the man throughout her life? (Father/Husband/Son)? Why do you think so?

II. Hopes, aspirations, expectations

A. *For children:*

1. If you were granted a wish from God, what would you wish for?
2. What do you wish/hope for your sons and daughters when they grow up?
3. What kinds of jobs/work would you like your children to do when they grow up?
4. Do you think you are able to fulfil all the needs of your children?

5. Do you think it is expensive to rear a child?
6. What do you expect from your children? From boys; from girls?
7. Do you consider any of your child's activities/behaviour as wasteful/improper? Which are those activities or behaviours?
8. What are the things that your son/daughter does well?
9. What are the qualities that you like in your children?
10. What are the qualities that you dislike in your children ?
11. Do you think children bring joy to sorrow? Why do you think so?
12. Why and at what times do you think children bring joy and/or sorrow/ why do you think so?
13. Do you think your children are happy/satisfied? Why do you feel so?
14. About 10-15 years from now what kind of a life will your children be leading?

B. For Self:

15. If you had money/power to bring about changes in your own life/living conditions, what would you like to do most?
16. What is your favourite memory—a day or event you enjoyed more than any other?
17. Was there any time in your life—as a child or even now—when you said to yourself—"I wish I had been born a boy?" Why do you wish so?
18. Which stage of life do you feel is best/pleasant—Childhood, Adolescence, soon after marriage, motherhood, Old age? Why?

III. Disciplining

1. How do you and your husband deal with the children when they misbehave?
2. Are the children more obedient with you or with their father? Why is if so?
3. If you are pleased with your child's performance how do you express your approval?
4. Should children be disciplined? Why?

IV. Health

1. What do you do for common illness like fever, cold/cough? Go to the doctor or prefer home remedies? Or just let be?
2. What do you do for major illness?
3. Do you think boys and girls need equal health care?
4. Do you think children should be vaccinated?

V. Education

A. Mothers of school going and non-school going children:

1. How much have you studied?
2. Why did't you study further?
3. Do you wish you had studied more? Why
4. Would you like to study/learn no? What would you like to learn? If not, what is the reason?
5. Do you think education is equally important for boys and girls? Why?
6. How much do you want your children to study?
7. Do you ever visit your child's school?
8. What is your opinion about the school? How is it?
9. Does any one help the child with studies ? How is it?
10. Who is more keen on educating children?
11. What kinds of difficulties do you face in educating your children?

B. Mothers of non-school going children:

12. (a) Did your child ever go to school?
    (b) If yes, why did she/he leave school?
    (c) If no, why didn's she/he go?
13. Does your child regret not having studied?
14. Does your child help in the house? In what ways does she/he help?
15. Do you think not being educated will make a difference in your child's life?

V1. Cultural Influences

A. Religion:

1. Do you do pooja in the house?
2. Do you visit the temple along with your children?
3. What festivals do you celebrate?
4. Do you fast? Why?
5. What other rituals do you practice?
6. When small-pox comes does it mean devi is angry?
7. Is 'pooja' necessary to prevent small pox or is vaccination alone effective/sufficient?

B. Marriage and child birth :

8. At what age do you plan to get your sons/daughter married?
9. (a) Would you approve of a young woman wishing to remain single?
   (b) If yes, Why?
   (c) If no, Why?

10. Should the parents seek the child's consent in the choice of a marriage partner? Suppose the parents select a husband for their daughter, and she says she does not like him; she does not want to marry him. Should the parents take objection? What about a son? Should his opinion be considered?
11. What kind of a husband would you choose for your daughter?
12. What are the qualities that a good wife should possess?
13. Suppose a girl and a boy are from two different castes, but they want to get married, would you approve of it in your family?
14. When a daughter gets married do you think parent should be obliged to give a dowry? Why do you think so? What if the parents are poor?
15. Should a widow/divorcee be allowed to remarry? Why?
16. When is a woman considered untouchable? (e.g. after delivery).
17. What care should be taken during pregnancy and delivery?
18. Suppose a woman's daughter is going to have a baby, should the mother advice her to register from maternity care, or do you think it is unnecessary?
19. How do people treat a barren woman? Why?
20. Suppose a woman produces no children, should her husband remarry? Why?
21. Suppose a woman produces no male children should her husband remarry? Why?

C. Recreation :

22. Does your family go for outings? How often? Where do you generally go?
23. Do you all, as a family, engage in any particular activity together? How often?
24. Does your child have any special interests/hobbies? If yes, what are they?
25. Do you have any free time?
26. What do you generally do in your free time? What do you like doing?

VII. Daily Life : Household Activities

1. What time of the day/household chores do you most look forward to? Why?
2. Does anybody help you in housework? Who?
3. Does your husband help in housework? How?
   What does he help in? Do you think he should?
4. Who works harder according to you, man or woman? Why do you say so?

5. Do you discuss household matters with your husband? How often-in a day/week, eg., buying books, clothes for children etc.?
6. Do you have a difference of opinion at such times? What happens? What does your husband do? How do you react?
7. Who takes decisions regarding various family matters, viz., children's education, marriage, disciplining, food, clothing, and daily routine matters (e.g. cooking)?
8. Do you believe that a woman should eat after her husband?
9. Who do you seek help/advice from when necessary?
10. Do you have any savings?
11. If yes, approximately how much do you have? Where do you keep the saving?
12. Do you ever spend money on personal items like saree, bangles etc.?

VIII. Employment

1. (a) Do you approve of a woman working outside home/farms?
   (b) If yes, Why?
   (c) If no, Why?
2. What kinds of jobs/work do you think are suitable for women?
3. Would you like to learn any income-generating skills? e.g. tailoring?
4. Would you prefer to earn money by doing some activity at home rather than go out and work?
5. Can you think of any tasks that can be done at home which fetch money?
6. Would you rather be fairly well off and not work than work and be quite well off?
7. Do you think employment brings with it a higher status? At home? In the community?
8. Do you think women should only remain at home (and look after the house and children)?

Questions for Employed Women

9. What work do you do that brings in money?
10. How much does your work pay you?
11. Who decided that you ought to go for labour?
12. Are you satisfied with your work? Do you like it?
13. Who looks after the children while you are away at work/farms?
14. Do you get any benefits from your work? If yes, what are they?
15. Do you think your wages are appropriate for your work?

16. What kinds of problems do you face as a result of your working?

IX. Political Awareness

1. Have you heard of any women leaders in your country?
2. Do you think women should enter politics? If yes, Why?
3. If a man and woman with the same qualifications were to contest in the elections, who would you vote for?
4. If a man belonged to one political party, say the Congress (I), and the woman belonged to another party, say Janata, then should the woman change her party in favor of the husband?

X. Perception of Change

1. How does your life differ from that your mother/grand mother (in terms of education, food, less segregation of sexes, respect for elders, and general way of living)?

XI. Opinions regarding the community Settings

1. Since how long have you have been residing here?
2. What is your opinion about the community/village (physical setting, people)?
3. What are the facilities you would like to have?

46A (25)

Title of the Instrument : **Semi-Structured Interview Schedules for Children and Parents on Development of Social Competence.**

Authors : Sophia Gir, and Prema Sharma, Guide : T.S. Saraswathi.

Availability : Department of Human Development and Family Studies, M.S. University, Baroda-390002.

Language : English.

Uses : The interview schedule can be used by researchers, counsellors, parents, and teachers, to identify factors that help the development of competence in children. This would also help identify the factors that can be strengthened to encourage competent behaviours in children.

Levels : Children aged 12-15 years and parents of children.

Main Features : Questions concerning home, school, peers, community, role of self, and other related matters. Questions are framed in order to obtain information regarding the type of competencies, skills, and abilities that the above mentioned socialization agents help to promote in the child and the ways and means adopted for the same.

Reliability : No reliability indices have been reported.

Validity : No validity indices have been reported.
Norms : Scoring norms in the manual.
References : 1. Gir, S. (1979) : Development of Competence related personality characteristics and coping strategies of competent boys. Unpublished Master's dissertation, M.S. University, Baroda.

SEMI STRUCTURED INTERVIEW SCHEDULES FOR CHILDREN & PARENTS

I. For Children :

1. What does your father do?
2. Does your mother work at present?
3. (a) What about your brothers and sisters—What are they doing?
   (b) Do you get together—what kind of activities you do when you are together? Any common interest you all have?
   (c) Do you think any brother or sister of yours helped you to develop interest in something or encouraged some ability in you?
4. Are there any relatives living with you? Did they stay with you at any time in past? What do you remember doing with them?
5. (a) When you all get together as a family what are the activities in which you generally indulge in?
   (b) Any particular interest or hobbies your father and mother have—sports, music, books?
6. (a) What do your parents like you to do?
   (b) How do they encourage you to do things according to their liking?
7. (a) What do your parents dislike you doing?
   (b) How do they express their dislike?
8. Do you think you were strictly brought up?
9. Whenever you have any problems or you are happy about something whom do you approach to tell your feelings?
10. Do you feel close to any one of your parents?
11. As you have your preference among your parents, do your parents have any preference among you all brothers and sisters?
12. (a) How do you remember your parents when you were small
    (b) What kind of activities you used to do together?
    (c) Who spent time with you—father or mother?
    (d) Did your parents feel that you had to be taken care of more or

less fairly closely or left you to yourself?

13. Do your parents feel strongly about your doing well in school? What do they encourage you to do besides studies? How are you doing in your class?
14. (a) In which area do you feel your parents encouraged you most?
    (b) Do you think your parent encouraged you to develop some of your abilities? If yes, what did they do?
15. Are you interested in reading?
16. Do you think anybody influenced you to develop this interest in reading books?
17. Since when have you been reading books?
18. (a) What sort of books do you read?
    (b) What do you like in the books that you read?
19. Any memorable book? What did you like best in that book?
20. Did you feel any change in yourself after you started reading books?
21. (a) From where do you get books?
    (b) Is there a library in your school?
22. What do you remember about that school?
23. What about this school? What, in your opinion, are the most outstanding features of your school?
24. (a) What are you mainly interested in studying at school?
    (b) How did you develop interest in this particular subject?
25. (a) What do you think about the extra-curricular activities in your school?
    (b) What activities do you participate in?
    (c) Do you think anybody influenced you to develop interest in these activities?
26. (a) Are there any committees or organisations in your school run by students?
    (b) Are you a member of any one of them?
27. What sort of activities do you like best in your school?
28. What is the general environment that prevails in your school?
29. How are the teachers in your school?
30. Is there any particular teacher who influenced you in any way? If yes, how?
31. Are you interested in participating in social activities?
32. Do you have a big group of friends or you move around with a selected group of friends?
33. What sort of activities do you all indulge in?

34. What activity or activities do you most enjoy doing with them?
35. What is it that you like most about your friends?
36. Do you feel any one friend in particular influences you more than others?
37. If yes, in what way does he/she do so? What specific types of abilities are being promoted?
38. What sort of activities do you engage in during vacation.
39. Do you have any particular hobby?
40. What do you think of the general atmosphere of the community in which you live?
41. What sorts of facilities are available in your community?
42. Do you promote your personality growth? If so, How?
43. What are the general attitudes and expectations of the people in your community?
44. Do they in any way encourage the development of some abilities?
45. Do you feel at any stage you made or are making a conscious effort to develop your abilities?
46. Till now what do you think—you had more of satisfactory experiences or unsatisfactory experiences? In which area were you most satisfied?
47. What do you think were your most satisfactory experiences, what gives you the most pleasure?
48. What do you think were the most unsatisfactory experiences?
49. If you were given your life again would you like to lead it in the way you have led it, or you would like some changes? What are your future plans?

II. For Parents

1. (a) Have you all been living as a single family always or was there some relative living with you?
   (b) How close were they?
   (c) Do you think you prefer a single family or a joint family?
2. What are the activities each family member is interested in?
3. (a) What are the times the family gets together as a group?
   (b) Do you feel it necessary to do so? Why?
   (c) What are the activities done together? What do you generally talk about?
4. (a) What are your views on disciplining your child?

(b) What are the types of things you are strict about and don't like?

(c) What are the types of things you like your child to do and what do you encourage him/her to do?

5. Do you feel any one of your children is more lovable and admirable? Why?

6. Does any one of your children prefer you—say, in order to share their experiences or discuss their problems? Why?

7. How were your children when they were small?

(a) Did they give you trouble, asking for constant attention or... Why?

(b) Did you leave them on their own for certain things? What things you left them alone for? Why?

(c) Did you get to spend time with your child? Whenever you spend time with your child what did you usually do?

8. Is your child closer to anyone of his/her siblings?

9. (a) Did you consciously try to promote some habit, some interest or happy in your child? Why?

(b) How did you do so?

10. What do you deal about your child's performance in school?

11. What do you like him/her to concentrate on at school? Why?

12. (a) Did your child always study in this school or in some other school also?

(b) If other—which school do you prefer? Why?

13. How does your child do in school?

14. What are the subjects he/she is mainly interested in studying at school?

15. (a) Does he/she participate in any extra or co-curricular activities?

(b) What are they?

(c) Does he/she do so on his/her own or do you encourage him/her?

(d) How do you encourage him/her?

16. (a) What are your child's hobbies and interests?

(b) Do you think its admirable to encourage him/her?

17. (a) Is your child on any one of the school committees or organisations?

(b) What does he/she do in these?

18. (a) What does the family generally do in vacations?

(b) How does your child generally spend his vacations?

19. (a) Is your child more interested: In indoor activities or outdoor activities?
    (b) In social outings or quiet hobbies?
20. What do you feel about the general environment at school?
21. What are the facilities available in the school?
22. What is your opinion of the teachers?
23. Do you think any particular teacher influenced your child more than the others? How?
24. (a) Does your child have a big group of friends or small?
    (b) What does he usually do with them?
25. What do you like best about his friends?
26. Do you think your child learnt any thing new after befriending them?
27. What is your opinion about the locality you live in?
28. How do you find the people?
29. What are the facilities available?
30. (a) Do you think living in this community is conducive to the growth and development of your child?
    (b) In what way? Why?
31. (a) Do you feel your child has at any stage made a conscious effort to develop his abilities?
    (b) In which area and how?
32. What are the areas he/she derives most satisfaction from?
33. What is he/she dissatisfied about?
34. (a) Do you think you have been able to provide all that you wanted for your children?
    (b) How?
35. (a) Do you feel happy about your child?
    (b) Is he/she happy?
36. What are your plans for your child's future? What would you like him/her to be most?

46A (26)

Title of the Instrument : **Interview Schedule on Child's Life at Home and Child's Handling by Mother.**

Authors : A.Verma, Pramilla Phathak, A. Mehta, Anjani Patel, and V. Mistry.

Availability : Department of Human Development and Family Studies, M.S. University, Baroda.

Language : English

Level : Mothers of young children.

Uses : Information collected on the basis of the interview schedule would have important consequences for the development of a home based mother education programme and even for guidance and counselling of mothers.

Main Features : This test schedule is divided into five sections dealing with different aspects of the child's life at home and mother's handling of the child. Each section includes a number of questions related to that particular aspect of a child's life.

Reliability and Validity : No reliability and Validity indices have been reported.

Norms : Scoring and interpretation given in the manual.

References :

1. Gambhir, S. (1972) : Child's life at home from birth to five years with special reference to social interactions. Unpublished Master's dissertation, M.S. University, Baroda.

INTERVIEW SCHEDULE ON CHILD'S LIFE AT HOME AND CHILD'S HANDLING BY MOTHER

Name of the child :	Mother's Name
Code No. :	Address
Birthdate :	Date of Interview
Age of the child :	Changes in income

Changes in the family composition

	S*[1]	N*[2]	A*[3]	Remark
I. Feeding				
1. The baby is				
(a) breast or top fed				
(b) breast and external feed (liquid)				
(c) breast and additional feed (solids)				
(d) top-fed/only liquids				
(e) top-fed liquids and solids				

*[1] S = Seldom

*[2] N = Never

*[3] A = Always

(Contd.)

	S*[1]	N*[2]	A*[3]	Remark
(f) given specifically prepared adult food				
(g) given adult food				
2. The child's feeding is done by				
(a) mother alone				
(b) mother and other adults				
(c) mother and sibling				
(d) sibling alone				
(e) servants				
(f) anyone				
(g) self				
3. When the child eats without any help, the child				
(a) does not eat much but plays with the food				
(b) spills food all over				
(c) eats with slight spilling or tradiness				
(d) eats tolerably neatly				
(e) eats like an adult				
4. The child is given food				
(a) at regular intervals				
(b) Whenever the child wants (cries)				
5. The child is given food				
(a) when alone				
(b) with other children but with special attention				
(c) with other children but separately from adults				
6. The child is given snacks				
(a) not given				
(b) whenever the child asks for it or cries				
(c) whenever the child has to go out				

(Contd.)

	S*1	N*2	A*3	Remark
(d) whenever the child is available at home				
(e) at the scheduled time				
7. The child is given sweets				
(a) to coax the child to do as desired				
(b) to keep the child engaged				
(c) to pacify when the child is crying or is unhappy				
(d) as a reward for good behaviour				
(e) any other reason (specify)				
8. The child is reminded and coaxed				
(a) for routine intake				
(b) for special necessary items of food				
9. When the child refuses to take the necessary food, the child is				
(a) coaxed to eat by				
(i) bribing				
(ii) talking to				
(iii) running after				
(iv) directing				
(v) praising				
(vi) taste and try				
(b) forced to eat				
(c) allowed not to eat				
10. When the child does not eat special or new food, the child is				
(a) requested to taste and try				
(b) forced to eat				
(c) allowed not to eat				
11. Toilet Training				
1. The child indicates the need for elimination : Yes/No if yes, by				
(a) discomfort or by making sounds				

(Contd.)

	S*[1]	N*[2]	A*[3]	Remark
(b) pointing to the place (toilet) or panty				
(c) moving towards the toilet or removing the panty				
(d) speech				
(e) goes to toilet independently				
The control of bowel movements				
The child has:				
(a) no control				
(b) momentary control control for short period				
The control of bladder movement				
The child has				
(a) no control				
(b) momentary control control for short period				
(c) prolonged control				
The child has bowel control				
(a) only when the child is awake				
(b) even when the child is asleep				
The child has bladder control				
(a) only when the child is awake				
(b) even when the child is asleep				
The child is helped to gain bladder and bowel control by				
(a) taking the child to toilet at regular intervals				
(b) being watchful about the child's indications				
(c) leaving the child alone to learn by self				
When the child loses control, the mother				
(a) remains relaxed				
(b) cleans and dresses the child in dry clothes				

(Contd.)

	S*[1]	N*[2]	A*[3]	Remark
(c) explains the need of control to the child				
(d) reminds the child of the centrol the child had				
(e) shows indifference				
(f) shouts at the child				
(g) threatens the child				
(h) punishes by depriving				
(i) physically punishes the child				
(j) ignores the child				
III. Sleeping				
1. The child sleeps for				
(a) 20 to 23 hours				
(b) 16 to 19 hours				
(c) 12 to 15 hours				
(d) 10 to 12 hours				
(e) 8 to 10 hours				
(f) less than 8 hours				
2. In addition to the night, the child sleeps in				
(a) morning; no. of hours				
(b) afternoon; no. of hours				
(c) evening; no. of hours				
(d) does not sleep during the day				
3. The child usually sleeps				
(a) early and gets up early				
(b) late and gets up late				
(c) any other pattern				
(d) nothing regular				
4. The child's sleep is				
(a) sound				
(b) disturbed (nightmares, talking in sleep, sleep-walking, teeth grinding etc.)				
5. If the child wakes up at night, the child is				

(Contd.)

	S*[1]	N*[2]	A*[3]	Remark
(a) fed				
(b) given a drink of water				
(c) cuddled to sleep				
(d) patted and rocked to sleep				
(e) not given attention				
(f) made to sleep by introducing fear				
(g) scolded or punished				
6. The child normally sleeps with				
(a) no one				
(b) siblings				
(c) mother				
(d) any adult				
7. The child indicates a dream by speaking				
(a) about the dream				
(b) about things that did not happen				
8. The child goes to sleep				
(a) with help such as:				
(i) rocking and patting				
(ii) special clothing article (mother's sari, etc.)				
(iii) own pillow				
(b) dell or a favorite toy				
(c) by sucking				
(d) by giving sleep inducing medicine				
(e) while hearing a story or song by an adult				
(f) while talking and playing with siblings				
(g) independently without help or it				
IV Bathing, Washing and Dressing				
1. The child is bathed by				
(a) mother				
(b) mother or adult relatives				
(c) sibling				

(Contd.)

	S*[1]	N*[2]	A*[3]	Remark

(d) servant
(e) anyone else
(f) self

2. The child is given massage before bath
   (a) regularly
   (b) on some special occasions
   (c) seasonally
   (d) never
3. The child takes bath
   (a) at specific timings
   (b) according to convenience
   (c) whenever the child pleases
4. The child is helped in dressing
   (a) all clothes
   (b) difficult clothes
   (c) buttoning and tying
   (d) combing hair
   (e) not at all
5. The child is helped in dressing by
   (a) mother
   (b) other adult
   (c) servant
   (d) sibling
   (e) anyone else
   (f) independent, not helped at all
6. The child is dressed in
   (a) children's common dresses of both sexes (zabhla)
   (b) suitable to the sex of the child
7. The dress of the children is selected by
   (a) elders
   (b) siblings
   (c) the child
8. The child's clothes are taken care of by

(Contd.)

	S*1	N*2	A*3	Remark
(a) mother				
(b) any other adult				
(c) siblings together with the child				
(d) the child				
9. The child is washed and cleaned				
(a) when the child gets up in the morning				
(b) before meals				
(c) after meals				
(d) whenever the child gets dirty				
(e) before going to bed				
10. The child is normally washed and cleaned by				
(a) mother				
(b) any other adult or sibling				
(c) self, with help from adults				
(d) self, with help from sibling				
(e) independently				
V. Socialization				
(a) Play				
1. The child's play contents are				
(a) sound producing objects and toys, e.g. rattlers etc.				
(b) wooden toys				
(c) constructive toys, blocks, clay				
(d) vehicles and outdoor material				
(e) human and animal toys				
(f) mechanical toys				
(g) odds and ends				
(h) books, cuttings, crayons				
(i) anything else (specify)				
2. The child gets toys when				
(a) not given toys at all				
(b) purchased on occasions (birthdays, new year etc.)				
(c) as a reward				

(Contd.)

	S*[1]	N*[2]	A*[3]	Remark
(d) given as gifts by relatives and visitors				
(e) the child asks for them				
(f) needed				
3. The child is allowed to play with toys				
(a) according to mother's wish				
(b) according to specific instruction and guidance				
(c) as the child pleases				
4. The child is given the toys to play				
(a) occasionally				
(b) whenever the child desires				
5. The child is responsible for				
(a) preserving and keeping the toys in order				
(b) sharing the toys				
(c) giving away and discarding toys				
(d) not responsible for anything				
6. The child's hobbies (e.g. pictures, feather, stamps, etc.) are				
(a) encouraged				
(b) shown indifference to				
(c) discouraged				
7. The child is helped				
(a) to collect. . . (pictures, stamps etc.)				
(b) to classify and preserve				
(c) to use. . .				
8. The child is allowed to play				
(a) in the house				
(b) at neighbours				
(c) common courtyard				
(d) garden or nearby playground				
(e) in the street				
9. The child is allowed to play with children				

(Contd.)

	S*1	N*2	A*3	Remark
(a) who are socially desirable				
(b) who are chosen by parents				
(c) whom the child likes				
(d) siblings and their friends				
(e) siblings alone				
(f) anyone				
(B) Communication				
1. (i) The child indicates needs and desires by				
(a) requesting				
(b) flattering				
(c) shouting angrily				
(d) being sulky				
(e) temper tantrums (kicking, beating, etc.)				
(ii) Mother responds to the child's needs				
(a) by giving what the child desires				
(b) by diverting the child's attention				
(c) depending upon convenience				
(d) scolding				
(e) verbal assurance				
2. When in need, the child usually goes to				
(a) mother				
(b) father				
(c) any other adult				
(d) servant				
(e) siblings				
(f) friends				
(g) no one				
3. The child mostly asks questions to				
(a) mother				
(b) father				
(c) any other adult				

(Contd.)

	S*[1]	N*[2]	A*[3]	Remark
(d) servant				
(e) siblings				
(f) friends				
4. The child's questions are				
(a) always replied to				
(b) replied to at times				
(c) usually replied to				
(d) not replied to				
5. The child always desires to be in company of				
(a) mother only				
(b) father only				
(c) any other adult				
(d) siblings				
(e) pears				
(f) anyone else (specify)				
6. The child often seeks				
(a) physical contact				
(b) follows some adult (specify)				
(c) presence of the adult				
(d) no one special				
(e) remains alone				
(C) Expected Social Behaviour				
1. The child communicates in socially approved manner with				
(a) parents				
(b) adults in the family				
(c) siblings-young/elder				
(d) other family acquaintances				
(e) strangers				
(f) servants				
2. The child seeks permission to				
(a) go out				
(b) give things to friends				
(c) use things belonging to others				
(d) use common belonging of the family (food, musical instruments, etc.)				

(Contd.)

	S*[1]	N*[2]	A*[3]	Remark
3. The child interferes in adult's talk and activities				
4. When the child interferes, the child				
(a) seeks undue adult contact				
(b) demands attention by expressing needs				
(c) asks questions				
(d) disturbs adults by				
(i) making noise				
(ii) creating mess				
(e) becomes aggressive towards others				
(f) any other (specify)				
5. The child says false things (lies)				
(a) because the child does not know the facts				
(b) because the child wants to show off				
(c) to save self from punishment or blame				
(d) to throw blame on someone else				

46A (27)

Title of the Instrument : **Knowledge Content of Mothers for Efficient Mother Craft.**

Authors : M. Khattar, M. Pandey, M. Bhattacharjee, J. Mewar, and N. Devi, Guide : P. Dave.

Availability : Department of Human Development and Family Studies, M.S. University, Baroda.

Language : English, Gujarati, and Nepalese.

Uses : The test can be used by community development workers to identify the areas in which mothers lack knowledge. This can in turn have useful implications in planning of intervention programs.

Levels : Mothers of children upto five years of age.

Main features : The test consists of 78 statements regarding knowledge essential for mothers, covering the areas of child development. Each statement is to be rated on a four point rating scale: 100%, 75%, 50%, and 25% — indicating how much the rater agrees with the correctness of the statements.

Reliability and Validity : No reliability or validity indices have been reported.

Norms : Scoring norms available in the manual.

References :Available in the manual.

Mother should know that/about	100%,	75%	50%	25%
1. The importance of prenatal clinics, prenatal medical checks and importance of following the doctor's advice.				
2. Normal body movement and exercises are essential for easy child birth.				
3. Taking drugs indiscriminately during the first three months of pregnancy may lead to congenital malformations.				
4. Mother's nutrition during pregnancy directly influences the growth and development of the foetus.				
5. Mother's nutrition during lactating period influences the quality and quantity of milk she can supply to the child.				
6. The technique of breast feeding the child.				
7. The importance of hygiene of breast feeding.				
8. The duration of breast feeding for proper growth of child.				
9. When to introduce top feeding.				
10. The nutritive needs of the child during the process of weaning.				
11. It is necessary that the food of the child should be varied and enough.				

(Contd.)

Mother should know that/about	100%,	75%	50%	25%
12. The introduction of supplementary and complementary food in the diet of the child.				
13. Both overfeeding and under feeding are harmful for the child.				
14. What and how much the child eats is important for his total growth and development.				
15. Water is an important requirement for the infant.				
16. How to detect gross sensory defects at the primary stage such as visual defect, hearing defect, etc.				
17. The hereditary diseases that run in the family.				
18. The importance of preparing a child for a visit to a doctor.				
19. Periodic health check up of the child helps to ensure the child's healthy growth.				
20. Utmost care should be taken to avoid child's contact with contagious diseases.				
21. When the child starts moving freely, his surroundings should be free of dangerous objects.				
22. Drugs, medicines, insecticides and poisonous liquid should be properly stored out of reach of the child.				
23. Opium and sleeping drugs for the infant are detrimental to his health.				
24. Habits of health involves washing of hands before meals and brushing of teeth after meals.				
25. Habits of health involves washing hands after using the toilet				

(Contd.)

Mother should know that about	100%	75%	50%	25%
26. The clothes of the child should be light, loose, comfortable and preferably of cotton.				
27. Good physical environment consists of good ventilation and sanitation.				
28. The habits of health involves regular open air play.				
29. The habits of health involves regular and sufficient sleep hours.				
30. Habits of health involves regularity in toilet.				
31. In the early years of life maturation plays an important role in toilet training.				
32. The new-born needs protection from extreme temperatures.				
33. The broad developmental milestones are age of sitting, standing and walking.				
34. Each child will be different from any other child in reaching each stage of general growth pattern within the limits of normality.				
35. No two children will respond identically to the same situation.				
36. Rigidity in handling the child should be avoided.				
37. Pressurizing the child for higher achievements without him being ready for it or not having the ability for it, leads to maladjustments.				
38. Within limits of supervision child needs freedom to commit errors, practice and learn.				

(Contd.)

Mother should know that/about	100%,	75%	50%	25%
39. The age related normal behaviour with special reference to his understanding.				
40. Children are imaginative and have their own way of expressing it, such as through make/believe play.				
41. Modelling is a good aid to the development of habits.				
42. A child learns a number of things by imitating others.				
43. Imitative play provides opportunity for the child to express his understanding about social roles.				
44. Making the desirable behaviour a pleasant experience for the child, helps in establishing habits.				
45. Safety of child while playing with toys and play materials is an important issue while selecting the toys.				
46. Age related normal play behaviour.				
47. Looking through the picture books and telling stories is important for the language development of the child.				
48. Language is an important tool of communication and expression.				
49. Age related normal behavior with special reference to his communication.				
50. During prelanguage stage, other people's talks with the child helps the child to understand and learn language.				
51. Having questions in mind (curiosity) is an important indication of a growing mind.				

(Contd.)

Mother should know that/about	100%,	75%	50%	25%
52. Answering the child's questions honestly in the language he can understand is important for his knowledge.				
53. To arouse curiosity of child is an important aid of child's learning.				
54. Stories provide opportunity to raise questions in child's mind.				
55. Taking the child out for visits to different places stimulates his curiosity.				
56. Age related normal behaviour with special referernce to his secial behaviour.				
57. Constant interaction with child is necessary for proper growth and development.				
58 The traditional and current roles and responsibilities of a mother in the subculture she belongs to.				
59. A relaxed attitude and giving proper attention to child helps to a great extent in forming good habits.				
60. Punishment of the child should have a sound reason.				
61 Punishment, its type, and intensity should be related to the cause.				
62 Child should know why he is being punished.				
63. The difference between a reward and a bribe.				
64. How rewards help in developing routine habits.				

(Contd.)

Mother should know that/about	100%,	75%	50%	25%
65. A child's emotions are aroused easily.				
66. A child needs occasional affectionate physical contact.				
67. A child needs the feeling of affection, security and being wanted, for the attainment of his potentials.				
68. A child should be wanted by the parents.				
69. Quarrels and disputes in the family affect the development of the child negatively.				
70. Parental disharmony affect the development of the child negatively.				
71. Mother's various positive and negative attitudes towards work, play and people may affect the child's development.				
72. A child's handling of genitals is natural and mothers should be relaxed about it.				
73. Mother's role is to stimulate and guide the child's course of development, not to control or restrict it.				
74. Mother should allow for the child's individuality and imperfection of skills.				
75. Organizing her work to save time for the child's care.				
76. Sending a child to preschool is not a matter of social trend, but, it is in the interest of the proper growth and development of the child.				
77. Overemphasizing the problem increases the problematic behaviour of the child.				

(Contd.)

Mother should know that/about	100%, 75% 50% 25%
78. When and where to seek professional help in handling the child's development.	

46A (28)

Title of the Instrument :**Story Situations Assessing Understanding of Population Issues**

Authors : C. Dave, and Guide : A. Verma

Availability : Department of Human Development and Family Studies, M.S. University, Baroda-2.

Language : Hindi and English.

Uses : The set of story situations may be used to collect bench-mark data prior to planning a population education programme. This may also be used as a post-test measure to gauge the effect of a given population education programme.

Levels : Children in their late childhood or early adolescence.

Main features : The measure consists of eight story situations encompassing different aspects of the population.

Reliability and Validity : No reliability or validity indices have been found.

Norms : Scoring norms and interpretation has been given in the manual.

References :

1. Dave, C. (1982) : Population education programme for secondary school students. Unpublished doctoral dissertation, M.S. University, Baroda-2.

STORY SITUATIONS ASSESSING UNDERSTANDING OF POPULATION ISSUES

EXPECTED OR DESIRED RESPONSES WITH FULL EXPLANATIONS

Situation I

1. I will ask him not to come to Bombay because (a) he may not got the job easily; (b) as it is we are so busy and he may not be able

Note : Actual story situations have not been provided by the author.

to adjust with this fast life; (c) who will look after the farm there?

2. Like Ram, if many people come to Bombay the population of Bombay will increase, which will lead to other problems like: (a) housing; (b) food; (c) unemployment; (d) environmental pollution; (e) overerowdedness and accidents; etc.

Situation II

3. Mrs. Sharma — because in small family the expenditure in bringing up children is less and so the happiness is more — the standard of living is higher, the health of all members is good, etc. There is no guarantee that if one has more children they will all help in business.
4. Either by comparing the merits of small families with the large families or comparing two families (one large and one small) from the neighbourhood and comparing them on the points like - standard of living (health of all members, education, food, happiness, income vs. expenditure, etc.).
5. The knowledge should be shared with others so that everyone comes to know from each other on population dynamics. By discussing amongst themselves they are better convinced to adopt small family norm.
6. Yes. This helps to develop insight into the different issues of population dynamics.
7. Yes, it should be offered to all students at this age because; (a) this is the age when they build up their opinions and so at this age if they are taught this course they will form desirable opinions towards small families; (b) mostly girls leave the educational field after this age and boys, mainly from middle and lower class, may not join the regular classes or college — and may start earning while learning. So they may either join night colleges or appear privately for examinations. Comparatively few would go for college education; (c) to have small families both boys and girls (future husbands and wives) should have the same opinions. Hence, this is the right age when majority of them (boys and girls) are studying and are in the process of developing their opinions for future life. So if population education has to be part of formal education, this is the right age (IX, X, XI classes).

Situation III

8. No, because they are not fully matured : (a) to take the desirable decision independently; (b) to take the responsibilities of parenthood.
9. A girl should be 20-22 years when she completes her graduation and can be said to be matured in her thinking and behaviour. A boy should be 24-26 years when he completes his education and has started working. If he has not taken up any kind of job then he could be still little older.
10. The age difference of 2-4 years is preferable so that developmentally they are not too far off in their meturity.
11. They should be informed about marriage, sex, family planning, etc., so that they plan their families accordingly and at the same time enjoy their married life also.
12. This information could be given either by parents or by friends or by teachers.
13. Preferably it should be given in the formal ways so that all get the knowlege at the right time and in a correct sense without any hesitation or hiding. As plain, clear facts of life, they can be explained in the class properly and doubts can be clarified easily by the teacher. Whereas in case of informal giving of information, all parents may not have correct knowledge and the parents or the children may not be very free with each other in order to tell or ask any thing or clear their doubts.

Situation IV

14. Both should have a small family, so that there is no inequality.
15. No. Even those who have more money to spend should also plan to have a small family, so that they can rear their children properly (provide them with all comforts and fulfil their needs) and the extra money that they feel like spending, can be used in some other way, or in helping the needy prople so that the gap between rich and poor is minimised and the whole country can pregress. The problem of over-population is also decreased and so are the other problems of food, housing, unemployment, etc., solved gradually.
16. Shyam should prefer 2-3 children, only the number that he can rear properly. Preferably one son and two daughters or two sons

and one daughter just to get the satisfaction of bringing up the children of both sexes. But if one has all 3 children of the same sex then just for the sake of having another male/female child one should not increase the number of children as this adds to their expenditure.

17. Preferably yes. But if one has all three daughters then one should not try for a son. Instead, one should satisfy oneself with whatever one has and should not increase one's expenditure. There is no guarantee that the fourth child will be a son only. If there is one son then the family name is continued but if there is none then also they should be able to manage to carry out the social and religious customs.
18. By performing 'Pooja' and taking 'Manata' one cannot have a son as these are not related to conception and sex determination in any way.

Situation V

19. This problem of unemployment is increasing day by day. Overpopulation is one of the main reason. Every year so many students pass-out that all cannot get employment.
20. The suggestions to solve this problem are: (a) to check the population growth, (b) to improve the educational system so that all need not go in for higher education. Only those who are very desirous may go in for higher education and the rest could got some technical training to start their own small scale industry or business etc., in other words, prepare themselves for varied types of jobs so that they can fit in wherever they feel competent.
21. Mr. Prakash should have his first child only after he gets a job so that he is able to bear the expenditure of raising a child.
22. He should have his second child after 2-3 years when the first child is little grown up and can express his needs so that both the second and the first child do not require the same amount of time and care.

Situation VI

23. I prefer Krishna's family because it is a small family. He has two sons to look after the farm and provides employment to other people when in need. So there is no constant expenditure of more

people in these family. The earning is same while the expenditure is less.

24. The standard of living of Krishna will be higher than that of Ram as the expenditure is less than in Ram's family. They will have more to spend on various types of expenditures.
25. In old age too, Krishna will be able to live happily as he will not have to warry about establishing his children. Financially, also he will be bettwe off and will be able to save for his old age.
26. In solving national problems such type of small families are desirable. They can solve the problems of over-population, unemployment, food, etc., and help to raise the standard of living.

Situation VII

27. She must discontinue the pregnancy because : (a) they did not plan for it; (b) it will add to their expenditure; (c) add to their work; (d) the second child will not be able to get adequate care and attention.
28. If she continues the pregnancy all the above mentioned problems will arise.
29. They should have used family planning devices if they wanted to have a gap between two children, or even undergone sterilization if they had decided not to have any more children.

Situation VIII

30. The reasons for their non-co-operation are : (a) ignorance of the benefits of small family; (b) lack of proper communication between the couple; and (c) national policy plans which resulted in compulsory sterilization.
31. Yes, because even those who did not have any children or are very young — married or unmarried had to undergo sterilization. Such mishaps have caused them to have no faith and respect in doctors.
32. Government should have just tried to develop awareness in them towards small family through various audio-visual aids and then only those who wish it should have been operated instead of making it compulsory. The decision of choosing the method of family planning should be left to the couple so that without using any type of compulsion, all may understand the need for small families and thereby try to control their family size.

46A (29) by Ritu Mehra and P. Kulhara

DEPARTMENT OF PSYCHIATRY PGIMER, CHANDIGARH

Measurement of Social Support

Name_____________________ Age _____ Sex ______ MS_______
Education__________Occupation________Income________
Religion ________________
Address ____

Instructions — Read each statement carefully and tick mark (✓) in the proper column of each item to indicate your personal judgement. There are no right or wrong answers. These items are related to emotional/support one gets when one faces a stressful situation.

Example — How much do you agree with the following statement :-

Statement	Agreement			
1. There are some people who can always be counted upon	Extremely 4	Quite a bit 3	A little 2	Not at all 1

If you agree with the satement extremely mark (✓) at Extremely (4)

If you agree with the Statement quite a bit mark (✓) at (3) Column

If you agree with the Statement a little mark (✓) at (2) Column

If you don't agree with the Statement mark (✓) at Not at all (1) Column

Please indicate your true and honest choice.

Thank you

	How much do you agree with the following Statements ?				
	Extremely	Quite a bit	A little	Not at all	Score
Statements	4	3	2	1	
1. No one cares much about what happens to me.					

(Contd.)

Statements	4	3	2	1
2. I am treated with respect.				
3. I feel as if, people don't really listen to what I say.				
4. People often go out of the way to help me.				
5. Real friends are hard to find.				
6. I wish people close to me could understand me better.				
7. It is usually best to tell your boss at job or elders at home what they like to hear.				
8. If I am not handling my problems responsibly there is always some one in my life who will bring it to my notice.				
9. The people with whom I work at office/at home always help each other.				
10. I don't know anyone who has the same values/beliefs in life as I have.				
11. My colleagues/superiors at work/my elders at home admire my good work.				
12. People don't usually let me down.				
13. I am criticized unfairly (without any reason) at work/at home.				
14. It's hard to find people you can trust.				
15. I have few relationships in my life on whom I can depend.				
16. I feel better after I have discussed my problems with some one.				
17. There does not seem to be enough time to have fun.				

(Contd.)

Statements	4	3	2	1
18. I often feel alone even among friends.				
19. When I do something for others they appreciate it (Praise me).				

46A (30)

Title of the Instrument : **Style of living.**

Authors : B.A. Parikh, and Others.

Availability : Departmant of Psychology, M.T.B. Arts College, Surat-395001.

Language : English.

Uses : Measures the attitude of people and their style of living.

Levels : Students.

Main features : The items were 25 in number and the students were asked to indicate their likes and dislikes. The items were listed in a form and the subject had been asked to indicate his response in oneout of three categories-'like', 'less like', or 'dislike'. The analysis of the data has been made in terms of percentage of like, and dislike, of the two groups — the boys as well as the girls.

46A (31)

Title of the Instrument : **The Influence of Parents in Choice of Certain Items by the Students.**

Authors : B.A. Parikh, and Others.

Availability : Department of Psychology, M.T.B. Arts College, Surat-395001.

Language : English.

Uses : Measures the influence of parents in the choice of certain items by the students.

Levels : Students.

Main features : The subject has to select or give their opinion regarding certain things like : 1. clothes, 2. friends, 3. study, 4. job, etc. The items of choice are varied. They are related to personal and social life. Analysis of data reveals that all areas of choice the percentage of students making choice only 'under the influence of parents' is much less.

Scales of 46 A (31) is printed on page 620

46A (32)

Title of the Instrument : **Relation with the members of the opposite sex.**

Authors : B.A. Parikh, and Others.

Availability : Department of Psychology, M.T.B. College, Surat-395001.

Language : English.

Uses : Measures the attitude of the younger generation's relation with the members of the opposite sex.

Levels : Students of the College level.

Main features : Contains 10 statements, The range of scores for this inventory is from 10 to 36.

ATTITUDE TOWARDS RELATION WITH MEMBERS OF THE OPPOSITE SEX

(1) Do you welcome co-education?

(2) Do you accept that young boys and girls students should mix with each other?

(3) Do you object to having friends of opposite sex?

(4) What do you think of sex relation before marriage?

(5) What type of friendship relation with the opposite sex would you accept?

(6) Is the friendship with members of the opposite sex a hindrance in study?

(7) It is so that friendship with members of the opposite sex contributes to the healthy development of the individuals.

(8) Do you believe that experiences of friendship with the members of the opposite sex are helpful for adjustment in the marital life?

(9) Does the heterosexual friendship relation lead to moral and character falls?

(10) Having no heterosexual friendship relation is a narrow and a backward outlook.

46A (33)

Title of the Instrument : **Status of Women.**

Authors : B.A. Parikh, and Others.

Availability : Department of Psychology, M.T.B. Arts College, Surat-395001.

Language : English.

Uses : Measures the nature and direction of the attitude of the students and their parents regarding the status of women in our society.

Levels : Women from Indian Society.

Main features : Consists of 20 statements. The statements in the inventory are related to various aspects of a woman's life.

ATTITUDE TOWARDS STATUS OF WOMEN

1. The woman who serves after marriage tries to escape from her duties of looking after the home and the children.
2. The woman should have freedom to bring an end to her marriage and get divorce when she desires to do so.
3. Man and woman are equal. So if the woman is doing a job, the man should share the responsibility of home management.
4. Women are soft and agile, so they cannot be given top executive posts of responsibility.
5. Like men; women also should have an independent career.
6. Women should have freedom to manage their income as they like.
7. Women cannot have marriage and job both together.
8. Women should not join politics.
9. The worthwhileness of a woman is in her becoming a good mother and a good housewife.
10. The woman should have freedom to decide when and how many children she should have.
11. The woman is the root cause in most of the difficulties of man.
12. It is a matter of joy that in India women are placed on high posts.
13. It is proper that parents put more restrictions over girls than over boys.
14. Widows should live a simple and restricted life.
15. Women should have equal rights in property.
16. Secoindary school education is sufficient for women. There is no need of higher education for them.
17. If more women do jobs the social, and economic problems will be solved.
18. Woman's place is in the home. It is not desirable that she should

join public life or do a job.

19. Society in which women are backward will remain backward.
20. The present status of women is satisfactory, so there is no necessity of giving them more freedom.

46A (34)

Title of the Instrument : **Intercaste Marriage.**

Authors : B.A. Parikh and Others.

Availability : Department of Psychology, M.T.B. Arts College, Surat-395001.

Language : English.

Uses : To find out the attitude of the younger generation as well as the parents for inter caste marriages.

Levels : Parents as well as the students or the younger generation.

Main features : For each statement in the inventory for measurement of attitudes for intercaste marriage the subject had to choose any one of the six categories of responses arranged in a progressive manner showing from most negative (1) to most positive (6) direction of the attitude.

ATTITUDE TOWARDS INTERCASTE MARRIAGE

1. Breaking the caste traditions in doing a marrige harms social organisation.
2. One should marry within one's own caste.
3. One cannot get a suitable mate from one's caste's narrow circle, so intercaste marriages should be encouraged.
4. Intercaste marriages are useful for social unity, so they should be encouraged.
5. The social reformers should recognise and honour the young men and women entering into intercaste marriages.
6. Intercaste marriages do not turn out to be happy, for the husband and wife come from different social, cultural groups.
7. Intercaste marriages reduce class distance.
8. The progress of India is arrested, because it cannot come out of narrow groups of the castes.
9. In today's industrial and urban society intercaste marriages are suitable.
10. In schools and colleges young boys and girls get ample opportu-

nities for coming into contact. Therefore, it is improper to insist on marriage within the caste.

11. There is no harm in choosing a suitable mate from other castes.
12. Marriage should be negotiated only after knowing and getting consent of each other. It does not matter if the two come from different castes.
13. It is tolerable that a girl marries a boy of a caste higher than her, but she should not marry a boy from a caste lower than her.
14. It is tolerable that a boy marries a girl of a caste higher than his, but should not marry a girl from a caste lower than his.
15. Intercaste marriage is a healthy social trend, becuase it breaks the bad traditions like dowry, bride-price, etc.

B

46B (1)

Title of the Instrument : **Maternal Attitude and Maternal Adjustment during Pregnancy (M.A. M.A) Questionnaire in Hindi.**

Purpose : To measure maternal attitude and maternal adjustment during Pregnancy (M.A. M.A.) Questionnaire in Hindi speaking population.

Authors : Karobi Das, P. Kulhara, Department of Psychiatry, PGIMER, Chandigarh - 160012.

Language : Hindi.

Availability : From the Author.

Uses : To assess maternal attitudes and maternal adjustment during pregnancy.

Levels : Educated persons. Illiterates can take it orally.

Main Features : 39 items in 4 point scale (1 to 4).

Reliability : Test-retest reliability is 0.90 ($P<0.01$). Split-Half reliability on five areas – 1. Body image = 0.57, 2. Somatic symptoms = 0.57, 3. Marital relations = 0.08, 4. Attitudes towards sex = - 0.22, 5. Attitude towards pregnancy and body = 0.08.

Validity : Because of low split-half reliability of 3 sub-scales, these sub-scales items were subjected to item analysis using E 1/3 method.

Time Limit : 10-15 minutes.

Norms : Second order factor analysis done on 206 pregnant women.

Reference : Unpublished. Will be soon published in a paper and also being used in the Ph.D. thesis of Karobi Das under the guidance of P. Kulhara.

46B (2)

Title of the Instrument : **Anushasan Mapani.**
Purpose : To measure the attitude towards dicipline.
Author : Shashikala Singh.
Language : Hindi.
Availability : Department of Psychology, Faculty of Social Sciences, Banaras Hindu University, Varanasi - 221005.
Uses : Dicipline measurement.
Levels : Adolescents.
Main Features : Likert type, consisting of 33 items.
Reliability : Split-half reliability coefficients by Split half method was = 0.67, and by Test-retest method was = 0.64.
Validity : Nil.
Time Limit : 15 minutes.
Norms : Not available. In the process of getting done.
References : Unpublished thesis entitled "A Study of the Certain Psycho-Social variables on the Attitude of Children towards discipline." Awarded by the L.N. Mithila University.

46B (3)

Title of the Instrument : **Measure of Approving Parent.**
Author(s) : Ravi Ambast and Narendra K. M. Tripathi.
Availability : Manovaigyanik Parikchhan Sansthan. U.H.B.-28; Sanjay Nagar Colony, Chowka Ghat, Varanasi - 2.
Uses : Measures the parental behaviours i.e. approval and disapproval behaviour of parents.
Language : Hindi.
Level : Parents having children in the range of 6-12 years.
Main Features : Has 48 items which are to be answered in 'Yes' or 'No'. 24 statements were positively cued and rest were negatively cued, and half were related with disapproving behaviour. There are two statements related with each parental behaviour.
Reliability : Test-retest reliability 200 subjects were retested after a gap of one month. Correlation coefficient obtained from the two sets of scores was 0.59 with an index of reliability of 0.77.

Split-half reliability correlation coefficient between the two halves was found to be 0.67 (N = 500). The self correlation coefficient of the whole test was found to be 0.80 with an index of reliability = 0.89.

Validity : Content validity as well as intrinsic validity were found.
Norms : Available.
Time Limit : No time limit.
References :

1. Johnson, R.C. & Medinnus, G.R. *Child Psychology : Behaviour and Development*. (3rd ed.) N.Y. : John Wiley Sons, Inc., 1974.
2. Rohner, R.P. *They Love Me, They Love me not : A Worldwide study of the Effects of Parental Acceptance and Rejection New Haven*, HRAF Press, 1975.
3. Rohner, R.P. *Worldwide Tests of Parental Acceptance Rejection Theory : An Overview*. Behaviour Science Research, 1980, 15, 1-21.
4. Schaffer, E.S. A Circumplex Model for Maternal Behaviour. *J of Ab. and So, Psy.*, 1959, 59, 226-335.
5. Sinha, D. *Socialization of Indian Child*, New Delhi : Concept Publishing House, 1981.

46B (4)

Title of the Instrument : **Home Environment Inventory (HEI)**
Author : Karuna Shankar Misra.
Availability : Ankur Psychologyical Agency, 22/481, Indira Nagar, Lucknow - 16.
Uses : Measures the psycho-social climate of home as perceived by children. Provides a measure of the quality and quantity of the cognitive, emotional and social support that has been available to the child within the home.
Language : Hindi.
Levels : Students of VIII to X classes.
Main Features : Contains 100 items related to 10 dimensions of home environment. Each dimension has 10 items belonging to it. Pupils have to tell the frequency with which a particular parent-child interaction behaviour has been deserved by them in their homes.
Reliability : Split-half reliabilities Coefficients for 10 dimensions of Home Environment as measured are given in Table Format in the manual.

Inventory Dimension		Reliability Coefficient
A	Control	0.879
B	Protectiveness	0.748
C	Punishment	0.947
D	Conformity	0.866
E	Social Isolation	0.870
F	Reward	0.875
G	Deprivation of Privilages	0.855
H	Nurturance	0.901
I	Rejection	0.841
J	Permissiveness	0.726

Validity : Home Environment Inventory has been found to possess content validity as measured with the help of views expressed by judges criterion related validity could not be established because of the lack of appropriate external criteria.

Norms : Percentile norms for girls as well as boys for 10th, 25th, 50th, 75th and 90th percentile scores have been given.

Time Limit : No time Limit.

46B (5)

Title of the Instrument : **Women Social Freedom Scale.**

Purpose : To measure women's desire for social freedom.

Author : L.I. Bhushan, Professor of Psychology, Bhagalpur University, Bhagalpur.

Language(s) : Manual in English and test booklet in Hindi.

Availability : M/s National Psychological Corporation, 4/230, Kacheri Ghat, Agra - 282004.

Uses : Useful in understanding attitudes, values, and social problems of female subjects.

Levels : Adolescents and adult females.

Main Features : The scale contains 24 highly discriminative items (including 6 negative items) selected out of 60 items in form of simple statement. Each item has two categories ('Agree', 'Disagree') of alternative responses, selected on the basis of DP items determined in terms of χ^2 (Chi-square) and Phi-coefficient.

The test items are related to (1) freedom from control or interference of parents and husband, (2) freedom from social taboos and rituals, (3) freedom from marriage and stereo-typed sex roles, and (4) social freedom and social equality.

Reliability : The test possesses high internal and temporal stability as detailed below :

Split-half reliability coefficient

Odd vs even	0.86 (N = 100)
1st half vs 2nd half	0.90 (N = 100)
Test-retest reliability	0.79 (N = 80)

Validity : The predictive and construct validities of the test have been ensured. Scores on WSF - Scale correlated positively and significantly ($r = 0.436$, $p < 0.01$) with the Hindi version of Eysenck's Radicalism Scale (derived from his Social Attitude Inventory).

Time Limit : 5 to 7 minutes.

Norms : Percentile norms on responses collected from college girl students of Bhagalpur University are provided in the Test manual.

References : Bhushan, L.I. (1981): Women Social Freedom Scale, *Psychologia* 24, 239-243.

46B (6)

Title of the Instrment : **Family Relationship Inventory.**

Author (s) : G.P. Sherry and J.C. Sinha.

Availability : National Psychological Corporation, 4/230, Kacheri Ghat, Agra-4.

Language : Hindi.

Levels : Hindi Speaking school or college students.

Uses : It discriminates the individuals who feel emotionally accepted, over protected, or rejected by their parents. It is especially helpful to the school counsellors and clinical psychologists to identify the mal-adjusted cases.

Main Features : Contains 150 items classified into three patterns of mother and father separately. Response is given in 'True' or 'False' whatever is applicable to the subjects.

Reliability : Test-retest reliability was determined on a sample of 100 intermediate students.

Validity : Inter correlation of scales, Criterion-oriented validity and group comparision was done.

Norms : Stanine norms, percentile norms are available.

Time Limit : No fixed time limit for the response. Usually 40-50 minutes is taken by the subjects.

References : 1. Brunken, R.J. and Crites, J.O. (1964) : An inven-

tory to measure the parental attitude variables in Roe's theory of vocational choice. *J. Counsel Psychol*, 11, 3-12.
2. Brunken, R.J. (1965) : Perceived Parental attitudes and Parental Identification in Relation to field of vocational choice. *J. Counsel Psychol.*, 13, 304-402.
3. Byers, A.P., and Zaccaria, J.S. (1963) : Recalled early parent-child relations, adult needs and occupational choice : A test of Roe's theory. *J. Counsel Psychol.* 12(4), 379-383.
4. Bhatia, Lilly (1975) : Relationship between parent child Relationship, Socio-economic status and vocational Interest of the students. Unpublished M.Ed. Dissertation, Agra University.
5. Arora, Neemu (1976) : Perceived parental attitudes and personal values of the students pursuing person oriented and non-person oriented occupations. Unpublished M.Ed. Dissertation, Agra University.
6. Medvene, A.M. (1970) : Person oriented and non-person oriented occupations in Psychology, *J. Counsel Psychology,* 17 (3), 243-246.
7. Roe, Anne (1957) : Early Determinents of vocational choice. *J. Counsel Psychol*, 4, 212-217.
8. Sinha, J.C. (1968) : Role of the family as a psychological unit in the vocational development. Research paper submitted to N.I.E. Delhi for the associateship course.
9. Saxena, M.S.L. Adjustment Inventory - A Manual.
10. Super, D.E. (1957) : *Psychology of Careers.* Harper and Brothers.

46B (7)

Title of the Instrument : **Parent Child Relationship Scale.**
Author(s) : Harish Chand Sharma and N.S. Chauhan.
Availability : National Psychological Corporation, 4/230 Kacheri Ghat, Agra - 282004.
Language : Hindi.
Level : Parents.
Uses : Used as a diagnosis and guidance tool related to children and

their parents.

Main Features : 11 points for 8 dichotomous dimensions of basic parent child relationship. For better planning, proper growth of the self or the child.

Reliability : 200 parents' test-retest reliability was found. Table of reliability coefficients :

S.No.	Dimension	(r)	Dimension	(r)
1.	Rejection	0.73	Acceptance	0.79
2.	Carelessness	0.82	Over protection	0.82
3.	Negligence	0.87	Over indulgence	0.79
4.	Strong realism	0.83	Utopian expectation	0.80
5.	Lenient standards	0.78	Severe moralism	0.84
6.	Total Freedom	0.76	Severe discipline	0.73
7.	Marital conflict	0.86	Marital adjustment	0.89
8.	Faulty role expectation	0.72	Realistic role expectation	0.70

Validity : Not mentioned.

Norms : Not available.

Time Limit : No time fixed.

References :

1. Aldous, J. and Kell, L. (1956) : Child Rearing Values of Mothers in Relation to their Children's. Perceptions of their Mother's Control : An Exploratory Study, *Marriage Fam. Liv.* 18, pp. 72-74.
2. Allport, G.W. (1961) : *Pattern and Growth in Personality*. Holt, Rinehart and Winston Inc., New York.
3. Antonvsky, H.F., (1959) : A contribution to Research in the area of Mother-Child Relationship. *Child Development*, 30, pp. 37-51.
4. Bakwin, H. (1948) : Pure Mother Over Protection. *J. Pediat*, 33, pp. 788-794.
5. Bakwin, H. (1949) : Emotional Deprivation in Infants, *J. Pediat* 35, pp. 511-521.

46B (8)

Title of the Instrument : **Radicalism and Conservatism Questionnaire.**

Purpose : To discriminate individuals and groups on R-C mental sets.

Author : V.K. Mittal.

Language : Hindi.

Availability : Publisher : Manovignan Kendra, 249, Noonia Street, Meerut Cantonment.

Uses : Study of individual and group differences and research.

Levels : 15 years plus, Degree and Post-graduate levels.

Main Features : Questionnaire contains only 40 items. 20 statements are in radical and 20 in Conservative forms. All items are highly discriminative. Agreement on radical items gets score value = 0.

Reliability : Split-half reliability after SB correlation = r = 0.87, 2. Test-retest reliability coefficient = r = 0.80.

Validity : Criterion related validity against rural and urban groups = r bis = 0.63.

Time Limit : 10 minutes.

Norms : Centile norms and Z scores.

References : Tool has been developed in connection with ICSSR project.

46B (9)

Title of the Instrument : **Violence-Non Violence Scale.**

Purpose : To discriminate individuals and groups on V-NV behaviour and beliefs.

Author : V.K. Mittal.

Language : Hindi.

Availability : Publishers : Manovignan Kendra, 249, Noonia Street, Meerut Cantonment - 250001.

Uses : Study of individuals and group differences and research.

Levels : Degree and PG Students.

Main Features : Guttman type undimensional scale containing 18 items each with four alternatives, out of which one is to be checked.

Reliability : 1. Coefficient of Reproductivity = 0.82, 2. Split-half after Spearman Brown Correlation r = 0.80.

Validity : 1. Content validity. Items are represented of six characteristics as given by Gene Sharp.

2. Criterion related validity against classification of students into broad groups by their teachers, rbis = 0.73.

Time Limit : No time limit for this test.

Norms : Z scores and Centile norms.

References : Nil.

46B (10)

Title of the Instrument : **Knowledge Inventory on Population Issues.**
Author : A. Karnnick and C. Dave. Guide : A. Verma.
Availability : Department of Human Development and Family studies, M.S. University, Baroda.
Language : Hindi.
Uses : It may be used to collect benchmark data in order to develop a curriculum on population education for secondary school students. It may also be used as a post-test measure to assess the effectiveness of the population education programme given to the students.
Level : Secondary school students in India.
Main Features : It consists of two parts : Parts A and B. Part A consists of questions related to subjects background information and Part B consists of 40 multiple choice questions of major population issues.
Reliability and Validity : No reliability or validity indices have been found.
Norms : Scoring norms available in the manual.
Reference : Dave, C : (1982) : Population education programme for secondary school students. Unpublished doctoral dissertation, M.S. University, Baroda.

46B (11)

Title of the Instrument : **A Law Scale.**
Author : I.A. Khan, C.C. Centre, Aligarh.
Language : English.
Availability : *Journal of Personality*, and *Clinical Studies*, 1989, 5, (1), 101-104.
Uses : To encourage interdisciplinary research and also to measure objectively the opinion of people toward law, to understand the attitudinal changes and to know the implications of such changes on the psychological health of the people.
Level : All classes of people.
Main Features : Likert type of a scale of the answers. 17 items are included in the final list.
Reliability : The split-half reliability technique was used to find out the reliability of the scale. ($Y = 11 = 0.924$, $df = 23$, $p < 0.001$).

Validity : Validity of the scale was decided empirically and it was found to be fairly high.

Norms : Given.

Time Limit : No fixed time limit.

References : Given in the manual.

46B (12)

Title of the Instrument : **Family Planning.**

Author : B.A. Parikh and others.

Availability : Department of Psychology, M.T.B. Arts College, Surat - 395001.

Language : English.

Uses : The nature and direction of the attitude of the students and the parents, towards family planning can be studied.

Level : Students as well as parents, as well as couples.

Main Features : The inventory consists of 15 statements. These statements are related to various aspects of the family planning programmes. The responses have to be chosen from the six alternatives given.

C

46C (1)

Title of the Instrument : **Measurement of Social and Political Attitudes.**

Author : R.N. Singh.

Language : Hindi.

Availability : Manovaigyanic Seva Kendra, Professors' Colony, Sakalenabad, Ghazipur - 233001.

Uses : Measures 7 attidutes of social importance.

Level : Adults and adolescents.

Main Features : T.B. of 84 items, separate AS and scoring key, Profile sheet, N sten norms.

Reliability : Split-half reliability of each factor = 0.54 to 0.72, Repeat reliability of each factor = 0.65 to 0.82.

Validity : Construct validity, internal validity and external validity ensured.

Time Limit : About 40 minutes.
Norms : N Sten norms provided.
References : Seven references provided.

46C (2)

Title of the Instrument : **Assessment of Maternal Disciplinary Practices.**
Authors : I. Kaur, D. Takkar, R. Kapadia, and C. Bhatnagar and Guide: T.S. Saraswathi.
Availability : Department of Human Development and Family studies, M.S. University of Baroda, Baroda.
Language : English.
Uses : Besides being a research tool for collecting information on material disciplinary practices, the tool can be used for obtaining base line data for planning mother education programmes. The interview schedule may also be used by teachers for obtaining background information of problem children in the classroom and/or for establishing approaches to teaching children or prior to application of principles of behaviour modification in the classrooms. With minor modifications, the same tool can be used to interview mothers/fathers.
Level : Children aged 10-15 years.
Main Features : The test consists of 15 life situations which occur very commonly in the every day family routine and where mothers are likely to use some disciplinary technique. For all these situations there is a list of 12 possible reactions of the mother.
Reliability : Test-retest reliability for the measure has been established (a 90 per cent agreement was obtained). A rank order correlation of 0.67 has been reported between the two sets of power assertion scores.
Validity : Comparision of responses on the structured vs. unstructured response lists has shown an 80 per cent agreement in scores.
Norms : Given
References : 1. Bhatnagar, C. (1978) : Perceived Maternal Disciplinary practices and their relation to development of moral judgement in 10 to 15 years old girls from the lower middle classes. Unpublished master's dissertation, M.S. University of Baroda, Baroda.

D

46D (1)

Title of the Instrument : **Bengali Adaptation of Moor's Menstrual Distress Questionnaire.**

Author : A.N. Chowdhury and N.N. Roy Chowdhury.

Language : English.

Availability : *Indian Journal of Psychomatic Obstetrics and Gynaecology*, Vol. 8, June 1987, No. 1, pp. 13-30.

Uses : Measures the mentrual distress in women.

Levels : Women.

Main Features : MDQ is a 49 item (symptom) questionnaire on a 6 point rating scale, ranging from no experience (1) to severe or acute experience. Moos by inter-correlation and factor analysis has 47 symptoms on a sample of 889 women, identified 8 groups of symptom subscales, 46 symptoms are located within this 8 symptom-scales because one symptom "change in eating habits" could not be located.

Reliability : Test-retest reliability method was adopted.

Validity : Construct validity of Bengali MDQ.

References :

1. Sutherland, H. & S Tewart, I : *Lancet*, 1, 1180, 1965.
2. Clare, A.W. : *Brit. J. Psychiat.*, 135, 576, 1979.
3. Moos, R. : *Psychosom. Med.*, 30,853, 1968.
4. Moos, R. : Mentrual Distress Questionnaire manual. Social Ecology Laboratory, Department of Psychiatry and Behavioural Science, Stanford University and Veterans Administration Medical Center, Palo Alto, CA., 1977.
5. Moos, R. : Perimentrual Symptoms : A manual and overview of research with the mentrual Distress Questionnaire. Social Ecology Laboratory, Stanford University School of Medicine, Palo Alto, CA, 1985.
6. Corradi, I., Chiarini, G.; Brunori, I. *et al.* : *Bollettimo di Psicologia Applicata*, 155,212, 1980.
7. Abdel-Khalek, A.M. : *Res. Behv. Personality*, 3, 13,1983.

8. Most, A.F.; Woods, N.F.; Dery, G.K. *et al.* : *Int. J. Nursing*, 18,61, 1981.
9. Dopico, O.F. : *Revista dc Psychologia Genl. Y. Applicada*, 30,773, 1981.
10. Moos, R. : Personal Communication.

INSTRUMENT INDEX

Note : Page Number show in Italic

AUTHOR INDEX

Note : Page Number show in Italic.

ADDENDA

11A (8)

LH-SCALE
(English Version)

Name ____________ Age ______ Sex ______

Occupation ____________ Education ____________ Date ______

Instructions

There are fifteen sentences in this scale related to some social and behavioural problems. Against each item mark tick (✓) Right/Wrong/ Uncertain according to your choice. This is not a test of Your intelligence or abilities, Your responses will be kept fully confidential.

1. I do not try to change some bad customs of society even though I can do so. Right/Wrong/Uncertain.
2. I do not console a crying man despite my sympathy for sufferers. Right/Wrong/Uncertain.
3. I am not eager to help a mishapped person even when I can do so. Right/Wrong/Uncertain.
4. At times I doubt my ability even when I know I am capable. Right/Wrong/Uncertain.
5. I can not teach young children despite my wishing. Right/Wrong/Uncertain.
6. I do not address a meeting easily even though I can do it satisfactorily. Right/Wrong/Uncertain.
7. I try to be unfamiliar to a person whom I have already met several times. Right/Wrong/Uncertain.
8. When someone does not appreciate my good work, I get sad. Right/Wrong/Uncertain.
9. I do not participate in gatherings even though I am capable of doing so. Right/Wrong/Uncertain.

10. If I meet a familiar person on road, I try to avoid him though I do not want to do so. Right/Wrong/Uncertain
11. I hesitate in talking to elders without any reason. Right/Wrong/Uncertain
12. I do not help people in trouble even though I am in a position to do so. Right/Wrong/Uncertain.
13. Inspite of having self confidence, my trust in capability is lessened while facing difficult situations. Right/Wrong/Uncertain.
14. Inspite of having the capability to take decisions, many times I fail to decide. Right/Wrong/Uncertain.
15. I cannot work properly in front of my elders even though I can do so. Right/Wrong/Uncertain.

15 B (3)

Title of the Instrument : **Projective Test of Achievement Motivation (nAch).**

Authors : P. Deo and A.Mohan.

Availability : National Psychological Corporation, 4/230, Kacheri ghat, Agra.

Language : English and Hindi.

Uses : To measure achievement motivation.

Level : Adolescents.

Main Features : The test consists of five pictures for two sets separately for the group of boys and girls, of these two depicted academic situation, one technical, one sports and one music of the five pictures, one is common for both boys and girls.

Reliability : The Test-retest Reliability = .41; the score-rescore consistency = .82; The inter scorer Reliability was between; 84 and 91 with three groups of scorers.

Validity : Face validity and concurrent validity established.

Time Limit : Five pictures are to be shown and each picture is shown for 30 seconds. For writing response stories, 4 minutes are to be given for each picture giving one minute to each of the four questions. There is an interval of 15 second between two pictures.

Norms : Norms are published in the manual.

References :

1. Atkinson, J.W. (1950) "The Projective measures of Achievement Motivation." Unpublished Ph.D.

Thesis, Michigan. In McClelland, D.C. (Ed.) "Measuring Motives in fantasy : The Achievement Motive". In *Studies of Motivation*, Appleton Century Crofts, Inc, 1955, pp. 401-412.

2. Atkinson, J.W. (Ed.) (1958). "Motives in Fantasy Action and Society : A Method of Assessment and Study," D.Van Nostrand Co. Inc., 873 (East-West Student Edition, (1966).
3. Bending, A.W. "Predictive and Postdictive Validity of need achievement measures." *J. Edu. Res*, 52, p. 119-120.

21 B (1)

Title of the Instrument : **Rao's Social Maturity Scale (RSMS)**
Purpose : To Measure Personal, Interpersonal and Social Adequacy.
Author : Nalini Rao.
Languages : English/ Hindi/ Kannada.
Availability : "RSMS" (A complete set of Manual of instructions, Scale Protocol, Scoring Blank and Scoring Template)1986. Available with: National Psychological Corporation, Bhargava Bhavan, 4/230, Kacheri Ghat, Agra- 282 400, India. [Kannada Scale available with the Author.]

Uses :
1. Useful to obtain a Comprehensive, dependable and practical means of Social maturity.
2. It can be used in researches in the field of Psychology, Education and Sociology since the scale is developed applying the interdisciplinary logistics.

Levels for whom it is meant : High School and collage students.

Main Features.
(1) Tool consists of nine sub-scales clustered under three dimensions of personal Adequacy, Interpersonal Adequacy, and Social Adequacy, each with three sub-scales
(2) The scale has 90 items.
(3) It is a four point Likert type attitude scale.

Reliability :
1. Test-retest reliability coefficient by Pearson Product Moment correlation range from, .63 to .91 on the sub-scales.
2. Internal consistency of the scale dimensions ranges

from .105 to .603 and established on upper primary, secondary and pre-university student samples.

Validity : 1. Criterion validity established against teacher ratings on the attributes of social maturity.
2. Concurrent validity on the three different language forms of Hindi, English, and Kannada Yielded Coefficients of Correlation ranging from .97 to .99.
3. Content validity also established.

Time required for administering : No time limit; It has been found to take not more than 35 to 40 minutes to answer 90 items.

Norms : No

Development of the Instrument : The scale has been standardized on a total sample of 2132 students from grades VI through XII employing rigorous psychometric procedures.

References : Sources : "A study of the Socio-Psychological correlates of social development of high school children in Grades VIII, IX & X in some high schools of Bangalore City", Unpublished Doctoral Dissertation in Education, Bangalore University, 1978.
(2) "Socialization of Children and Youth (in press). Agra : Bhargava Book House.

22 A (3)

Interview Schedule-Cum Checklist for Assessing some Aspects of Academic Stress and Symptoms in 10-16

YEAR OLD STUDENTS

1. In what way does education help you ?
2. What should be the role of schools?
3. Are the schools fulfilling these roles? Why/Why not?
4. Do you look forward to going to school? Why/Why not?
5. What is your reaction towards examinations - before, during and after taking them?
6. Do examinations try to assess your academic performance? Why/Why not?
7. Are you satisfied with the examination system? Why/Why not?
8. Can you suggest any variation in the examination system?
9. What, according to you, are the merits of home work?

10. What are the demerits of home work?
11. Does home work help in learning? If yes, how?
12. Are you satisfied with the kind of home work that is given?
13. Can you suggest any other type of home work that can be given?
14. How much time (on an average) does it take you to finish your home work daily?
15. Do you get time to play or for pursuing hobbies or leisure activities after school work?
16. What are the consequence of not doing your home work?
17. Are you afraid of the consequences?
18. Why are you (or are you not) afraid of the consequences?
19. What are the characteristic that you look for in a teacher?
20. What types of students are preferred by a teacher?
21. Do you fall in that category? Always sometimes Rarely
22. Rate the teacher who teach you on following scale :
    a. They come prepared for the class : Always Sometimes Rarely
    b. They are partial to some students : Always Sometimes Rarely
    c. They try to make an effort to understand you and your problems : Always Sometimes Rarely
    d. You discuss your problems with them : Always Sometimes Rarely
    e. You have been reluctant to come to school because you feel your teacher (s) do not like you or they might punish you : Always Sometimes Rarely
    f. Your teacher punishes if you do not do the work given to you : Always Sometimes Rarely
    g. The teachers use corporal punishment : Always Sometimes Rarely
23. What kind of expectation do your parent have with regard to academic achievement : High Average Low
24. Do you feel you come up to their expectations : Always Sometimes Rarely
25. Do you get tensed up or worried about getting good marks in exams : Always Sometimes Rarely

26. Do your parents or siblings help you with school work : Always Sometimes Rarely
27. How do your parents react if you do not do well in exams. or in school : Harsh reaction Feel upset No reaction
28. Do your parents expect you to do well in school because your sibling(s) do (or have done) so : Always Sometimes Rarely
29. For relieving your tensions and worries due to school or academics, what do you do?
30. At the thought of going to school, have you ever got :
    (a) Headaches (b) Stomachaches (c) Fever
    (d) Constipation (e) Diarrhoea (f) Any other.
31. When you have not done your home work, have you ever got :
    (a) Headaches (b) Stomachaches (c) Fever
    (d) Constipation (e) Diarrhoea (f) Any other.
32. During examinations, have you ever got :
    (a) Headaches (b) Stomachaches (c) Fever
    (d) Constipation (e) Diarrhoea (f) Any other.
33. Do you feel tense due to pressure of school work : Always Sometimes Rarely
34. Do you find it difficult to attend to the teacher in class due to too much work in school : Always Sometimes Rarely
35. Before the examinations, do you feel any of the following :
    a. Get nightmares/ bad dreams : Always Sometimes Rarely
    b. Feel tensed : Always Sometimes Rarely
    c. Feel anxious : Always Sometimes Rarely
    d. Feel irritable : Always sometimes Rarely
    e. Sleeplesseness : Always Sometimes Rarely
36. Do you feel afraid of failure in exams : Always Sometimes Rarely
37. Do you thing many of your friends are doing much better than you in school work? How do you feel about it?
38. What do you feel when you don't do well in you examinations?
39. Have school related problems been reason for your :
    a. Inability to sleep : Always Sometimes Rarely
    b. Restlessness : Always Sometimes Rarely
    c. Daydreaming : Always Sometimes Rarely

e. Aggressiveness (verbal or physical) : Always Sometimes Rarely

f. Fighting with your friends : Always Sometimes Rarely

g. Difficulty in adjustment with your school : Always Sometimes Rarely

h. Difficulty in adjusting at home : Always Sometimes Rarely

i. Missing school : Always Sometimes Rarely

j. Feeling that you are a misfit in school : Always Sometimes Rarely

k. Comparing yourself with your siblings or friends : Always Sometimes Rarely

l. Not being accepted by your peer group : Always Sometimes Rarely

m. Not wanting to continue studies : Always Sometimes Rarely

31 A (26)

Title of the Instrument : **The Learned Helplessness Scale.**

Purpose : To Measure Learned Helplessness (LH) of employees in organisations.

Authors : D.M Pestonjee and K. Prathap Reddy

Language : English.

Availability : Dr. D.M Pestonjee, L&T Professor of Organisational Behaviour & Chairman, OB Area, Indian Institute of Management, Ahmedabad- 380015

Uses : The present scale can be used to assess the type and extent of learned helplessness existing in employees of all levels in organisations

Levels : It may be administered to any level of employees operating in different types of organisations.

Main features : It is a 24-items scale in which each statement is rated on a 6-point scale. In all, 8 dimensions of learned helplessness are sought to be measured.

Reliability : Nunnally's (1967) reliability test was used to assess the reliability of each of the eight dimensions. Reliability of the items was also tested by calculating inter-item correlations. The correlations suggested a fairly strong reliability of all the eight dimensions.

Validity : Established, available with the authors.

Time Limit : 20-25 minutes.

Norms : Not available.

References :

1. Abramson, L.Y., Garber, J., and Seligman, M.E.P. (1980) Learned Helplesness in Humans : An Attributional Analysis. In Garber and Selligman (Eds.) *Human Helpless*, New York : Academic Press.
2. Abramson. L.Y., Seligman, M.E.P., and Teasdale, J (1978). Learned Helplessness in Humans : Critique and Reformulation. *Journal of Abnormal Psychology*, 87, 49-74.
3. Pestonjee, D.M. and Redd, K.P. (1988). Development of a Psychometric Measure of Learned Helplessness. Working Paper No. 746, Ahmedabad: Indian Institute of Management.
4. Nunnally, J.C. (1967). *Psychometric Theory*. New York : McGraw-Hill

THE LEARNED HELPLESSNESS SCALE

1. Name of your Organization :
2. Your Highest Qualification :
3. Age :
4. Sex :
5. Designation :
6. Experience in The Present Post :
7. Total Experience :
8. Promotional Avenues :
9. Income :
10. Marital Status :
11. Number of Dependent :
12. Family Structure :

Instructions : Please indicate your agreement or disagreement with each of the following statements by putting appropriate number against the basket ( ), showing your degree of agreement with the statements given below....

Strongly Agree – 1
Agree – 2

Slightly Agree – 3
Slightly Disagree – 4
Disagree – 5
Strongly Disagree – 6

Your explicit responses will be very useful for this research work, Please do not conceal the facts, the responses would be treated in strict confidence and for research purpose only.

01. No matter what I do, some people do not like me. ( )
02. If I have more/less friends, it is mainly because I wanted to have more/less friends. ( )
03. There is a direct relation between how hard I work and what result I get. ( )
04. Honesty, hardwork and truthfulness are not our way of life, and there is hardly anything one man can do to change this. ( )
05. There are many undesireable elements in the culture of my organization, but I feel helpless to correct them. ( )
06. I do not struggle hard to overcome my faults because I know that I will not be able to correct them. ( )
07. I know many things are bad in my organization but I am unable to do anything to correct them ( )
08. I do not like my present job but I can not quit it because I can not be able to get a better job. ( )
09. It is not always wise to plan too far ahead because many things turn out to be a matter of good or bad luck any way. ( )
10. I do not like many aspects of my job, but what can I do about it. ( )
11. When I fail to do as well as I am expected to in my organization, it is usually due to lack of effort on my part. ( )
12. If I succeed on a task, it is usually because I am lucky or am helped by other people. ( )
13. If I were to fail in a task, it would probably be because I lacked skill in that area. ( )
14. If I am not successful in my organization it is because of lack or expertise to do well on my job. ( )
15. Even if it urgent, there is no use trying to do something in this organization, if it is against rules. ( )
16. If I were not successful in my organization, it is because my Boss did not help me. ( )
17. If I really try hard, I can become an expert of computer science in no time. ( )

18. It seems to me that getting along with people is a skill. ( )
19. There is no use in working very hard in this organization, because whatever rewards I get are in no way related to my performance. ( )
20. If I were not successful in my organization, it is because the culture of my organization does not facilitate me to succeed. ( )
21. My life is mainly shaped by my efforts. ( )
22. Many time I feel that I have little influence over things that are happening to me. ( )
23. Weather or not I get in to an accident depends mostly on how careful I am while walking or driving on road. ( )
24. When I can not understand something it is usually because it is too hard to understand for me as well as for others. ( )

46 A (15)

P.G.I. YOGA ATTITUDE SCALE

Name.. Date..............................

Age........................ Sex...................... Psy.No..........................

Instructions : Given below are a few sentences about Yoga. Of these To which ones do you agree....and....to what extent....

		Strongly agree	Agree	Un-certain	Dis-agree	Strongly disagree
1.	Yoga benefits everyone.	☐	☐	☐	☐	☐
2.	Yoga makes a person emotionally stable.	☐	☐	☐	☐	☐
3.	Yoga can cure all diseases.	☐	☐	☐	☐	☐
4.	Yogic principles are very difficult to follow in real life.	☐	☐	☐	☐	☐
5.	Yoga is meant only for Sadhus, Sanyasis or Saints who live alone in the jungle.	☐	☐	☐	☐	☐

	Strongly agree	Agree	Un-certain	Dis-agree	Strongly disagree
6. Yoga is only for those incompetent or weak people who cannot face difficulties in life.	☐	☐	☐	☐	☐
7. Yoga is essential for spiritual progress.	☐	☐	☐	☐	☐
8. Yoga is essential for good health.	☐	☐	☐	☐	☐
9. Yoga gives peace, strength and unity to the whole life.	☐	☐	☐	☐	☐
10. Yoga brings success to life.	☐	☐	☐	☐	☐
11. You can overcome mental conflicts or problems.	☐	☐	☐	☐	☐
12. Yoga can make a person more intelligent.	☐	☐	☐	☐	☐
13. There are many other ways besides yoga by which a person can obtain peace and happiness.	☐	☐	☐	☐	☐
14. Yoga gives many ways by which a person can strengthen or build character.	☐	☐	☐	☐	☐
15. Even bad habits like stealing, gambling etc. can be checked by yoga.	☐	☐	☐	☐	☐
16. Yoga brings discipline into life.	☐	☐	☐	☐	☐

46A (31)

THE INFLUENCE OF PARENTS IN CHOICES OF CERTAIN ITEMS

Instructions : To whose opinion would you give more importance in making your choice regarding the following items. The respondent is to select one of the three alternative responses : (i) parents' opinion (ii) one's own as well as parents' opinion, and (iii) one's own opinion.

Items : Choice of	Parents	Both	Self
1. Clothes			
2. Friends			
3. Study			
4. Job/Business			
5. Friendship with opposite sex			
6. Choice of a mate			
7. Hobbies/Interests			
8. Leisure time activities			
9. Recreation			
10. Obeying parents			

AUTHOR INDEX

Note: Page Number [illegible]